Granada, San Juan del Sur & Southwest Nicaragua

FIRST EDITION

GRANADA, SAN JUAN DEL SUR & SOUTHWEST NICARAGUA

A Great Destination

Paige R. Penland

The Countryman Press
Woodstock, Vermont

OPPOSITE: *Trails through Mombacho National Park's cool cloud forest are steep and misty.*

This book is dedicated to my aunt Patricia Mouton, who dedicated her life to books. As an English teacher; president of the board of directors for the Syracuse, New York, school district; avid reader; and inspiration, she and my uncle Steve taught me to respect good writing and love a great book. Thanks so much, Aunt Pat, I love and miss you.

Granada, San Juan del Sur & Southwest Nicaragua
ISBN 978-1-58157-113-4

Interior photographs by the author
Book design by Joanna Bodenweber
Composition by Chelsea Cloeter
Maps by Erin Greb Cartography, © The Countryman Press

Published by The Countryman Press, P.O. Box 748, Woodstock, VT 05091

Distributed by W. W. Norton & Company, Inc., 500 Fifth Avenue, New York, NY 10110

Printed in the United States of America

10 9 8 7 6 5 4 3 2 1

THE ADIRONDACK BOOK
THE ALASKA PANHANDLE
ATLANTA
AUSTIN, SAN ANTONIO
  & THE TEXAS HILL COUNTRY
BALTIMORE, ANNAPOLIS & THE CHESAPEAKE BAY
THE BERKSHIRE BOOK
BIG SUR, MONTEREY BAY
  & GOLD COAST WINE COUNTRY
CAPE CANAVERAL, COCOA BEACH
  & FLORIDA'S SPACE COAST
THE CHARLESTON, SAVANNAH
  & COASTAL ISLANDS BOOK
THE COAST OF MAINE BOOK
COLORADO'S CLASSIC MOUNTAIN TOWNS
COSTA RICA: GREAT DESTINATIONS
  CENTRAL AMERICA
DOMINICAN REPUBLIC
THE FINGER LAKES BOOK
THE FOUR CORNERS REGION
GALVESTON, SOUTH PADRE ISLAND
  & THE TEXAS GULF COAST
GUATEMALA: GREAT DESTINATIONS
  CENTRAL AMERICA
THE HAMPTONS
HAWAII'S BIG ISLAND: GREAT DESTINATIONS
  HAWAII
HONOLULU & OAHU: GREAT DESTINATIONS
  HAWAII
THE JERSEY SHORE: ATLANTIC CITY TO CAPE MAY
KAUAI: GREAT DESTINATIONS HAWAII
LAKE TAHOE & RENO
LAS VEGAS
LOS CABOS & BAJA CALIFORNIA SUR:
  GREAT DESTINATIONS MEXICO
MAUI: GREAT DESTINATIONS HAWAII
MEMPHIS AND THE DELTA BLUES TRAIL
MICHIGAN'S UPPER PENINSULA

MONTREAL & QUEBEC CITY:
  GREAT DESTINATIONS CANADA
THE NANTUCKET BOOK
THE NAPA & SONOMA BOOK
NORTH CAROLINA'S OUTER BANKS
  & THE CRYSTAL COAST
NOVA SCOTIA & PRINCE EDWARD ISLAND
OAXACA: GREAT DESTINATIONS MEXICO
OREGON WINE COUNTRY
PALM BEACH, FORT LAUDERDALE, MIAMI
  & THE FLORIDA KEYS
PALM SPRINGS & DESERT RESORTS
PHILADELPHIA, BRANDYWINE VALLEY
  & BUCKS COUNTY
PHOENIX, SCOTTSDALE, SEDONA
  & CENTRAL ARIZONA
PLAYA DEL CARMEN, TULUM & THE RIVIERA MAYA:
  GREAT DESTINATIONS MEXICO
SALT LAKE CITY, PARK CITY, PROVO
  & UTAH'S HIGH COUNTRY RESORTS
SAN DIEGO & TIJUANA
SAN JUAN, VIEQUES & CULEBRA:
  GREAT DESTINATIONS PUERTO RICO
SAN MIGUEL DE ALLENDE & GUANAJUATO:
  GREAT DESTINATIONS MEXICO
THE SANTA FE & TAOS BOOK
THE SARASOTA, SANIBEL ISLAND & NAPLES BOOK
THE SEATTLE & VANCOUVER BOOK
THE SHENANDOAH VALLEY BOOK
TOURING EAST COAST WINE COUNTRY
TUCSON
VIRGINIA BEACH, RICHMOND
  & TIDEWATER VIRGINIA
WASHINGTON, D.C., AND NORTHERN VIRGINIA
YELLOWSTONE & GRAND TETON NATIONAL PARKS
  & JACKSON HOLE
YOSEMITE & THE SOUTHERN SIERRA NEVADA

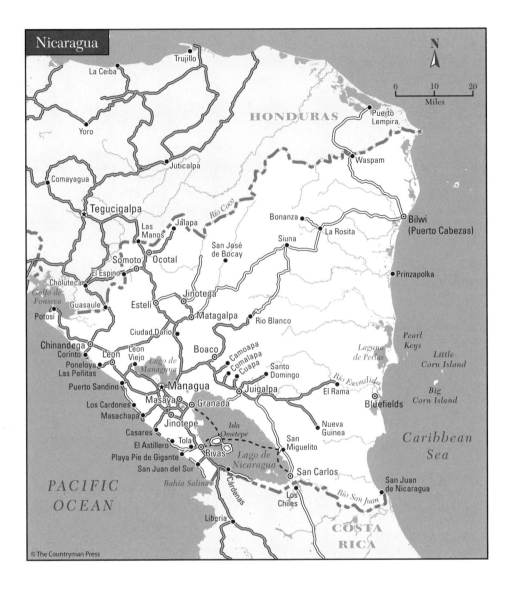

Nicaragua

La Ceiba
Trujillo
Yoro
HONDURAS
Puerto Lempira
Comayagua
Juticalpa
Waspam
Tegucigalpa
Las Manos
Jálapa
Río Coco
Bonanza
La Rosita
Bilwi (Puerto Cabezas)
Somoto
Ocotal
San José de Bocay
Siuna
El Espino
Choluteca
Jinotega
Prinzapolka
Golfo de Fonseca
Estelí
Matagalpa
Guasaule
Ciudad Darío
Río Blanco
Potosí
Laguna de Perlas
Pearl Keys
Chinandega
Corinto
León
Boaco
Camoapa
León Viejo
Lago de Managua
Comalapa
Cuapa
Santo Domingo
Río Escondido
Little Corn Island
Poneloya
Las Peñitas
Puerto Sandino
Managua
Juigalpa
El Rama
Big Corn Island
Los Cardones
Masaya
Granada
Bluefields
Masachapa
Jinotepe
Isla Ometepe
Nueva Guinea
Caribbean Sea
Casares
Tola
El Astillero
San Miguelito
Playa Pie de Gigante
Rivas
Lago de Nicaragua
San Carlos
San Juan del Sur
San Juan de Nicaragua
PACIFIC OCEAN
Bahía Salinas
Cárdenas
Río San Juan
Los Chiles
Liberia
COSTA RICA

N

0 10 20
Miles

© The Countryman Press

Contents

Acknowledgments   9

Introduction   9

The Way This Book Works   10

1

History and Culture
12

2

Planning Your Trip
28

3

Managua and the Managua Beaches
Capital of Lakes and Volcanoes
50

4

Masaya, the Pueblos Blancos, and Carazo
Music and Dance, Art and Soul
80

5

Granada
"Granada is Nicaragua, the rest is only countryside"
118

6

San Juan del Sur
Summertime, and the Living's Easy
164

7

RIVAS AND THE TOLA BEACHES
Pristine Bays, Empty Waves
202

8

ISLA OMETEPE AND LAKE NICARAGUA
Isle of Myth and Magic
232

9

SUGGESTED READING
269

INDEX   273

MAPS

Nicaragua Country Map   6
Southwest Nicaragua   30
Managua   52
Carazo and the Pueblos Blancos   82
Masaya   83
Granada   120
San Juan del Sur   166
Rivas   205
Isla Ometepe   234

Acknowledgments

I could not have done this book without a great deal of help, beginning with Kim Grant, who got me this gig, and Kermit Hummel, Lisa Sacks, Eric Raetz, Doug Yeager, Erin Greb, and the rest of the crew at Countryman Press. Thanks to my mother who, as always, kept my affairs in order while I was on the road.

I had an amazing support group here in Nicaragua, including Nadene Holmes, Janik Keddy, Amadis de Gaula, Kathy Johnson, Neil Cusacovich, Alvaro Miranda Bouillé, Jessica Schugel, Colin Allen, Mike King, Salad Steve, Carlos Corea, Anne Thorne, Allan Blandon, Gustavo Ramirez, Enrique, Angela Lehman, Sarah Fahey, Karen Emanuel, Natasha and Jacob Follwell, Marlowe Mackenzie, Alexis Calderon, Andrew and Justin of the Whiteboard Project, and many, many others who helped me out along the way. Thanks to you all!

Introduction

This is Southwest Nicaragua, the warm heart of the Americas. It is a lush and tropical land, defined by sculpted bays and sundrenched beaches, sparkling lakes and volcanic islands, where proud Spanish cities rise in a graceful architectural symphony above this epic landscape.

"*Pase adelante*," step right in, past the oversized wooden doors and centuries-old adobe façades, today painted in dazzling hues. Granada's Colonial mansions, built for conquistadores and Spanish nobility, surround marble courtyards and exuberant gardens with a 16th-century elegance that these days seems all but forgotten. Horse-drawn carriages clip-clop past, and can take you to cathedrals that house miraculous virgins, or markets where you'll find fresh, ripe fruits unlike any you've ever seen.

Or head to the soft sands, swaying palms, and rolling waves of Nicaragua's magnificent Pacific shore. The classic beach town is San Juan del Sur, inset into a deep horseshoe bay, protected by dramatic headlands. It still has a laid-back surfer vibe, but as the pretty city grows and goes inexorably upscale, more wonderful restaurants, relaxed nightlife options, and sophisticated resorts and hotels are opening for business.

If you are seeking a more secluded shore, fear not. Nicaragua remains much less developed for tourism than its more popular neighbors, though this is changing. Despite being Central America's safest country, its reputation suffered in the wake of the brutal Contra War of the 1980s. Almost as soon as the guns were silenced in 1988, however, adventurous travelers began making their way here, to enjoy world-class surfing on empty waves, climb active volcanoes, or swim in sparkling crater lakes.

Today, plush hotels and ecoresorts are clustered in the most popular spots, accommodating even the most demanding travelers as they take day trips to less developed destinations: horseback rides through misty mountaintop coffee plantations, boat tours through 365 tiny *isletas* topped with gleaming resorts and delicate white herons, or day trips to the hammock workshops of Masaya, handicrafts capital of Nicaragua.

Though the southwest is the most developed corner of the country, there are still plenty of easily accessible escapes off the beaten path. North and south of San Juan del Sur, the scalloped Pacific shore protects an array of broad beaches, where you'll find quaint fishing villages, protected sea turtle nesting grounds, and tiny surf communities where you'll be welcomed with simpler pleasures.

Or visit Nicaragua's most impressive natural treasure, Isla Ometepe. Formed from two volcanoes, one of them active, this hourglass-shaped island is littered with pre-Columbian statues and petroglyphs, and lined with shady, pearl gray beaches. Considered sacred for centuries, and recently named a UNESCO Biosphere Reserve, this magical, isolated spot is simply unforgettable.

Southwest Nicaragua seems small, and it is, with good roads that connect the splendid beaches, active volcanoes, and Spanish Colonial cities within a few hours. Even business travelers working in the sprawling, underrated capital of Managua are within 45 minutes of several national parks and the ancient, fascinating villages of the cool, mountainous Meseta Central.

Yet it has so much to offer. It is the perfect destination for a short vacation for those eager to experience classic Central American treasures in a week or less. Other visitors, enchanted by its warm, friendly culture and endless choice of activities, end up spending the rest of their lives here. Come visit, and you'll understand why.

THE WAY THIS BOOK WORKS

This book covers the southwestern portion of Nicaragua. Nicaragua is the largest country in Central America, at 130,373 square km (50,337 square miles) about the same size as Greece or the U.S. state of New York.

Southwest Nicaragua refers to that slender isthmus of land separating Nicaragua's two massive inland lakes, Lake Managua (Xolotlán) and Lake Nicaragua (Cocibolca), from the Pacific Ocean. It was raised from the seas by its backbone of volcanoes, several still active. The region also encompasses the Meseta Central, a fertile, rolling plateau rising to the west of the tectonic landscape. The Pacific Coast is a series of deeply scalloped bays, with beaches gradually growing longer and broader as you head north.

Managua is the nation's capital, known as the "city without a center." Its once cosmopolitan downtown was ruined by earthquake and war, and today the city sprawls haphazardly along the shores of Xolotlán (Lake Managua). Though there is much to recommend it—including safe, attractive neighborhoods with great hotels, dining, and nightlife; as well as pretty, less touristed beaches—Managua is for the most part difficult to navigate and dodgy. Adventurous travelers will enjoy exploring, but most visitors head straight to Granada or San Juan del Sur.

To the southwest of Managua is what many consider the spiritual heart of the nation, the cool, tropical highlands of the Meseta Central. The ancient handicrafts villages of this fertile region—**Masaya, the Pueblos Blancos, and Carazo**—are a great destination for culture lovers and are known for their fine churches, indigenous traditions, and array of colorful handicrafts. Beyond the beautiful pottery, fine leatherwork, and world-class hammocks are natural attractions as well. Fuming Masaya Volcano and Laguna de Apoyo, a postcard-perfect protected crater lake, are the most famous destinations, but there are many other outdoorsy escapes.

Granada, the "Gran Sultana" of Lake Nicaragua, is considered one of Central America's most beautiful cities, and makes an excellent base for exploring the region. Its fantastic Spanish Colonial architecture is now inhabited by wonderful hotels and restaurants for every budget, tour operators, and museums, inviting culture lovers to stay for a week or lifetime.

To the south, on the Pacific, lies **San Juan del Sur**, Nicaragua's most popular beach town. The village itself, within a picturesque bay, is small and delightful, offering great lodging, dining, surfing, and a laid-back nightlife scene. The wilder beaches to the north and south are easily accessible from town, and offer even more options.

Rivas and the Tola Beaches covers the isthmus less traveled. Rivas, despite its Spanish Colonial pedigree and convenient position as a transportation hub between Granada, San Juan del Sur, and Isla Ometepe, is rarely considered a destination. It's a great little escape, however, and also the gateway to the gorgeous Tola beaches. Well known to surfers, but long isolated by poor roads, it is now undergoing huge changes as the developers roll through.

This book saves the best for last, exquisite Isla Ometepe, rising from Lake Nicaragua to two bounteous volcanic peaks. It is well worth the ferry ride to visit this unique paradise of archaeological treasures and natural wonders.

Understanding Lodging and Dining Codes

Rather than give specific prices, this guide rates dining and lodging options within a range.

Cost of lodging is based on an average per-room, double occupancy rate during peak season (December through April). Nicaragua's 15 percent sales tax and gratuities are not included; note that paying cash sometimes results in taxes being waived. Prices are much higher during the Christmas holidays and, to a lesser extent, Semana Santa (Easter Week), when you should have reservations.

The following restaurant prices are based on the cost of a dinner entrée with a nonalcoholic drink, not including the recommended 10 percent tip (sometimes included in the bill). Note that in listings, business hours are not specifically given. Instead, the abbreviations B, L, or D are used to denote breakfast, lunch, and dinner.

Code	Lodging	Dining
Inexpensive ($)	Up to US$25	Up to US$5
Moderate ($$)	US$25 to US$60	US$5 to US$10
Expensive ($$$)	US$60 to US$100	$10 to $20
Very Expensive ($$$$)	US$100 and up	US$20 or more

I've also added a ✪ symbol next to places that are personal favorites, but keep in mind that your tastes may differ from mine.

1

HISTORY AND CULTURE

NATURAL HISTORY

Geology

The Central American isthmus is young. It was until recently a volcanic archipelago, marking the active fault line where the motionless Caribbean Plate and expanding Cocos Plate crash.

As the ocean-soaked Cocos moves eastward from the Middle American Trench, it is subducted beneath the Caribbean Plate, and melts into steam-filled lava. Lighter than bedrock, this lava rises—producing the string of volcanoes that define Southwest Nicaragua. Sediments have collected around these islands, and around three million years ago created a viable land bridge between North and South America.

Many of the region's most important geological features were created much later, including Cocibolca (Lake Nicaragua) and Xolotlán (Lake Managua). These were formed when a *graben* (a valley created by parallel fault lines pulling a continent apart) filled with water, perhaps as recently as 12,000 years ago. The Isletas de Granada date to around the same time, when a massive eruption of Volcán Mombacho created the Asese Peninsula.

Cocibolca and Xolotlán used to be a single lake, but water levels have dropped at least 15 meters over the centuries. Today, they are separated by the fertile Tisma wetlands—usually. During the nightmare torrents of Hurricane Mitch in 1998, the two lakes were once again briefly but devastatingly joined.

Lake Nicaragua is slowly draining to the Caribbean via the Río San Juan, and this can be measured on a human scale. A walk from Granada's current lakeshore toward the old city center on Calle La Calzada is, for architecture buffs, a walk back in time.

Earthquakes and volcanic activity continue to shape the region. Managua in particular, which sits within the lake graben, is regularly rocked with profound consequences. In many ways the 1972 earthquake that destroyed the capital led to the 1979 revolution.

Biology

Southwest Nicaragua is primarily dry tropical forest, though the volcanoes rise to rain- and cloud-forested altitudes. This biome is characterized by deciduous trees, which shed their leaves during the dry season (December through April), much as they do during winter at higher latitudes.

This ecosystem is, however, much more diverse than those at temperate latitudes. Some 70 tree species can be found within 1/10 of a hectare (1/4 acre). It is home to almost half of Nicaragua's 694 bird species, three types of monkeys (howler, spider, and capuchin or whiteface), giant anteaters, pizotes, squirrels, deer, iguanas, boa constrictors, caimans,

Mombacho Volcano still keeps watch over the Isletas de Granada, cast into Cocibolca some 12,000 years ago.

sloths, dozens of bats, and 250,000 types of insects. The **Alianza para Las Areas Silvestres (ALAS)** (Alliance for Wild Areas; 2552-4528; www.avesnicaragua.org) maintains exhaustive online bird and mammal lists.

Nicaragua's Pacific Coast provides important nesting grounds for four kinds of sea turtle, while Lake Nicaragua is famously home to bull sharks—a stout, vicious creature that happily consumes human beings. Cocibolca's populations were heavily depleted during the Somoza era, however, when their fins were sold to China; today, you'd have to be very unlucky to see one. Bull sharks are unique in that they can manipulate the amount of salt in their bloodstream as they move between saltwater and freshwater—in this case between the Caribbean and Lake Nicaragua along the Río San Juan.

The dry tropical forest is one of Central America's most devastated biomes, as it is easily burned off and used for farms and ranches. However, Nicaragua has an extensive national park system administrated by **MARENA** (Ministry of Environment and Natural Resources; www.marena.gob.ni), while several private preserves are part of the **Red de Reservas Silvestres Privadas Nicaragua** (Network of Private Wildlife Reserves; www.redrspnica.com).

History

Pre-Columbian Nicaragua

The first human beings probably arrived in Southwest Nicaragua around 12,000 years ago, Chibcha-speaking peoples originally from Colombia and Venezuela, who cultivated *yuca*, or manioc, in the region.

Many businesses display ceramics and petroglyphs found on their grounds, such as this collection at Finca Venecia on Isla Ometepe.

Nahuatl-speaking peoples arrived from what is now Mexico much later, in three major waves. The first settled here around 300 A.D., a branch of Chorotegas called the Mangues, who spoke a dialect of Nahuatl, cultivated corn and used *metates* (corn grinders), and had a complex and hierarchical political system. Another massive immigration of Chorotegas flowed in during the sixth and seventh centuries, bringing with them technologically advanced weapons, tools, and ceramics.

Finally, the Nahuas made the journey south in the ninth or tenth century, from the mythical cities of Ticomega and Mahuatega (probably Tula, Mexico). Their language, political system, and religion soon came to dominate the region. They carved statues dedicated to Aztec and Olmec deities, and worked with jade, gold, and ceramics using Mayan techniques.

All of their descendants contributed to the culture of Gran Nicoya, a unified political and economic region that covered Nicaragua's Pacific side, as well as the Guanacaste Province of Costa Rica. Different *cacicazgos*, or city-states, engaged in political struggles, such as

Nahuas of Jinotepe and the rival Chorotegas of Diriamba. However, they spoke mutually intelligible languages and relied on one another for trade.

Oddly, the name Nicaragua probably isn't an indigenous word. It's more likely a combination of "Nicarao," name of the *cacicazgo* that dominated the Isthmus of Rivas, and the Spanish word for water, *agua*.

The Spanish Conquest

When Spanish conquistador Gil González Dávila first reached what is now Nicaragua, he called a meeting with Cacique (Chief) Nicarao, leader of Nicarao Callí, a major city just east of Rivas. The spot where they met January 21, 1522, is marked by the Cruz de España, near San Jorge. There, the two men famously discussed technology, astronomy, and religion.

González gave Nicarao an ultimatum: Convert to Christianity, or be destroyed. Nicarao, who had almost certainly heard about González's bloody conquests in Costa Rica and Panama, had one thousand of his warriors convert on the spot. The Spanish destroyed them anyway.

The conquistadors would go on to occupy the port city of Xalteva, now a neighborhood of Granada, in 1524; they submitted as well, and were soon violently dominated and controlled by the Spanish, their culture destroyed. Word of the slaughter moved fast in Gran Nicoya, and by the time González reached the Meseta Central, the locals were prepared.

In April 1529, González arrived at the Chortega capital of Diriá, where he gave 27-year-old Cacique Diriangén the same ultimatum: Christianity or death. Diriangén, who had raised an army of thousands while watching the brutal occupation of the lowlands, chose not to sell his soul so cheaply.

On April 17, he met the Spanish in battle, but within half a day his troops were utterly destroyed. Diriangén, however, not González, has been immortalized in statues, place names, and popular songs, and he is remembered as "Nicaragua's first freedom fighter."

In Managua, some 40,000 people simply disappeared into the Northern Highlands rather than convert or fight. The Spanish moved right in to their old homes and farms. The Maribios of what is now León put up a mighty resistance, fighting for years before the Spanish finally subdued them. On Isla Ometepe, the locals apparently got on pretty well with the Franciscans, who (very unusually) left ancient stone idols erect right next to their church.

And on the wild Caribbean Coast, the Miskito Indians formed an alliance with the British and Dutch pirates, who used their territory, along with Isla Ometepe, as a base for attacking the Spanish throughout the 1600s and 1700s. Even as European wars weakened Spain itself, repeated pirate attacks on Granada and throughout Latin America gradually undermined the Spaniards' hold on the Americas. On September 1821, Mexico and Central America declared themselves independent from Spain.

Central American Republic and Civil War

The decades following independence were turbulent, as different groups tried to assert their dominance over Central America. The Mexicans went so far as to found the First Mexican Empire in 1822, sending troops to conquer the newly liberated Central American isthmus. This failed, however, and five countries—El Salvador, Guatemala, Honduras, Nicaragua, and Costa Rica—formed the Central American Republic.

A network of bitter power struggles conspired to pull the young republic apart. Wealthy families were split, with Liberals demanding a federalist government, like the United

States, and considerable autonomy for member states. Their champion was Salvadoran hero Manuel José Arce, chosen as the republic's first president, who abolished slavery and instituted democratic reforms.

Conservatives, made up of landowners and powerful businessmen, wanted a strong central government, with laws handed down from Antigua (read: from them) binding the entire isthmus. They pressured Arce into abandoning the Liberal cause, even as civil wars flared up across Central America.

Granada, historically a city of merchants, was firmly Conservative. León, Nicaragua's administrative capital under Spain, was decidedly Liberal. As the republic disintegrated, the two proud cities entered a brutal civil war to decide which would be Nicaragua's capital. The war would drag on for decades.

The cost was incalculable. The Nicaraguan province of Guanacaste, paying taxes to León, yet having their sons drafted by Granada, voted to become part of Costa Rica. In 1852, diplomats attempted to stop the fighting by naming the small city of Managua as the capital. Both sides agreed to the cease-fire, yet the war continued. León surreptitiously hired a mercenary army, led by Tennessean and Mexican-American War veteran William Walker.

Walker arrived with his *filibusteros,* or private military contractors, in 1855, and his band of hardened vets made short work of Granada's exhausted conscripts. Rather than turn the city over to the Liberals, however, Walker set up headquarters in Granada and declared himself president. Desperate for money, he reinstated slavery in an attempt to secure funding from Southern U.S. politicians—themselves gearing up for the U.S. Civil War.

He also betrayed his former benefactor, railway and steamship tycoon Cornelius Vanderbilt. The robber baron had provided Walker's mercenaries free passage to Nicaragua on his Accessory Transit Company, a steamship-rail-steamship route across Lake Nicaragua that connected New York City with the gold fields of California.

Walker, with his new presidential powers, "nationalized" the railways and gave them to Vanderbilt's competitors, Garrison and Morgan. He famously sent them all a note: "Gentlemen: You have undertaken to cheat me. I won't sue you, for the law is too slow. I'll ruin you. Yours truly, Cornelius Vanderbilt."

Vanderbilt armed, trained, and funded anyone willing to take on Walker, whose legalization of slavery profoundly offended civilized Central American sentiment. The Salvadoran, Honduran, and Costa Rican militaries all began preparations. When Walker's men invaded Costa Rica, unaware of their new military strength, President Mora defeated them within 14 minutes—then chased them back to Rivas. There, Walker made his stand, and was defeated when a young school teacher named Emmanuel Mongalo Rubio (in the Costa Rican version of the story, it was a young Tico drummer boy named Juan Santamaría) gave his life to toss a torch into their flammable position.

Walker fled Nicaragua, burning Granada to the ground in his vindictive retreat. He would later be executed by a Honduran firing squad. Granada (in ruins) and León (in shame) finally agreed to honor Managua as the new capital.

The United States Takes an Interest

Throughout the Nicaraguan civil war, Vanderbilt had operated the "Nicaraguan Route," which carried adventurers from the U.S. East Coast to the gold fields of California via the Río San Juan and Lake Nicaragua. This was one of two shipping routes, much faster and safer than crossing the massive U.S. overland; the other was through Panama.

The French were already planning to build a canal in Panama, and had begun paying

Vanderbilt $56,000 per month to keep the Nicaraguan route closed. When the U.S. government began contemplating a Nicaraguan Canal that would compete with the French, they sent a sly French lobbyist to the scientifically illiterate U.S. Congress, and showed them a Nicaraguan postage stamp that portrayed erupting Volcán Momotombo, far from the site of the canal. Congress, convinced by the ruse, postponed their plans.

The French were unable to complete the Panama Canal themselves, however, and the U.S. eventually took over the project. In 1903 the Panama Canal opened. Nicaragua's economy went into a tailspin, and they began planning their own canal. Now it was the U.S. that didn't want the competition.

In 1914, U.S. President Taft and Conservative Nicaraguan President Diego Manuel Chamorro signed a controversial treaty that gave the U.S. control over any future canal, and the right to "protect U.S. interests" in Nicaragua.

The U.S. Marines had already invaded the country a few years earlier to "protect U.S. interests"; U.S. General Smedley Butler's account of the occupation is illuminating. After taking Coyotepe, near Masaya, U.S. troops carried Nicaragua's mortally wounded General Benjamín Zeledón in a cart to Catarina to be executed. The spectacle was, according to local legend, witnessed by a young man from Niquinohomo, "Valley of the Warriors," Augusto C. Sandino.

Revolution

Sandino, who apparently realized his destiny after seeing Nicaraguan hero General Zeledón so disrespected, was forced to flee Nicaragua soon after the U.S. Marines attacked. He had tried, and failed, to shoot the son of a prominent Conservative politician who had insulted his mother. Sandino's subsequent adventures took him Mexico, where he was exposed to socialism, revolution, and wealthy benefactors such as artists Frida Kahlo and Diego Rivera. Upon returning to Nicaragua in 1926, Sandino decided to join the half-hearted Nicaraguan rebellion against U.S. interests.

Other revolutionaries, who were winding down their revolt under pressure from the better-armed U.S. Marines, refused to take the slight man seriously. So a group of Puerto Cabezas prostitutes purchased weapons for Sandino and his "Crazy Little Army" themselves. Soon Sandino was a force to be reckoned with, and he eventually controlled the vast Segovia Mountains in north-central Nicaragua. Despite tactics that included the first aerial bombing of civilian targets, the U.S. Marines never were able to capture the "General of Free Men." As the Great Depression took hold, and taxpayer funding dried up, the military was forced to return home.

They left behind an English-speaking bureaucrat, Anastasio Somoza García, as head of the U.S.-controlled National Guard. Somoza invited Sandino to dinner at the presidential palace on February 21, 1934, for peace talks. Though they had a safe-conduct agreement, the National Guard assassinated Sandino and his men as they left the house. Two years later, Somoza forced the elected president to resign and took control of the country. For the next 42 years, he and his two sons would control Nicaragua.

In the late 1960s, a group of young people (mostly university students) calling themselves "Sandinistas" began mobilizing in the mountains. They had a bit of support from Cuba, but almost none from the wealthy and powerful Nicaraguan families who ran the country. Most people were disgruntled under the dictatorship, but didn't want to rock the boat.

After the 1972 earthquake that destroyed Managua, however, Anastasio Somoza Debayle (Somoza García's son) went too far. He declared martial law and took control of all international aid money, which he funneled toward his friends and supporters. Even the wealthy classes were miffed.

The Sandinista Revolution began in earnest, with widespread support from Nicaraguans across the political and economic spectrum. When the National Guard murdered *La Prensa* publisher Joaquín Chamorro, the Sandinistas called a general strike that immobilized the country. The subsequent bloody Monimbó Insurrection—when young guerrillas wearing the masks used to perform the indigenous, anti-Spanish play *El Güegüense* hurled home-made grenades at the heavily armed National Guard—inspired countrywide urban rebellion.

On July 19, 1979, the guerrillas took control of Managua. Somoza fled to Miami, then Paraguay, where he was assassinated. While the vast majority of Nicaraguans supported, and still support, the revolution, atrocities followed the change of power. For instance, several members of Granada's ruling families, who had supported Somoza during the revolution, were marched out to the tip of the Asese Peninsula, executed, and buried in a mass grave.

The fall of the Somoza dictatorship was celebrated by Nicaraguans of all political stripes, and a coalition government was formed. The Sandinista-led Junta of National Reconstruction received wide international support, and initiated successful literacy and health care campaigns throughout the impoverished countryside. They called it *Nicaragua Libre* (Free Nicaragua), a phrase emblazoned on their license plates, passports, and the national consciousness.

The Contra War

While U.S. president Carter made no moves to undermine the Sandinista-led government, his successor, Ronald Reagan, was another story. One of his first acts as president was to order support for the resistance movement, or Contras, who he later compared to the founding fathers of the U.S.

The Contras were strongest on the Caribbean Coast, formerly controlled by the British. The isolated Afro-indigenous populations have historically been quite autonomous from the Pacific side, and many people don't even speak Spanish. Exiled members of Somoza's National Guard found safe haven there, and began organizing their own revolution. The Reagan administration supplied them across the Honduran border.

When the Democrat-controlled Congress tried to limit Reagan's expenditures, passing the Boland Amendment (which specifically forbade U.S. tax dollars being used to overthrow the Nicaraguan government), the U.S. president approved a black-ops mission to support them instead, funding the Contras with a convoluted mess now known as the Iran-Contra Affair.

For seven long years, the Contra War raged, destroying what was left of Nicaragua's fragile infrastructure and killing some 60,000 people. Though Granada was relatively untouched—it was a safe city for the families of leaders on both sides—refugees poured in from regions with heavy fighting.

The May 1986 Esquipulas Accords, signed by President Daniel Ortega, began the peace process, but it was only after a Contra supply plane flown by a U.S. citizen was shot down on October 5 of that year, exposing the illegal affair, that U.S. support for the Contras was finally cut off. Fighting continued in remote regions, but by the end of the decade, Nicaragua was at peace.

Presidential elections in 1990 did what the Contras never could, and unseated the Sandinistas, or FSLN (Sandinista National Liberation Front) from power. Violetta Chamorro,

Sandinistas and Liberals do come together when it's important, such as at a baseball game at Dennis Martínez National Stadium.

Rivas native and widow of slain *La Prensa* publisher Joaquín Chamorro, was elected the first female head of state in the Americas. While her administration is criticized for failing to reinvigorate the Nicaraguan economy, her peace held, and Nicaraguans once again had hope.

Nicaragua at Peace

With the wars behind them, Nicaraguans began a national reconciliation, in many ways symbolized by President Chamorro's family: Two of her children fought for the Sandinistas, two for the Contras. She herself had been a part of the original FSLN government, before quitting and becoming a publisher of *La Prensa*, which was pointedly critical of Ortega's administration.

The peace is surprisingly without bitterness, though the political parties remain polarized. With one of the freest presses in the world, battles are now fought on paper, or at flag-waving rallies. The vast majority of Nicaraguans are just grateful to have a chance to rebuild, and raise their families without fear.

Agriculture provides about 18 percent of the GDP, and 30 percent of Nicaraguan jobs—not including subsistence and part-time farmers.

Aid money—and to a lesser extent, international investment—began trickling into the country in the 1990s. Most was concentrated in Southwest Nicaragua, which had survived the war with its infrastructure relatively intact. Tourists began crossing the Costa Rican border as well, and soon there were surf camps set up along the Pacific Coast and fine hotels in Granada. By the mid-2000s, Nicaragua was being pitched by developers as the "next Costa Rica, with ocean-view lots available now!"

The global economic collapse in 2008, combined with the election of former FSLN guerrilla Daniel Ortega, put a crimp on international investment, but Nicaragua's reputation as the safest, cheapest destination in Central America keeps bringing in tourists and adventurous would-be expats.

Despite the modest economic growth, Nicaragua remains the second-poorest country in the hemisphere, after Haiti. Since the war, it has suffered more than its share of natural disasters, such as Hurricane Mitch in 1998, which destroyed three-quarters of the nation's infrastructure. There have been man-made ones as well, such as corpulent President Arnoldo Alemán, who stole millions of dollars but escaped prison by signing "El Pacto" with President Daniel Ortega.

The Pact allowed Ortega, a controversial figure on a good day, to win the 2006 presidential elections with just 38 percent of the vote; his split opposition didn't even come close.

While foreign investors and developers worried the old die-hard socialist would start nationalizing businesses, or using "land reform" legislation to repossess foreign-held properties, the FSLN 2.0 has been much more moderate.

Ortega is certainly still a rebel, and an enthusiastic member of the Bolivarian Revolution led by anti-U.S. firebrand and Venezuelan President Hugo Chavez. But while continuing to criticize U.S. policy and "wild capitalism," the FSLN has also streamlined visas, residencies, and investment requirements, making Nicaragua one of the easiest tropical spots for U.S. citizens, and everyone else, to buy property or retire.

The FSLN, and Daniel Ortega in particular (many Nicaraguans will tell you pointedly that they are Sandinista, but not "Danielista"), is criticized for the very fishy 2008 midterm elections, with allegations of widespread fraud, as well as a stringent abortion policy that forbids the procedure even in cases of rape, incest, and danger to the woman. The FSLN also changed—legally and democratically, but still—the constitution, allowing President Ortega to run for reelection in 2011.

Despite widespread disillusion with the current president, at press time Ortega looked like a shoo-in. Even the opposition press is predicting that he'll win with 54 percent of the vote, beating the same batch of lackluster candidates more easily than the last time. Either

Although school is free, books and uniforms are prohibitively expensive for some families; several aid organizations in Granada and San Juan del Sur accept donations, if you'd like to help out.

While it's easier to decribe Colonial buildings such as Hotel Spa Granada as adobe, a tough mix of straw and mud, walls are made of much sterner stuff at their core.

way, the one thing Sandinistas and Liberals always agree on is that increased tourism and foreign investment are actively benefiting Nicaragua. Expect to see both sides work toward further improvement of access and infrastucture for visitors to their beautiful country.

CULTURE

No matter their political stripe or economic class, Nicaraguans are profoundly proud of their rich cultural heritage, and make a great deal of effort to keep their traditions alive. From the very indigenous fiestas still celebrated in the old Chorotega capital of Diría, to Granada's International Poetry Festival, there is the sense that Nicaragua is important, and has a depth of spirit that offers much to the rest of the world.

At the same time, there is frustration with the lack of natural resources, infrastructure, and educational opportunities . . . a sense that the unique gifts their children display will go to waste.

And there is a lot of love here. Family is of utmost importance, and spending time with friends and loved ones, no matter how humble the setting, is considered life's greatest joy. People are warm with each other, and with guests; everyone who visits seems touched by these smiles.

Architecture

Architecture buffs are in for a real treat, with wonderful Spanish Colonial cities scattered throughout the countryside. Masaya, Rivas, and the Pueblos Blancos all have remarkable examples of the style, but Granada is the star of the show. Recently repainted in rich tropical hues, the harmonious architecture of the "Gran Sultana" is considered one of the loveliest in Central America.

While the style is usually called "Spanish Colonial," most of the city was rebuilt in the late 1800s, after William Walker's fiery retreat. The floor plans, many interior walls, and a handful of buildings date to the 1500s. But most buildings display a mix of more modern styles: neo-Colonial, with modest ornamentation, small windows, oversized doors, *tejas*-tiled roofs, and interior courtyards; Baroque, with more stylized details and squared towers; and what some call "coffee-boom" architecture, dating to the late 1800s and early 1900s, when newly wealthy coffee growers incorporated Art Deco and other modern influences.

Clothing

Most Nicaraguans wear simple, comfortable clothing—perhaps inexpensive and worn, but always spotlessly clean and neatly pressed. Older women never wear shorts, and if you want to be taken seriously (for instance, if you're working), stick to skirts or pants hemmed below the knees. Things are more relaxed close to the beach.

It is almost never OK for men to go topless away from the beach. In rural areas, men and women swim fully clothed. Standards for formal dress, including business meetings and upscale events, are fairly relaxed; think casual Friday.

Most Nicaraguans have long since abandoned traditional clothes like those still worn in Guatemala or Mexico, even in indigenous communities. You'll still see folkloric costumes worn at festivals. Probably the most traditional Nicaraguan item worn regularly these days are Rolter sandals, those cheap plastic shoes you'll see everywhere.

Tasty traditional Nicaraguan street food is available at central parks all over the country—or go for the hot dogs.

Food

Traditional Nicaraguan cuisine is simple and wholesome. The classic Granada dish is *vigarón*, a pile of mashed *yuca* (manioc, a starchy root vegetable), *chicharrón* (fried pig skins), and spicy cabbage salad, served on a clean banana leaf all over the city.

A typical breakfast is usually *gallo pinto* (rice and beans), served with eggs and *maduros*—sweet, fried, ripe plantains. You could also try plantains prepared as *tejadas* (sometimes called *verdes*), or chips, often topped with meat, cheese, and more cabbage salad, something like Nicaraguan nachos; or *tostones con queso*, green plantain medallions fried and served with cheese.

There's a lot of fried food here, the best served at *fritangas*, outdoor barbecues that set up at around sunset all over the country. These usually offer your choice of grilled chicken or beef (in nicer restaurants called a *parrillada* or *churrasco*), served with *gallo pinto*, *tejadas*, *papas* (fried balls of mashed potatoes and cheese), *tacos* (meat or beans wrapped in tortillas and fried), or other greasy goodness, all served on a banana leaf and topped with the ubiquitous cabbage salad.

Other traditional dishes worth trying include *baho* (steamed meat, *yuca*, and plantains simmering in huge, banana-leaf-topped kettles in parks and markets); *nacatamales*, thick pork tamales packed with rice and vegetables, usually available on weekends; *quesillos*, "burritos" made with white cheese, sautéed onions and cream sauce; *salpicón*, a minced meat and vegetable salad, often served cold; and *indio viejo,* a rich, traditional Easter dish made with shredded meat, vegetables, mint, and cornmeal.

Enjoy yours with *tiste* or *pinolillo,* sweet, somewhat gritty corn beverages traditionally served in a carved jícaro (similar to a coconut) shell; or a *fresco,* sweetened fruit juices (you may want to ask for yours *sin azucar,* without sugar). These are available at not only restaurants, but also in parks and bus lots, served in plastic bags with straws. Finish up with a *cajeta*—natural candy made with caramelized fruit, coconut, and sometimes milk—most famously produced in Diriomo.

Music and Dance

The Meseta Central is famed for its folkloric dances, today performed in a swirl of skirts and masks all over the country. The most striking is *La Gigantona*, performed by a dancer costumed as an enormously tall Spanish woman with her much shorter indigenous companion, *El Enano Cabezón*, who even ducks between her legs. It is often used as social satire.

El Güegüense, a scalding musical comedy written in the 1500s, has been recognized by UNESCO. The play, performed in masks, pits a witty *Mestizo* (mixed Spanish and indigenous) merchant against a group of clueless Spanish tax collectors, often performed with current political problems in mind. *El Viejo y La Vieja* describes the courtship of an older

Nicaraguan cuisine may not have a lot of heat, but spicy chileros (jars of pickled chiles and vegetables) on the table at most restaurants and markets let you add a little extra.

In markets, bus stops, and parks all over the country, to-go sodas and frescos (sweetened fruit drinks) are served in baggies with straws.

man and woman, followed by the gentleman flirting with young ladies in the audience. In a country that lost 10 percent of its men to war and emigration, this too is used as social commentary.

The most traditional Nicaraguan music is the *marimba,* performed on a sort of wooden xylophone that has its origins in Africa. Mexican mariachis, German polkas, Dominican merengue and *bachata,* Jamaican reggae, Miami reggaeton, and the smooth rock ballads of the 1980s (expect to hear more Journey and REO Speedwagon than you have in years) are also part of the musical landscape.

The most famous modern artists are the brothers Carlos Mejia Godoy and Luis Enrique Mejia Godoy, who provided the soundtrack to the Revolution—but are currently in litigation with the modern FSLN to get them to stop using their tunes for rallies and political ads.

Other popular performers at press time include the rock bands Momotombo, División Urbana, and Perrozomopo; classic rock cover bands Déjà vu (popular in Granada) and Milly Majuc (in Managua); and La Cuneta Son Machín, a mix of all of the above.

Sports

Nicaragua does have a soccer league, the Federación Nicaraguense de Futbol (www.fenifut .org.ni), but the real national passion is *beisbol*. Introduced to the nation in 1888, baseball grew in popularity during various waves of U.S. intervention, when the Marines sponsored games and perhaps teams.

Today, the national stadium is named after Nicaragua's most famous player, Dennis Martínez, or "El Presidente." The *Bóer* of Managua, founded in 1905, pack the stadium regularly, going up against the *Tigres* of Chinandega, *Leones* of León, and the Granada *Orientales* (more often called by their cooler original name, the *Tiburones* [Sharks]). They play home games at Estadio Roque Tadeo Zavala. Tickets cost around US$2.

2

Planning Your Trip

Nicaragua is located in the heart of the Americas, within four hours of Miami, Atlanta, or Houston on a direct flight. While the country overall suffers from severe infrastructure issues—this is the second poorest nation in the hemisphere, and was at war for most of the 1970s and 1980s—the region covered in this book is developing quite rapidly.

This is, in a large part, due to tourism and foreign investment, enthusiastically supported by government initiatives. It's certainly not Cancún, but roads are good, transportation is reliable, and tour operators and hotels can help smooth the way for less intrepid travelers.

Managua, the capital, is not a particularly convenient base for seeing the country. The city of 1.4 million sprawls, and while a few people enjoy its gentle chaos, most catch the first bus out. If you're here, however, day trips around the country are easy to arrange.

Most travelers base themselves in either **Granada**, a cultural gem with museums, good restaurants, and a fine lakefront; or **San Juan del Sur,** a relaxed Pacific beach town with festive nightlife and great surfing. Both have hotels for every budget, several tour operators, and good transport connections.

Rivas and **Masaya, the Pueblos Blancos, and Carazo** are also convenient bases, with excellent transportation and a small selection of hotels and restaurants geared mostly to Nicaraguans. They aren't as well set up for tourism, yet—which might be just your speed.

Isla Ometepe is a beautiful lake island with wonderful hotels and natural attractions, but rather inconvenient transportation, which makes it a poor base for day trips. It's better to schedule at least two days just for Ometepe to justify the extra travel time. The **Tola beaches** and **Carazo beaches** are less accessible than those close to San Juan del Sur, so factor in extra travel time for them as well.

Southwest Nicaragua is small, with good, well-signed major roads, reliable bus service, and comfortable private shuttles between the major tourist destinations. While I strongly recommend carrying a Spanish phrasebook with you at all times, you'll almost always find English speakers in Granada and San Juan del Sur—and to a lesser extent Isla Ometepe and the city of Masaya—who can help you out.

Tourist Offices and Information

Many destinations, including Managua, Masaya, Jinotepe, Granada, Rivas, and San Juan del Sur, have official **Intur** (www.intur.gob.ni; www.visitanicaragua.com; open 8 AM–1 PM Mon. through Sat.) offices, run by the Nicaraguan Institute of Tourism. These vary in quality, ranging from absolutely useless (San Juan del Sur) to marginally helpful (Granada, Managua).

Private tour offices and hotels happily take up the slack, offering vast collections of

Centros turísticos, or "tourist centers," are government owned and usually a bit scruffy—but always safe, inexpensive, and family friendly.

brochures, free maps, English-speaking staff, and good advice—though you'll probably be steered toward their tours. Your hotel can usually provide information.

In small, rural towns, the place to go is the *alcaldía,* or mayor's office. Usually located on the central park, they can usually point you (in Spanish) toward local guides, guesthouses, and destinations.

ONLINE RESOURCES

Nicaragua has scores of tourism-related Web sites, and I've listed more at the beginning of each destination chapter. Some are in Spanish only, but Google Translate makes them accessible to everyone. Many businesses use Facebook as their primary Web site. Also check out general travel sites such as **Trip Advisor** (www.tripadvisor.com) and **V!va Travel Guides** (www.vivatravelguides.com), with lots of great Nica information.

Between the Waves (www.wavesnicaragua.com) Free, quarterly, English-language maga-zine offers its excellent articles and useful tourist information online.

Centroamerica (www.gocentroamerica.com) Poorly designed, Spanish-only Web site is an absolute wealth of information, with excellent coverage of Southwest Nicaragua.

Go To Nicaragua (www.gotonicaragua.com) Well-written and designed Web site offers English-language news, articles, links, a forum, and much more.

Guía Turística Nicaragua (guiaturisticanicaragua.com) Comprehensive, Spanish-language guide is like the Yellow Pages for tourists.

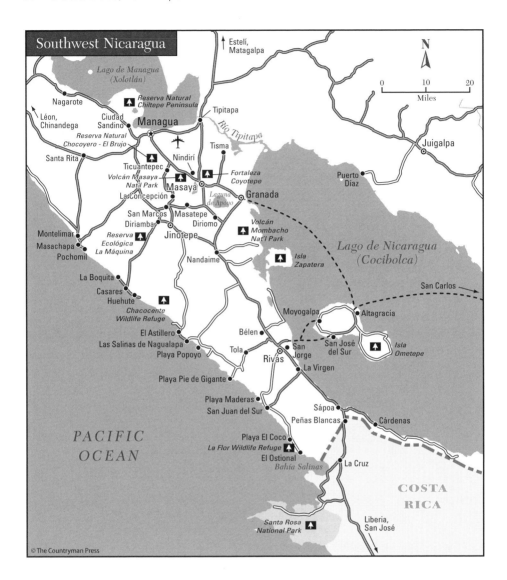

Southwest Nicaragua

↑ Estelí,
Matagalpa

*Lago de Managua
(Xolotlán)*

Nagarote

Léon,
Chinandega   Ciudad
Sandino   **Managua**

*Reserva Natural
Chiltepe Peninsula*   Tipitapa

Río Tipitapa

Juigalpa

Santa Rita   *Reserva Natural
Chocoyero - El Brujo*

Tisma

Ticuantepec   Nindirí

*Volcán Masaya
Nat'l Park*   **Masaya**   Fortaleza
Coyotepe   Puerto
Díaz

La Concepción   *Laguna
de Apoyo*   Granada

San Marcos   Masatepe
Diriamba   Diriomo   Volcán
Mombacho
Nat'l Park   *Lago de Nicaragua
(Cocibolca)*

Montelimar   **Jinotepe**

Masachapa   *Reserva
Ecológica
La Máquina*   *Isla
Zapatera*

Pochomil   Nandaime

La Boquita   San Carlos →

Casares
Huehute   *Chacocente
Wildlife Refuge*   Moyogalpa   Altagracia

El Astillero   Bélen

Las Salinas de Nagualapa   Tola   San
Jorge   San José
del Sur   *Isla
Ometepe*

Playa Popoyo   **Rivas**

La Virgen

Playa Pie de Gigante

Playa Maderas
San Juan del Sur   Sápoa

Peñas Blancas   Cárdenas

Playa El Coco
La Flor Wildlife Refuge

El Ostional
Bahía Salinas   La Cruz

*PACIFIC
OCEAN*

COSTA
RICA

*Santa Rosa
National Park*   Liberia,
San José

© The Countryman Press

N

0   10   20
Miles

⊗ **Hecho** (www.hechomagazine.com) Bilingual, beautifully designed arts and culture magazine has a Web site with an events calendar, movie schedules, and hipsters galore.

IBW Internet Gateway (www.ibw.com.ni) Portal has listings for government, education, commercial, and tourism sites, as well as hospitals and NGOs.

Latin American Network Information Center (www1.lanic.utexas.edu/la/ca/nicaragua) Academic portal has links to university, tourism, culture, media, economics, sports, and political sites.

⊗ **Manfut** (www.manfut.com) Huge, messy Web site is a great source of photos, videos, and articles about every corner of Nicaragua, most in Spanish.

Nica Living (www.nicaliving.com) Popular expat forum offers a wealth of knowledge, information, gossip, and absurdities that offer real insights into your new favorite country.

Nica Times (www.nicatimes.net) This English-language weekly has humorous articles, tourism information, and, sometimes, actual hard-hitting journalism.

✪ **Nicaragua Guide** (www.nicaragua-guide.com) Fantastic resource for long-term visitors.

✪ **ViaNica** (www.vianica.com) When travel guides finally disappear forever, we can blame excellent Web sites like this one, with beautifully presented, bilingual information about destinations, hotels, restaurants, and more.

TOUR OPERATORS

These are just a few of the outfitters offering tours in Nicaragua; many more can be found online. Also check the destination chapters, listing local operators.

Bohdin Adventure Services (www.bodhin.com) Upscale outfit offers pricey wellness tours, including yoga workshops and luxury ecolodges.

Un Buen Viaje (612-386-0839 (U.S.); www.tourstonicaragua.com) Adventurous, all-inclusive tours offer inroads and insight into the Nicaragua less traveled.

Cocopeli Tours (2270-6497, 8479-1530; www.cocopeli-tours.com) Small outfitter offers full-custom tours to unusual, difficult-to-reach destinations.

Hijuela (8698-1439; www.hijuela.com) Specializes in multiple-day tours to the cool northern Nicaraguan Highlands, not covered in this book but well worth seeing.

I Do! Bodas (2266-6405; www.idobodas.com; Bolonia, Nicaragua) Plans destination weddings and corporate events.

Gray Line Tours Nicaragua (2552-6000; www.graylinenicaragua.com) Seasoned international operator offers plush bus tours all over Nicaragua and Central America.

Solentiname Tours (2270-9981; www.solentinametours.com) Operator specializes in the other side of Lake Nicaragua and the magical Solentiname Archipelago and Río San Juan.

CRIME

Nicaragua is the safest country in Latin America (tied with Uruguay), but it is also the poorest. "Rich tourists" are sometimes targeted for theft.

Most crime is nonviolent and opportunistic, such as overcharging for cabs, giving incorrect change, and stealing items off beaches. While the majority of hotel workers are honest, there is no reason to tempt someone making US$5 per day by leaving cash and electronics out in the room. Keep valuables in a safe or locker, with the front desk, or otherwise secured out of sight.

Pickpockets, camera snatchers, and other thieves work the markets, buses, festivals, and central parks, so don't let your belongings dangle or keep a wallet in your back pocket. Make a photocopy of your passport to carry, and leave valuables at your hotel. If anyone tries to distract you by spilling something on you, tugging your sleeve, or even starting a conversation in a chaotic situation—such as a bus terminal ("I want to practice my English"), these are red flags, warning you to stay alert, survey your surroundings, and keep your belongings close.

Armed muggings do happen, particularly in Managua and around San Juan del Sur. Ask business owners about recent security issues, and avoid carrying anything you wouldn't cheerfully hand over at knifepoint.

Most taxis in Nicaragua are shared—that is, they will pick up new passengers while en route to a destination. This is usually safe, but one popular trick in Managua at press time begins with a friendly stranger, often a woman who approaches you on a bus, offering to share a cab to a destination. After the mark is in the taxi, other "passengers" get in and immobilize him or her, usually by cramming them into the middle of the back seat or (if the victim is in the passenger seat) holding a knife to their throat. They will then drive them to several different ATM machines until their account is drained, and dump the victim (usually unharmed) far from town. When I travel in Managua, I like to sit directly behind the driver, and will feign nausea if anyone tries to take my window seat.

You may be offered illegal drugs, usually marijuana and cocaine. If you purchase them, note that every *vago* (bad guy) in town will know within the hour, making you a woozy target for theft and sexual assault.

Prostitution is illegal in Nicaragua, though widespread and generally tolerated. Pedophiles having sex with children under 18, however, are vindictively pursued and gleefully prosecuted to the very full extent of the law.

If you are pulled over for a traffic offense, the police officer can take your driver's license until you pay the fine, usually at an inconveniently located bank. You can ask, "*¿No hay una multa que podría pagar aquí?*" (Is there a fine I can pay here?) Bribery is illegal, and your offer may well be refused. However, the going rate for minor traffic offenses is around US$10.

If you are accused of a more serious crime, police have the right to keep you 48 hours before you are charged, so be friendly and polite; they will generally return the favor. You do not get a call, you cannot see your lawyer, and if you go to jail on a Friday, you'll be there until Monday. If you are taken to jail, keep cash on your person; cops may let you order out for pizza, which you should share.

CLIMATE

Nicaragua has two seasons. *Verano*—literally "summer" but better translated as "dry season"—runs from November through April. Streams dry up, trees lose their leaves, and you can count on hot, sunny days. *Invierno*, "winter," is the rainy season, with showers most afternoons from May through October, with the heaviest rains in September and October.

Southwest Nicaragua is warm, generally between 18°C (64°F) and 32°C (90°F), with March and April in the high 30s (100s). The rainy season can be cool at times, with November and December the coolest months. The Meseta Central and tops of cloud forested volcanoes can get chilly, dropping into the low 10s (50s). Bring a sweater or light jacket.

INFRASTRUCTURE ISSUES

Nicaragua is a developing nation, and both water and electricity can go out for several hours at a time. Better hotels have water tanks and generators; budget places usually do not. Bring a flashlight, candles, and perhaps wet wipes or antibacterial gel.

Tap water is potable in Managua, Granada, Masaya, and the cities of the Pueblos Blancos. On Isla Ometepe or at any of the beaches (including San Juan del Sur), it's best to drink bottled water.

Even the dry tropical forest is lush in its way—with pitahaya plants, rather than the cloud forest's more familiar bromeliads, making their homes in the trees.

Nicaragua Facts and Figures

Capital: Managua

Size: 130,373 square km (50,337 square miles)—largest country in Central America

Population: 5,700,000 (over 1 million live abroad)

Race: 69% Mestizo, 17% White, 9% Black, 5% Amerindian

Religion: 58.5% Roman Catholic, 21.6% Evangelical, 15.7% Agnostic/Atheist; 1.6% Moravian; 2.6% Other Religions

Currency: Córdoba (C$)

Country Code: 505

Time: GMT–6

Electricity: 110 Volts AC/60Hz and 220 volts (US-style electrical plugs, but many have only two prongs; bring an adapter)

Useful Phone Numbers

Fire Department 115, 911

Police 118, 126

Red Cross 128

Information 113

International Operator 116

SOCIAL UNREST

While modern Nicaragua is a notably nonviolent country, it has the some of the most liberal free speech laws in the world. Protests are common and can be a bit scary, particularly when teenagers bring out their "mortars," or homemade projectile launchers. These are basically glorified fireworks, but you wouldn't want to get hit by one.

If a protest or strike happens near you (and the 2011 elections will surely be preceded by plenty), the best thing you can do is walk in the other direction. Bystanders are never targeted, but there's always the chance of some overenthusiastic little drip firing his mortar in the direction of a cop, and you don't want to get caught up in the ensuing melee.

CENTROS TURÍSTICOS

The government operates several *centros turísticos,* or tourist centers, left over from the more socialist Sandinista administration of the 1980s. They often occupy land once owned by the Somoza inner circle, and are always in a spectacular natural setting, perhaps a crater lake or particularly nice beach.

They're usually on the scroungy side, but have amazing playground equipment, lots of benches and trees, inexpensive restaurants and bars, and sometimes basic lodging. They usually charge US$0.25 to enter, US$1.25 with a car.

LODGING

Nicaragua does not have the same range of top-end accommodations offered in more developed destinations, but that's changing. Managua, Granada and San Juan del Sur all have luxury hotels, which are bargains by international standards.

Midrange travelers will find comfortable hotels and B&Bs throughout Southwest Nicaragua. For US$30 to US$80, you can enjoy spotless, attractive accommodation in modern buildings or beautifully refurbished Colonial mansions with fabulous views, wonderful patios and gardens, pools, and most modern amenities—except, perhaps, hot showers. Ask if that's important to you.

Budget travelers will be in heaven—you can find your own room in major tourist destinations for US$10, a dorm bed for US$5, or even less off the beaten path. You'll have your choice of internationally operated backpacker spots with free coffee, wifi, and cheap tours—or family-run hotels geared to Nicaraguan travelers, which are generally much more basic, private, and cheap.

RESTAURANTS AND FOOD PURVEYORS

Nicaragua isn't exactly a foodie destination, but you'll find restaurants serving international cuisine, vegetarian food, and gourmet meals in Managua, Granada, and San Juan del Sur.

In less touristy spots, you'll probably be limited to fresh seafood and well-prepared Nica cuisine, served at *comedores,* simple eateries offering inexpensive set plates; *bufetes* or *comida a la vista,* steam-table buffets where you point to your preference; and on the street, where you'll usually find *quesillos, vigarón, baho, fritangas,* hot dogs, and *raspados*—Nicaraguan snow cones.

Food is generally hygienically prepared, and few people have stomach problems visiting Southwest Nicaragua. Those with delicate stomachs should avoid markets, street stands, and fresh, unpeeled fruits and vegetables.

Rooms in authentic Colonial hotels can vary a great deal in size, shape, and natural light; some are quite beautiful, like this room in Granada's Hotel La Bocona.

Despite the growing upscale market, budget travelers can still find rooms with amenities such as "Dude, they'll throw a cold beer right up to your hammock!"

Meals at a sit-down restaurant are a luxury to most Nicaraguans, thus some ceremony is involved. First, order just your drinks. Service is sometimes slow, but you're supposed to be enjoying yourself, right? Only after drinks arrive is it considered polite to ask for appetizers, and then your meal. Afterward, they won't bring your check until you ask for it, either verbally (*"la cuenta, por favor"*) or by using international sign language, holding an invisible pen in the air and squiggling.

Every major city has a municipal market, often next to the bus lot, while vendors in smaller villages usually sell produce, baked goods, and other items in the central park.

SHOPPING

Nicaragua's artisans produce several very fine *artesanías*, or handicrafts. The most popular (and pricey) place to shop is the **Masaya Old Market**, with top-quality crafts from all over the country, including the famed naïve paintings from Solentiname and black pottery of Jintoga. The city of Masaya and surrounding towns are well known for their family workshops, which you can visit with a tour or on your own.

Nicaragua's signature handicrafts are Masaya's hammocks, considered among the best in the world—and well worth the struggle getting home. Fine woodwork, export-quality leather goods, and beautiful ceramics (have the store wrap them up) are also great gifts. Some of your friends, however, may prefer Nicaragua's famous cigars, coffee, and Flor de Caña rum.

If you've always wanted to see the inside of a third-world prison, try removing pre-Columbian artifacts from the country. If you purchase replica Chorotega pottery, keep the receipt to show at immigration.

MAPS

Unfortunately, the easiest map to find outside the country is **ITMB Nicaragua** (US$10), which has potentially dangerous errors. Order **Mapas Naturismo** (www.mapas-naturismo.com; US$10) instead, also available in Nicaraguan shops. If you have a compatible system, **GPS Travel Maps** (www.gpstravelmaps.com) has downloads, US$24.95 for a basic map, US$49.95 with routable functions.

Once you're in the country, you'll find loads of excellent, free maps at **Intur** offices, hotels, tour operators, and rental car companies. **Bosawas Maps** (www.bosawas.com), available all over the country and online, and **Tierra Tour** (www.tierratour.com) in Granada, have the best city maps for top destinations. Intur makes the most useful country

Many restaurants, particularly in rural destinations, still use wood-fired stoves; allow time for a leisurely meal.

map, with handy regional inserts for top destinations. The best free map of San Juan del Sur is inside the weekly *Del Sur News*.

Serious map lovers can visit **INETER** (Nicaraguan Institute for Territorial Studies; 2249-3890; in front of the Hospital Metrópoli Xolotlán; 9 AM–12 PM and 1 PM–5 PM), in a really sketchy part of Managua (take a cab), with scores of different maps for sale that are also viewable online.

Getting Around

Air

Aeropuerto Internacional Augusto C. Sandino (MGA; 2233-1624; www.eaai.com.ni; KM11 Carretera Norte) is Nicaragua's only international airport, with an adjacent terminal for national flights on **La Costeña Airlines** (www.lacostena.com.ni) to Caribbean destinations. Recently remodeled, it is Central America's most modern. The US$35 departure tax is usually included in your ticket.

There is an unmanned Intur desk inside the international terminal, with free maps and brochures, and another information desk close to the ticket counters, with English speaking staff and a phone to make hotel reservations. There are several ATM machines, souvenir shops, bookstores, cell phone stores, and rental car companies (see the Managua chapter) next to ticketing. Note that there's a one-time fee of US$10 for renting cars at the airport. Inside the terminal, there is an anemic selection of duty free shops and souvenir stores, and **Café las Flores,** with a smoking section and pretty good hummus.

There are several airlines serving MGA, including:

Aerocaribbean (2277-1591; www.cubajet.com) Daily flights to Havana, Cuba
Aeromexico (2266-6997, 2233-2875; www.aeromexico.com; Plaza España, de la Óptica Visión, 1 cuadra este) Four weekly flights to Mexico City
American Airlines (2255-9090; www.aa.com; Plaza España, 3 cuadras sur) Daily flights to Miami
Continental Airlines (2233-1624; www.continental.com) Daily flights to Houston
Copa Airlines (2267-0045; www.copaair.com) Daily flights to Guatemala City, San José (Costa Rica), San Salvador, and Panama City
Delta Airlines (2233-9943, 2254-8130; www.delta.com; rotonda El Güengüense, 1 cuadra este) Daily flights to Atlanta
Spirit Airlines (2233-2884; 2233-2886; www.spiritair.com) Budget night flights to Fort Lauderdale, Florida
TACA (2266-6698, 2263-1929; www.taca.com; Plaza España, Edificio Málaga) Daily flights to Argentina, Belize, Brazil, Canada, Chile, Colombia, Cuba, Ecuador, Guatemala City, Los Angeles, Mexico City, Miami, New York, Peru, Panama, and San Salvador

Taxi Transportation from the Airport

Look for the red shirts right outside the door to find ✪ **Taxis Oficial Aeropuerto** (8811-1816), which offers safe, private taxis for up to four people to central Managua (US$16), Masaya (US$30), Granada (US$45), León (US$80), and other destinations.

Cheaper shared taxis wait across the street from the airport, and charge US$5 per person to take you into Managua. These are usually safe, but your bags and newbie status do make you a juicy target for theft.

Private Shuttles from the Airport
Several companies provide comfortable, air-conditioned shuttles from the airport to popular tourist destinations. These should be reserved in advance.

Adelante Express (8850-6070, 2568-2390; www.adelanteexpress.com) Serves San Juan del Sur and the surrounding beaches

Nica Express (2552-8461, 8988-8127, 8883-8127 (Sun.); www.nica-adventures.com; Granada, Calle La Calzada) Runs shuttles to Granada, San Jorge, San Juan del Sur, and the Costa Rican border

Paxeos (2552-8291, 8465-1090; www.paxeos.com; Granada parque central, blue house next to the cathedral) Serves Granada, León, San Juan del Sur, and San Jorge (Isla Ometepe)

Flying into Costa Rica
Because Costa Rica receives more international flights than Nicaragua, it's often significantly cheaper and more convenient to fly into Liberia's **Aeropuerto Internacional Daniel Oduber Quirós** (LIR; www.liberiacostaricaairport.net), an hour by taxi from the Nicaraguan border; or San José's **Aeropuerto Internacional Juan Santamaría** (www.alterra.co.cr), four hours by taxi, or six hours by bus, from the border.

Until recently, **Nature Air** (www.natureair.com) offered direct flights from both San José and Liberia to **Aeropuerto Granada** (GRA), which is currently closed. Check to see if that's changed.

International Buses
Several international bus lines have offices in Managua, with connections to all Central American capitals. You can also get buses to Costa Rica and Panama from Granada, Masaya, and Rivas, and there's a ticket office in San Juan del Sur. You should buy tickets in advance, in person, with your passport in hand.

Central Line (2254-5431; del antiguo Cine Cabrera, 2.5 cuadras arriba sobre Avenida 27 de Mayo) Three daily buses to San José (US$23; 4:30 AM Tue. through Sun., 10 AM Mon.)

Cruceros del Golfo (2222-3065; www.kingqualityca.com; Sector Bolonia, Cine Dorado 200 metros este) The only direct bus to Guatemala City (US$50; 2:30 AM) and a 5:30 AM bus to San Salvador (US$27)

King Quality (2228-1454; www.kingqualityca.com; Sector Bolonia, Cine Dorado 200 metros este) Luxury line has buses to San José (US$32; 2 PM); Honduras (US$43; 5 AM, 11 AM); San Salvador (US$52; 3 AM, 5 AM); and Guatemala City (US$94; 5 AM, 11 AM)

Tica Bus (2222-3031; www.ticabus.com; Sector Bolonia, Cine Dorado 200 metros arriba) Popular, reliable line has a convenient hostel ($) in Managua, three buses to Costa Rica (US$20; 6 AM, 7 AM, and noon); and a 5 AM bus to Tegucigalpa, San Salvador, and Guatemala City (US$72)

Transnica (2270-3133; Rotonda de Metrocentro, 3 cuadras al lago, 50 metros arriba) Buses to San José (US$20; 5:30 AM, 7 AM, 10 AM, 3 PM); Tegucigalpa (US$40; 2 PM), and San Salvador (US$50; 5 AM, 12:30 PM); one executive bus to San José (US$40; noon)

Crossing the Costa Rican Border

Just 24 km (15 mi) south of Rivas and 40 km (25 mi) from San Juan del Sur is the Sapoá–Peñas Blancas border with Costa Rica. Whether you need to "renew" your visa with a 72-hour vacation, are flying out of a Costa Rican airport, or just want to see what the neighbors are up to, this is the easiest place to cross.

Going south across this border is much easier on an international bus, which will guide you through the somewhat confusing process. International buses leave for Liberia and San José, Costa Rica, from Granada, Jinotepe, Managua, Masaya, and Rivas. (If you're headed north, it's much more convenient to leave from Managua.)

If you do it on your own, the bus from Rivas will drop you in Sapoá, a chaotic strip of food stalls, about one block from the poorly signed door through the border fence. There, a guard will charge you US$1 for municipal taxes.

Once inside the border, you will be accosted by pint-sized touts offering to help you navigate customs. This isn't a bad idea—they have the forms you'll need (and pens), and can carry your bags for a bit more. Otherwise, head to the first official looking building and go to the outside window (look for the lines of people carrying luggage), where you will pay US$2, in córdobas or dollars, to leave Nicaragua. (It's US$7 to enter.) There is a public bathroom behind the bank (with an ATM), as well as mediocre duty free shops and people selling snacks and hammocks.

From here, you'll walk or take a pedicab about 1 km across the border, stopping once to have your passport, and maybe bags, checked. On the Costa Rican side, you enter the building to have your passport stamped. It is free to enter or leave Costa Rica. This side of the border has a good restaurant with clean restrooms, and an ATM.

While you can exchange Costa Rican *colones* fairly easily in Granada or San Juan del Sur, Nicaraguan *córdobas* are generally useless outside Nicaragua. If you exchange money at the border, note that the *coyotes* (money changers) are notoriously dishonest. Know the exchange rate ahead of time, and approximately how much you should be getting back.

Buses leave right from the border post to Liberia, Costa Rica (US$2, 2 hours), every 45 minutes or so. Buses leave to San José (US$6, 6 hours), the capital, every hour. Taxis wait to take you to Liberia (US$50 for four). On the Nicaraguan side of the border, travelers must leave the border zone to find Rivas buses, which leave every 20 minutes. Taxis cost about US$20 to San Juan del Sur, US$30 to San Jorge (Isla Ometepe).

Driving cars over the border is time-consuming, but straightforward; it's US$22 to drive into Costa Rica, US$15 to return to Nicaragua. Some rental car companies, including Alamo (www.alamo.com), allow you to take rental cars over the border for a fee.

Online Resources

Touristy Costa Rica is practically a bilingual country, and it's easy to navigate without a guidebook. These sites have all the information you'll need, in English. *Pura vida!*

Go Visit Costa Rica (www.govisitcostarica.com) Huge, comprehensive guide to the entire country

ICT (www.visitcostarica.com) Excellent, official Instituto Costarricense de Turismo site

Liberia, Costa Rica (www.liberiacostarica.com) Information on top-end hotels, private transportation, and area beaches

Liberia, Costa Rica Info (www.liberiacostaricainfo.com) This site isn't as pretty, but is more useful, with a great map, bus schedules, and hotel listings for every budget

✪ **Nicoya Peninsula** (www.nicoyapeninsula.com) Beautiful Web site covers Nicoya, jutting out into the Pacific just south of the border

Addresses

While streets in most major Nicaraguan towns have recently been named (or in Managua's case, numbered), these are only used, occasionally, in Granada. Most people give addresses using the traditional, and rather confusing, system of directionals.

Each town has certain well-known landmarks, many of which will be recognizable to tourists, such as the central park (*parque central*) or important churches. Others are more esoteric, such as Piedra La Bocona, a stone statue that was Granada's first mailbox; or mundane, for instance, Curacao department store—or, if Curacao closed several years ago, the address might be given from "*de donde fue Curacao,*" where Curacao used to be.

Addresses give the number of blocks (or meters, *varas,* or kilometers,) and direction (usually north, south, east, and west) from these locally known landmarks. For instance, Restaurant El Garaje's Granada address is "*del Convento San Francisco 2.5 cuadras al lago,*" i.e., "from Convento San Francisco, 2.5 blocks toward the lake."

Toward the lake? What lake? What convent? These are legitimate questions. In Managua, the lake is north; in Granada, it's to the east. The convent is mentioned in this book, so you could theoretically find the restaurant yourself using directionals. Other addresses aren't quite as easy. This is why I've given most addresses in Spanish, so you can ask taxi drivers and locals to point you in the right direction.

Addresses outside of towns are often given as a kilometer measurement, usually from Managua, on major highways called *carreteras.* For instance, Viva Guesthouse is at *KM14 Carretera Managua-Masaya,* i.e., 14 km from Managua on the road toward Masaya.

Units of Measurement

Cuadra: city block, sometimes designated (imprecisely) as "100 metros"
Metro: meter
Vara: 0.83 meters

Directions

Abajo: Down (usually "west," but sometimes "downhill")
Al lago: Toward the lake
Arriba: Up (usually "east," but sometimes "uphill")
Contiguo: Next to
Este: East
Frente: Across from
Mano derecha/izquierda: Right/left side
Norte: North
Oeste: West
Sur: South

Landmarks

Barrio: Neighborhood
De donde fue [Cine Cabrera]: Where [Cabrera Cinema] used to be
Entrada: Entrance (the exit off a carretera into town)
Puente: Bridge
Rotonda: Traffic circle
Semáforos: Traffic lights

Car

Nicaragua is a relatively inexpensive country (by Central American standards) to rent a car, and most major roads to destinations covered by this book are very good. Some secondary routes, including those to popular Pacific beaches, are well maintained dirt roads.

In the dry season, most of these are passable with normal cars. In the rainy season, some roads can be impassable even in four-wheel-drive vehicles. After heavy rains, it's worth asking if the road is open: "*¿Se puede pasar por Playa Gigante?*"

You'll be sharing the road, including the Panamerican Highway, with oxcarts, horse-drawn carriages, three-wheeled motor taxis, herds of cattle, and so on. Don't expect to get anywhere quickly.

To rent a car, you must have a driver's license (foreign licenses are good for one month after entering Nicaragua), passport, and credit card. In general, you must be over 25 years old. Local operations may offer a little leeway. Your credit card probably covers at least two weeks of car insurance, but call to make sure. Regardless, you are required to buy very basic insurance for US$13 per day; optional policies provide better coverage.

Most rental car agencies are based in Managua, but there are also desks in Granada, San Juan del Sur, Isla Ometepe, and elsewhere.

Taxis

Most taxis are shared, i.e., they will stop to pick up passengers en route to your destination. This presents certain security issues; see the Crime section in this chapter for more. Always check for a taxi license on the dash, and compare the photo to the driver. If anything seems off, there are hundreds more cabs to choose from.

Settle on a price before getting in the taxi. Taxi drivers will often try to overcharge foreigners. I usually ask local businesses about appropriate fares: "*Cuanto cuesta un taxi por [Tica Bus]?*" ("How much is a taxi for [Tica Bus]?") Then, when the driver quotes a much higher fee, I can say, "*Me dijo la señora 30 córdobas*" ("The lady told me 30 córdobas"). In Granada, taxis have a set fare of 10 córdobas (US$0.50) anywhere in the city.

Buses

Buses are frequent and inexpensive. In general, there are two types of intercity buses. Full-size buses, usually Bluebirds, are cheaper and more frequent, but stop for anyone on the side of the road, which slows you down. Smaller microbuses, or minivans, cost a few córdoba more but are safer and faster. These usually leave when full, rather than having a set schedule.

Buses are generally safe, although you should always keep a close eye on your valuables. Keep documents and valuables in your moneybelt and a smaller, separate backpack in case they need to move your larger bag. You may be asked to put big backpacks and suitcases in the back of the bus, which is usually safe, but stay close if you can.

Board the bus and take a seat. Once you're rolling, someone will come to collect the money. If he gives you a ticket, keep that safe—you'll need to show it later.

Intercity buses do not have restrooms; plan ahead. Buses usually run from about 4 AM—7 PM. **Central America Bus Schedules** (www.horariodebuses.com) has bus schedules throughout the country.

Boats

You'll need to take a ferry to get to Isla Ometepe, the Zapatera Archipelago, and hotels in the Isletas de Granada. Boat taxis are also convenient along the Pacific Coast, particularly from San Juan del Sur to the surrounding beaches. Kayaking is popular in Granada, Isla Ometepe, and Laguna de Apoyo.

Public boats do not routinely hand out life jackets, but you can ask for one. The lake can be choppy; consider taking Dramamine for longer trips.

Bicycles

Nicaraguans use bicycles as a primary means of transportation on any road, including the Panamerican Highway, so drivers will see you. You can rent bikes easily in Granada, San Juan del Sur, and Isla Ometepe.

PRACTICAL MATTERS

Bathrooms and Showers

First: *Never flush toilet paper.* There are a handful of hotels with special plumbing, but if there's a wastebasket beside the toilet, that's where your paper goes. If you forget and the toilet overflows, let management know what happened, as that will expedite repair. You will never forget again.

In the midrange and budget categories, there may not be hot water, so ask, if that's important to you. Hot showers are more common on the cooler Meseta Central, often using electric water heaters installed directly on the showerhead. Rather ominous-looking plastic bulbs with wires sticking out, they are colloquially known as "suicide machines" and require a delicate touch.

Before starting the shower, put it on the hottest setting, usually indicated by two blackened ovals on the far left of the switch. Turn on the water until you hear an electric hum. The trick is to turn the water to the lowest possible flow while maintaining the hum, for a hot, or more likely lukewarm, shower. Do not touch the heater until you are dry.

Public bathrooms can be a bit basic at markets and bus stops; plan ahead.

In very basic hostels and markets, you may run into bucket-flush toilets. The handle won't work, and there will be a large barrel of water with a smaller bucket nearby. Fill the smaller bucket, raise the toilet seat (if there is one), and pour about a gallon of water into the bowl from chest high. Voila! Now you're flushing like a local.

Communications

International Calls

You can make convenient, cheap, international calls at the chain **Llamadas Heladas** (www.llamadas.com.ni), with air-conditioned private booths. They have a blue logo, and are usually close to the central park in most major Nicaraguan cities, including Granada, Masaya, Managua, and Rivas. They also recharge cell phones.

Most Internet cafes also offer inexpensive international calls. You'll sometimes see credit card payphones specifically for international calls, but these are ridiculously expensive.

Cell Phones

It's inexpensive to purchase a cell phone while in Nicaragua, or simply buy prepaid chips for your own phone. There are two major networks, **Claro** (www.claro.com.ni) and **Movistar** (www.movistar.com), both of which have *recargas,* or chip recharging stations, in every tiny town in Nicaragua.

Internet Access

Wireless Internet is widely available at hotels geared to international travelers, as well as some cafés, restaurants, and malls. Some hotels lie about having wifi; check before paying if it's important. Internet cafés can be found in even the smallest towns.

Mail

Correos de Nicaragua, the post office, can be found in most towns of any size, usually within a few blocks of the central park. DHL has offices in Managua, Granada, and Masaya.

Embassies and Consulates

Most countries have embassies or consulates in Managua; you can find a complete list at **Embassies Abroad** (www.embassiesabroad.com/embassies-in/Nicaragua).

Gay and Lesbian Travelers

In 2002, President Chamorro criminalized homosexuality, probably to secure much-needed aid money from the Catholic Church and religious entrepreneurs. The law was rarely enforced, and in 2008 the FSLN repealed it, though homosexuality still remains something of a social taboo.

Many gays and lesbians live fairly openly in Managua, where the **March for Sexual Diversity** is held each year. Tourist areas, including Granada and San Juan del Sur, have become safe havens for Nicas who are out and about. In smaller towns, it's polite to play down your sexuality; violence or even negative reactions are rare, but you might make older people uncomfortable.

There a few Web sites to help you find the scene, including **Gay Nicaragua** (www.gaynicaragua.net), **Global Gayz** (www.globalgayz.com), and **Purple Roofs** (www.purpleroofs.com), with recommendations for gay-friendly businesses.

In **Managua**, there are at least two prominent gay bars, **Tabú** (Bolonia, de Intur 0.5 cuadras al oeste), a big disco with broad appeal, and the more upscale **Q** (Calle 27 de Mayo, semaforos 200 metros este), both convenient to Plaza Inter. **Viva Guesthouse and Spanish School** (8743-3700; www.vivanicaraguaguesthouse.com; KM14 Carretera Masaya; $$; wifi) provides information and lodging.

It's easy for adventurous types to arrange artesanal fishing anywhere, but San Juan del Sur has the widest choice of professional sportfishing outfits.

Granada doesn't have exclusively gay bars, but the scene is very gay-friendly, with spots like **Café Nuit, El Club, Disco Mi Tierra, Restaurant Omix**, and **La Pantera** in the centro turístico well known among revelers. The centro turístico is a "meet and greet" spot for local men in the afternoon. **Hotel Joluva** (www.joluvanicaragua.com) is a good source of information.

Similarly, San Juan del Sur lacks a gay and lesbian "scene," but **Pelican Eyes** and other businesses are very welcoming of gay and lesbian travelers.

Special Needs Travelers

Nicaragua has very little specific infrastructure for wheelchairs or the blind. However, as with any country recovering from a major war, there are plenty of locals with disabilities, so people are used to helping out. You'll find haphazardly placed ramps in the uneven streets, and many hotels can prepare rooms with temporary ramps and reconfigured furnishings if you give them advance notice. I have referred to this type of access throughout the book as "challenging."

HEALTH CARE

Nicaragua has a two-tiered health care system that provides free medical services to everyone, including tourists and illegal immigrants. They don't even ask to see your ID. If you'd rather spend money for more comfortable care, there are better private hospitals in Managua, and a network of private clinics throughout the country.

Pharmacies (*farmacías*) serve as de facto clinics, and can diagnose and treat minor medical problems. They have a *Libro de Contraindicaciones* for clients. It can be hard to find some medications and brands, so bring what you'll need from home.

While no special vaccinations are required for travel to Nicaragua, make sure that your hepatitis A, hepatitis B, and tetanus vaccinations are up to date. Malaria is present but very rare in Southwest Nicaragua, so antimalarial pills are not usually necessary.

Also rare but present is dengue, another mosquito-borne illness. It can be deadly, but more commonly means two painful weeks under close medical observation. If you become feverish (fair skinned people flush noticeably red), seek medical attention. Unfortunately, there is no medication for dengue, so bring DEET-based mosquito repellent (not usually available in Nicaragua) and sleep under a mosquito net or a fan.

Public Care

Major cities, including Managua, Masaya, Jinotepe, Granada, and Rivas, have free, full-service hospitals, while smaller populations, including San Juan del Sur, Isla Ometepe, and the Pueblos Blancos, have public clinics, called *Centros de Salud*.

The care itself is actually pretty good, thanks to Nicaragua's close relationships with Cuba and Miami. Many doctors speak some English, equipment is usually modern, and service is by most accounts efficient, thorough, and professional.

Remember that this generous hospitality comes courtesy of the second poorest country in the hemisphere. Accommodations can be grimy, there's no food service (stands set up outside every hospital), and if they don't have the medication you need, you'll have to purchase it at a pharmacy.

Nicaraguans come prepared, with money (to send out for pizza and meds), a towel and/or sheet (seriously), and nothing that could be stolen while they sleep.

Private Care

Nicaragua also has a network of private hospitals and doctors' offices that provide (theoretically) better care in much more comfortable, hygienic conditions. There are also excellent private clinics; **Guía Nicaragua Médica** (www.suguiamedica.com) has listings. Wealthy Nicaraguans use the private system almost exclusively, while poorer folks augment incomplete public care with paid services.

A private consultation runs US$7 to US$40, while a stay in a private hospital can cost several hundred dollars per day.

Managua

Most private hospitals are in Managua, including excellent, modern ✪ **Hospital Metropolitano Vivian Pellas** (2276-2142; www.metropolitano.com.ni), considered the best in the country; and **Hospital Bautista** (2264-9020; www.hospitalbautistanicaragua.com; Barrio Largaespada, costado Sur del Recinto Universitario Carlos Fonseca Amador), which is older, but still known for quality care.

There are better-than-average public hospitals as well. The best are **Hospital Militar Dávila** (2222-2763; Loma de Tiscapa); **Hospital Salud Integral** (2266-1707; www.hospital saludintegral.com.ni; Montoya, 1 cuadra al lago, 1 cuadra abajo), and **Hospital Antonio Lenín Fonseca** (2266-6547; Residencia Las Brisas), with the country's best trauma unit.

Granada

Outside Managua, Granada has the widest range of treatment geared to foreigners. Public **Hospital Amistad Japón** (2552-7049; direccion conocida) is well known for good care, dirty sheets, and the dogs and cats in the courtyard waiting area. **Hospital Privado Cocibolca** (2552-2907; KM45 Carretera a Masaya) is private hospital, but you must have a doctor's referral to visit.

There are several good private clinics, including **Clínica de Especialidades Piedra Bocona** (2552-5989; Calle La Libertad), operated by English-speaking Dr. Francisco Blanco; **Dr. Pedro Pablo Iglesias** (2552-4179; Calle Aravesada, frente Farmacía Los Angeles), specializing in internal medicine; and **Dr. Yelka Martínez** (8855-2481; Calle Consulado, frente Movistar), who deals with women's issues.

MONEY

The official Nicaraguan currency is the córdoba (C$), denominated in C$1, C$5, and C$10 coins, and brightly colored C$10, C$20, C$50, C$100, C$200, and C$500 bills. It is difficult to change large bills outside major destinations.

U.S. dollars are widely accepted throughout the country; most businesses do their accounting in dollars. Bills must be in good condition; those with tears or markings may be refused. Euros, Canadian dollars, and other currencies can sometimes be exchanged in major tourist areas, but rates will be poor.

It is safe to change money on the street with *coyotes,* or money changers, in Granada (near banks and the market) and Managua (Plaza España). Coyotes are generally honest, but definitely know the exchange rate going in.

Credit Cards

Credit cards are widely accepted throughout the country. Some businesses, particularly in San Juan del Sur, will charge a 5 percent credit card processing fee. This is technically illegal (they're supposed to take the loss themselves), but common.

If you need a cash advance, Banco America Central (BAC) provides the best service to international travelers, with withdrawals of up to US$2,000 per day.

Debit Cards

ATM machines can be found in most major cities, and provide both dollars and córdobas. Be careful, particularly in Managua, when withdrawing cash in the evening; malls and supermarkets are your safest bets.

Tips

Nicaragua is a tipping country, and it is customary to leave a 10 percent tip at full-service restaurants (usually included with the bill, so check) unless service is truly terrible. Larger tips are appropriate at better restaurants and for exceptional service.

Guides should be tipped at least a few dollars, as this is often their primary income. Tipping maids, and other hotel staff, is appreciated as well. Taxi drivers are not usually tipped.

Visas

Nicaragua is happy to have you, and only requires visas (usually easy to get) from about 40 countries, listed by the **Ministerio de Relaciones Exteriores** (www.cancilleria.gob.ni). Citizens of most nations—including Australia, Canada, European Union member states, New Zealand, the U.S., and all Latin American countries except Cuba—do not require a visa. Fellow members of the C-4 Union (El Salvador, Guatemala, and Honduras) require only ID.

Your passport must be valid for six months after arriving. You'll need to buy a US$5 tourist card, which is good for 90 days. You can extend the visa for up to 90 more days (US$10 per month) at any Ministerio de Gobernación office; Sandino Park in Granada and MetroCentro Mall in Managua are convenient.

You can renew your visa unlimited times by leaving the country for 72 hours. Note that other C-4 countries do not count, so Costa Rica is usually the most convenient destination.

Nicaragua has extremely favorable requirements for residency and investment, but building your dream home and retiring to paradise isn't quite as simple as some realtors would have you believe. There are several books with advice for long-term residents; see Suggested Reading for listings.

A handful of companies offer consultations and information on the latest changes to residency laws, saving you time and money. Try **Details Management** (8432-4724; mavericks_granada@yahoo.ca; Calle El Arsenal, Tres Mundos, 50 metros oeste).

LANGUAGE

While many people working in the tourist industry speak some English, I highly recommend investing in a Spanish phrasebook; you'll be glad you did.

Nicaragua is an excellent place to learn Spanish, as classes are inexpensive and competitive, and people speak much more slowly than in, say, Mexico. Spanish schools are listed in all destination chapters. If you already speak Spanish, you'll be learning *Nicañol,* or Nicaraguan Spanish, which drops the "s" on many words and uses *vos* rather than *tu* in conversation.

EVENTS

These events are celebrated nationally, but each city has its own festivals, listed in those chapters and well worth making the effort to attend.

January
New Year's Day (January 1) Most businesses close.

March–April
Semana Santa (one week before Easter) "Holy Week" is the biggest event on the
    Nicaraguan social calendar. It starts on Palm Sunday, a spectacular followed by daily
    processions and special Masses, most poignantly the Stations of the Cross on Good Fri-

day. Many inland businesses close Thursday through Sunday, when everyone who can swing it heads to the beach, where rates rise, rooms fill, and revelry ensues.

May

Labor Day (May 1) Many businesses close.

Día de la Cruz (May 3) Day of the Cross is celebrated all over the country with pilgrimages up tall cross-topped mountains.

July

Anniversary of the Revolution (July 19) The anniversary of the 1979 triumph of the Sandinista-led Revolution packs Managua with FSLN faithful.

September

National Day of the Nicaraguan Entrepreneur (September 8) Officially honors martyred coffee magnate Jorge Salazar Argüello, but is really the conservative Liberal Party's answer to July 19.

Batalla de San Jacinto (September 14) Commemorates this key 1856 battle with William Walker's *filibusteros.*

Independence Day (September 15) Celebrates Central America's 1821 independence from Spain with marching bands, parades, and fireworks.

October

Día de la Raza (October 12) Christopher Columbus's arrival in the New World is celebrated with mixed emotions.

November

Día de los Difuntos (November 2) All Soul's Day is a family holiday, celebrated in cemeteries to honor lost loved ones.

December

La Purísima (December 8) The week leading up to the feast day of Nicaragua's Patron is filled with beautiful processions and special masses, culminating in *La Gritería,* when the crowd asks, "Who causes so much happiness?" and then answers, "The conception of María!"

Christmas (December 25) Many businesses close on December 24 and 25.

3

Managua and the Managua Beaches

Capital of Lakes and Volcanoes

Though they call Managua the "city without a center," Nicaragua's sprawling, lakefront capital has plenty of heart. It's rarely love at first sight, but give this lush city time to work its sultry charms and you'll discover a fascinating urban landscape of arts, business, music, and poetry—as well as revolutionary-topped volcanoes, relaxed ferry rides, huge markets, the country's best nightlife, and so much more.

The vast majority of tourists, intimidated by Managua's gritty expanse, skip the capital entirely to head for more accessible destinations. Adventurous souls, however, tempted by its shady streets, festive nightlife, and creative collection of monuments, may have some fun.

Enjoy a drink along the *malecón*, overlooking the silvery surface of Xolotlán, today called Lake Managua. The broad Pacific beaches of Masachapa and Pochomil, 15 gorgeous kilometers of golden sand, are a mere 45 minutes away in a private car.

The oldest footprints in the Americas, made some 6,000 years ago, are preserved by the lake's quiet shore. The new cathedral, however, is so emphatically modern that few people can even guess what it is. Upscale neighborhoods offer glittering malls, gourmet restaurants, five-star hotels, and exclusive clubs. General Sandino dominates the city skyline, standing atop Volcán Tipitapa; Managua is the only capital city in the world with a volcano right downtown.

"Downtown" is something of a misnomer in this fractured city. Managua once had Central America's most sophisticated city center, with high-rises and shops that glittered along the lakefront, inspiring Guy Lombardo's smooth anthem, *Managua:* "Every day is made for play and fun / 'cause every day is a fiesta . . . ."

Then, a few minutes after midnight on December 23, 1972, a series of strong earthquakes climaxed in a 6.5-magnitude monster that leveled the city. Managua's hospitals, police headquarters, and city center were reduced to rubble. Hundreds were still trapped in the wreckage that Christmas, capping a year of crop failure, constitutional crises, and social unrest by literally breaking Nicaragua's heart.

The holiday tragedy earned international attention, and millions of aid dollars poured in. Former President Anastasio Somoza Debayle, third in the series of Somozas to run the country, used his position as head of the National Guard to declare martial law, take control of the aid money, and enjoy his first taste of absolute power.

Much of the city was never rebuilt, as funds were channeled to the best-connected fami-

Managua is the greenest capital city in Central America, including shady neighborhoods like Los Robles—home to many of the capital's best hotels.

lies. Somoza's excesses began earning him the enmity of rich and poor alike. The Sandinista-led rebellion blossomed into a full-fledged revolution, and in 1979 the dictatorship was violently ousted.

Exhausted, cheering young rebels filled the crumbling remains of the Plaza de la República, which they pledged to rebuild. Instead, they would spend the next decade embroiled in a proxy Cold War nightmare.

The wealthy rebuilt on the outskirts of town, today the upscale Los Robles and Altamira neighborhoods. The old city center is still called the "Ruins of Managua," where transient *maquilladora* workers and desperately poor families make their precarious homes.

Renovations over the past few years, however, have cleaned up the old city center, and today shady walkways connect the old cathedral and national theater, surrounded by monuments and important buildings. The lakefront, boasting brand-new centro turistico, Puerto Salvador Allende, is once again bringing families and fiesteros (party people) to the shores of Lake Managua.

Online Resources

Managua Alcaldía (www.managua.gob.ni) The mayor's site has city maps and Spanish-language information on area attractions, monuments, and government news.

Click Managua (www.clickmanagua.com) Online scene magazine has a great events calendar, information on restaurants, clubs, musicians, artists, concerts, movies, and much more.

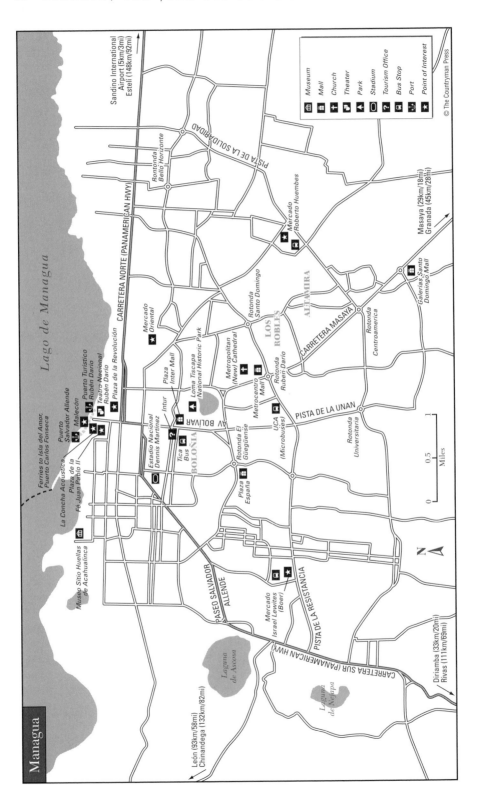

Managua

Lago de Managua

Sandino International
Airport (5km/3mi)
Estelí (148km/92mi)

CARRETERA NORTE (PANAMERICAN HWY)

PISTA DE LA SOLIDARIDAD

Rotonda
Bello Horizonte

Mercado
Roberto Huembes

Masaya (29km/18mi)
Granada (45km/28mi)

ALTAMIRA

Galerías Santo
Domingo Mall

Rotonda
Santo Domingo

LOS
ROBLES

CARRETERA MASAYA

Rotonda
Centroamerica

Mercado
Oriental

Plaza
Inter Mall

Metropolitan
(New) Cathedral

Loma Tiscapa
National Historic Park

Rotonda
Rubén Darío

Rotonda
Universitaria

PISTA DE LA UNAN

Metrocentro
Mall

UCA
(Microbuses)

AV BOLÍVAR

Intur

Estadio Nacional
Dennis Martínez

Tica
Bus

BOLONIA

Rotonda El
Güegüense

Plaza
España

Ferries to Isla del Amor,
Puerto Carlos Fonseca

La Concha Acústica

Plaza de la
Fe Juan Pablo II

Puerto
Salvador Allende

Malecón

Puerto Turístico
Rubén Darío

Teatro Nacional
Rubén Darío

Plaza de la Revolución

Museo Sitio Huellas
de Acahualinca

PASEO SALVADOR ALLENDE

Mercado
Israel Lewites
(Boer)

PISTA DE LA RESISTANCIA

CARRETERA SUR (PANAMERICAN HWY)

León (93km/58mi)
Chinandega (132km/82mi)

Laguna
de Asoxsa

Laguna
de Nejapa

Diriamba (33km/20mi)
Rivas (111km/69mi)

N

0   0.5   1
Miles

Museum
Mall
Church
Theater
Park
Stadium
Tourism Office
Bus Stop
Port
Point of Interest

© The Countryman Press

CRIME AND OTHER CONCERNS

While Managua is the safest Central American capital on paper, "wealthy tourists," are targeted for theft, most famously in the backpacker ghetto of Bolonia, usually called "Tica Bus" (for the bus station) or sometimes Barrio Marta Quezada.

Bag snatchers are the biggest problem, so leave your valuables in the hotel and don't let anything dangle. Armed muggings also occur, often on the walk from the Tica Bus neighborhood to Plaza Inter Mall. Thieves are looking for easy marks, so walk confidently and make it obvious that you are aware of your surroundings. The ATM at the Esso across from Plaza Inter Mall is well known for attracting clueless tourists, so use it carefully.

The taxi scam described in the Planning Your Trip chapter, under Crime, is a real problem in Managua. There are hundreds of taxis, so there is never any reason to let a stranger choose your cab for you. Your hotel has trusted drivers whom they can call.

You should take all big-city precautions anywhere in Managua, which has extremely poor neighborhoods, but ripping off tourists is less of an industry elsewhere in town. The lakefront malecón is pretty run down, but there's plenty of security, particularly at family-friendly Puerto Salvador Allende. The posh Altamira and Los Robles districts are generally very safe, even walking around at night.

TOURIST INFORMATION

Intur (2254-5191 ext 237; gloria@intur.gob.ni; from Crowne Plaza, 1 block south and 1 block east, Sector Bolonia; open from 8 AM–1 PM Mon. through Fri.). Convenient to Plaza Inter Mall, Tica Bus, and Sector Bolonia, the Ministry of Tourism's flagship tour office is the best of the bunch, with attentive staff, lots of flyers and free maps, and more.

GETTING AROUND

Managua is Nicaragua's transportation hub. It is home to Nicaragua's only international airport, **Aeropuerto Internacional Augusto C. Sandino** (MGA; 2233-1624; www.eaai.com.ni; KM11 Carretera Norte), and most international bus terminals, both covered in the Planning Your Trip chapter. Buses throughout the country leave from five major terminals.

Managua sprawls. While some maps show numbered sidestreets, only the names of major carreteras are used. Addresses are given in directionals, which are even more complicated here than elsewhere. Excellent free maps are available at the airport, Intur, and most hotels; get one. Shared taxis ply the streets, and they can get you where you need to go—show them the address as it's written in this chapter.

Car

Managua can be challenging in a car, but the major roads—Carretera Masaya, Avenida Bolivar, Carretera Sur—are fairly well signed and easy to navigate, as long as you have a map (most rental car companies have great free ones) and are prepared to deal with *rotondas,* or traffic circles.

Gas stations are everywhere in Managua proper, but there's only one by the beaches, between Masachapa and Pochomil. These are just a few of the rental companies available.

Alamo (2277-1117; www.alamonicaragua.com; Hospital Militar 100 varas arriba) Offices at the airport, Granada, and San Juan del Sur; they'll let you drive to Costa Rica for a US$25 fee.

Auto Express (2222-3816; www.aexpress.com.ni; Rotonda Plaza Inter, 1 cuadra al lago, 2.5 cuadras abajo) Nicaraguan company is convenient to Tica Bus.

✪ **Budget** (2255-9000 (airport), 2270-9669 (Holiday Inn Managua), 2278-9504 (Carretera Masaya), 800-758-9586 (U.S.); www.budget.com.ni) Offices in Granada, Peñas Blancas (Costa Rican border), Estelí, Chinandega, and Matagalpa. Will let you drive to Costa Rica for a fee.

Dollar (2552-8515; www.dollar.com.ni) Offices in Granada, Peñas Blancas, Estelí, Matagalpa, and León.

Lugo (2266-5240, 305-897-1805 (U.S. and Canada); www.lugorentacar.com.ni; Bolonia, Canal 2, 2 cuadras al lago, 3 cuadras abajo) Local company has offices on Carretera Masaya.

Toyota Rent a Car (2266-3620, 2233-2192 ext 2357; www.toyotarentacar.com; rotonda El Güegüense, 3 cuadras sur)

U-Save Auto Rental (2251-8860; www.usaveca.com; KM9.5 Carretera Norte)

Buses

There are five rather chaotic bus terminals sending buses throughout Nicaragua. While city buses connect them, take taxis when transporting luggage.

The city bus system is useful and cheap (US$0.30 anywhere in town), but crowded and intimidating, so most tourists take cabs. If you're up for it and speak a bit of Spanish, ask at your hotel or area businesses for information on getting to your destination.

MERCADO HUEMBES (MERCADO CENTRAL)
Granada US$0.50; every 15 minutes
Masatepe US$0.50; every 20 minutes
Masaya US$0.40; every 15 minutes
Nandaime US$0.50; every 30 minutes
Rivas US$1.50; every 30 minutes
San Jorge US$2; every 30 minutes
San Juan del Sur US$2.75; every 30 minutes

MERCADO MAYOREO
Bilwi (Puerto Cabezas) US$15; noon and 5 PM
Boaco US$1.50; every 30 minutes
Estelí US$2.25; every 30 minutes
Jinotega US$3.75; every hour
Matagalpa US$2; every 30 minutes
San Carlos (Costa Rican border) US$7.50; six times daily

MERCADO ISRAEL LEWITES
Chinandega US$2; every hour
Diriomo US$0.60; every 45 minutes
Jinotepe US$0.50; every 20 minutes

La Paz Centro (León Viejo) US$0.75; every 15 minutes
León via Ciudad Sandino and Laguna Xiloá US$1; every 30 minutes
Masachapa and Pochomil US$1.15; every 30 minutes

MERCADO ORIENTAL

Minibuses run between this huge, notoriously dangerous market and many destinations covered in this book, but it is not recommended for most tourists—particularly with luggage.

✪ TERMINAL UCA

Minibuses are fast and convenient, leaving every 20 minutes or so, when the van is full.

Diriamba US$1.15
Granada US$1
Jinotepe US$1.15
León US$2
Masaya US$0.50
Rivas US$2
San Marcos US$0.60
Ticuantepe US$1.15

MANAGUA BEACHES

Buses leave Israel Lewites for Masachapa, Pochomil, and Pochomil Viejo (US$1.15) every 30 minutes. Avoid buses that go via Villa Carmen, which adds an extra hour to your trip. Most hotels are located close to the bus line, while *triciclos turisticos* (bicycle rickshaws) provide inexpensive transport.

Taxi

Taxis in Managua are unmetered and, with the exception of pricey cabs at the airport and in front of some malls, shared. Taxistas almost always try to overcharge foreigners (and Nicaraguans), so feel free to haggle.

LODGING

Managua, unsurprisingly, has the widest range of lodging in the country, from US$5 budget backpacker accommodations close to the Tica Bus terminal (the de facto name of the neighborhood; tell your taxi driver "Tica Bus") in Bolonia, to the only real five-star accommodations in Nicaragua, most in the Los Robles and Altamira neighborhoods. At the beach, Montelimar is the only real full-service, all-inclusive beach resort in the country.

This chapter lists only a fraction of the great hotels available around town.

Lodging Price Code

Cost of lodging is based on an average per-room, double occupancy rate during peak season (December through April). Nicaragua's 15 percent sales tax and gratuities are not included; note that paying cash sometimes results in taxes being waived. Prices are much higher during the Christmas holidays and, to a lesser extent, Semana Santa (Easter Week), when you should have reservations.

Inexpensive ($)	Up to US$25
Moderate ($$)	US$25 to US$60
Expensive ($$$)	US$60 to US$100
Very Expensive ($$$$)	US$100 and up

SECTOR BOLONIA

This popular neighborhood for travelers has two main areas where hotels cluster. Close to Plaza España, a shopping center near Rotonda El Güegüense, there are several midrange boutique properties in a relatively safe residential neighborhood.

The more popular tourist quarter, close to Plaza Inter Mall and most international buses, is usually called "Tica Bus" for the Tica Bus terminal at its center, though it is sometimes labeled Barrio Marta Quezada. While there are a few upscale properties, closer to Plaza Inter, most are scraping the bottom of the budget category (see Other Hotels, later).

If you arrive on an international bus, touts will offer to lead you to hotels that pay them commission. They may say your preferred hotel is closed or full, but this probably isn't true.

CROWNE PLAZA HOTEL MANAGUA

General Manager: Dagoberto Silva
2228-3530
www.ichotelsgroup.com
Octava Calle Suroeste 101
Price: Very Expensive
Credit Cards: Yes
Handicap Access: Yes
Wifi: Free in the lobby, US$6 per day in rooms

A Managua landmark, this replica Mayan pyramid was one of the few buildings to survive the city's devastating 1972 earthquake. The upscale neighborhood that once surrounded Loma Tiscapa has since moved to Los Robles and Altamira, but this five-star InterContinental property remains.

It has recently been remodeled with soothing color schemes, fabulous bedding, and all the luxury amenities you'd expect. Upgrading to a suite or executive level accommodations gets you more perks; Howard Hughes was hiding out in the presidential suite when the earthquake hit.

On-site steakhouse **The Place** (2228-3530; L, D; $$–$$$) also belongs in a nicer neighborhood, with its handsome architecture, warm brick columns, and salto ceramic tile floors. Enjoy USDA Angus beef, U.S. or Brazilian cuts with one of more than one hundred different wines. There's also a US$8 all-you-can-eat Mongolian buffet at lunch.

HOTEL EL CONQUISTADOR

2222-4789
www.hotelelconquistador.info
gerencia@hotelelconquistador.info
De Plaza Inter, 1 cuadra sur, 1 cuadra oeste
Price: Moderate to Expensive
Credit Cards: Yes
Handicap Access: Challenging
Wifi: Yes

Though close to Tica Bus, this midrange beauty is a class act. A huge, breezy lobby with handmade rocking chairs and leafy murals is a great place to enjoy your complimentary breakfast, though the Spanish-style courtyard patio in the back might be nicer on a steamy afternoon.

Rooms aren't quite luxurious, but are comfortable and well decorated, with muted paint schemes, attractive furnishings, and original art. All the modern amenities, including hot baths, are provided as well.

HOTEL MOZONTE

Owner: Carlos Alvarado
2266-0686, 8864-1125, 786-350-4360 (U.S. and Canada)
www.hotelmozonte.com
info@hotelmozonte.com
Entrada a PriceSmart, 1.5 cuadra al lago
Price: Moderate
Credit Cards: Yes
Handicap Access: Yes
Wifi: Yes

This charming boutique hotel close to Plaza España is convenient to restaurants and grocery stores, well away from the backpacker ghetto. The theme is Spanish Colonial, with rooms on two floors fronted by a patio surrounding the pool and garden. Rooms boast lots of gleaming hardwood accents and cool white tile. They aren't quite plush, but are spotless and modern, offering air-conditioning, private hot baths, phones, cable TV, desk areas, and complimentary breakfast. You may hear some noise from the pool at night.

✿ MANSIÓN TEODOLINDA
Manager: Neville A. Cross
2228-1050
www.teodolinda.com.ni
hotel@teodolinda.com.ni
De Intur, 1 cuadra al sur y 1 cuadra abajo
Price: Moderate to Expensive
Credit Cards: Yes
Handicap Access: Yes
Wifi: Yes

The Teodolinda is an absolute gem, close to Plaza Inter and most Bolonia nightlife, but without a hint of grunge. The whitewashed building is modern and safe, surrounding the best pool in the neighborhood. There are plenty of places to relax within its walls, including a small gymnasium and **Los Girasoles Restaurant** (B, L, D; $$), serving light international cuisine, steak, and seafood.

Rooms are clean and comfortable, if not extravagant, with white tiled floors, wood accents, frilly bedspreads, and good hot water (some rooms have tubs).

LOS ROBLES/ALTAMIRA
CASA NARANJA
General Manager: Carlos Morales
2277-3403
www.hotelcasanaranja.com
info@hotelcasanaranja.com
KM4.5 Carretera Masaya, de Tip Top 75 metros oeste, frente Pro-Nicaragua
Price: Expensive
Credit Cards: Yes
Handicap Access: Yes
Wifi: Yes

The lush gardens and patios at the heart of this boutique hotel, along with the plants and flowers throughout, may make you forget that you're staying in the capital. Though this is a newer building, the wood-accented arcades and archways that dominate its architecture seem faithfully Spanish, with tiled patios and living areas decorated with antiques.

All the rooms are different, but have attractive handmade furnishings, outstanding beds, and luxury amenities. The suites are more like apartments, with full kitchens and private entrances. If you're a golfer, note that they work with Nejapa Golf Club.

HILTON PRINCESS MANAGUA
Manager: Moises Figueroa
2255-5777
www1.hilton.com
KM4.5 Carretera Masaya, frente MetroCentro
Price: Very Expensive
Credit Cards: Yes
Handicap Access: Yes
Wifi: Yes

Hilton doesn't disappoint with its Managua location, with an ornate lobby, professional service, and five-star rooms with world-class amenities, perfectly patterned décor, and plush furnishings.

The gym and event/meeting centers are excellent, the pool area small but clean. There's a restaurant (the buffet breakfasts get raves) and bar. Two executive levels have higher quality amenities and a VIP lounge with great city views.

✪ HOTEL LOS ROBLES
Owner: Walter Buhler
2267-3008, 2277-2153, 2277-2157, 786-345-5195 (U.S.)
www.hotellosrobles.com
info@hotellosrobles.com
Del Restaurante La Marseillaise, 30 m al sur, Los Robles
Price: Very Expensive
Credit Cards: Yes

The InterContinental's executive floors offer outstanding views over Managua—to Momotombo Volcano on a clearer day than this.

Handicap Access: No
Wifi: Yes

It's like an elegant Spanish Colonial Granada hotel in Managua's nicest neighborhood, with its polished wooden columns, gleaming antiques, and shady green courtyard. It's a small hotel with a subtly inspiring artistry, from the handwoven bedspreads to the traditional metalwork, all positively glowing as the late afternoon sun.

Some rooms are a bit small, but all are outfitted to satisfy the most discriminating travelers. Bathrooms have hand-painted tiles and bathtubs, while rooms come equipped with upscale amenities, including a complimentary cell phone. The **restaurant** (B, D; $$$–$$$$) is excellent.

REAL INTERCONTINENTAL METROCENTRO MANAGUA

Sales: Ramiro Lorio
2276-8989, 2276-8988
www.ichotelsgroup.com
Frente Metrocentro, Carretera Masaya
Price: Very Expensive
Credit Cards: Yes
Handicap Access: Yes
Wifi: US$15 per day

This is Managua's finest luxury hotel, flawlessly professional from the moment you stroll into the exquisitely decorated, marble-floored lobby. Rooms are decidedly business oriented, with tasteful décor, flatscreen TVs, fluffy robes, huge windows and, on the executive floors (with a VIP lounge and better amenities), the best views in the city. The gym is solid and pool outstanding. You're conveniently right across from MetroCentro Mall.

ELSEWHERE IN MANAGUA
BEST WESTERN LAS MERCEDES
General Manager: Roberto Cruz Sequiera
2255-9910
www.lasmercedes.com.ni
reservaciones@lasmercedes.com.ni
KM11 Carretera Norte
Price: Expensive
Credit Cards: Yes
Handicap Access: Yes
Wifi: Yes

Location, location, location: Las Mercedes is a two-minute walk to the international airport, making this the logical spot to stay before or after a long flight. Happily, it's also a very nice hotel. The grounds are soothing, with a great pool, fountains, and palm trees to drown out plane noise, and with wooden cabanas scattered throughout. This is an older hotel, and while the smallish bungalows have been remodeled to international specifications—air-conditioning, 42" cable TV, hot baths, great bedding, coffeemakers—it's not as nice as some newer options.

CAMINO REAL
General Manager: Alvaro Dieguez
2255-5888, 2255-5900
www.caminoreal.com.ni
reservashcr@caminoreal.com.ni
KM9 Carretera Norte
Price: Very Expensive
Credit Cards: Yes
Handicap Access: Yes
Wifi: Free in the lobby, US$5.75 per day in rooms

About 2 km (1.2 miles) from the airport, this luxury property sprawls across manicured grass lawns, where you'll find a large pool with a bar and kids' area, tennis courts, gymnasium, spa (the sauna and steam room are free for guests), and even a nursery for deer. Rooms are large, modern, and fabulous, with a nature theme and wooden furnishings, faux marble accents, and all the amenities you'd expect, plus one you might not: It's attached to a 24-hour Pharaoh's Casino, for all your gambling needs.

✪ CASA DEL SOL HOTEL BOUTIQUE
Owner: Darios Sarmiento
2265-0307, 2265-3221
www.hotelcasadelsol.com.ni
reservaciones@hotelcasadelsol.com.ni
Carretera Sur, semáforos del 7 Sur, 100 metros al sur, 0.5 cuadra oeste
Price: Expensive to Very Expensive
Credit Cards: Yes
Handicap Access: Challenging
Wifi: Yes

On a hill above the southwestern edge of the city, this place is a gem, convenient to both the U.S. Embassy and Carretera Sur. The remodeled plantation mansion is geared toward business travelers, with a sleek elegance and professional demeanor.

Soothing color schemes, elegant wooden furnishings, pre-Columbian art, and some rooms with private gardens are complimented with workstations, beautiful bathrooms, minibars, and satellite TV. There's a small pool and the upscale **restaurant** (B, L, D; $$$) is well regarded for its imported steaks and international seafood dishes.

MANAGUA BEACHES
BARCELÓ MONTELIMAR
General Manager: Walter Martino
2269-6769, 2269-7669
www.barcelomontelimarbeach.com
montelimar.beach@barcelo.com
Playa Montelimar
Price: Expensive to Very Expensive
Credit Cards: Yes
Handicap Access: Yes
Wifi: Yes

Nicaragua's only full-on, all-inclusive resort occupies an old Somoza property on an absolutely idyllic beach, with decent surfing and even a few petroglyphs. It's not the Four Seasons, but it's pretty darned nice—with 204 comfortable bungalows, 88 tasteful luxury rooms (go for the bungalows), four truly amazing pools, tennis courts, windsurfing, a casino, an airstrip, and unlimited alcohol. You either like these places or not, so suffice it to say that this beauty is a great deal.

GRAN PACIFICA BEACH AND GOLF RESORT

President: Martin G. Roberts
2270-3856, 800-959-6422 (U.S. and Canada)
www.granpacifica.com
info@granpacifica.com
Playa Montelimar
Price: Expensive to Very Expensive
Credit Cards: Yes
Handicap Access: Yes
Wifi: Yes

Still under construction at the time of research, this luxury development—with hotels, condos, full-sized vacation homes, pools, surfing, a beach club, and more—promises to be the finest on the Nicaraguan coast. It's geared to long-term guests with both **Las Perlas** (www.lasperlasdegran pacifica.com), with fully equipped condominiums and spectacular views, and plush vacation homes priced by the week rather than night.

In addition to the 7 km (4 mi) of exquisite beach, the development will have 3 nine-hole golf courses. One, the Tommy Haugen-designed Emerald 9, which can be played as 13 holes, was open for play at press time.

✪ HOTEL SUMMER

Owners: Alberto Vega Rizo, Ruth Luna
2268-7754, 2278-0045 (Masachapa), 8608-3283 (Pochomil)
Playa Masachapa, Pochomil Centro Turístico
Price: Moderate
Credit Cards: Yes
Handicap Access: Challenging
Wifi: No

There are two Hotel Summers to choose from, one in Masachapa and another in the Pochomil Centro Turístico, and both highly recommended for their pretty accommodations, excellent service, and (in Masachapa) the best seafood ✪ **restaurant** (B, L, D; $$–$$$$) on the Managua beaches.

The original Masachapa property is colorfully painted and decorated with seashells, and offers fantastic views from the breezy restaurant—as well as small but immaculate rooms with excellent beds, private cool baths, and some with private balconies overlooking the street.

A second, newer Hotel Summer has the same cheerful paint schemes but larger, more private bungalows with SkyTV, air-conditioning, and cheerful art from the Meseta. It's at the north end of the centro turístico, set apart from the rest of the rather ramshackle complex.

✪ HOTEL VISTAMAR

Management: DETURPASA SA
2265-8099 (reservations), 2269-0431 (hotel)
www.vistamarhotel.com
reservaciones@vistamarhotel.com
Playa Pochomil
Price: Expensive
Credit Cards: Yes
Handicap Access: No
Wifi: In the lobby

Beautifully crafted in tropical pastels, these Caribbean-style wooden bungalows overlook a serene stretch of Playa Pochomil, well away from the centro turístico. Go for the slightly pricier second floor units, with private porches overlooking the serene gardens, four pools—and that wide, beautiful beach. All have spacious interiors, handmade furnishings, satellite TV, solar-heated private baths, air-conditioning, and needlessly pretty details such as river rocks and seashells embedded into the construction.

An attentive **restaurant** (B, L, D; $–$$) serves international, Nicaraguan, and vege-tarian items. Pool service and an all-inclusive option reinforce that laid-back resort feel. There's also an on-site paslama (olive Ridley) sea turtle nursery.

Other Hotels

Bolonia/Tica Bus

There are dozens of budget hotels within a few blocks of Tica Bus; if none of these appeals, most offer basic accommodation with private bath for around US$8. Ask to see a room before committing.

Casa de Huespedes Santos (2222-3713; Tica Bus 1 cuadra al lago, 1.5 cuadras abajo; cash only; $) Bright yellow backpacker beacon offers a vast, cleanish collection of relaxed lounge areas and tiny, misshapen rooms offering OK beds, cable TV, and private cool baths featuring creative plumbing solutions.

✪ **Casa Vanegas** (2222-4043; casavanegas@cablenet.com.ni; Tica Bus 1 cuadra este; cash only; $; wifi) Charming, spotlessly clean, family-run *hospedaje* has excellent rooms, great mattresses, and computers for guests. Some rooms have shared baths, others have air-conditioning.

Hotel Los Cisneros (2222-3535, 2222-7273; www.hotelloscisneros.com; loscisneros @hotmail.com; Tica Bus 100 metros norte; credit cards accepted; $$; wifi) Walled off from the backpacker ghetto, colorful, air-conditioned apartments have full kitchens, terraces, air-conditioning, cable TV, and hot baths.

Hostal Dulce Sueño (2228-4125; www.hostaldulcesueno.com; hospedaje_dulcesueno @yahoo.es; Tica Bus, 75 varas arriba; cash only; $; wifi US$1 per day) Nica-Dutch couple has nicer-than-average rooms with fans and cable TV, plus a shared kitchen and second-floor hammocks with views over the ghetto drama.

Hostal San Felipe (2222-3178; Tica Bus, 0.5 cuadras norte; cash only; $; wifi) Not to be confused with well-known Hotel Los Felipe (though that's probably the idea), this basic spot a stone's throw from Tica Bus has big, clean rooms with great mattresses and big private tiled baths—cheap.

✪ **Villa Angelo** (2268-0764, 786-380-4430 (U.S.); www.hotelvillaangelo.com; villa .angelo@hotmail.com; de Mansión Teolinda, 30 varas abajo; $–$$; wifi) Flashpacker crash pad costs a bit more, but it's a great space, with big, bright, fresh rooms boasting great beds and furnishings, air-conditioning, private hot baths, big closets, and a patio with plenty of plants. An apartment with full kitchen sleeps four.

Los Robles and Altamira

Hotel Ejecutivo (2277-4211; mitzijaen@hotmail.com; Altamira, de Pizza Hut 1 cuadra abajo, 1.5 cuadras al lago #238; credit cards accepted; $$; wifi) The best deal in Altamira is this family-run, five-room charmer. It's not fancy, but spacious, air-conditioned rooms with soft beds, wicker furniture, cable TV, shared kitchen on the mellow porch, and private machine-heated baths are just fine.

Hotel El Gran Marquez Bed and Breakfast (2270-9858; www.hotelgranmarquez.com; hotelgranmarquez@cablenet.com.ni; Monte España 2 cuadras al lago, 2 cuadras arriba, 20 varas al lago; credit cards accepted; $$–$$$; wifi; wheelchair access) Solid boutique hotel close to Zona Hippos has 12 bright, tiled rooms with small living areas, cable TV, air-conditioning, machine-heated private baths, and a nice interior courtyard.

Hotel La Pyrámide (2278-0687; www.lapyramidehotel.com; pyramide@ibw.com.ni; Reparto San Juan, del Gimnasio Hércules, 3.5 cuadra sur, 1 cuadra este; credit cards accepted; $$–$$$; wifi) The suite is in the apex of this huge, suburban pyramid, with simpler rooms in the corners and a normally shaped second building. Rooms are simple, with private bath and pyramid-themed furnishings. Staff can prepare fresh, healthy meals with vegetarian options, or ask to use their kitchen.

Hostal Real (2277-0021, 2277-1214; www.hostalreal.com.ni; info@hostalreal.com.ni; de los semáforos de la entrada principal de Los Robles 50 varas oeste, 3 cuadras sur; credit cards accepted; $$$; wifi) Rather like staying in an overstocked antique shop, this is a great choice for arts and crafts lovers. Rooms have all the usual top-end amenities, and are uniquely decorated with a theme (Thai, Mexican).

Hotel Sol y Luna B&B (2277-1009, 2278-6006; solyluna@cablenet.com.ni; Los Robles, de Zona Hippos, 3 cuadras sur, 10 varas abajo, curva de calle #16; credit cards accepted; $$–$$$; wifi) Modern boutique property on a quiet Los Robles side street has large rooms with wooden accents, low beds, cable TV, and air-conditioning; some have minifridges. Communal spaces and gardens are great.

Managua Beaches

The Pochomil Centro Turístico has several much more basic hotels, offering simple, cement, fan-cooled rooms with shared bath for around US$7.

La Cueva de la Sirena (2269-0433, 8499-6492; Pochomil Centro Turístico; credit cards accepted; $$) On the northwest side of the centro turístico, the "Mermaid's Cave" has a long wooden hallway—painted sea green for a cavelike ambiance—and dark, clean (but slightly dank) air-conditioned rooms with private baths. The beachfront restaurant is great.

Escuela Hoteleria y Turismo Masachapa (8353-2693; yunier.rodriguez@gmail.com; entrada Masachapa, mano derecha; credit cards accepted; $$$) Set to open at press time, this surprising elegant, Mexican resort-style boutique hotel at the entrance to Masachapa is operated by a Spanish tourism school. Rooms are beautiful, as is the rancho-style restaurant, all outfitted like an upscale ecolodge with lots of natural fibers, bamboo, flagstone-paved outdoor showers, and a great pool.

✪ **Hospedaje El Cangrejo** (8460-7903; Centro Turístico Pochomil; credit cards accepted; $) At the heart of the centro turístico, this wooden, two-story building has clean, cheap, breezy rooms with thin mattresses and shared baths. One room has air-conditioning and a private bath.

✪ **Hotel Villa Ordoñez** (8851-5483, 2475-7006; www.hotelvillaordonez.com; Playa Pochomil Viejo; credit cards accepted; $$–$$$) South of the centro turístico is much more exclusive Pochomil Viejo—check out expresident Arnoldo Alemán's enormous spread. There are a few guesthouses, but just one hotel. The wooden Victorian has cool, comfortable, white-tiled rooms with new furnishings, hot baths, large cable TVs, and minifridges; pay US$12 more for a balcony. A beachfront tiki bar overlooks a huge tidal pool, where local churches hold baptisms.

Hotel Vista al Mar (2269-0115, 2244-0736; Playa Masachapa; cash only; $$) Right on the waves at the end of the road from Managua, this spot has several different types of rooms, all due to be remodeled before this book hits the shelves.

RESTAURANTS AND FOOD PURVEYORS

Nicaragua's best selection of fine dining and international cuisine, not to mention fast food and classic traditional eateries, is unsurprisingly right here in the capital.

Restaurant and Food Purveyor Price Code

The following prices are based on the cost of a dinner entrée with a nonalcoholic drink, not including Nicaragua's mandatory 13 percent restaurant tax and "suggested" 10 percent tip, which is usually included with the final bill (so check).

Inexpensive ($)	Up to US$5
Moderate ($$)	US$5 to US$10
Expensive ($$$)	$10 to $20
Very Expensive ($$$$)	US$20 or more

Restaurants

LA CASA DE LOS NOGUERAS
2278-2506
Los Robles, Avenida Principal #17
Price: Very Expensive
Cuisine: Mediterranean
Serving: L, D
Credit Cards: Yes
Child's Menu: No children under 10
Handicap Access: Challenging
Reservations: Recommended

When Managua's upper crust wants to splash out on quality Spanish cuisine, they come to this gorgeous old Los Robles mansion. At lunch, the place is packed with smooth talking businessmen in tailored suits. In the evening, when the linen-draped patio sparkles with fairy lights, it becomes a much more romantic experience; make reservations to dine al fresco. Proper attire is required.

EL GARABATO
2278-3156, 2278-2944
Los Robles, Hotel Seminole 2.5 cuadras sur

Price: Moderate to Expensive
Cuisine: Nicaraguan
Serving: L, D
Closed: Sun.
Credit Cards: Yes
Child's Menu: No
Handicap Access: No
Reservations: Yes

The theme is "traditional Nicaraguan culture," and it comes on strong, with very authentic menu items, including some you won't find anywhere else, all beautifully prepared. There's Nica music in the background, and a very interesting souvenir shop. The porch is convivial, the gardens out back more romantic.

RESTAURANTE INTERMEZZO DEL BOSQUE
2271-1428
www.intermezzodelbosque.com
Colegio Centroamérica 5 km al sur
Price: Expensive to Very Expensive
Cuisine: Gourmet Nicaraguan
Serving: D Mon. through Fri., L, D Sat. through Sun.
Credit Cards: Yes
Child's Menu: No
Handicap Access: Challenging
Reservations: Yes, recommended on weekends

If you need an enchanted evening, climb into the clouds atop the cool, forested mountains just west of the city, to this century-old hacienda with fantastic views over Managua's flickering breadth. Prices are steep—the recommended Thai coconut shrimp with ginger sauce runs about US$18, while a salmon Caesar salad is a more manageable US$8. Or just enjoy some sangria or a slice of maracuya cheesecake. It's romantic. Groups can book "Noches Nicaragüenses," with live music and folkloric dance.

LIKUN PAYASCA
2222-3586, 8924-7411

Puerto Salvador Allende
Price: Expensive
Cuisine: Nicaraguan
Serving: L, D
Credit Cards: Yes
Child's Menu: No
Handicap Access: Challenging
Reservations: Yes

While the lakefront malecón has several restaurants and bars, Likun Payaska (Lagoon Breeze) is my pick, inside family-friendly Puerto Salvador Allende's popular centro turístico. The fine flagstone patio overlooks Xolotlán and the ferry terminal, and there's sometimes live music on weekends. Seafood is the specialty, but they also do fried rice dishes and Nica cuisine.

MAREA ALTA
2278-6906, 2270-7959
marealta@ibw.com.ni
Los Robles, Hotel Seminole 2.5 cuadras sur
Price: Moderate to Expensive
Cuisine: Seafood
Serving: L, D
Credit Cards: Yes
Child's Menu: No
Handicap Access: Challenging
Reservations: Yes

Classic Managua landmark is as popular for its scene as seafood, with a relaxed, chatty patio that fills up as sunset approaches. Some say it's a tad overpriced, but you're paying for the location and vibe as much as the fresh, well prepared fish dishes. Options on the bilingual menu range from inexpensive and tasty canastas (baskets) of fried shrimp, calamari, and sea bass, to pricier platters such as Alaskan king crab legs and lobster risotto. Try the French fries.

MARHABA HOOKAH HOUSE
2278-5725
hookahhouse@yahoo.com
Zona Hippos, Los Robles
Price: Moderate

Cuisine: Middle Eastern
Serving: D
Credit Cards: Yes
Child's Menu: No
Handicap Access: No
Reservations: Yes

With its low, cushioned seating, Persian music, and linen curtains billowing in the breeze, this is a great choice when you need something completely different. Hookahs can be loaded with your choice of 50 flavors of tobacco.

There are meals on the menu, or order several small dishes, such as tabouli, fatoush, falafel, or various kebabs. There's a very full bar, or go for the Arabic-style coffee with cardamom. On weekends at 9:30 PM, belly dancers swirl through.

LA MARSEILLES
2277-0224
catsa100@gmail.com
Los Robles, Calle Principal
Price: Expensive
Cuisine: French
Serving: L, D
Credit Cards: Yes
Child's Menu: No
Handicap Access: Yes
Reservations: Recommended

For more than half a century, this landmark restaurant (literally—most addresses in the neighborhood are given from La Marseilles) has been fastidiously preparing Managua's most elegant evening out. French cuisine is served with aplomb in the beautiful dining room, a great way relax after too long in the hinterlands.

✪ OLA VERDE
2270-3048
www.olaverdesa.com
KM4 Carretera Masaya, del Tip Top, 2 cuadras abajo
Price: Moderate to Expensive
Cuisine: Healthy Organic and Vegetarian

Serving: L, D
Credit Cards: Yes
Child's Menu: No
Handicap Access: Challenging
Reservations: Yes

This serene spot in shady Altamira serves healthy and mostly organic cuisine, with plenty of creative vegetarian choices. The menu changes frequently, but you can expect such items as spicy baba ganoush, fresh vegetable soups, or delicate sea bass carpaccio—before moving onto mains like the organic beef in coconut and soy, or greens and goat cheese lasagna. The Ola Verde also has a deli stand, serving a limited menu of less expensive items, at **Alter Eco** (see Shopping).

LA TERRAZA PERUANA
2278-0013, 2278-0031
medicinamoran@cablenet.com.ni
Planes de Altamira, de Pastelería Sampson,

100 varas al lago
Price: Expensive
Cuisine: Peruvian
Serving: L, D
Closed: Mon.
Credit Cards: Yes
Child's Menu: Yes
Handicap Access: No
Reservations: Yes, recommended on weekends

This relaxed wooden dining area with trickling fountains, white tablecloths, and gilded religious paintings in classic Cuzco style is a fine place to enjoy one of the world's great cuisines. If you've never tried Peruvian food before, begin with the ceviche, served with corn and sweet potato, or causa, a structural potato salad laden with stewed meats or seafood. The aji de gallina, shredded chicken in a sweet, rich yellow pepper sauce, is a classic entrée, but it's all great.

The new Puerto Salvador Allende Centro Turístico on Lake Managua offers inexpensive pleasure cruises around Isla del Amor.

Food Purveyors

If you're staying in Bolonia's backpacker quarter, you'll find good *fritangas* and other cheap eats all over the neighborhood, with a cluster of nicer restaurants and bars just uphill from the Intur office and Plaza Inter Mall, which has a food court.

Asian

✪ **Jui Fook Restaurant** (2278-8623; Los Robles, frente Restaurante Marsellaise; credit cards accepted; L, D; $$–$$$) Serves San Francisco–style Chinatown cuisine, like dim sum (starting at 11 AM daily), spare ribs, Szechwan chicken, and even Peking duck with an hour's notice. There's an atmospherically decorated, air-conditioned VIP room and a small selection of Chinese groceries and medicines for sale.

Palace of Korea (2266-8968; Del Hospital Militar, 1 cuadra abajo, contiguo a Western Union; credit cards accepted; B, L, D; $$$) This fabulous white mansion with lots of marble is Bolonia's favorite Korean restaurant, serving tabletop barbecues and other Korean *típica,* as well as Chinese and Japanese dishes.

Royal Tepanyaki (2228-3530; Crowne Plaza, Bolonia; credit cards accepted; L, D; $$$–$$$$) Elegant restaurant at the Crowne Plaza pyramid serves what may be Nicaragua's best Japanese food.

El Tercer Ojo (2277-4787; www.eltercerojo.com.ni; del Hotel Seminole, 2.5 cuadras sur, Zona Hippos; credit cards accepted; L, D; $$–$$$) The Managua branch of Granada's most exotic evening out has the same cool, Far Eastern theme and eclectic fusion menu, including sushi and Thai dishes.

Bakeries

Pastelería Sampson (2277-0096, 2277-0096 (delivery); Altamira, de Optica Matamoros, 2 cuadras abajo; B, L, D; $) Landmark bakery specializes in fancy cakes, but also has pastries, tiramasu, salads, and sandwiches enjoyed on the flagstone garden patio. There's another branch in Bolonia (2254-4882; Rotonda El Güegüense, 1 cuadra al lago, 1 cuadra arriba).

Tonalli (2222-2678; Tica Bus, 3 cuadras arriba, 0.5 cuadra sur; cash only; B, L; $; closed Sun.) Popular bakery run by a women's collective also sells fresh yogurt, salads, quiches, and light meals.

Cafés

Bisou Bisou (2278-1865; KM7.5 Carretera Masaya; credit cards accepted; L, D; $$) Eatery filled with fresh flowers and cool art serves more than 30 types of crepes, a dozen creative salads, and rich gelato to finish it off.

Café Le Poeta (2267-5005; KM4.5 Carretera Masaya, del Restaurante La Pizzeta, 1 cuadra abajo; credit cards accepted; B, L, D; $–$$$) Poetry-themed café serves espresso beverages and creative Nicaraguan cuisine, from pastries to steamed sea bass in a red wine–mushroom sauce. There are poetry readings on Thursdays at 5 PM, when you should have reservations.

Café Mama Quilla (2279-8325; www.cafemamaquilla.com; KM12.7 Carretera Masaya; credit cards accepted; B, L, D; $$) Hip, upscale café has quite a list of organic espresso and coffee beverages, plus teas, smoothies, milkshakes, pastries, paninis, and light meals.

Latin Cuisine

Santa Fe (2268-9344; Bolonia, Rotonda El Güegüense, 1 cuadra norte; credit cards accepted; L, D; $$–$$$) Family-style Mexican restaurant and steakhouse serves hefty portions in the air-conditioned dining room.

Mesón Español (2276-5293; Galerías Santo Domingo; credit cards accepted; L, D; $$$–$$$$) Don't let the mall location deceive you—this is one of Managua's oldest, best-loved restaurants, formerly located in Bolonia. There's a good tapas menu, tasty fish dishes, and of course paella.

Moon River Burritos (2277-5017; Los Robles, Monte de los Olivos 1.5 cuadra norte, contiguo Librería San Jerónimo; cash only; L, D; $) "California-style" Mexican fast food, like big burritos and soft tacos, is served up fresh.

Nicaraguan

⊘ **Al Di La** (2291-2359, 2291-2210; Parque El Crucero, 200 metros, Las Nubes; cash only; open 1 PM–5 PM Sunday; $$$$) Make reservations to enjoy a US$30, multicourse meal in a private mansion overlooking the city. It's about thirty minutes west of Managua proper, in the chilly altitudes of *Las Nubes* ("The Clouds").

⊘ **Coctelería Vuelve de Vida** (2249-3536; Calle Principal tope sur, Ciudad Jardín; credit cards accepted; L, D; $$) Festive, open-air bar and restaurant in this downscale neighborhood serves seafood cocktails, ceviche, beer, and live music on Sunday afternoons.

Grill 50 (2278-3287; rgonzalez@grill50.com; del Hospital Monte España, 2 cuadras al lago, 2 cuadras arriba; credit cards accepted; L, D; $$) Ranchero-style churrasco joint—try the *puyasu*—also serves quesadillas and seafood patacones. The executive lunch is a good deal, or go upscale on "Wine and Piano" Tuesdays, with live music starting around 6 PM.

El Quesillazo (2277-4100; contiguo a Claro Altamira; cash only; B, L, D; $–$$) The specialty is huge *quesillos*, but they serve other traditional treats like *indio viejo* and top-notch *nacatamales*.

Cocina de Doña Haydée (2270-6100, 2270-0426; www.lacocina.com.ni; Planes de Altamira, de la óptica Matamoros, 1 cuadra al oeste; credit cards accepted; L, D; $$) Staff outfitted in Nicaraguan traditional costumes serve up some of the finest renditions of classic Nica cuisine anywhere.

Pizza and Italian

Pane y Vino (2278-4442; Altamira, Enitel Villa Fontana 200 metros al norte; credit cards accepted; L, D; $$–$$$) Popular family restaurant serves wood-fired, thin-crust pizzas, big salads, fresh pastas, sinful desserts, and perhaps something from the full bar.

Pizzería Rock Munchies (2276-1294; primera entrada Las Colinas, detras de Gasolinera Esso; credit cards accepted; L, D; $$) Loads of fresh toppings, two-for-one deals at lunch, and delivery anywhere in town—their Facebook page has a menu.

Valenti's Pizza (2278-7474; De Shell Plaza el Sol, 5 cuadras al sur, Los Robles; credit cards accepted; L, D; $$–$$$) Local chain has good pizza, clean dining rooms, and several other franchises all over Managua; their Facebook page has locations.

Vegetarian

Ananda (2228-4140; Bolonia, Reparto El Carmen, esquina apuesta a Montoya; cash only; B, L, D; $) The outstanding juice bar is the star attraction, but this unpretentious restaurant also serves good, inexpensive vegetarian food. Penny pinchers should drop by for the lunch buffet.

Culture

The first people probably arrived at Lake Managua, called Xolotlán after the God of Corn, around 12,000 years ago. Perhaps 6,000 years ago they even left their footprints in the soft lake mud. By the time the Spanish arrived in 1528, the city was already a bustling trade center and port of perhaps 40,000.

The residents, who had apparently already heard about the conquistadors, evacuated the city prior to their arrival. Spanish settlers took over their abandoned farms and homes, and by 1750s had their own little lakefront town with churches and schools. Managua didn't really merit much attention, however, until after independence from Spain in 1821 and the collapse of the Central American Republic a few years later.

Nicaragua's two wealthiest cities, Granada and León, fell into decades of civil war to decide which would lead the nation. In an effort to end the pointless struggle, Managua—located between the rival cities—was declared the nation's new capital in 1852. Only after William Walker humiliated León and burned Granada to the ground in 1856, however, was this designation taken seriously.

Managua tried to grow into a wealthy, cosmopolitan city, by inviting industry and investment. This unfortunately contaminated the lake with chemical waste in 1927. (Only now is this being cleaned up, thanks to a water treatment plant donated by Germany). Worse, the city lies within the massive fault-ridden graben, the rift pulling Nicaragua's lakes apart. In 1885, 1931, and 1968, earthquakes destroyed entire neighborhoods. In 1972, a massive 6.5-magnitude quake leveled the city.

The subsequent Sandinista-led revolution and war with the Contras absorbed any funds that might have gone toward repairing the capital. Destructive flooding from Hurricane Mitch destroyed what work had been done.

Today, the city seems to be slowly but finally recovering, in the wealthy neighborhoods anyway. But the majority of the city's 1.8 million souls remain desperately poor, and it's a problem no political party or president has the power to fix, not anytime soon.

Architecture and Monuments

Slowly but surely, the old city center and lakefront *malecón* are making a comeback, thanks to revitalization efforts such as new **Puerto Salvador Allende,** a sparkling new centro turístico with restaurants and ferry rides; someday, perhaps, you'll even be able to swim here.

You can't miss the enormous white wave of the 1985 **La Concha Acustica,** a most unusual stage overlooking **Plaza de la Fé Juan Pablo II,** where Pope John Paul II addressed his Nicaraguan fans.

Several important buildings surround the **Plaza de la Revolución;** today they contain mostly government offices. To the east is the shattered French Gothic-Romanesque façade of the 1931 **Cathedral Santiago,** severely damaged in the 1972 earthquake and never repaired. To the south is the **Palacio Nacional de la Cultura,** with a good museum. To the north is the former presidential palace, renamed the **Palacio de los Pueblos de America Latina** by current President Daniel Ortega.

To the west are the 1899 **Plaza de la República** and the **Tomb of Comandante Carlos Fonseca,** a philosopher and fighter in the Sandinista-led revolution, now honored with an eternal flame. Continue north toward the lake, and you'll find **Monumento Rubén Darío,** honoring Nicaragua's greatest poet, as well as the Teatro Rubén Darío and a park currently filled with exhibits about **Darío** and **General Sandino.**

Still erect despite decades of neglect, Managua's long-suffering Old Cathedral currently serves as a political billboard.

Nearby, the 1990 **Parque de la Paz**, marked by a lighthouse, has thousands of guns, and at least one tank, that former Presidenta Violeta Chamorro collected after the Contra War and had encased in concrete. Nearby the **Statue of the Unknown Guerrilla**, topped with a Sandinista flag, is close to the **Monument to the Nicaraguan Worker,** erected by the opposition Liberal Party.

Other important Managua buildings include the 1993 **Catedral Inmaculada Concepción de María** (2278-4223; catedralmga.blogspot.com) or New Cathedral, a surprisingly modern, stamped-cement edifice designed by Mexican architect Ricardo Legoretta; the domes represent Nicaragua's diocese. The stark, gray interior with surprising pink and yellow panels is oddly pretty, sublime in a way. Managua's other point of pilgrimage and prayer is the 1948 **Estadio Nacional Dennis Martínez** (Avenida Salvador Allende), a 40,000-person stadium where baseball and soccer games are held.

Museums

There are several tiny museum displays around town, including **Biblioteca Roberto Incer Barquero** (2265-0500; Semáforos del 7 Sur, 300 metros este; admission free; open 8:30 AM–6 PM, Mon. through Sat.), with 67,000 books, a newspaper and magazine reading library, and small numismatic museum; and **Museo del Departamento de Malacología**

The 63 cúpulas atop Managua's New Cathedral, representing Nicaragua's 63 dioceses, soften the light within.

Ciencias Naturales, a snail museum at the UCA (University of Central America). The following are full-sized museums.

MUSEO NACIONAL DE NICARAGUA DIOCLESIANO CHÁVES
2222-2905
Palacio Nacional de la Cultura, costado sur de la Plaza de la Revolución
Admission: US$4/2/1 foreigner/student/Nicaraguan
Open: 9 AM–4 PM daily

The Palace of Culture was originally built in 1935, and not quite destroyed in 1972. Today the rebuilt palacio houses this interesting museum, with recently expanded exhibits covering natural history—such as panda bears, giant sloths, and mastodons—and human history, with a really top-notch collection of ceramics, stonework, jewelry, tools, and other pre-Columbian artifacts.

The murals in this place are unreal—ask to go upstairs and see the one depicting the 1972 earthquake.

MUSEO SITIO HUELLAS DE ACAHUALINCA
2266-5774
De las bodegas Delgadala María, 1 cuadra al lago

Admission: US$4/2/1 foreigner/student/Nicaraguan
Open: 9 AM–4 PM daily

In an impoverished neighborhood on the northwest corner of town is one of the most important archaeological sites in Central America, the Footprints of Acahualinca. They were left in the soft mud of the lakeshore between 6,000 and 8,000 years ago by a family of 10–12 people, a deer, and a raccoon.

The prints were uncovered by accident in 1874, and Japanese forensic scientists believe that these were tall people, unhurried in their passage, not fleeing an eruption. Researchers hypothesize that one of the area volcanoes erupted after they'd passed through, covering the prints in hot volcanic ash that "fired" them, like ceramics.

There's not much else to see, as they've closed the forensics display, but for some a visit will be well worth the time and expense of a taxi.

Nightlife

Managua has the country's best nightlife scene. This is just a smattering of what's on; check **Click Managua** (www.clickmanagua.com), **Vianica** (www.vianica.com/thisweek), and **Hecho Magazine** (www.hechomagazine.com), with events listings, theater schedules, and venue reviews.

BELLO HORIZONTE

Downscale but safe neighborhood is known for its wandering mariachis, smoky casinos, and **Pizzería Los Ídolos** (2249-0517; Rotonda Bello Horizonte; credit cards accepted; L, D; $$–$$$) with basalt statues, cold beer, great pizza, and party people who can go all night.

The Huellas de Acahualinca, footprints dating to between 6,000 and 8,000 years old, were buried beneath 14 layers of ash.

BOLONIA

El Caramanchel (8931-4199; Bolonia, del Hospital Militar 3 cuadras al norte, 0.5 cuadras oeste; open 6:30 PM–3 AM Wed. through Sun., closed Mon. through Tue.; $$) Artsy, soft-lit bar brings in hipsters with live music, alternative film screenings, art exhibits, and cheap mojitos.

Casa de los Mejía Godoy (2222-6110; www.losmejiagodoy.com; Rotonda Plaza Inter, 2.5 cuadras sur; credit cards accepted; B, L, D; $$–$$$) Legendary singers, songwriters, and brothers Carlos and Luis Enrique Mejía Godoy have a wonderful thatch-roofed bar where they and their friends perform.

Mirador Tiscapa (2222-5945; Pista Benjamin Zeledon; credit cards accepted; L, D; $$–$$$) Popular, very local nightspot has a big dance floor, views over the crater lake, and huge variety platters of tasty Nica cuisine.

Ruta Maya (2268-0698; www.rutamaya.com.ni; Estadio Nacional, 1.5 cuadras oeste; L, D Mon. through Sat., closed Sun.) Musical hot spot attracts top musicians from all over the country and world; check their Facebook page for events.

LAKE MANAGUA

Puerto Turístico Rúben Darío, the scroungier and more fun side of the lakefront, has a strip of pizzerias, coctelerías, and breezy bars with huge dance floors that go until dawn on weekends, including popular **Bar El Muellecito** and **Playa de los Romanticos**.

ZONA HIPPOS

Upscale Los Robles has a cool scene, centered on beloved sports bar **Zona Hippos** (2267-1346; www.zonahippos.com; Calle Principal, Los Robles; credit cards accepted; L, D; $$–$$$), serving cold beer and U.S./Mexican-style happy hour cuisine, such as beef super nachos. There are a dozens of great restaurants with wide patios and porches within just a few blocks, like **La Pirata** (2278-3817; $$$)—which has a buccaneer theme, great piña coladas, and pricey seafood dishes.

ZONA VIVA

Glittering **Galerías Santo Domingo Mall** (KM7 Carretera Masaya) has a popular, polished outdoor dining and nightlife plaza that will make even the most nervous travelers feel safe and secure. Things start up at around noon and go until late.

There are lots of bars, including **Cigars Zone** (2276-5377; www.cigarszone.com) serving cocktails and fine Estelí cigars; **Moods** (2276-5276; moodsmanagua.com; open 9 PM–3 AM Wed. through Sat.), Managua's hottest nightclub at press time; and **MVP Sports Bar** (2276-5308; open 4 PM–1 AM), with a chrome-accented, neon-lit lounge and huge TVs.

Across the street, **Hipa Hipa** (2278-8504; www.elhipa.com; KM7.5 Carretera Masaya; open 9 PM–5 AM Wed., Fri., and Sat.) is a massive dance club that gets packed with a young, trendy crowd. Pricey.

Spanish Schools

Viva Spanish Schools (2270-2339; www.vivaspanishschool.com; vivaspanish@btinternet .com; detras de Metrocentro, del Edificio FNI, 2 cuadras al sur) Spanish school close to MetroCentro Mall offers private and group lessons, plus a very comfortable, good-value, gay-friendly **guesthouse** (2270-2339, 8743-3700; www.vivanicaraguaguesthouse.com;

vivanicaraguaguesthouse@yahoo.com; KM14 Carretera Masaya; credit cards accepted; $$; wifi) with better weekly rates.

Cinema

There are several movie theaters in Managua, most at major malls. **Cinemark** has air-conditioned theaters at **MetroCentro** (2271-9039), **Plaza Inter** (2222-5122), and **Galerías Santo Domingo** (2276-5065). A free, glossy magazine, **Movie Review** (www.moviereview nica.com), has schedules—click "Cines y Horarios."

Theater

Teatro Rubén Darío (2222-7426; www.tnrubendario.gob.ni; contiguo al malecón) Nicaragua's national theater remains one of the best nights out in Managua, with a fairly impressive stage, great acoustics, and top-notch performances from all over the world. Click "Cartelera" on the Web site for a schedule. Prices vary, but are very reasonable; a recent performance by **Ballet Folklórico Nicaragüense** (www.balletfolklorico nicaraguense.com) cost US$10 for the best seats, US$5 for the third balcony.

Teatro Justo Rufino Garay (2266-3714; www.rufinos.org; contiguo parque Las Palmas, de Montoya, 3 cuadras oeste, 15 metros norte) The nicer of two small theaters on the park, this shows mostly local and Latin American troupes.

Theater Victor Romeo (2266-6738; frente parque Las Palmas, de Montoya, 3 cuadras oeste, 50 metros norte) Black box auditorium showcases alternative Nicaraguan and international performers.

RECREATION

National Parks and Protected Areas

EL CHOCOYERO–EL BRUJO NATURAL RESERVE
2276-7810, 2276-7811
Ticuantepe de la vuelta de Telcor, 75 meters al este
Open: 24 hours
Admission: US$7

This pretty preserve, just 29 km (18 miles) from Managua, has several hiking trails through the steep and forested hills. A family-friendly, half-hour stroll brings you to 18-meter (59-foot) El Chocoyero Waterfall, best known for the thousands of parakeets (chocoyos) that nest in its walls; the best time for birders to visit is dawn or dusk.

A steeper, more difficult hike brings you to El Brujo (Bewitched) Waterfall, which seems to disappear into the sandy earth. A six-hour trail takes you to a mirador (overlook) across Managua and the volcanoes; mandatory guides charge US$10. There's a **campsite** ($), but bring your own tent.

✪ LOMA TISCAPA NATIONAL HISTORICAL PARK AND LAGUNA DE TISCAPA
Bolonia, uphill from Plaza Inter
Admission: US$1/free foreigners/Nicaraguans
Open: 7 AM–6 PM Mon. through Sat., 9 AM–6 PM Sun.

Thousands of chocoyos *nest at Reserva Natural Chocoyero-El Brujo and in the crater walls of Volcán Masaya, where little else can survive.*

Loma Tiscapa, an active volcano only a few thousand years ago, offers awesome city views that could once be enjoyed only from the presidential palace perched atop the crater rim. The ruins of the palace and dungeons, today a small museum, also mark the spot where Anastasio Somoza García posed for photos with General Augusto C. Sandino, before having the "General of Free Men" assassinated. They hid Sandino's body, to avoid a martyr's funeral and pilgrimage site, and forbade the display of his image.

Today, the loma (hill) is topped with an iconic 18-meter (60-foot) Sandino statue that glows at night, and is now Managua's most recognizable landmark. There's also a small canopy tour, a few rusty tanks, and poetry for the fallen hero.

If you enter from the other side of the crater, you can swim in (or hike around) **Laguna de Tiscapa** (Avenida Colan; open daily; US$1), but it's apparently not very clean.

Other Parks and Natural Attractions

Arboretum Nacional Dr. Juan Bautista Salas Estrada (2222-2558; giomen@ns.uca.edu.ni; Avenida Bolívar, de Plaza Inter, 1.5 cuadras norte; open 8 AM–4 PM Mon. through Fri., closed Sat. through Sun.; US$0.50) Rather run-down arboretum between Plaza Inter Mall and the Lake Managua *malecón* is a shady place to relax, with more than two hundred Nicaraguan plant species.

Montelimar Cave (Barceló Montelimar) This shallow cave's ceiling is covered with blue and red petroglyphs. Visit with **Inspiration Tours** (8379-7440; www.inspirationtours .org).

Montibelli Private Wildlife Reserve (2270-4287; www.montibelli.com; Ticuantepe de la vuelta de Telcor, 75 meters al este; open Tue. through Sun., reservations requested) Private, 165-hectare preserve offers 6 km of well-maintained, family-friendly trails through a swath of reforested coffee plantation. Spend the night at **Eco-albergue Oropendola** (credit cards accepted; $$–$$$), with attractive fan-cooled cabins.

Xiloá (Jiloa) Lagoon (open 8 AM–9 PM daily, US$0.30 pedestrian, US$1.25 car) Located 12 km (7 miles) northeast of the city, Chiltepe Peninsula has two crater lakes: easily accessible Xiloá, with a centro turístico, and higher-altitude Apoyeque, to which you can hike. The easiest way here is by taxi (US$10 each way), but you can also take a bus to Ciudad Sandino, and catch a cab there.

Zoológico Nacional Nicaragüense (2279-9073; sacasmarina1@yahoo.com; KM16 Carretera Masaya; open 8:30 AM–5 PM Tue. though Sun., closed Mon.; US$0.75/0.50 adult/child, US$0.75 for butterfly and orchid gardens) This isn't exactly a world-class zoo, but it's a great place to see Nicaraguan wildlife, most brought here for rehabilitation. There are three species of monkeys, four native wildcats, tapirs, sloths, caimans, pizotes, anteaters, and peccary. There are also lions, tigers, butterflies, and Pipo, the resolute chimpanzee.

Activities

✪ **Canopy Tours Nicaragua** (8886-2836, 8872-2555; www.canopytoursnicaragua.com; Tiscapa National Historical Park; US$15/11.50 foreigners/Nicaraguans) In Sandino's

Augusto C. Sandino, "General of Free Men," stands atop Managua's downtown Loma de Tiscapa, surveying the city and lake below.

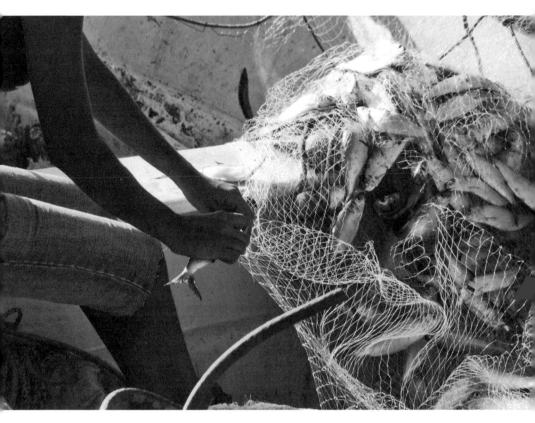

Bringing in the day's catch is work for the whole family.

shadow above Tiscapa Crater Lake is this awesome little canopy tour. There are three
cables totaling 1,250 meters (4,100 feet) that cross the dramatic volcanic crater at
speeds of up to 80 km per hour.

Horseback Rides Silvio Balaque (8633-3838) Rents horses on Pochomil Beach for US$6
per hour. It's best to call ahead, but you'll usually be able to find them on the sand.

Paintball Las Colinas (8440-6128; 2 entrada Las Colinas, 0.5 cuadra al este, 50 varas al
norte; open 1 PM–6 PM Tue. through Fri., 9 AM–6 PM Sat. through Sun., closed Mon.) As
you may have guessed from the political billboards, paintball is a popular Managua
diversion.

Boat Tours

Puerto Salvador Allende (2222-2745, 2222-3543; apxolotlan@epn.com.ni; www.epn.com
.ni; open 8 AM–11 PM; free, US$0.50 parking) is home port for **Ferry La Novia de Xolotlán**.
The two-level tour boat takes a 45-minute jaunt around **Isla del Amor**, a small (five square
blocks) island off the coast of Peninsula Chiltepe. Formerly owned by the Somozas, it is
being developed into a centro turístico. Currently, you'll just cruise past for the views.
Tours run Tuesday through Sunday at 9 AM, 11 AM, 1 PM, 3 PM, 5 PM, and 6:30 PM, US$4/2
adult/child (lower deck), US$5/3 adult/child for the glassed-in upper level.

A five-hour trip to **Puerto Carlos Fonseca**, an isolated port town on Xolotlán's northern shore, includes three hours to wander around town, known for pastries, organic soaps and shampoo, and thermal springs. The trip leaves at 10 AM and 1 PM Saturday and Sunday only, US$10/5 adult/child.

Also here is **Nicán Park Peréz Noguera** (open daily; rides US$0.30–50), a parking-lot amusement park with rickety carnival rides; and the **Bus Turístico** (2222-2745, www.epn .com.ni; 9 AM–7 PM; US$0.50), which makes a 40-minute round trip to Loma Tiscapa in an old school bus with most of the roof removed. Bring sunscreen.

Golf
Gran Pacifica Beach and Golf Resort (2270-3856, 800-959-6422 (U.S. and Canada); www.granpacifica.com) This plush resort on Masachapa Beach, about 65 km (40 miles) from Managua, specializes in golf.

Nejapa Country Club (8883-4252; ngcc@alianza.com.ni; exit KM11.5 Carretera Masaya) Since 1940, Nicaragua's only private golfing club has carpeted the shores of Laguna Nejapa, at a crisp altitude above the city. Green fees run US$62.50 for 9 holes, US$117 for 18; there's also a pool, restaurant, and tennis courts.

Surfing
The Managua beaches are not well known for surfing, but there's a long, sandy beach break that extends well up the coast and left off the rocky point in front of Montelimar. Meat Grinder is apparently the most famous wave, a shallow reef break that gets hollow barrels midtide to high tide.

In the Pochomil Centro Turístico, rent boards for US$10 per hour from **Amaru** (8606-2437; johana.lanza@yahoo.es), usually at **Restaurant Los Ranchitos** (8606-2431; de rotonda 300 varas).

Los Cardones Surf Lodge (8364-5925, 8618-3147; www.loscardones.com; infoloscar-dones@yahoo.com; Carretera Montelimar KM49, 15 km al oeste; $$$) Isolated, eco-friendly surf cabins and great food are about 15 km (9 miles) northwest of Masachapa. They access sandy-bottomed beach breaks perfect for beginners, as well as serious waves.

SHOPPING
Expats come from all over the country to shop Managua, with foreign brands and consumer goods that are hard to find elsewhere.

Banks and ATMs
In Managua proper, ATMs are plentiful. The Managua beaches, however, have one Visa/Plus ATM, at the Barceló Montelimar, which costs US$5 for nonguests to use.

Groceries
The best place to find brands from home are at Managua's huge supermercados, particularly **La Colonia Galerías Santo Domingo** on Carretera Masaya, and enormous **PriceSmart** (2254-4700; Rotonda el Güegüense 1.5 cuadras este, Bolonia; open daily), near Plaza España. If you're staying by Tica Bus, the closest grocery store is a US$1 cab ride (or 20-minute walk), **La Colonia** at Plaza España.

The beaches have plenty of basic *pulperías,* but the closest supermarket is **Palí** in San Rafael del Sur, 11 km (7 miles) east of Masachapa.

✪ **Fabríca de Chocolate Momotombo** (2278-4918; www.chocolatemomotombo.com; Altamira, de Pasteleria Sampson 1 cuadra al sur) offers the finest chocolate in Nicaragua, while **Enoteca Vinos y Mas** (2276-5113; www.enotecavinosymas.com; KM7 Carretera Masaya) has one of the country's best wine selections.

Markets

There are dozens of markets in Managua, but you'll probably find everything you need at ✪ **Mercado Roberto Huembes**, with a relatively orderly maze of housewares, vegetable stands, eateries, and great selection of souvenirs. Conveniently, this is also where you catch buses to Granada and San Juan del Sur.

Mercado Israel Lewites, with buses leaving to the White Towns and Carazo, is also a large, friendly market, as is **Mercado Mayoreo**, on the east end of town.

The mother of all markets is the **Mercado Oriental** (Barrio Los Angeles), Central America's largest, with a (deserved) reputation for pickpockets and worse that discourages most tourists. But smart shoppers know there's no better selection: After a 2009 military coup evicted former Honduran President Zelaya without his signature cowboy hat, Nicaraguan President Ortega brought him here to buy a new one. If you decide to visit, take the usual precautions (e.g., emergency cab fare in your sock) and stay alert, you'll probably be fine.

Malls

Managua is also home to several good malls, with ATM machines, movie theaters, and free wifi.

Galerías Santo Domingo (www.galerias.com.ni; KM7 Carretera Masaya) Nicaragua's largest and most exclusive mall boasts more than 130 stores, including a Mac Center (2278-0226; no Genius Bar). **Zona ViVa**, with dozens of outdoor bars and restaurants in an outdoor complex, gets packed.

Metrocentro (Carretera Masaya) This popular mall is convenient to the cathedral and upscale Altamira and Los Robles, with more than one hundred shops, a massive food court, and a cinema.

Multicentro Las Americas (www.lasamericas.com.ni; Bello Horizonte) Nicaragua's second largest mall has a supermarket, food court, and more.

Plaza Inter (Bolonia, Rotonda Plaza Inter) Convenient to the backpacker hotels near Tica Bus, this scruffy but air-conditioned mall has 65 stores, a solid food court, and a cinema.

Books

The national library, **Biblioteca Roberto Incer Barquero** (2265-0500; biblioteca.bcn.gob .ni; Semáforos del 7 Sur, 300 metros este; closed Sun.) has a reading library with international magazines and newspapers, plus free wifi.

Centro Nicaragüense de Escritores (2267-0304; escritor@ibw.com.ni; del Hotel Seminole, 2 cuadras sur, Galería Casa de los 3 Mundos; closed Sat. through Sun.) Groovy gallery and shop offers an eclectic selection of Nicaraguan magazines and books.

✪ **Frontera Books** (2270-2345; fronterabooks@ibw.com.ni; Semáforos Entel Villa Fontana, 200 varas al lago, contiguo a Pan e Vino; closed Sun.) Fabulous bilingual bookstore in Altamira has a great selection in English, including a children's section, yoga and lifestyle books, and new and used travel guides.

Gonper's Librerías (www.gonperlibrerias.com) Nicaragua's largest bookstore chain has mostly Spanish-language books; there are branches at MetroCentro, Plaza Inter, and elsewhere in town.

Librería Hispamer (2278-1210; portón UCA, 1 cuadra este, 1 cuadra sur) Huge academic bookstore near the university has a small selection in English.

Handicrafts

For comprehensive, updated gallery listings for Managua, check out **Nicaragua Art Gallery** (www.nicaartgallery.com).

AK47 Tattoo (2278-9869; www.dorianserpa.blogspot.com; chuckfsc@hotmail.com; Altamira, de la Vicky 5 cuadras al sur, Sonya's Plaza) Managua's premier tattoo parlor offers Nicaraguan art that will last a lifetime.

✪ **Alter Eco** (altereconicaragua@gmail.com; Semáforos Enitel Villa Fontana, 1.5 cuadras al Lago; closed Sun.) Cool collection of artsy, woman-owned shops under one roof includes **Spices and Sugar** (8429-0961), with flowing, flattering fashions at great prices; **Cocos** (8370-5897), selling locally designed beachwear; and **Ola Verde** (see Restaurants) with organic coffee and light meals.

Joya de Nicaragua (2266-5766; www.joyadenicaragua.com.ni; de Rotonda El Güegüense, 1 cuadra este, 2 cuadras norte) Some of the world's finest cigars.

Mama Delfina (2267-8288; titulacayo@hotmail.com; Altamira, Semáforos Enitel Villa Fontana, 2 cuadras al Lago) Near Alter Eco, this store sells creative, high-quality Nicaraguan folk art from all over the country, as well as videos about Nicaraguan handicrafts.

EVENTS

Managua may not do "quaint" well, but the city goes all out with serious fiestas on national holidays and the **Anniversary of the Revolution** (July 19), when Plaza de la Revolución is a sea of Sandinista red and black.

Fiestas de Agosto (August 1–10), more properly known as the Fiestas Patronales Santo Domingo, is Managua's biggest party, with live music, horse parades, traditional dance, political grandstanding, heavy drinking, and religious festivities.

4

Masaya, the Pueblos Blancos, and Carazo

Music and Dance, Art and Soul

The Nicaraguan heartland is cool and green, its rolling hills carpeted with fertile farms and wild countryside that cradle an ancient community of adobe villages. This is the Meseta Central, Nicaragua's most productive region—famed for its flowers, handicrafts, and swirling costumed dances, the "Cradle of Culture" for the nation.

The Meseta, or Central Plateau, is most famous for the bustling city of Masaya, and rightly so. This unpretentious town hasn't received any sort of dramatic facelift, thus many of its classic Colonial buildings are still a bit war-torn and rent with regular earthquakes, courtesy of Volcán Masaya fuming above town. But there is still so much beauty to be discovered beneath the cracked and pockmarked surface.

Most people just visit on a day trip to the famous Masaya Old Market, an enormous 1881 edifice designed to resemble a Spanish castle. Today its thick basalt walls are filled with tidy rows of handicraft shops, selling the very finest *artesanías* from every corner of Nicaragua. But if you take the time to wander around town, you'll find family-run workshops where Masaya's famous hammocks, woodwork, leather goods, and other crafts are made before your eyes.

Most tours also visit two of the Meseta's most impressive natural wonders: the precipitous edge of Volcán Masaya's Santiago Crater, pouring its endless clouds of sulfurous gas across the sky; and Catarina Mirador, overlooking sparkling Laguna de Apoyo, a wondrous and protected crater lake.

But there is so much more to this magical region, a land of myth and music that rises from Masaya's steamy plains to mountains of chilly coffee-growing altitudes. These towns, the Pueblos Blancos and cities of Carazo, were founded long before the Spanish arrived, and still boast their old names—Masatepe, Niquinohomo, Diriamba. Their memories are long.

The mighty warrior Diriangén, Cacique of the Mountains, is still celebrated in the land of his sacrifice. Though he lost his battle against the Spanish, the dances and artwork of his Chorotega people still thrive beneath a Catholic veneer.

Masaya and the Meseta's civic fiestas are renowned for their color. The wooden saints they celebrate may be several centuries old, but the dances around them are more ancient

Masaya's magnificent 1881 Old Market houses one of the most beautiful collections of handicrafts in Central America.

still. And when you have had your fill of culture, head west for relaxation. The pastoral landscape plunges from the cool Meseta to broad Pacific beaches that, like so much of this amazing region, are almost undiscovered.

CRIME AND OTHER CONCERNS

Carazo and the Pueblos Blancos constitute one of the safest and best-developed regions in the country, with potable water, excellent roads, ATMs, grocery stores, and (usually) reliable electricity.

Since it isn't a tourist destination, you won't really find the usual contingent of hustlers and petty criminals, even at the beaches. Still, there's no reason to be careless. Count your change, watch your wallet at the markets, and don't leave anything unattended on the beach.

The lack of specific tourist infrastructure may be frustrating for folks who don't speak Spanish. If you plan to travel much farther than Masaya, Catarina, and San Juan del Oriente, keep your Spanish phrasebook handy.

GETTING AROUND

Though this region has beautifully paved, well-signed roads and speedy, convenient bus and taxi transportation, it isn't the easiest part of Nicaragua to navigate. Masaya is a major city on the tourist routes, but the rest of the Pueblos Blancos (Catarina, Diriá, Diriomo,

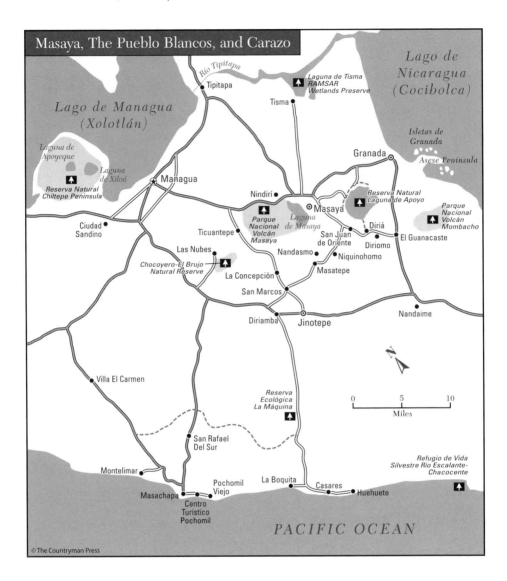

Masatepe, and Niquinohomo, among others) and Carazo towns (Diriamba, Jinotepe, and San Marcos) are scattered around the rolling countryside and connected by pastoral roads. The beaches are only accessible via Diriamba.

Drivers will need a good map and enough Spanish to ask, "*¿Donde está [Niquinohomo]?*" (Where is [Niquinohomo]?) Buses, vans, and collective taxis run throughout the region frequently, but are not always well signed for tourists. If an attraction is outside town (for instance, the Diriá Mirador or El Pochote in Masatepe), you'll need to take a tiny three-wheeled mototaxi.

Most people book guided day trips from Granada, which usually visit the Masaya Old Market and either Masaya Volcano or the Catarina Mirador and San Juan del Oriente. Some companies specialize in handicraft tours of the Pueblos Blancos. The easiest way to Laguna de Apoyo is via the private shuttles that leave daily from Granada hotels.

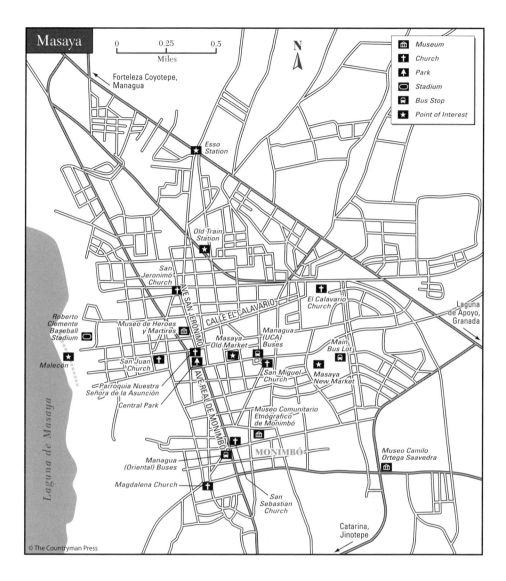

Car

The Meseta Central enjoys the best road system in Nicaragua, with good signage and lots of gas stations, restaurants, and smooth pavement. Renting a car is the ideal way to see the region, and more easily accomplished in Managua or Granada. **Madera's Inn Hotel** (2552-5825; www.hotelmaderasinn.com; Bomberos, 2 cuadras sur) rents cars.

Note that Masaya, Diriamba, and Jinotepe are large, confusing cities with one-way streets and traffic, so stay alert and try to arrive well before sunset.

International Buses

Tica Bus (www.ticabus.com) Has offices in **Masaya** (2522-0445; frente Farmacia Aguilar) and **Jinotepe** (2532-2721; parque central 1.5 cuadras norte), both with daily buses to San José, Costa Rica.

Transnica Masaya (2522-4585, 8353-3955; bomberos, 25 varas sur) Four buses head south to Liberia and San José, Costa Rica, (US$34.50) at 5 AM, 7 AM, 10 AM, and 1 PM; one runs north to Tegucigalpa, Honduras, (US$28.25) daily.

Buses

There are several different bus, minibus, and *colectivo* taxi lines between the cities of the Meseta Central, many of them independently operated. Masaya is the regional transportation hub.

MASAYA

Most buses and minivans leave from Masaya's sprawling, chaotic bus lot, adjacent to the New Market.

Catarina US$0.20; every 30 minutes
Chinandega US$2; 5:15 AM
Diriomo US$0.30; every 20 minutes
Estelí US$2; 5:45 AM and 6:45 AM
Granada US$0.40; every 18 minutes
Jinotepe and San Marcos US$0.35; every 20 minutes
Jinotepe US$0.65; every 15 minutes
Laguna de Apoyo (rim) US$0.35; every 40 minutes
Laguna de Apoyo (crater lake) US$0.50; 6:30 AM, 10:30 AM, and 3:30 PM, returning from Apoyo at 6:30 AM, 11:30 AM, and 4:30 PM
Managua Huembes US$0.30; every 20 minutes. Microbuses to **Managua Mercado Oriental** (US$0.60; every 15 minutes) leave from San Sebastian Church in Monimbó; to **Man-**

Online Resources

Alcaldía Catarina (www.catarina.gob.ni, www.catarina.info.ni) All Pueblos Blancos alcaldías, or mayor's offices, have launched Spanish-language sites featuring "Mis Atractivos Turísticos" (My Tourist Attractions) with listings and photos, and "Mi Cultura" with dance and handicraft information, events calendars, and more. These cover Catarina.

Alcaldía Masatepe (www.masatepe.gob.ni, www.masatepe.info.ni) Covers the famed furniture town.

Alcaldía Masaya (www.masaya.gob.ni) Masaya's Alcaldía needs to add more information.

Alcaldía Niquinohomo (www.niquinohomo.gob.ni, www.niquinohomo.info.ni) Covers Sandino's birthplace.

Alcaldía San Juan de Oriente (www.sanjuandeoriente.gob.ni, www.sanjuandeoriente.info.ni) Covers Nicaragua's most important ceramics center.

Diriamba Online (www.diriamba.info) Good Spanish-language site has cultural information and tourism listings.

✪ **Laguna de Apoyo** (www.lagunadeapoyonicaragua.com) Useful English-language site has links to all lodging options on the crater lake.

Masatepe Online (www.masatepe.org) Spanish-language city guide has listings, cultural information, and photo galleries of the woodworking capital.

Masaya Viva (www.masayaviva.com) Regularly updated Spanish-language blog has cultural articles.

Often the cheapest, easiest way around the Pueblos Blancos and Carazo towns is in a mototaxi, even more fun than it looks.

agua UCA (US$0.60; every 10 minutes) from Parque San Miguel, one block east of the Old Market.

Masatepe US$0.25; every 20 minutes
Matagalpa US$2.30; 6 AM, 6:45 AM
Nandasmo US$0.30; every 20 minutes
Niquinohomo US$0.30; every 30 minutes
Pacaya US$0.30; every 15 minutes
Tipitapa US$0.40; every 20 minutes

CARAZO BEACHES
All beach buses leave from Diriamba.

La Boquita and Casares US$0.35; every 30 minutes
Huehuete US$1; buses leave Diriamba at 6 AM, 6:45 AM, 10:40 AM, 1 PM, 3:30 PM, and 4:30 PM; returning at 5:40 AM, 6 AM, 9 AM, 12:20 PM, 1 PM, 3:30 PM, and 4:30 PM

CATARINA AND SAN JUAN DE ORIENTE
Buses and microbuses pass the Catarina *empalme,* or exit, on the main road every 20 minutes or so, signed to **Granada, Jinotepe, Masaya, Nandaime,** and **Managua.** The stop is

several steep blocks from Catarina Mirador (US$0.25 mototaxi) and about 1 km from San Juan de Oriente (US$0.50 mototaxi).

DIRIAMBA

The main bus lot is on the main *carretera* at the main entrance to town, across from the **Torre Reloj** (clock tower). Some buses and minivans leave from just outside the station. Mototaxis charge US$0.25 anywhere in town, US$0.75 to Jinotepe or San Marcos.

La Boquita and Casares US$0.35; every 30 minutes
Huehuete US$1; 6 AM, 6:45 AM, 10:40 AM, 1 PM, 3:30 PM, and 4:30 PM
Jinotepe US$0.40; every 20 minutes
Jinotepe Microbus US$0.60; every 20 minutes (leaves from behind the Basilica)
Managua US$0.90; every 15 minutes
Managua Microbus US$1.15; every 15 minutes
Masatepe US$0.40; every 20 minutes
Masaya US$0.70; every 20 minutes

JINOTEPE

Jinotepe, not Masaya, is the Panamerican Highway's main stop on the Meseta. Though it's a chore getting to Granada from Jinotepe, there are fast, easy connections to Rivas and Managua.

Diriamba US$0.40; every 20 minutes
Diriamba Microbus US$0.60; every 20 minutes
Managua UCA US$1.15; every 20 minutes
Managua Israel Lewites US$0.50; every 20 minutes
Masaya US$0.65; every 15 minutes
Nandaime US$0.45; every 30 minutes
Rivas US$2; every hour
San Marcos US$0.35; every 20 minutes

LAGUNA DE APOYO

Buses leave the **Masaya Municipal Market** every 40 minutes (US$0.35) for the *rim* of the crater, but only three buses go down to the Laguna (US$0.50), leaving Masaya at 6:30 AM, 10:30 AM, and 3:30 PM, returning at 6:30 AM, 11:30 AM, and 4:30 PM. It's a steep half-hour walk to the lake from the crater rim.

Several hotels in Granada offer inexpensive shuttle service to different Apoyo accommodations, and happily arrange day trips and overnights at the lake. You can hire private taxis from Granada (US$12), Masaya (US$7), or anywhere else.

MASATEPE

Masaya–Jinotepe buses (US$0.40; every 15 minutes) drop passengers off on the highway, close to the furniture market. Other buses leave from two blocks north of the Masatepe Central Park for **Diriamba** (US$0.30; every 20 minutes), **Jinotepe** (US$0.35; every 20 minutes), and **Managua** (US$0.60; every 30 minutes).

SAN MARCOS

Microbuses leave from the central park, while full-sized **Masaya–Jinotepe buses** (US$0.30; every 15 minutes) pass through town on the main road.

Diriamba US$0.25; every 6 minutes
Jinotepe US$0.30; every 10 minutes
Managua US$1; every 15 minutes

TOURIST INFORMATION

Casa El Güegüense (2534-2132, 8607-8191; www.diriamba.info2532-0298; lissethaburto @hotmail.com; De Kodak, 1 cuadra sur, Plazita Rolando Orozco) Carazo's information booth is at the handicrafts market.

Masaya Intur (2522-7615, 2522-2251; masaya@inturžgob.ni, uh.morales@hotmail.com; opuesta iglesia San Francisco; open 11 AM–4 PM Mon. through Sat.) Helpful office has free maps and can recommend hotels.

Nicadventure Jinotepe (2532-2344, 8837-4355; www.nicadventure.net; BAC, 1 cuadra norte) Private Jinotepe outfitter also has information on Facebook.

Servitour Monimbó (2522-7404; servitour_monimbo@hotmail.com; Plaza Pedro Joaquin Chamorro, 75 varas al este) Private Masaya operator offers the usual tours plus more in-depth exploration of workshops and cultural sites.

LODGING

The Meseta Central simply doesn't offer the same range of lodging as major tourist destinations, which is part of its charm. You're here to experience the real Nicaragua, right? This may include hotels that are geared to real Nicaraguan travelers.

Budget and midrange travelers have the most to choose from, and your money goes a lot further on the Meseta. Masaya has a huge selection of quality backpacker hotels, and you'll also find clean, inexpensive spots in Catarina, Masatepe, Diriamba, Jinotepe, and the Carazo beaches.

Luxury lovers may feel more comfortable basing themselves in Granada, but also consider a night in Casa Catarina, a tasteful 2.5-star property in cool Catarina; or Diriamba's even nicer Mi Bohio, which holds its own against most top-end Granada hotels.

Lodging Price Code

Cost of lodging is based on an average per-room, double occupancy rate during peak season (December through April). Nicaragua's 15 percent sales tax and gratuities are not included; note that paying cash sometimes results in taxes being waived. Prices are much higher during the Christmas holidays and, particularly on the beaches, Semana Santa (Easter Week), when you should have reservations.

Inexpensive ($)	Up to US$25
Moderate ($$)	US$25 to US$60
Expensive ($$$)	US$60 to US$100
Very Expensive ($$$$)	US$100 and up

Hotels

MASAYA

HOTEL BESA-FLOR
Owners: Guisela Chavarría and Johannes Füssel
8634-9970, 8652-5214
www.hotel-besa-flor.de
jo@hotel-besa-flor.de
KM 19.8 Carretera Managua, pulpería San Antonio 300 metros Sur
Price: Moderate
Credit Cards: No
Handicap Access: Yes
Wifi: Yes

This pretty, German-Nica owned escape lies in the hills of Nindirí, on the border of Masaya National Park. While the setting is natural—they're even conserving a small tract of land, Castillo del Duende Guarda-barranco Finca Silvestre Forestal—the whitewashed rooms are quite comfortable, with modern cool baths and good beds. They're very involved in the local community, and can arrange fully customized regional tours.

✪ HOTEL IVANIA

Owner: Ivania Vega
2522-7632
www.hotelivanias.com
hotelivanias@hotmail.com
de la Iglesia Calvario, 3.5 cuadras oeste
Price: Inexpensive to Moderate
Credit Cards: Yes
Handicap Access: Yes
Wifi: Yes

Slightly underpriced hotel caters to NGOs and missionary groups, and meets high standards with their clean, tiled, air-conditioned rooms, eclectic Masatepe furnishings, and machine-heated baths. Some rooms have refrigerators. You'll also enjoy the mosaic-tiled courtyard patio, with lots of hammocks and a small fountain. It's three blocks from the Old Market.

HOTEL MASAYA

General Manager: Cristhian Fajardo
2522-1030, 2552-0981
www.hotelmasaya.com
fajacris@hotmail.com
Entrada Principal, 50 varas norte
Price: Moderate
Credit Cards: No
Handicap Access: Yes
Wifi: No

The City of Flowers' first Harley Davidson—themed hotel doesn't actually rent motorcycles (though they'll arrange it), but they do have a diamond-tuck front desk and Harley photos everywhere. Eleven rooms are large and very clean, with air-conditioning, machine-heated private baths, decent beds, and cable TV.

✪ HOTEL MONIMBÓ

Administrator: Karen José Aguilar
2522-6867, 8460-4326
hotelmonimbo04@hotmail.com
Plaza Chamorro, 1 cuadra este
Price: Inexpensive to Moderate
Credit Cards: Yes
Handicap Access: Challenging
Wifi: Yes

In the heart of Monimbó—several blocks from the Old Market but surrounded with workshops making marimbas, leather shoes, and fine guitars—is this excellent hotel. Follow the signs from San Sebastián church to the whitewashed stucco compound. Behind the walls, you'll find a tidy courtyard garden with huge ferns and a wooden shared porch with murals, hammocks, and restaurant service.

Relaxing rooms are clean and modern, with air-conditioning, cable TV, machine-heated baths, telephones, great mattresses, and attractive furnishings. It's popular with businesspeople and tour operators, so make reservations.

MADERA'S INN HOTEL

Owners: Johanna and Roger Velázquez
2552-5825
www.hotelmaderasinn.com
maderasinn@yahoo.com
Bomberos, 2 cuadras sur
Price: Inexpensive to Moderate
Credit Cards: Yes
Handicap Access: No
Wifi: Yes

This homey guesthouse right downtown has, for many years, offered rooms of all shapes, sizes, and decorative themes within a maze of handicraft-strewn hallways. All the rooms have private baths, and one room is air-conditioned. Definitely ask to see a

You'll appreciate the effort that goes into seemingly simple artesanías *by visiting Masaya's workshops, like this one behind Museo Ortega Saavedra.*

couple before choosing (and check the mattresses, some are new). The hotel also offers city and workshop tours in both Spanish and English, as well as airport shuttles (US$10) and other information.

PUEBLOS BLANCOS (CATARINA, DIRIÁ, DIRIOMO, MASATEPE, NIQUINOHOMO, SAN JUAN DE ORIENTE)

CASA CATARINA
Owner: María Julieta Choiseal
2558-0261, 2558-0199
www.hotelcasacatarina.net
reserve@hotelcasacatarina.net
Catarina, Parque Central
Price: Moderate to Expensive
Credit Cards: Yes
Handicap Access: No
Wifi: Not yet

Catarina, enrobed in all its colorful flowers above the laguna (lagoon), needed a classy hotel. Now it has one, right on the adorable central park, three blocks downhill from the famous Catarina Mirador, the scenic overlook above Laguna de Apoyo crater lake. Rooms are on the small side, but very comfortable and tastefully decorated, with large hot-water baths, big TVs, and lots of dark hardwoods and taupe fabrics. There's a good restaurant (B, L, D; $–$$) serving quality Nicaraguan food on-site.

Though most of the three-story building, hung with huge ferns, is entirely modern, its historic heart was built in 1903 with materials brought by oxcart from Granada. The hacienda was later confiscated by the FSLN, and used as a military base during

Cool and breezy Catarina Mirador, overlooking stunning Laguna de Apoyo, is the perfect place to relax.

battles memorialized in murals at the ✪ **bar**. After the perfectly coiffed, and understandably miffed, former owner won her family home back from the Sandinistas in court, she decided that opening a successful business would be the best revenge.

✪ FLOR DE POCHOTE

Owners: Ove Forbis and Rosario Duarte
8885-7576, 8617-2894, 8600-0652
www.flordepochote.com
faurby@ibw.com.ni
About 3 km (1.8 miles) north of Masatepe
Price: Inexpensive
Credit Cards: Yes
Handicap Access: No
Wifi: No

This is a very special property, with the view of Volcán Masaya that lays out how huge that fuming crater really is. It's rustic: Cabins and dorms are a fair walk from the lodge, and constructed with volcanic stones, wood, and bamboo. Rooms have OK private baths, and hand-hewn beds have new mattresses. Your porch, strung with hammocks, has truly epic volcano views, which you can explore on three separate trails through the forest.

Residents of the neighboring village of El Pochote (the hotel also arranges homestays; $) can take a guide to Masaya Lagoon and up the back side of the volcano. Day-trippers (US$1) can visit with reservations, though guided hikes cost extra. A mototaxi from Masatepe costs US$0.50.

HOTEL HACIENDA PUERTA DEL CIELO

8336-4912, 8927-0112
www.haciendapuertadelcielo.com

info@haciendapuertadelcielo.com
Outside Masatepe
Price: Moderate to Very Expensive
Credit Cards: Yes
Handicap Access: No
Wifi: No

This romantic, resort-style escape has five relatively plush casitas, all overlooking a truly fabulous pool with the steaming Masaya Volcano behind it. Spacious, comfortable villas are adults-only, designed for upmarket international travelers. The palapa-topped buildings are painted with brilliant tropical colors, and feature Masatepe's finest furnishings and all the modern amenities. Packages are all inclusive, with three gourmet meals—and there's a spa on-site.

CARAZO (DIRIAMBA, JINOTEPE, AND SAN MARCOS)

HOTEL CASA BLANCA
Manager: Roger González
2535-2717, 8851-2990
www.casablanca.com.ni
oxford@ibw.com.ni
San Marcos, Iglesia Católica 3 cuadras este
Price: Moderate
Credit Cards: No
Handicap Access: No
Wifi: Yes

The most comfortable option in San Marcos proper is this venerable midrange spot, three blocks from the central park. Large wooden rooms have high ceilings, big windows, and hot baths, all surrounding a mellow courtyard terrace. It's geared toward groups (but accepts individuals), and can arrange meals and tours.

ECOPOSADA EL JARDÍN TORTUGA VERDE
Owner: Roberto Rappaccioli Lacayo
2534-2948, 8862-6252
www.ecolodgecarazo.com
rorappal@turbonett.com.ni

Diriamba, KM40.5 Carretera Sur
Price: Moderate
Credit Cards: Yes
Handicap Access: No
Wifi: Yes

Just outside Diriamba, within a rambling maze of tropical gardens and flower nurseries, is a uniquely beautiful option. There are only five rooms hidden throughout the greenscape, each handcrafted and filled with eclectically mismatched furnishings and original art.

It's not upscale, but private machine-heated baths, cable TV, and air-conditioning in two rooms make it quite a comfortable oasis. The casita, which sleeps six, has a full kitchen. Breakfast is included and other meals can be arranged, or take a mototaxi into town (US$0.25).

✪ HOTEL Y SPA MI BOHIO
Owner: Socorro Chávez
2534-4020
www.hotelmibohio.com
mibohio@cablenet.com.ni
Diriamba, Costado Este de la Policia Nacional
Price: Moderate
Credit Cards: Yes
Handicap Access: Yes
Wifi: Yes

This beautiful new boutique property is the best hotel on the Meseta, its entirely modern construction cast in rather opulent Colonial style. Tiled courtyard porches and slender wooden columns surround a courtyard garden and trickling fountains. Rooms are sweet, with perfect hot-water bathrooms, huge cable TVs, great bedding, fine Masatepe furnishings, and all the amenities you'd expect at twice the price in Granada. There's even a tiny gym and spa, with a steam bath and Jacuzzi (US$5 per hour).

A light continental breakfast is included, but don't skip their popular ✪ **restaurant** (2534-2347; L, D; $$–$$$), serving hearty

Nicaraguan classics—try the jalapeño chicken—and all sorts of fresh seafood in a classic bamboo rancho. They also sell local coffees, jams, and candies.

HACIENDA SAN PEDRO HOTEL BOUTIQUE
Owner: Viviana Nissen
2535-2860
hotelhaciendasanpedro.com/web
hotelhaciendasanpedro@gmail.com
San Marcos, Iglesia Católica 3.5 cuadras al norte
Price: Moderate to Expensive
Credit cards: Not yet
Handicap Access: Challenging
Wifi: In restaurant

Just north of San Marcos, this 120-year-old Italian-style villa sits on a 60-manzana (100-acre) property that was once a successful coffee farm. After the government seized it during World War II (the family was originally from Germany), they ran it into the ground. Today, however, the artsy owners offer eight good rooms—all individually furnished with antiques, original fine art, and European-style duvets.

There are plans to develop the old beneficio (coffee processing plant) into a swimming pool and tennis courts. An open-air **restaurant** (B, L, D; $$$) serves your complimentary breakfast on a wonderful rambling wooden porch.

HOTEL CASA MATEO
Manager: Lynn Schweitzer
2532-3284, 8839-5214, 410-878-2252 (U.S.)
casamateo2000@yahoo.com
Jinotepe, De BDF, 2 cuadras abajo
Price: Moderate
Credit Cards: Yes
Handicap Access: Challenging
Wifi: In the lobby

The appealingly gritty city of Jinotepe (population 30,000) may not have many hotels,

but there's plenty of room at this great place, run by a Christian ministry. It's huge, with 38 rooms on three floors of spacey, late-1960s architecture, surrounding an atrium where their recommended restaurant, ✪ **El Jardín de los Olivos** (2532-3284; B, L, D; $$–$$$), serves Nica and international dishes.

The hotel is past its prime, but rooms are very clean and well maintained. Budget accommodations have decent beds, private warmish baths, and excellent balconies—or pay a few dollars more for better furnishings, air-conditioning, bathtubs, and other comforts.

CARAZO BEACHES
The Meseta Central drops almost 900 meters (3,000 feet) in just 35 km (22 miles), from the cool coffee-growing hills of Diriamba to Carazo's enticing collection of broad Pacific beaches.

When you arrive at the sea, take a right for **Centro Turistico La Boquita**, an agreeably scruffy, government-run "tourist center" with budget lodging. Go left for the fishing village of **Casares**, with two unusual boutique properties. Mostly undeveloped **Huehuete** is a few kilometers farther south.

HOTEL EL CASINO DE CASARES
Owner: Patrice Glo
8651-6589, 2532-8002
pglo2005@yahoo.es
Casares Centro, on the beach
Price: Inexpensive to Moderate
Credit Cards: Yes
Handicap Access: Yes
Wifi: Not yet

On a white-sand beach strewn with cheerfully painted fishing boats, this comfortable boutique hotel seems an anomaly. The lobby is a work of art, packed with fantastic paintings and sculptures beneath starry, arched cathedral ceilings. An unfinished casino and nightclub are gearing up to go at of press time.

Rooms aren't quite as extravagant as the entrance, but have small balconies, great beds, modern baths, cable TV, and more art. Those facing the sea have air-conditioning, or save on a fan-cooled room with views over the tiny town.

HOTEL LUPITA
Owner: José Felix Navarrete Palacios
8856-8207
hotellupita@yahoo.com
Casares, 800 metros de la parada de auto-buses
Price: Moderate
Credit Cards: Yes
Handicap Access: No
Wifi: No

Rising to remarkable solitude atop smooth, wave-crashed cliffs, this isolated hotel offers utter escape from the world. Rooms set into the steep property are spacious, with high wooden ceilings, handcrafted bamboo furnishings, air-conditioning, freshly painted private bathrooms, and TV—

though there's no cable or cell phone signals. There's no beach, either, though the huge swimming pool overlooks steep cliffs, which you can descend down—past precariously hanging cactuses—to tide pools at the bottom.

✪ HOTEL Y RESTAURANT SULEYKA
Owner: Giocanda Sánchez
8904-4502, 8698-3355
Centro Turistico La Boquita
Price: Inexpensive to Moderate
Credit Cards: Yes
Handicap Access: No
Wifi: Not yet

Centro Turístico La Boquita's best rooms are right on the waves, at this well-run hotel with options for everyone. Basic, fan-cooled cement rooms with private baths and new foam mattresses are just US$15, but pay a bit more for one of her better air-conditioned units upstairs—with cute furniture, real mattresses, and a balcony overlooking the waves and river.

Other Hotels
None of these hotels has wireless Internet, wheelchair access, or accepts credit cards unless specifically noted.

Masaya
Hotel Cailagua (2522-4435; cailagua@ibw.com.ni; KM30 Carretera Masaya; credit cards accepted; $$) Right on the carretera, this convenient midrange choice offers large rooms with private baths, air-conditioning, cable TV, complimentary breakfast, and a pool.

Hostal Santa María (2522-2411; www.hostalsantamarianic.com; info@hostal santamarianic.com; del BanPro 1 cuadra este, 0.5 cuadras sur; credit cards accepted; $–$$) Freshly updated hostel offers 16 small, immaculate rooms with frilly details, private baths, cable TV, soft beds, and handmade furniture—some with air-conditioning. There's a pool in the gardens.

✪ Hotel California (2522-2831, 8672-8403; rigo_cabezas@hotmail.com; de la Curacao 20 metros al norte; $) Pretty budget spot has cane ceilings, handsome wicker furnishings, and seven simple but comfortable rooms.

Hostal Mi Casa (2522-2500, 8874-9999; mantonabermudes@hotmail.com; Curacao 50 varas norte; $; wifi) Behind Fruti Fruti, this friendly, family-style budget hotel has great gardens and comfortable rooms with fans, soft beds, and a shared machine-heated bath.

Hotel Regis (2522-2300; La Curacao, 0.5 cuadra norte; $) At just US$4 per person for clean rooms with fans and shared bath, this is a budget traveler's first choice.

Pueblos Blancos (Catarina, Masatepe, Nindirí)

Las Cabañas Encantadas (8474-6854; KM25.5 Carretera Masaya; credit cards accepted; $$; wifi) Few people stay in historic Nindirí, but this clutch of modern wooden cabins may tempt you with wonderful views, full kitchens, air-conditioning, original art and handicrafts, and a small pool.

Hospedaje Euros (2558-0045; mtalavera2009@yahoo.com; Iglesia Católica, 1 cuadra oeste; $) Catarina's cavernous, chaotic, cheapest choice rents acceptable cement rooms with soft beds, shared baths, and volcano themes.

Hotel Faleiros (8690-0965; hotelfaleiros.nicahoteles.com; Masatepe, de Petronic 30 varas al este; $; wifi) Close to the Masatepe entrance and furniture market, this surprisingly nice, family-run hotel has clean rooms with charming furnishings and art, modern hot baths, big TVs, and a shared outdoor kitchen.

Hotel Jaaris (8640-5427; jackybenazirm24@yahoo.es; Catarina, Iglesia Bautista, 1 cuadra este, 50 metros sur; cash only, $) Next door to Euros in Catarina, this spot is a bit more expensive, but offers more privacy and character.

Carazo (Diriamba, Jinotepe, and San Marcos)

San Marcos has several guesthouses offering rooms to long-term students, but most will let you stay for around US$10 per night. Look for private homes displaying small signs saying *se aquilan cuarto* or *se renta habitaciones*.

Base Camp International (8336-9755; www.basecampcenters.com; Jinotepe, Parque Central, 2 cuadras oeste, 0.5 cuadras sur; $; wifi) Run by Volunteer Abroad, this coffee-boom mansion with cool courtyard gardens is geared to groups, but anyone can enjoy the spacious fan-cooled dorms and private rooms with sturdy beds, full kitchens, and machine-heated baths. They also arrange Spanish classes and volunteer opportunities.

Casa Concepción Navarro (8848-5939; San Marcos, frente BAC; credit cards accepted; $) Signed San Marcos guesthouse has huge rooms with private baths and breakfast.

Posada La Viña (2534-2162, 8478-6941; Diriamba, del Hospital San José, 1 cuadra oeste; $) Diriamba's best budget spot has a love hotel vibe (mirrored headboards, low lighting) but is very clean, professional, and freshly painted—with bamboo furnishings, private baths, and cable TV. Take a mototaxi (US$0.25), as it's several blocks from the city center.

Quinta Lupita (2534-3399, 8856-8207; hotellupita@yahoo.com; KM42.5 Carretera Sur Diriamba-Carazo; credit cards accepted; $$; wifi) Outside Diriamba, this stately, columned plantation mansion offers nine enormous, uniquely decorated rooms that still echo the coffee-boom decadence of the early 1900s. All have private hot baths, antiques, and shared kitchens—but you're really here for the huge swimming pools fed by a natural artesian well. Day-trippers (US$1.50; open 7 AM–6 PM) are welcome. It's a US$0.25 mototaxi ride from Diriamba.

Carazo Beaches

Huehuete did not have any hotels at press time, but customers can camp or hang a hammock for free at **Restaurant-Bar Don Segundo Cruz** (with restrooms). **ANDEN** (National Teachers Association; 2266–1471; www.cgten-anden.org.ni) was building cement bungalows on the beach that they plan to rent to tourists.

El Buen Gusto (8403-8805; La Boquita Centro Turistico; $) The cheapest acceptable rooms on the beach are behind this beachfront restaurant (B, L, D; $$–$$$) small, cement boxes with private baths, fans, and thin foam mattresses.

Olas Escondidas (8359-0025; La Boquita Centro Turistico; $$) Run by local surf champ Dennis Muñez, Carazo's only surf lodge has two huge, tiled rooms with air-conditioning, cable TV, safety boxes, good beds, and a friendly dog named Tsunami—all on a headland just above the beach. **Rancho Brava Mar**, on the beach, can hook you up.

Villas del Mar (2552-5825; villasdelmar@yahoo.com; La Boquita, 200 metros sur del Centro Turistico; credit cards accepted; $$) This new, modern hotel has spotless tiled rooms, large bathrooms, orthopedic mattresses, cable TV, and air-conditioning, all just outside La Boquita.

RESTAURANTS AND FOOD PURVEYORS

While every small town has its collection of inexpensive *comedores* and bakeries, the classic places to dine on the Meseta are **Catarina Mirador** or **Diriá's Mirador el Boquete**, both offering several restaurants overlooking Laguna de Apoyo. Family-friendly *restaurantes campestres* (country restaurants) scattered along the road between Catarina and Masatepe have gorgeous gardens, playground equipment, and excellent traditional cuisine.

Restaurant and Food Purveyor Price Code

The following prices are based on the cost of a dinner entrée with a nonalcoholic drink, not including Nicaragua's mandatory 13 percent restaurant tax and "suggested" 10 percent tip, which is usually included with the final bill (so check).

Inexpensive ($)	Up to US$5
Moderate ($$)	US$5 to US$10
Expensive ($$$)	$10 to $20
Very Expensive ($$$$)	US$20 or more

Restaurants

MASAYA

There are a few acceptable midrange restaurants geared to international tourists in and around the Handicrafts Market, and lots of cheap *comedores* at the New Market.

EL BUCANERO

2522-7550
KM26.5 Carretera Masaya
Price: Moderate
Cuisine: Nicaraguan
Serving: B, L, D
Credit Cards: Yes
Child's Menu: No
Handicap Access: Challenging
Reservations: No

Perched on the rim of Masaya's own crater lake, this popular restaurant is just outside town, off the Panamerican Highway toward Managua. Views from the open-air patio over the laguna and volcano can be enjoyed with well-prepared Nicaraguan cuisine, burgers, steak, and seafood. They often have live music, and there's even a swimming pool. Take a mototaxi from town.

✪ LOS CHORREDORES FRITANGA AND GRILL

2522-2291
gmcj13@gmail.com
de DGI, 0.5 cuadras oeste
Price: Moderate
Cuisine: Nicaraguan Fusion
Serving: L, D
Credit Cards: Yes

Child's Menu: Yes
Handicap Access: No
Reservations: For groups

Rather sophisticated spot with an elegantly rustic dining room serves what they call "fritanga fusion," with updated takes on classic street cuisine like churrasco (grilled beef), tejadas (plantain chips), and gallo pinto (rice and beans). The Nicaraguan owners lived abroad for many years, and their polished, professional kitchen also turns out international favorites such as carpaccio and fajitas. Cool place.

DON PEPE
8614-4119
Avenida Real San Jerónimo, de Iglesia San Jerónimo 2.5 cuadras sur
Price: Expensive to Very Expensive
Cuisine: Nicaraguan
Serving: L, D
Credit Cards: Yes
Child's Menu: No
Handicap Access: Yes
Reservations: For groups

In a beautifully refurbished Italian-style villa, this romantic spot has fresh flowers, chandeliers, candles, and crisply attired waitstaff, perfectly presented as the sun sets over the courtyard gardens. The menu is short, with churrascos and steaks; try the res con jalapeño in a creamy hot pepper sauce. There are also a few chicken and seafood dishes, plus Chilean wines.

TAQUERÍA LA JAROCHITA
2522-4831
Costado este del parque central 75 metros norte
Price: Moderate
Cuisine: Mexican
Serving: L, D
Credit Cards: Yes
Child's Menu: No
Handicap Access: No
Reservations: For groups

A fine spot for a fiesta with family or friends, this brightly painted Mexican restaurant serves up a cheery ambiance and large portions of good Mexican cuisine. Specialties include the tacos (try with carnitas), pozole (hominy and pork stew), chicken in mole, and several vegetarian options.

PUEBLOS BLANCOS (CATARINA, DIRIÁ, DIRIOMO, LAGUNA DE APOYO, NANDASMO, MASATEPE, NIQUINOHOMO, SAN JUAN DE ORIENTE)
The classic Pueblos Blancos dining experience is at the **Catarina Mirador,** where restaurants serve overpriced steak and Nica cuisine with magnificent lake views. **Restaurante Brumas de Apoyo** (2558-0251; credit cards accepted; B, L, D; $$$) has big windows, while **Restaurant Los Faroles** (8734-0150; credit cards accepted; B, L, D; $$–$$$) is a bit more downscale.

More festive lake lovers, however, head to the row of restaurant-bars along the **Diriá Mirador,** which open around noon and close when the last customers go home.

EL LIBRO CAFÉ
2558-0014
Mirador Catarina, just left of the entrance
Price: Moderate
Cuisine: Nicaraguan
Serving: L, D
Credit Cards: Yes
Child's Menu: No
Handicap Access: Yes
Reservations: For groups

Though most international visitors pay top dollar at one of the Catarina Mirador restaurants right on the crater rim, you'll often get better value (and better food) on the other side of the parking lot.

This simple spot, away from the fine views, is consistently recommended as the best restaurant in town. Sit down at one of the plastic tables to enjoy very tasty jalapeño beef steak, pollo rostizado (fried chicken), and other Nica cuisine.

LA OLLA DE BARRO

2523-2698
KM52 Carretera Masaya–Naindame,
between Masatepe and Niquinohomo
Price: Moderate to Expensive
Cuisine: Nicaraguan
Serving: L, D
Credit Cards: Yes
Child's Menu: Yes
Handicap Access: Yes
Reservations: For events

This popular, enormous restaurant
campestre has been serving Nica families
for three decades. Though you can order a
meal, most folks come for the appetizers—
in particular the tejadas (plantain chips)
and tostones (plantain medallions) topped
with meats and cheeses, as well as Masatepe's signature mondongo (cow stomach
stew—much better than it sounds). Or just
turn the kids loose in the Dr. Seuss–style
playground while you enjoy a cocktail.

MIRADOR EL POLLO

8856-9554, 8830-8434
KM41 Carretera Masaya–Naindame
Price: Moderate
Cuisine: Nicaraguan
Serving: B, L, D
Closed: Wed.
Credit Cards: No
Child's Menu: No
Handicap Access: No
Reservations: No

There are several other spots with Laguna
de Apoyo views, such as this shady little
dive across the highway from San Juan del
Oriente. The menu is short, the specialty is
chicken wings (alas) or tostones con queso,
and the view is incredible.

The restaurant, well signed from the
road between Diriá and Catarina, is about
300 meters from the turnoff to San Juan del
Oriente, a 10-minute walk from the bus
stop.

Carazo (Diriamba, Jinotepe, and San Marcos)

BISTRÓ LAYHA

2532-2440, 2532-0243
bistrolayha@gmail.com
Jinotepe, Parroquia Santiago 2.5 cuadras
al sur
Price: Moderate
Cuisine: Nicaraguan Fusion
Serving: L, D Thu. through Sun.
Closed: Mon. through Wed.
Credit Cards: Yes
Child's Menu: No
Handicap Access: Challenging
Reservations: Yes

Fabulous little bistro in downtown Jinotepe
serves sophisticated cuisine in stylish environs. Sleek furnishings are dressed up with
fresh flowers and original art. A great place
to enjoy espresso beverages and light bistro
cuisine such as grilled sandwiches, creative
pasta dishes, and great salads.

✪ LA CASONA COFFEE SHOP

2535-2798, 8688-1002
www.lacasonasanmarcos.com
San Marcos, de Enitel 1 cuadra norte
Price: Moderate
Cuisine: International
Serving: B, L, D
Credit Cards: Yes
Child's Menu: No
Handicap Access: Yes
Reservations: For groups

This San Marcos landmark, "where la gente
cool hangs out," caters to the university
crowd. The cozy wooden interior and gardens are perfect for enjoying lazy afternoons and long nights filled with strong
coffee, cheap beer, and live music. The food
is tops, from hefty grilled sandwiches (try
the Fran special) to Nica bocas (bar snacks)
and big nachos, which fill you up on student
prices.

The real draw, however, is the scene.
This is the perfect spot to start your night

out on the town, though more often than not the best music in Carazo is right here.

PIZZERÍA COLÍSEO

2532-2150, 2532-2646
Jinotepe, BanCentro, 1 cuadra norte
Price: Moderate
Cuisine: Italian
Serving: L, D
Closed: Mon.
Credit Cards: Yes
Child's Menu: No
Handicap Access: Challenging
Reservations: Yes

Though Jinotepe's cuisine scene leaves much to be desired, this famed pizzeria serves tasty thin-crust pies and other more upscale Italian items. The atmosphere, in an old coffee-boom mansion, is romantic and service is very good. There's a full bar and decent selection of wines.

CARAZO BEACHES

There are a few basic seafood restaurants in Casares, but most day-trippers come to dine at **Centro Turístico La Boquita.** Beachgoers can base themselves at one of several rancho restaurants, most of which accept credit cards, serve beer and rum, and will watch your stuff while you take a swim—or even let you pass out in a hammock overnight. Local specialties include *sopa marinero* (seafood soup), *langosta rellena* (lobster stuffed with cheese and shrimp), and massive *surtidos*

(variety platters) for groups.

Upon arrival, you'll be (too) enthusiastically greeted by half a dozen touts, all offering discounts on menu prices. Ambiance ranges from simple, like breezy, wooden **Bar-Restaurante Eliath** (8947-7419, 8905-2319; $$–$$$), with plastic tables on the sand; to downright elegant, such as **Restaurant Los Jicaritos** (8368-0181; $$–$$$), with its finely made rancho, private dressing rooms for swimmers, colorful tablecloths, production kitchen, and attentive hostess, Susy. Take your pick, then relax and make a day of it.

RESTAURANT-BAR DON SEGUNDO CRUZ

8439-2855
Huehuete
Price: Moderate
Cuisine: Seafood, Nicaraguan
Serving: B, L, D
Credit Cards: Not yet
Child's Menu: No
Handicap Access: Challenging
Reservations: No

The stunning white-sand beach of Huehuete, only recently accessible via paved road, still doesn't have much development. Don Segundo Cruz, however, has been bringing folks all the way out here for years with cold beer and big plates of whatever's fresh that day—shrimp, grilled fish, conchas negras—served right on the sand.

Food Purveyors

Asian
The Meseta has its share of inexpensive, edible Chinese food.

Restaurant Casa Blanca (8886-0057; Jinotepe, KM49 Carretera Sur; credit cards accepted; L, D; $$) Has a huge menu and bigger portions.

La Pagoda de Oro (2534-4087; del Reloj Público, 1 cuadra sur, 2.5 cuadras oeste; credit cards accepted; L, D; $$) Walking distance from the Basilica.

Restaurante Yuan-Lin (8993-4140; Masaya, de la Curacao 1 cuadra norte; credit cards accepted; L, D; $$) Masaya's Chinese restaurant is actually pretty good.

Bakeries

Panadería Brenes (8832-0409; Masatepe Central Park; cash only; $) Enjoy a sweet snack after perusing Masatepe.

Panadería Central Quintanilla (8898-8763; Catarina, frente Hospedaje Euros; cash only; B, L; $) Family-run bakery sells inexpensive bread and pastries.

✪ **Panadería Norma** (2522-6629; northwest corner of Masaya Old Market; cash only; B, L, D; $) Excellent bakery, convenient to the Old Market, sells delicious pastries, sandwiches, and more.

Reposteria Adelita (2532-2974; San Marcos; cash only; $) Sweet and savory baked goods across from the university.

Cafés

Café Negro (2535-2506; San Marcos, 1 km Carretera La Concha; D Sun. through Wed., L, D Thu. through Sat.; $$) Just outside San Marcos, sink into a leather chair and enjoy this popular bar and café. There's live music on Saturday.

Fruti Fruti Smoothies (2522-2500; Curacao, 50 metros norte; cash only; B, L, D; $) Masaya juice bar offers a huge selection of smoothies, juices, and milkshakes, as well as coffee and bistro cuisine.

Momentos Café (8647-5568; Jinotepe, de Santa Maria 1.5 cuadras sur; credit cards accepted; open 2 PM–10 PM Tue. through Sun.; $) Around the corner from Hotel Casa Mateo, Momentos does Jinotepe's best espresso beverages, top-notch *batidos,* and sinful *meloso,* coconut-almond cake.

Nicaraguan

✪ **Casa de Cajetas** (Diriomo Centro; cash only; B, L, D; $) Diriomo's famous *cajetas,* traditional sweets made with candied fruits and other ingredients, are worth the trip.

✪ **Comida Buffet** (8438-2166; Masaya, costado Mercado Viejo; cash only; L, D; $) Next to Masaya Intur, this steam-table buffet sells cheap, vegetarian Nica and Asian cuisine—much of it involving soy "meat."

Restaurant Paraíso (2535-2712; San Marcos, de Texaco 1 cuadra norte, 0.5 cuadras oeste; credit cards accepted; L, D; $) Cavernous beacon to thirsty students serves barbecued chicken wings, *tostones,* and cheap beer. The US$3 lunch special is a deal.

Buen Gusto (2532-1145; Jinotepe, de Santa Maria, 1.5 cuadras sur; cash only; B, L, D; $) Enjoy good, cheap eats near Hotel Casa Mateo, with burgers, set plates, and ✪ *tejadas.*

Villa's Restaurant (2534-2159; Diriamba, Parque Central; credit cards accepted; B, L, D; $$) Local landmark offers well-prepared Nica cuisine in a grand old coffee-boom mansion, close to the Diriamba Basilica.

Pizza

Golden Pizza (2557-0467; Diriá, 1 cuadra del parque central; cash only; L, D; $–$$) Most visitors head to the mirador, but you can enjoy pizza, roast chicken, and burgers right in the old Chorotega capital.

Pizzeria Amigos (2535-2148; San Marcos, de Texaco 1 cuadra norte; credit cards accepted; L, D; $$) No college town is complete without a sprawling, beer-soaked pizzeria, and here it is.

Tele Pizza (2522-0170; Masaya, Iglesia la Asunción, 25 varas norte, Avenida San Jerónimo; credit cards accepted; L, D; $–$$) Everyone's favorite pizza has a Masaya branch, serving hefty salads, cheesy garlic bread, and cheap slices.

CULTURE

Masaya was declared the Capital of National Folklore in 2000, but the saying "If Nicaragua is my body, Masaya is my heart," is much older. It is the capital of the fertile Meseta Central, where several small, ancient villages have notably contributed to Nicaragua's rich artistic and musical traditions.

The **Pueblos Blancos** (White Towns) are named for the pale volcanic tuff originally used to build each village, today cheerfully painted and filled with colorful handicraft workshops. They are also called the *Pueblos Brujos*, or Bewitched Villages, for the spiritual wisdom and herbal tinctures of their *curanderos*, or faith healers—still open for business in fascinating **Diriomo.**

When conquistador Gil González Dávila first arrived on the Meseta, it was divided into *cacicazgos* (provinces) occupied by two Nahuatl-speaking peoples: the Nahuas, who controlled Masaya, Masatepe, and Jinotepe; and the Chorotegas, led by Chief Diriangén. His name meant "Ruler of the Mountain People," and it is preserved at his former capital, now called **Diriá**, and the loyal polities of **Diriamba** and **Diriomo.**

Diriangén welcomed the Spanish to his stronghold with gold, women, and meat, though the 27-year-old warrior understood exactly what was planned. He feigned interest in González's offer of peace in exchange for new Christian converts, but this was only to buy time to organize the troops he had been gathering since the Spaniards' bloody occupation of Nicarao (now Rivas) in 1523.

On April 17, 1529, "Nicaragua's first freedom fighter" met the Spanish in a terrible battle. The Spanish were victorious. It is Diriangén's statue that is erected throughout the Meseta, however, and his sacrifice that is immortalized in Carlos Mejía Godoy's anthem, "Nicaragua, Nicaragüita."

It is a region renowned for its rebellious nature, and many of Nicaragua's historic heroes and villains have hailed from the Meseta's cool heights. San Marcos was the birthplace of controversial former presidents Anastasio Somoza García and Arnoldo Alemán, while Niquinohomo ("Valley of Warriors") gave the nation Augusto C. Sandino and his ally from Masatepe, progressive President José María Moncada.

They say success of the Sandinista-led revolution was decided by the 1978 Monimbó Insurrection, a bloody street battle considered the *chispa* (spark) that finally set the rebellion alight on a national level. Young guerrillas disguised themselves with the masks of the *Güegüense,* but rather than pretending obedience like that sly folkloric hero, threw homemade hand grenades instead.

The Meseta has thus retained its cultural integrity, the deep roots of these pre-Columbian pueblos blossoming into Nicaragua's finest artistic, literary, and musical traditions. This is the land of the *marimba,* a type of wooden xylophone that provides the soundtrack of the nation, and the flaring skirts of spinning dancers celebrating each civic fiesta. Most international visitors simply breeze through the Masaya Old Market, but there is so much more to discover.

Masaya

The gateway to the Meseta is Masaya, which poet Rubén Darío called the City of Flowers. It boasts a fine collection of Colonial and coffee-boom buildings, most still scarred from years of warfare, earthquakes, and neglect. The only truly Colonial church is the simple, baroque 1751 **Parroquia Nuestra Señora de la Asuncion,** with a classic bell tower over-

Though most of Masaya's churches have been entirely rebuilt over the years, the 1751 Parroquia Nuestra Señora de la Asunción is original.

looking bustling **Parque 17 de Octubre,** packed with delightful outdoor eateries.

Masaya's famously extravagant religious processions usually begin at the 1928 **Parroquia San Jerónimo,** (Avenida San Jerónimo, del parque centra, 4 cuadras norte). Given almost any excuse, parades of dancers, musicians, saints, and costumed revelers will make their way through Masaya to the historic indigenous city of **Monimbó.** Now a Masaya neighborhood, it is marked by the stately, columned façade of the 1935 **Iglesia San Sebastián** (Avenida Real Monimbó, del parque central, 6 cuadras sur) and entirely modern **Iglesia Maria Magdalena** (de San Sebastián, 2 cuadras suroeste), where San Lázaro is famously honored by hundreds of costumed dogs.

Other architectural gems include the 1891 **Old Market,** 1926 **Train Station,** and in the mountains high above the old rail line, **Fortaleza Coyotepe.** Hire a horse-drawn carriage to the **Masaya Malecón,** the recently remodeled boardwalk overlooking **Laguna de Masaya** (no swimming) and fuming Santiago Crater. Nearby, the 1848 **Iglesia San Juan Bautista** marks Masaya's famous hammock-making neighborhood, well worth perusing.

The Pueblos Blancos

The best known of the White Towns is **Catarina,** with its refreshing and windswept mirador overlooking Laguna de Apoyo from 623 meters (2,043 feet) above sea level. Stroll down to

Though most people just visit Catarina's mirador, it's worth walking around town to see the city's famed flower nurseries.

the town center, with its kaleidoscopic *viveros* (flower nurseries) and old baroque church with some of the nicest gold-gilt *retablos* (altar pieces) in Nicaragua, dating to the 1700s.

Just south of Catarina, **San Juan del Oriente** is known for its ceramics workshops, some of which offer tours. **Masatepe,** nearby, is famed for its furniture, but check out the photogenic city center, where 18th-century **Iglesia San Juan Bautista** watches over a shady park apparently sponsored by Movistar phones.

Niquinohomo is best known as the birthplace of General Sandino, and his family home was once a museum. Townspeople are patiently waiting for First Lady Rosa Murillo to return their favorite son's boots, guns, typewriter, letters, clothing, and photos, but in the meantime Sandino's childhood home serves as a reading library. It is worth seeing the 1663 **Iglesia Santa Ana,** with a sturdy, baroque-meets-Mudéjar façade atop an indigenous cemetery.

The old Chorotega capital of **Diriá** is now a tiny town, best known for **Mirador el Boquete,** a couple of kilometers from the center with restaurants overlooking Laguna de Apoyo. **Iglesia San Pedro y San Pablo** marks the spot where Cacique Diriangén first confronted the Spanish, and today hosts indigenous-accented religious festivities. Neighboring **Diriomo** is best known for its *curanderos,* or faith healers. Stop by rather gothic **Iglesia Nuestra Señora de la Candelaria** to get in the witchy mood.

Carazo

Though the three cities of Carazo's **Triangulo de Oro,** or Golden Triangle, were important Nahual and Chorotega towns, the region most recently came into its own during the coffee-boom years of the late 1800s. Nicaragua's first coffee plants arrived here in 1858, and within a few decades these simple cities were being rebuilt with serious flourish: baroque columns, elaborate frescos, wrought-iron balconies, even Egyptian-inspired Art Deco.

The region remains most famous for a piece of local literature dating from the 1500s: *El Güegüense.* The musical play, originally composed in both Spanish and Nahuatl, is a comedy on the surface, with sharp social commentary underneath. The script changes, but always pits a sharp *Mestizo* merchant against a dandy band of Spanish tax collectors, all in blue-eyed masks.

The merchant, El Güegüense (Nahuatl for "wise man") never actually fights the nobility, instead using wicked double entendres and feigned obedience to avoid paying his fines, marry off his son to the governor's daughter, and continue running his business tax-free. It is performed all over the country, often to ridicule local politicians, but the classic version can be appreciated at Diriamba's **Fiestas Patronales de San Sebastián** (January 17–27).

Diriamba is worth visiting any time for the soaring 1932 **Basílica Menor de San Sebastián,** designed by Italian-born architect Mario Favilli. The ornate *retablos* dating from

The perfect gift for the libertarian in your life? A doll based on the Güegüense, *written in the 1500s as a protest against high taxes.*

the 1700s are the stars of the show, but paintings by John Fusch Holl and the "father of Nicaraguan modern painting," Rodrigo Peñalba, are also displayed. You can't miss the 1936 **Torre Reloj**, or clock tower, still keeping perfect time.

Jinotepe has much more of a city feel, with most architecture dating from the uninspired 1960s, though the 1860 **Iglesia Santiago Xilotepetl** (today the last word is usually spelled *Jinotepe*) is nice. It holds a statue of Apostle Santiago that was found floating in the waters of Huehuete in the 1740s, along with San Sebastian, patron of **Diriamba.**

San Marcos is best known for the Nicaraguan campus of **Ave Maria University** (2535-2314; www.avemaria.edu.ni; de Texaco, 2 cuadras sur), built by Catholic philanthropist and Domino's Pizza founder Tom Monaghan. It's one of the best universities in the country, and classes are conducted in English, so the party scene will have plenty of people eager to practice with you.

Museums
This region has several small museums, none of them particularly impressive, but offering a good excuse to explore.

Masaya
MUSEO COMUNITARIO ETNÓGRAFICO DE MONIMBÓ
Monimbó, dAdmission: By donation
Open: 9 AM—noon, Tue. through Sun.

Diriamba's beautiful basilica houses an image of San Sebastián found floating in Huehuete in 1751—along with Jinotepe's patron, Apostle Santiago.

You can't miss this tiny museum, painted bright Sandinista pink. Well, you probably can. It does its best to celebrate the FSLN past and present, with a few masks from the Monimbó Insurrection and papier-mâché cow and pigs, which symbolize the FSLN's 2009 "tax rebate," in the form of livestock. There are also some ceramics and handcrafts, including a festival dress painted with an image of San Jerónimo.

MUSEO Y GALERÍA DE HEROES Y MARTIRES
2522-4317, 2522-2194
www.masaya.gob.niAdmission: Free
Open: 7 AM–1 PM Mon. through Fri.
Inside the Masaya

Inside the Masaya Alcaldía, this is the best of the Masaya museums, its walls covered with photos of the "Heroes and Martyrs of the Revolution." There are also personal effects, old weapons, and other exhibits. But, if you've got time, the great value in this place is revealed by really studying the faces of those who gave their lives all those years ago.

FORTALEZA EL COYOTEPE
8694-9012
pmoreno21@yahoo.comAdmission: US$1/0.50 foreigner/Nicaraguan
Open: 8 AM–5 PM daily

Once fearsome, this fortress atop Masaya's "Hill of Coyotes" is one of Nicaragua's creepier destinations. The hill strategically overlooks the rail lines and freeway, and was for this reason fortified in 1893 by President José Santos Zelaya. He spent his administration fight-ing U.S.-based fruit companies, and though they chased him out of the country in 1909, it wasn't until October 4, 1912, that the U.S. Marines finally took his stronghold.

Coyotepe's current fortress was probably completed during World War I, while the sinis-ter underground dungeons were added in 1936. Both the Somoza and Sandinista govern-ments used it as a particularly brutal prison. Almost airless and lightless, this warren of tiny cement rooms was packed with criminals and political prisoners who covered the ver-min-infested floor when they lay down. The painfully cramped rooms, eerie graffiti, rumors of Satanic ritual use, and dead serious descriptions of torture and pain by your guide—all conspire to raise every hair on the back of your neck during the short tour.

In 1984, the whole mess was shut down for good—and returned to the Boy Scouts of Nicaragua, who had used it for their annual jamborees in the 1960s. Today, scouts offer tours of the fortress as well as **camping** (cash only; $) with reservations.

The entrance to the fortress is about 3 km (1.8 miles) north of Masaya at KM28 of the Carretera Masaya-Managua; any Managua–Masaya bus can drop you off for a 20-minute climb to the top. A taxi from Masaya costs US$3.

CASA-MUSEO COMANDANTE CAMILO ORTEGA SAAVEDRA
8902-9021Las Sabogales, Admission: By donation
Open: Daily, knock to see if they're home

Once a safe house for Sandinista rebels, this building's owners "disappeared" shortly before the Monimbó Insurrection. During the battle, President Ortega's brother, Camilo Ortega, was killed just four blocks away. Today, the tiny museum houses a few photocopied La Prensa articles and a wide-collared, polyester-blend dress shirt once owned by Camilo, plus a few other revolutionary mementoes. The people running it are sweet, and have a woodshop where you can watch them make bowls and jewelry.

Diriamba

Drop by **Casa El Güegüense** (2534-2132, 8607-8191; www.diriamba.info; 8 AM—5 PM daily) with an art gallery, tourist information, free coffee, and brightly costumed, masked figures that represent the region's renowned folkloric dances.

MUSEO ECOLÓGICO DE TRÓPICO SECO

2534-2129
www.adeca.org.ni/museo_eco
Costado Sur Policía Nacional
Admission: US$1.25
Open: 8 AM—4 PM Mon. through Fri.

This small but extremely well-presented museum is dedicated to the ecology of the dry tropical rainforest, today the most endangered Central American ecosystem. Excellent murals and exhibits include a detailed topographic map that marks active volcanoes with glowing LED lights. There are a lot of hands-on displays for kids. Check out the rubbings of an enormous **petroglyph** (rock carving) located about 1.5 km (1 mile) from the museum, at Poza del Mero, el Mango entrada. The museum may be able to find guides.

Nindirí

MUSEO DE NINDIRÍ CACIQUE TENDERÍ

8659-8218
Nindirí, one block from the parque central
Admission: US$2
Open: 9 AM—4:30 PM Mon. through Fri.

About 3 km from Masaya, this once important Chorotega town is best known for **Iglesia Santa Ana,** built in the late 1500s with fine retablos. One block away is Nindirí's oldest house, **La Casona,** and the city's museum.

Your fee includes a Spanish-language tour of their top-quality collection of ceramics and stone pieces. You can also arrange tours of the town, including a **cemetery** with a pre-Columbian sacrificial stone and the 19th-century **Iglesia El Calvario**—or even spend the night in a haunted house. Contact Justo Pastor Ramos (8659-8218; justopramos@yahoo.es).

Nightlife

Though there are plenty of places to satisfy your thirst on the Meseta, most towns just offer the usual local bars. Popular party destinations on weekends include the restaurant-bars at the **Diriá Mirador,** the public beach at **Laguna de Apoyo,** and the beachfront restaurants of **Centro Turístico El Boquete.**

Masaya has a few interesting options, with several discos at the **Malécon,** and **Rincón Romántico** (2522-4933; Masaya, Rotonda Las Flores, 200 metros al suroeste; open 6 PM—1 AM Fri. through Sat.) offering dancing on weekends. Mellower options include **La Ronda Bar Restaurant** (2522-3310; parque central; credit cards accepted; L, D; $$), which is right downtown and has a dance floor and outdoor seating, and **Mr. Lorch's Bar & Grill** (2522-7628; Curacao, 20 varas norte; closed Sun.) with karaoke.

San Marcos is a university town, with plenty of nightlife geared to students and party people; start at **La Casona** or **El Paraíso** to find out what's on.

Spanish Schools

Futuro Mejor Spanish School (www.futuromejor.org; La Conquista; US$200 per week, all inclusive) Brand new Danish-Nica Spanish school is in a small town near Jinotepe.

Estación Biológica FUNDECI/GAIA (8882-3992, 8665-9046; www.gaianicaragua.org; apoyo@gaianicaragua.org; Laguna de Apoyo) GAIA is a scientific research station that offers great value on professional Spanish classes, as well as U.S.-university-accredited tropical biology courses, at the bottom of a volcanic crater. Their relaxed wooden lodge has basic accommodations for students and visitors, and they also arrange scuba diving in the crater.

✪ **La Mariposa Spanish School and Ecohotel** (8669-9455; mariposaspanishschool.com; San Juan de la Concepción) This pricey school comes highly recommended for its professional, organized classes; quality tours; flowering gardens; healthy cuisine; and sunny wooden rooms with private hot baths. There are classes especially for children.

Masaya Spanish School (www.masayaspanishschool.com; Diriomito) About 15 minutes from Masaya, this school offers classes, homestay, and meals.

Spanish School Catarina (8876-4316, 2558-0140; www.spanishschoolcatarina.com; parque central, 1 cuadra oeste, frente Tienda Quintanilla) Study Spanish in Catarina, with homestays available.

Theater

Jueves de Verbena (Masaya Old Market; 7:30 PM Thurs.; admission varies, usually US$1) Masaya's famous handicrafts market hosts weekly folkloric performances, with live music, plucky marimbas, and traditional dances from all over Nicaragua, including the *Palo de Mayo* of the Caribbean Coast and *Güegüense* of the Meseta Central. Stands sell Nica cuisine. There are also *bailes tradicionales* (traditional dances) every Sunday.

RECREATION

National Parks and Protected Areas

✪ RESERVA NATURAL LAGUNA DE APOYO

2558-0456
www.amictlan.com
Between Granada and Masaya
Open: 24 hours
Admission: Usually free, but may charge US$0.25 for pedestrians, US$1.25 for cars

Deeply inset into a richly forested volcanic crater is Laguna de Apoyo, one of Nicaragua's loveliest natural treasures. Formed 23,000 years ago, the sparkling lake covers Central America's lowest point (Apoyo's bottom is 125 meters below sea level), with delightfully clean water fed by hidden fumeroles and saturated with minerals reputed to have therapeutic powers.

The crater is a natural reserve, threaded by beautiful trails. It is imperfectly protected—from poachers, loggers, and tourists—so tread lightly. In addition to being Central Amer-

Relax at the bottom of a thickly forested volcano, perhaps at Crater's Edge, overlooking mineral-rich Laguna del Apoyo.

ica's best swimming hole, this is also a much-needed habitat for sloths, giant anteaters, howler monkeys, jaguarundis, and others.

There are even half a dozen endemic fish, such as the arrow mojarra (Amphilophus astorquii), discovered in 1976. You can scuba down to see them, along with the dramatic crater topography, through **Estación Biológica FUNDECI/GAIA** (see Spanish Schools, earlier).

Three footpaths descend the steep crater walls: from **Mirador Catarina** (emerging near Hotel San Simian), **Mirador Diriá** (actually a four-wheel-drive road to Apoyo Camp, 2 km north of San Simian on a hiking trail), and the city of **Granada**, an 8-km walk that begins at the cemetery, emerging opposite the hotels. There have been armed muggings on all three, so go in groups, preferably with a guide, and leave your valuables at home.

Most people come to the Laguna on the paved road, signed from the Masaya–Granada Carretera, served by buses, taxis, and private shuttles from Granada (see Getting Around, earlier). You can chill on the public beach, with friendly restaurants serving Nica cuisine, including colorfully painted **Restaurante Monteverde** (8888-3705; credit cards accepted; B, L, D; $$) and neighboring **Apoyo Beach** (credit cards accepted; B, L, D; $$).

Most international travelers spend the day (or night) at one of a handful of hotels offering day passes, food service, lake access, and the most remarkable moonrises you'll ever see in your life.

At the "triangle," where the access road meets the lakeshore, make a right for Norome (1 km) and San Simian (1.3 km). Turn left and you'll see the Monkey Hut, Crater's Edge, the public beach, and GAIA within a few hundred meters, or continue toward La Orquidea (1.3 km) and La Posada Ecológica Abuela (2 km).

Apoyo Camp (8837-3990; www.apoyocamp.com; shamus_396prod@hotmail.com; $–$$) Well away from the other hotels (access is via the Diría Mirador), this mellow spot has surprisingly nice adobe rooms with good beds, wood accents, and private baths—plus cheap camping and hammock rental. There's a shared kitchen and wood-fired stove, and a beautifully landscaped terrace overlooking the lake and dock.

✪ **Crater's Edge** (8895-3202; www.craters-edge.com; cratersedge@gmail.com; credit cards accepted; $–$$; wifi) This laid-back flashpacker lodge is just about perfect, with lots of palm-shaded patio space, comfortable furnishings, hanging chairs, and a floating dock. Kayaks and inner tubes are complimentary, meals are out-of-this-world, and the breezy dorm one of Nicaragua's best. Julio Toledo offers Seeing Hands Blind Massage on-site. Crater's Edge offers inexpensive shuttle service from Granada at 10 AM and 4 PM daily.

La Orquidea Casa de Huésped (8872-1866; www.laorquideanicaragua.com; $$–$$$; wifi; day pass US$5) Colonial Revival–style B&B has flowing white stucco architecture, built-in furniture, a red-tiled roof, and lakefront gardens. The modern, tastefully decorated guesthouse has a tiled full kitchen, patio, and plunge pool, with two bedrooms rented separately or together as the entire house. Two smaller, less expensive rooms have air-conditioning and private baths—but the cheapest, "The Belltower," is the best; a tiny twin bed crammed into the top of a tower with windows on all sides.

Monkey Hut (8887-3546; www.thebeardedmonkey.com; monkeyhutlauna@gmail.com; $–$$; day pass US$6) This fun budget lodge has long been a backpacker favorite, but is no longer owned by the famous Bearded Monkey in Granada (it and La Libertad hostel still run daily shuttles). Regardless, the pleasant wooden rooms and dorms are still clean and comfortable, as is the romantic casita on the water. Kayaks, inner tubes, and other toys are included, and there's a snack bar (but no meal service) on-site.

La Posada Ecológica Abuela (8880-0368, 8966-4084; www.posadaecologicalaabuela.com; info@posadaecologicalaabuela.com; credit cards accepted; $$$; day pass US$10 which you can redeem at their restaurant) With wonderful murals and a top-notch dock, this comfortable hotel is among the laguna's most comfortable. Rooms are small but air-conditioned, with hot baths, CD players, and TV/DVDs; some have minifridges and balconies. Guests also have access to kayaks, mountain bikes, and more.

San Simian (8813-6866, 8850-8101; www.sansimian.com; contact@sansimian.com; credit cards accepted; $$–$$$; day pass US$5) Romantic spot on the edge of the untouched wilderness is landscaped with dark volcanic-rock terraces, botanical gardens, and very comfortable bungalows. It is associated with Hotel Casa San Francisco in Granada, and has similarly good rooms—excellent beds, Far Eastern accents, and even a plunge pool in the Mango Moon unit. Cuisine is creative, ranging from spicy vegetable curries to Caribbean-style fish in pineapple chutney.

Villas at Norome Resort (2552-8200 (reservations), 8867-7304 (hotel), 760-494-7331 (U.S.); www.noromevillas.com; info@noromevillas.com; credit cards accepted; $$$; wifi in lobby) The most luxurious property on the lake climbs the steep crater walls to several cavernous vacation villas designed for top-end travelers. They come in several different sizes and configurations, all with top-end décor, full kitchens, and views through the forest. The restaurant is stocked with sailboards and kayaks.

✪ PARQUE NACIONAL VOLCÁN MASAYA

2522-5415
nydiagut@ibw.com.ni
KM 23 Carretera a Masaya
Admission: US$4.50/1 foreigner/Nicaraguan
Open: 9 AM–4:30 PM; night visits can be arranged

The most heavily venting volcano in the world is Santiago Crater, the vast and gaping maw that marks the center of Volcán Masaya National Park. If you flew into Managua, you could not miss the blackened mountain, pouring its sulfurous burden into the sky.

The Spanish thought this was the gateway to hell, and erected La Cruz de Bobadilla at the high viewpoint to keep Satan from emerging. The simmering lava at the bottom has certainly taken many a political prisoner, criminal, and unlucky soul to their sudden demise.

You can drive right up to this rumbling pit, where eruptions still occur with some frequency. MARENA (Ministry of Environment and Natural Resources) advises you to stay only 20 minutes (they hand out masks on particularly gassy days), and park your car facing downhill. There are several trails from the parking lot to the cross still performing its somber duty above Santiago and to dormant craters nearby. The far parking lot, where you might see the famous parakeets that live in the otherwise uninhabitable crater walls, is currently closed to the public.

Every tour operator in the country stops at the crater, usually in conjunction with Masaya Old Market. Night tours offer the opportunity to see a tiny glimmer of red lava at the bottom; most people enjoy the day trip.

The park also offers some 15 km (9 miles) of outstanding hiking. Drop by their excellent visitors center, with a great little natural history museum, to arrange required guides. In addition to seeing wildlife, you can visit fantastic viewpoints, a lava tunnel, and Tzinaconostoc Cave—with bats.

There's no camping at the gates of hell, but ✪ **Hotel Volcán Masaya** (2522-7114; KM 23 Carretera Masaya; credit cards accepted; $$), at the park entrance, is a clean and comfortably rustic lodge surrounded by peaceful gardens. Rooms have air-conditioning, private hot baths, and pleasant porches in the gardens.

Note that it's a 7-km climb from the park entrance (where any Masaya–Managua bus can let you off) to the crater; most people hire taxis from Masaya.

TISMA LAGOON RAMSAR WETLANDS PRESERVE

2552-8721, 8974-9526
www.tisma.gob.ni, www.tisma.info.ni
de Tisma, 2 km noreste
Admission: Free
Open: 24 hours

The soft, fertile lowlands that separate Lake Nicaragua and Lake Managua are home to the ever-shifting humedal, or wetlands, of the Tisma Lagoon System.

Flocks of birds flit above the calm water, including zarcetas, pato chanchos, gallitos de agua, and many more. Beneath the surface are tasty guapote, tilapia, and the toothy gaspar, a "prehistoric fish" traditionally eaten during Semana Santa. Masatepe artisans come here to pick the reeds, tule and junquillo, that they weave into furnishings.

At the time of research, the tiny municipality of Tisma was constructing a breezy pavilion restaurant and 20 rustic, fan-cooled cabins about 2 km (1.2 miles) from the lagoon. (Ramsar, an international wetlands treaty, forbids building on the shoreline.) They'll cost around US$20, including access to flagstone-paved natural pools, one a warm thermal spring. They already arrange birding and fishing trips, guided hikes, and horseback rides.

There are no hotels in Tisma proper, but there are a couple simple comedores and shops. Buses (US$0.40) make the 14-km (9-mile) trip from Masaya to Tisma every 40 minutes, on a good paved road well signed from the Carretera Masaya. Check with the **Tisma Alcaldía** (contact information above) or the **Casa de Cultura Alejandro Martinez** (Tisma Central Park), with a small collection of cultural and archaeological artifacts, for information.

Other Parks and Natural Attractions

Catarina Mirador (open 8 AM–9 PM; US$1/0.10 foreigner/Nicaraguan) Gazing out over
  Laguna de Apoyo's impossibly photogenic crater is a national pastime, and at Catarina
  there's stadium seating. The overlook is now a friendly centro turístico, filled with
  lovers and families, at least a dozen restaurants, and plenty of souvenir stands, mari-
  achis, and photographers. Escape the crowds by walking around the flower-filled town
  of Catarina just outside the mirador, hiking down to the lake (2.5 hours round-trip;

Tisma Lagoon and Río Tipitapa form a fragile, fertile buffer between Lake Nicaragua and Lake Managua.

leave valuables at home), or along a dirt road to tiny Pacaya (3 hours round-trip) with a less trafficked mirador.

Petroglyphos del Cailagua (between Masaya and Nindirí; free) This 200-character petro-glyph field, next to an impressive but polluted waterfall, is hard to find on your own. Any hotel can arrange guides from both Masaya and Nindirí. You can either walk or take a cab most of the way.

Proyecto Parque Nacional Ecológico del Café (2534-2132, 8607-8191; ariciacerda@yahoo .com; Teatro Gozalez, 2.5 cuadras al oeste, Diriamba) At press time, the Carazo government and FUNDENATURA (a nature preservation fund) were developing a national park set into reforested coffee plantations. Contact them or **Casa El Güegüense** (2534-2132; www.diriamba.info) for information.

✪ **Reserva Ecólogica La Maquina** (8901-1989; KM58.5 Carretera Diriamba–La Boquita; open 8 AM–5 PM Tues. through Sun.; US$1) Just off the road from Diriamba to the beaches, this rather grandly named "ecological park" is centered on a cool, crashing 10-meter (30-foot) wide waterfall, with a couple of swimming holes and an old dam. There's a short trail, lined with ceiba trees and boulders, along the river, and a small **restaurant** ($$) serving Nica set plates. You can camp in the parking lot for US$3 per person.

Boat Tours

Most hotels on Laguna de Apoyo have kayaks, while the Monkey Hut and Norome rent sail-boats, and San Simian a catamaran.

Any hotel on the Carazo beaches can arrange sightseeing or fishing trips with local boat captains, but there's nothing geared specifically to foreign tourists. In La Boquita, **Rancho Brava Mar** (8947-7427; $$) arranges boats through the Río Acayo mangrove estuary—as well as fishing, surfing, and horseback tours.

Horseback Riding

Aquiler de Equinos (8978-5305; Mirador Catarina) Enterprising youths at Catarina Mirador offer several horse tours, ranging from 15-minute rides for screaming children (US$1.50) to guided treks down to the lake (US$20).

Volcano Ranch (8806-5123; www.volcanoranchnicaragua.com; Diriá) Luxurious ranch offers professional, guided horseback tours for all ages. They also rent a five-bedroom vacation home overlooking Laguna de Apoyo for around US$300 per night.

Surfing

There is surfing on the Carazo beaches, but very little information available. **Huehuete** evi-dently has a wave, and you can rent surfboards or arrange lessons at Centro Turístico La Boquita at Carazo's only surf camp, **Olas Escondidas** (see Lodging) or "Hidden Waves."

Water Parks

Hertylandia (2532-2156, 2532-3081; KM48 salida a San Marcos, Jinotepe; open 9 AM–5:30 PM Wed. through Sun., closed Mon. through Tue.; US$4.50) Just outside Jinotepe, Nicaragua's premier water park has seen better days, but its run-down collection of slides, pools, and playground equipment should keep kids happy. Inexpensive Nica food and cold beer are served.

SHOPPING

If you're the sort who saves souvenir shopping for the last minute, you'll find gifts for all your jealous loved ones—fast—at the amazing **Masaya Old Market,** with top-quality handicrafts from all over the country, conveniently featured on every tour that rolls through the region.

If you're the type who prefers to savor the shopping experience, and perhaps explore the Meseta's rich artistic heritage, operators like **Va Pues** (2552-8291; www.vapues.com) in Granada and **Servitour Monimbó** (2522-7404; servitour_monimbo@hotmail.com; Plaza Pedro Joaquin Chamorro, 75 varas al este) in Masaya specialize in visiting handicrafts workshops.

Or just wander around on your own. This is easy to do in Masaya's safe streets, lined with family-run craft studios creating hammocks, fine woodwork, marimbas, palm crafts, and more. If you're feeling adventurous, head out into the Pueblos Blancos, each with its own specialty. Don't be shy—artisans will often wave you over to watch them work, then try to sell you something for a fraction of what you'd pay at the Old Market.

Banks and ATMs

Most major towns on the Meseta Central have ATM machines, including Diriamba,

If you're walking from Masaya's Old Market to the laguna, it's worth taking a few minutes to wander around Barrio San Juan's hammock shops.

Jinotepe, Masaya, Masatepe, and San Marcos. The Carazo beaches do not have ATMs or banks, and credit cards are only accepted at the centro turístico. Come prepared.

Groceries

This region also has plenty of grocery stores, including **Palí** in two Masaya locations (on Carretera Granada and at the parque central), Diriamba (on the highway), Masatepe (Central Park), and Jinotepe (one block from the park, at the market). Jinotepe has a locally owned **Supermercado Santiago** as well, two blocks away.

Markets

Masaya Old Market (Avenida El Progreso; open 9 AM–6 PM) Constructed during the heady coffee-boom years of the late 1800s, the dark basalt towers of this faux medieval castle rise above the clogged streets like a Gothic anachronism. Within its well-ordered stalls you'll find the highest quality handicrafts from all over the nation: naïve paintings from Solentiname, Estelí cigars, Jinotega black ceramics, Masaya hammocks, as well as ATMs, and even a DHL desk. Come Thursday evening for *Jueves de Verbena,* with traditional music and dancing.

Masaya New Market (Mercado Municipal Ernesto Fernandez; Masaya Bus Terminal; open 4 AM–5 PM) The sprawling, chaotic New Market, adjacent to the dusty bus lot, has the usual rows of butchers and vegetable stands, but also sells serious *artesanías.* Quality is usually better at the Old Market, but if you just need standard souvenirs—leather wallets, wooden tableware, stuffed cane toads drinking tiny bottles of rum—you'll get better deals here.

Mercado de Artesanías Mazatepelth (Masatepe, across from the town entrance) If you're furnishing your vacation home, start at Masatepe's *muebles* (furniture) market, selling handmade wooden, reed, and wrought-iron furnishings. For a larger selection and better prices, visit the small studios all around Masatepe, Nandasmo, and Niquinohomo.

Ceramics

Though you'll find this ceramic center's distinctive pottery all over the country, it's fun and easy to visit **San Juan de Oriente**, just 1 km south of Catarina—take a mototaxi (US$1) from the mirador. The tiny town is lined with stands and workshops making the colorful pottery, the largest set up for tours.

The most popular style is molded earthenware, formed into wind chimes, flower pots, and speckled chickens—all brightly colored with lead-free mineral oxides and fired in a brick kiln. You'll also find smooth, deeply engraved stoneware, often with jewel-toned glazes depicting plants and animals; and replica pre-Columbian pieces, such as those sold at **Gallery Nica** (8981-0822; www.galerynica.com; de la Alcadía 0.5 cuadras este), run by UNESCO-recognized artist Helio Gutierrez.

Hammocks

The soft, wide hammocks of Masaya are legendary, with rich natural colors and elaborate fringes that have long been symbolic of the nation. You can find great Masaya hammocks at the Old Market, but you'll enjoy a wider selection and better prices anywhere else in town.

The traditional hammock-weaving neighborhood is in **Barrio San Juan**, not far from the Masaya Malecón. Begin at famed **Fabrica de Hamacas** (2522-4549, 8662-0032; elmers

San Juan del Oriente's colorful ceramics are for sale at shops and pottery studios all over town.

0601@turbonett.com.ni; Antiguo Hospital, 1 calle norte) or **Hamacas Vicente Sauzo** (2522-2502; vicente_sauzo692005@yahoo.com; Hogar San Antonio, 1 cuadra norte) to get an idea of what a top-quality, premium-priced hammock is supposed to look like.

Quality hammocks cost around US$20 for the simplest models; US$30–50 for hammocks with wooden poles, including hammock chairs; and up to US$100 for special orders. They'll wrap them for easier transport home.

Guitars

Masaya is known for its handmade guitars, with flamenco, classical, and mandolin styles available in a variety of tropical woods. Start at **Zepeda Guitars** (guitarraszepeda.com; de Union Fenosa Carretera Masaya, 200 meters oeste), producing some of Central America's finest instruments. Prices, which include a lifetime service warranty, begin at around US$100 for a basic classical guitar, and rise into the stratosphere.

EVENTS

Masaya, which relishes its role as the "Cradle of Nicaraguan Culture," puts on spectacular festivals from September through January, worth taking the time to see. The entire Meseta is known for its fantastic civic fiestas, with Catholic saints, indigenous dances, and horse parades (*hípicas*).

January

San Silvestre de Papa (Catarina, January 1) Catarina rings in the New Year with flowers and parades.

✪ **Fiestas Patronales de San Sebastián** (Diriamba, January 17–27) One of the country's most colorful festivals celebrates San Sebastián with music, dancing, hípicas, and performances of *El Güegüense.*

February

La Virgen de la Candelaria (Diriomo, February 2–8) The "Witch Capital of Nicaragua" sends its Virgin on her annual pilgrimage to Los Jirones.

March

Semana Santa (March or April; week before Easter) Masaya and other towns have notable traditional processions and events throughout the week. The beaches are packed.

Fiesta de la Virgen de la Asunción (Masaya, March 16) Annual procession reenacts the Virgin saving Masaya from a 1772 lava flow.

✪ **Fiesta San Lázaro** (Masaya, Sunday before Palm Sunday) Locals dress their dogs in costume and head to Iglesia María Magdalena, to celebrate the Feast Day of Saint Lazarus.

April

Hípica Casares (Casares, late April) The beach town goes cowboy.

May

Homenaje a La Santa Cruz (La Boquita, May 1) Religious festivities by the beach.

Hípica Tisma (Tisma, early May) Horse parades in Tisma, too.

Domingo de Trinidad (Masatepe, late May) The biggest *hípica* in Nicaragua peaks the last weekend in May with some serious parties.

June

Fiesta Cerámica (San Juan de Oriente, June) The ceramics capital of Nicaragua celebrates.

✪ **Fiestas Diriá** (Diriá, late June) Former Chorotega capita honors San Pedro and San Pablo with a *hípica,* fireworks, and folkloric dances involving dried bull penises.

Fiesta San Juan Bautista (Catarina, June 24) Catarina's biggest party marks the feast day of Saint John the Baptist, and solstice.

July

Hípica Jinotepe (Jinotepe, late July) Carazo's capital goes country.

Fiestas Niquinohomo (July 26) The "Valley of Warriors" honors its patron, Santa Ana.

Baile de Chinegros (Nindirí, July 27) Children's dance is the star of this festival.

August

Fiestas María Magdalena (Monimbó, August 15) Masaya's oldest neighborhood celebrates its patron.

Carnival (Masaya, August 27) Hey, any excuse for music, dancing, and parades.

September

✪ **Fiestas Patronales de San Jerónimo** (Masaya, September 20) Masaya begins three weeks of serious festivities dedicated to Saint Jerome; not to be missed.

October

Hípica Diriamba (Diriamba, mid-October) Diriamba's finest horses on show.

Procesión de Torovenado (Masaya, last Sunday) Costumed parade pokes fun at political figures.

✪ **Procesión de Los Ahüizotes** (last Friday) Not to be confused with Halloween, this traditional parade has kids costumed as Nicaraguan myths and legends.

November

Festival Folklórico (First Sunday) Masaya closes its epic civic fiestas with this folkloric festival.

Baile de los Diablitos (Masaya, last Sunday in November) Actually, Masaya continues to party well into the New Year; the excuse for this festival is a "Little Devils" dance.

December

Fiestas Virgen de Guadalupe (Jinotepe, December 12) Colorful celebration showcases the Dance of the Chinegros, with colorful costumes and indigenous flair.

Feria Navideña de Artesanos de Carazo (Diriamba, weekend before Christmas) Arts and crafts fair in Diriamba.

5

GRANADA

"Granada is Nicaragua, the rest is only countryside."

—*Granadino saying*

Rising in sun-drenched tropical color from the shores of Lake Nicaragua, "La Gran Sultana" is a city of aristocratic bearing, tempered but never humbled by her tumultuous five hundred years. Among the oldest European settlements in the Americas, Granada was founded in 1524 on the shores of what the Nahuals called Cocibolca, the "Sweet Sea."

For centuries, Granada has watched over this waterway, which the Spanish christened Lake Nicaragua—once the most important route between the Caribbean and Pacific. She has both profited and suffered for her station, and seen more than her fair share of war, grandeur, romance, and flames. Like the phoenix, however, she always rises again to more marvelous heights, mixing ashes into adobe brick that will build a more glorious future.

Granada's dazzling historic center is considered one of Central America's architectural masterpieces, comparable only to longtime northern rival León, and Antigua, Guatemala. It is the grace of steel, designed for defense, though the strength of her high, stuccoed walls and strategically placed stone churches is disguised with a soaring neoclassical confection of photogenic façades and shady plazas.

These still echo today with the clip-clop of horse-drawn carriages plying narrow, high-walled streets that are a kaleidoscope of Colonial façades, vigas, frescos, and ironwork detail. On the most elaborate buildings, you will find glazed ceramic plaques commemorating the residence of some historic figure—poet Rubén Darío, perhaps, or past president Violeta Chamorro.

At Granada's heart is the central park, presided over by luxuriant baroque arcades, the

Online Resources

Granada Nicaragua (www.granadanicaragua.net) Easy-to-use, informative, English-language site has information about hotels, buses, and more.

Discover Granada (discovergranada.net) Primarily covers budget hostels.

Find It Granada (www.finditgranada.com) Small site has information geared to expats and tourists.

Granada.com.ni (www.granada.com.ni) Information needs an update.

The Granada Blog (granadanicaragua.typepad.com) This is part of a nascent network of tourism blogs.

A fine way to enjoy Granada is in the back of a horse-drawn carriage.

cathedral's stately domes, and an ivory-and-maroon cascade of neoclassical columns—all backdrops to theater, music, and thousands of lives. Above it all soars the ragged crater of Volcán Mombacho, veiled in sparkling mists against an otherwise cloudless sapphire sky.

Hire a horse-drawn carriage to show you this city, its elegant churches and regal homes, before finally descending the ancient Calle La Calzada that connects the city to her lake. It is worth taking some time to contemplate this vast, volcano-studded sea—perhaps renting a boat to travel through the Archipelago of Asese, 365 tiny islands that unfurl from Granada's southern shore into the serene waters.

Return to the city center before 5:30 or so to climb the claustrophobic spiral staircase of Iglesia La Merced's bell tower, piercing the deepening blue. This is Granada's finest spot for a sunset.

End your evening beneath the stars, back on La Calzada, the heart of the city's dining and nightlife district. You may hear a dozen different languages over your drinks, as this city has become quite the international attraction in recent years. But this is nothing new, not for Granada; remember that she has been a sophisticated, cosmopolitan city for half a millennium—and she is making yet another comeback, to take her rightful place among the world's great beauties.

CRIME AND OTHER CONCERNS

Granada is an established tourist destination. While violent crime is rare, the usual rascally collection of pickpockets, touts, beggars, and drug dealers is out in force. The historic cen-

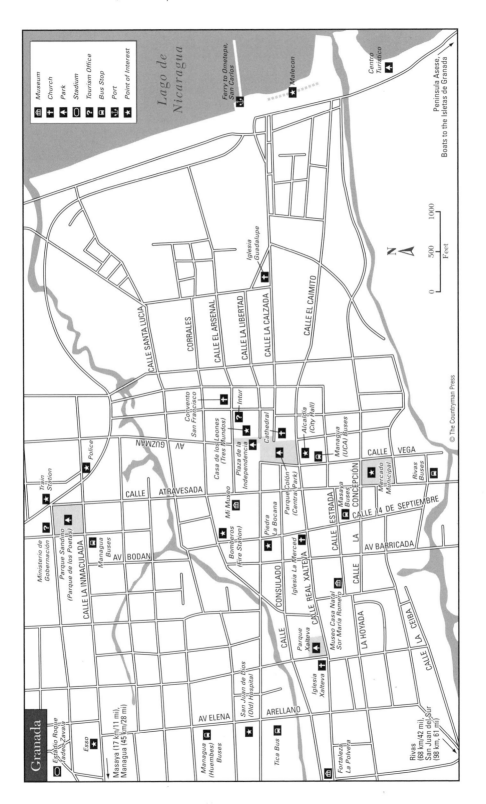

Granada

Museum
Church
Park
Stadium
Tourism Office
Bus Stop
Port
Point of Interest

Lago de Nicaragua

Ferry to Ometepe, San Carlos
Malecon
Centro Turistico
Peninsula Asese, Boats to the Isletas de Granada

Iglesia Guadalupe

CALLE SANTA LUCIA
CORRALES
CALLE EL ARSENAL
CALLE LA LIBERTAD
CALLE LA CALZADA
CALLE EL CAIMITO

N
0 500 1000 Feet

© The Countryman Press

Convento San Francisco
Intur
Casa de los Leones (Tres Mundos)
Plaza de la Independencia
Cathedral
Alcaldía (City Hall)
Managua (UCA) Buses
CALLE VEGA

AV GUZMAN
Police
Train Station
CALLE ATRAVESADA
Mi Museo
Parque Colón (Central Park)
Piedra La Bocana
Masaya Buses
LA CONCEPCIÓN
Mercado Municipal
Rivas Buses

Ministerio de Gobernación
Parque Sandino (Parque de los Poetas)
Managua Buses
AV BODAN
Bomberos (Fire Station)
CALLE CONSULADO
Iglesia La Merced
CALLE ESTRADA
CALLE LA
CALLE 14 DE SEPTIEMBRE
AV BARRICADA

CALLE LA INMACULADA
CALLE REAL XALTEVA
Museo Casa Natal Sor María Romero
LA HOYADA
CALLE LA CEIBA

Estadio Roque Tadeo Zavala
Esso
Masaya (17 km/11 mi), Managua (45 km/28 mi)
Parque Xalteva
Iglesia Xalteva
San Juan de Dios (Old Hospital)
CALLE

Managua (Huembes) Buses
AV ELENA
Tica Bus
ARELLANO
Fortaleza La Polvera
Rivas (68 km/42 mi), San Juan del Sur (98 km, 61 mi)

ter is quite safe for walking, though normal precautions apply. Taxis are also generally safe, and charge a flat US$0.50 for shared transport anywhere in town.

The much poorer surrounding neighborhoods are also safe, but don't tempt people with cameras and other valuables. Take a taxi between the center and lakefront bars at night, and avoid walking Diamante Road on the Asese Peninsula.

If you are robbed, the **Police Station** (2552-2977, 2552-2929; Calle La Immaculada, between Calle Atravesada and Avenida Guzmán, across from Parque Sandino) can file a report for your travel insurance, but probably won't try to recover your stuff. They do take violent crime and drug offenses seriously, however. Few officers speak English, so try to find a Spanish speaker to help make any report.

Local aid groups ask you to *not* give money to the legions of children begging on La Calzada. Families send their kids from as far away as Managua to work the strip, while Granadinos rent their children out. In Granada, **La Esperanza** (www.la-esperanza -granada.org) and **Carita Feliz** (www.caritafeliz.org) provide nutritious meals and educational opportunities to local kids, and accept donations. **Proyecto Mosaico** (www.pro mosaico.org) can arrange volunteer opportunities for a fee, while any Spanish school can usually find local, free volunteer positions.

TOURIST INFORMATION

Granada's official Ministry of Tourism office, **Intur** (2552-6858; Esquina opuesta Iglesia San Francisco, Calle El Arsenal; open 8 AM–1 PM Mon. through Fri.), is actually semiuseful, with flyers, maps, and other information. There are more than a dozen private tour operators and information offices in the historic center offering the same brochures, and attentive staff that may speak some English.

GETTING AROUND

Granada is an excellent walking town, and good free maps are available at hotels and tour offices. Though the city sprawls, most destinations are in the historic center, within a few blocks of the central park, also called Parque Colón. Horse-drawn carriages line up on the western side of the park, and offer inexpensive tours around town.

Streets have clearly marked names that are on all the maps, and house numbers are slowly being implemented. Addresses, however, are still usually given as directionals (see the Planning Your Trip chapter for an explanation of addresses). Just remember that the lake is east (in Granada, *al lago*) and you'll be fine.

The city is laid out on a logical Spanish grid around the central park, where you'll find the *alcadía* (mayor's office), cathedral, and other important buildings. To the east, Lake Nicaragua is connected to the historic center via Calle La Calzada, a pleasant 1-km stroll ending at the Muelle de Granada, with ferries for Isla Ometepe. Head south along the sandy lakefront to visit the centro turístico and Asese Peninsula, where you'll find boats for the Isletas de Granada.

The primary street heading west from the central park is Calle Xalteva, traversing the city's oldest neighborhoods for six blocks before reaching Iglesia Xalteva. La Fortaleza is two blocks farther west.

The main north-south road is Calle Atravesada, called Calle El Comercial as it passes the

Mercado Municipal, three blocks south of the central park. Heading north, Calle Atravesada ends at Parque Sandino (Parque de los Poetas), with its shuttered 1888 train station.

Calle La Inmaculada, on the northern edge of town, becomes the highway to Managua. It crosses Avenida Elena Arellana, which becomes the southbound highway to Rivas, San Juan del Sur, and Costa Rica. Both are well signed from Calle Xalteva, but may be easier to reach from Calle Atravesada at Parque de los Poetas (Parque Sandino). Conveniently, most rental car offices are at the corner of Arellana and Inmaculada, while all international bus offices are scattered along Avenida Arellana.

Aeropuerto Granada (GRA) is not currently receiving commercial flights.

Car

Granada can be a tricky place to drive, with narrow, one-way streets and poor signage—not to mention those horse-drawn carriages. Even if you've rented a car, it's usually worth grabbing a cab at night. Most rental car offices are thankfully located at the corner of Calle La Inmaculada and Avenida Arellana, the two main routes out of town.

Alamo (2277-1117; www.alamonicaragua.com; alamonicaragua@anccar.com; Hotel Colonial, parque central) International operator lets you cross the Costa Rican border for a fee.

Armadillo (8833-8663; www.armadillo-nicaragua.com; Shell Guapinol 4 cuadras norte, 1.5 oeste) Local operator gets high marks from expats.

Budget (2552-1789; www.budget.com.ni; granada@budget.com.ni; Shell Guapinol, Calle La Inmaculada and Avenida Arellano)

Dollar (2552-8515; www.dollar.com.ni; Plaza Colón Hotel, parque central)

International Buses

Three international carriers, all located on Avenida Elena Arellana, offer direct service from Granada. While this is convenient to Costa Rica and Panama, travelers headed north will find better connections from Managua. You must buy tickets in person, with your passport.

Central Line (2552-5299; Shell Guapinol, 1.5 cuadras sur) One bus to San José, Costa Rica (US$23; 5:15 AM)

Tica Bus (2552-8535; www.ticabus.com; Arellano Avenue, 0.5 cuadras del Antiguo Hospital) Two buses to San José, Costa Rica (US$20; 7 AM and 1 PM)

Transnica (2552-4301; Shell Guapinol, 1.5 cuadras sur) Three regular buses to San José, Costa Rica (US$23; 6 AM, 8 AM, and 11 AM); one nicer *ejecutivo* to San José (US$34.50; 2 PM) and one *ejecutivo* to Tegucigalpa, Honduras (US$28.75; 2 PM).

Buses

Most intercity buses leave from the Rivas lot, one block south of the market, but Managua and Masaya buses leave from elsewhere.

There are city buses, but most aren't really useful for the casual tourist. The Mercado-Hospital and Lago-Hospital lines connect centro turístico, Mercado Municipal, and Avenida Arellana. Special *colectivo* taxis to Puerto Cocibolca (on the far side of the peninsula, near Puerto Asese) run when full from Shell Palmira (by the market) for US$0.50 per person, compared to US$1.50 in a regular shared cab.

Diriá US$0.45; every 20 minutes
Managua UCA US$0.60; every 30 minutes. Minibuses leave from just south of the central

Make the claustrophobic climb to the bell towers of Iglesia La Merced for fantastic views over the Colonial city's tejas-tile roofs.

park (listen for touts yelling "managuamanaguamanagua") and Avenida Bodan, across from Parque Sandino.

Managua Huembes US$0.55; every 30 minutes. Buses leave from Calle La Inmaculada.

Masaya US$0.40; every 20 minutes. Buses leave from Calle 14 de Septiembre, one block west of the Mercado.

Nandaime US$0.45; every 20 minutes. It's sometimes faster to catch a Rivas-bound bus in Nandaime.

Rivas US$1.25; every hour

Private Shuttle

Private shuttles are safe and convenient, and can carry your luggage without a fuss. Make reservations at least one day in advance.

Nica Express (2552-8461, 8988-8127; www.nica-adventures.com; Calle La Calzada, 2.5 cuadras al lago) Shuttles to Managua at 4 AM, and to San Jorge, San Juan del Sur, and the Costa Rican border at 8 AM (US$15).

Nicarao Lake Tours (2552-3307 (Granada), 2568-2244 (San Juan del Sur); www.nicarao lake.com) Shuttles to San Jorge and San Juan del Sur for US$15 (US$20 round-trip).

✪ **Paxeos** (2552-8291; www.paxeos.com; parque central) Runs several daily shuttles to Managua, serving all MGA flights before 2 PM Monday through Saturday; arrange service for later and Sunday flights 48 hours in advance. They also offer daily shuttles to León (US$20; 9 AM) and Rivas, San Jorge, and San Juan del Sur (US$18; 8:30 AM).

Taxi

Shared cabs are plentiful throughout Granada, and generally very safe. At press time, the fare anywhere in town was US$0.50. Longer trips cost more, such as US$1.50 to Puerto Cocibolca (Puerto Asese), US$15 to Masaya, and US$30 to Managua.

Horse-drawn Taxi

Horse-drawn carriages line up on the west side of the central park, their colorful cabs and beribboned horses offering leisurely US$5 to US$20 tours or simple transportation around the city. Choosing cabs with the healthiest-looking horses, rather than lowest fares, provides a real incentive for drivers to treat their charges well.

Bicycle

Granada is an excellent place to see on a bike. The classic ride is out to Puerto Asese, on a good paved road. The 5-km (3-mile) unpaved trek to Laguna de Apoyo is fun on mountain bikes.

Several spots rent bikes, including ✪ **DeTour Viajes y Cultura** (2552-0155; www.detour-nicaragua.com; Calle El Caimito), which also organizes bicycle tours; **Hostal San Ángel** (2552-6373; mariacampos118@hotmail.com; parque central, 50 metros south); **Nahual Tours** (8988-2461; Calle La Calzada, del parque central 150 metros del lago); **Tierra Tour** (8862-9580; www.tierratour.com; Calle La Calzada); **Bikes For Rent** (8894-1545; Calle 14 Septiembre, casa verde, frente Palí); and **Nicaragua Dulce** (2552-6351; www.nicaraguadulce.com) at Marina Cocibolca.

Boat

Granada has three major ports on Lake Nicaragua. **Muelle de Granada**, at the end of Calle La Calzada, is a long pier (off limits except to ticketed passengers) where you catch the Sunday Cruceros Familiares Lago Cocibolca boat tours, and passenger ferries to **Isla Ometepe** (US$3; 4 hours) every Monday and Thursday at 2 PM, with continuing service to San Carlos; returning on Wednesday and Saturday from Altagracia at 12:30 AM (no typo). It is usually more convenient to take ferries from San Jorge, near Rivas. See the Isla Ometepe and Lake Nicaragua chapter for more information.

The other two ports are **Cabaña Amarilla**, on the south end of the centro turístico where Peninsula Asese begins, and **Marina Cocibolca** (2228-1223; www.marinacocibolca.net; open 8 AM–10 PM), on the far southern side of the peninsula, a US$1.50 cab ride from town. Both are primarily used for pleasure tours exploring the Isletas; see the Boat Tours section, later, for more information. Collectivo boats (US$8) leave for Isla Zapatera thrice weekly from Marina Cocibolca.

LODGING

Granada is famous for its historic Spanish Colonial mansions with thick adobe walls, ornate tile and woodwork, and beautiful interior gardens—today remodeled into hotels for every budget. Whether you're spending US$15 or US$150, remember that rooms in authentic Colonials tend to be dark, and vary widely in size and shape. If you don't like the first one you see, ask to see more.

Luxury lovers have a small but growing selection of hotels, from isleta getaways to truly historic buildings in the city center. Midrange travelers can find modern rooms with air-conditioning, cable TV, private baths, and good furnishings starting at around US$40, but a bit more money will get you gardens, breakfast, and that rarest of steamy Granada's amenities—hot showers.

There are dozens of budget spots, and you can easily score a dorm bed for US$5 or private room for US$10. Spanish schools can arrange homestays for nonstudents, around US$85 per week, including all meals.

Lodging Price Code

The cost of lodging is based on an average per-room, double occupancy rate during peak season (December through April). Nicaragua's 15 percent sales tax and gratuities are not included; note that paying cash sometimes results in taxes being waived. Prices are much higher during the Christmas holidays and, to a lesser extent, Semana Santa (Easter Week), when you should have reservations.

Inexpensive ($)	Up to US$25
Moderate ($$)	US$25 to US$60
Expensive ($$$)	US$60 to US$100
Very Expensive ($$$$)	US$100 and up

Hotels

HOTEL ALHAMBRA

General Manager: Juan Pasos Lacayo
2552-4486, 2552-2035
www.hotelalhambra.com.ni
hotalam@tmx.com.ni
parque central
Price: Moderate to Expensive
Credit Cards: Yes
Handicap Access: No
Wifi: In the lobby

The sentimental favorite, the Alhambra is the oldest continuously operating hotel in Granada, famed for its five-star location on the central park. The dramatic lobby—with antiques, art, and gleaming tiles—makes a promise not quite met by the rooms, which are small and fairly basic. All are recently remodeled, however, with air-conditioning, hot water, huge wide-screen TVs, telephones, and good beds. Definitely spring for a balcony room, with wonderful views over the plaza and cathedral. There's a small pool and very pretty 80-person events salon.

✪ HOTEL LA BOCONA
Director: Nadene Holmes
2552-2888
www.hotellabocona.com
hotellabocona@yahoo.com
Calle La Libertad
Price: Moderate to Expensive
Credit Cards: Yes
Handicap Access: Challenging
Wifi: Yes

Granada is historically a city enamored of its noblesse, and this hotel provides the perfect aristocratic experience. The immaculately restored mansion is a symphony of gleaming Spanish tiles, 8-meter-tall cane ceilings, and three fabulous courtyards that offer yoga spaces, spa rooms, a fine pool, handcrafted Masatepe furnishings, modern art, and other enticements that will keep you lounging happily through the heat of the day. On-site **CocoBerry Spa** (see Spas and Gyms, later) is one of Nicaragua's nicest.

Rooms are among the city's loveliest, spacious and airy, with enormous windows and mahogany canopy beds. Rates are lower than you'd expect because of the hotel's commitment to authenticity: Each room's large, modern private hot bath is located a few meters from the bedroom. A fluffy robe and slippers are provided to guests.

Despite the luxurious surroundings, half of all revenue goes to benefit **Carita Feliz** (www.caritafeliz.org), a great organization that helps local children. Guests can arrange to visit participating families, visit a private island, or even help piece together the past with the pre-Columbian pottery experts at affiliated **Mi Museo** (see museums).

BOHEMIAN PARADISE
Owner: Lucy Bartlett
2552-5892, 8877-1414
www.seecentralamerica.com
granada@seecentralamerica.com
Calle Corral, del Convento San Francisco, 2 cuadras al lago
Price: Moderate
Credit Cards: Yes
Handicap Access: Challenging
Wifi: Yes

Tucked away in a quiet corner of the historic city center, this option angles for a more authentic experience. The setting is typically Spanish, with colorful tiles and pretty gardens where you'll enjoy breakfast, which always includes very traditional treats such as *rosquillas*, or corn rings.

Five rooms all have air-conditioning, private hot baths, and cable TV—as well as locally made items such as the colorful Masaya bedspreads, for sale in their community-conscious souvenir stand. The second-floor suite has fine views.

HOTEL COLONIAL
General Manager: Etienne Vanoye
2552-7581, 2552-7299
www.hotelcolonialgranada.com
reservations@hotelcolonialgranada.com
parque central, 25 varas norte
Price: Moderate to Expensive
Credit Cards: Yes
Handicap Access: No
Wifi: Yes

This stylish entry, right off the central park, has been recently eclipsed by newer, more luxurious hotels. Still, the sprawling property offers 37 appealing rooms, which comfortably surround banana-shaded gardens and pools.

The least expensive are small, but well-amenitied, with hot-water baths, air-conditioning, artesanías, original paintings, and excellent furnishings. Larger rooms have more light, better bathrooms, and perhaps a private terrace or courtyard balcony; while suites have king-sized beds, carved stone lamps, Spanish tiles, and more—one has a Jacuzzi. Apartments have full kitchens. Breakfast is included, and the on-site tour office arranges excellent treks; they operate a private island in the Isletas, and have a fine boutique hotel on the Río San Juan.

HOTEL CON CORAZÓN
Owner: Freek Sanders
2552-8852
www.hotelconcorazon.com
correo@hotelconcorazon.com
Calle Santa Lucia 141
Price: Moderate
Credit Cards: Yes
Handicap Access: Challenging
Wifi: Yes

The "Hotel with Heart" was founded to fund local social programs, but would be a great choice for travelers anyway. Sixteen modern rooms have European styling, with slate floors, chrome fixtures, and sculptural furnishings—warmed up with handicrafts and photos of families involved in their various aid projects.

A sunny pool in the rear courtyard is surrounded by thatched rancheros with hammocks, while the original courtyard houses a **bar and restaurant** (B, L, D; open Tues. through Sat.; $$) serving quality Nicaraguan cuisine; even nonguests will enjoy their three-course, US$12 prix fixe dinners made with fresh, local ingredients—sometimes served with a side of live music. The hotel also offers unusual, community-conscious tours and an excellent selection of souvenirs.

HOTEL DARÍO
Owner: Paolo Manzoni
2552-3400
www.hoteldario.com
info@hoteldario.com
Calle La Calzada, 1.5 cuadras al lago
Price: Expensive
Credit Cards: Yes
Handicap Access: Yes
Wifi: Yes

The best address on Calle La Calzada, this elegantly refurbished neoclassical edifice dates from the early 1800s, and its fanciful and photogenic façade remains the backdrop to many upper-crust Granadino weddings. Architecture buffs will appreciate the Mudéjar-style woodwork and iron accents adorning the interior gardens; luxury lovers will enjoy the excellent (if small) rooms, with all the amenities you'd expect at this price—right down to the ironing boards, hair dryers, small gym, and sparkling pool.

El Tranvía (L, D; $$$–$$$$), the Darío's immodest fine-dining restaurant, occupies a splendid Colonial space with wide windows looking onto La Calzada. Spanish-accented dishes such as lobster in coconut sauce, filet mignon in red wine and mushrooms, paella, and other extravagant treats are always on the menu—but make reservations for Friday night marimba, when they serve upmarket takes on classic Nica recipes.

✪ LA POSADA DEL SOL
Managers: Lucia and Don Maximiliano
8451-8474, 2552-0442
www.laposadadelsol.com.ni
info@laposadadelsol.com.ni
Calle Caimito, 3.5 cuadras al lago
Price: Moderate
Credit Cards: Yes
Handicap Access: Challenging
Wifi: Yes

Though it's not quite as polished as some of the others on Calle Caimito's strip of great

One of the great joys of Colonial-style architecture is the interior garden, sometimes magnificently maintained—like this at Hotel Darío.

midrange hotels, Posada del Sol is a better deal, with larger rooms, air-conditioning, and real hot water. It's set up for long-term visitors, and rates drop for longer stays; some rooms have full kitchens.

The courtyard has some Granada style, with wide porches, cane awnings, lots of plants, and hammock chairs overlooking a huge, deep, clean lap pool. The two-story building is modern, and a bit rough around the edges. The huge rooms—set up so you can get a little privacy—are oddly shaped, with partial walls and big bathrooms, which is nice.

GRAN FRANCIA

Owner: Giesele Camille
2552-6002, 2552-6007
www.lagranfrancia.com

marketing@lagranfrancia.com
parque central
Price: Expensive
Credit Cards: Yes
Handicap Access: Yes
Wifi: Yes

The historian's choice is this technically restored, landmark mansion right on the central park, with interior walls dating from 1526 and rooms packed with museum-quality antiques. It was once the home of the foul French Duke Hugo Theobald, who fled to Granada after murdering his wife. It later served as an inn, where William Walker and his bloodthirsty crew long over-stayed their welcome.

Today, the Gran Francia has been painstakingly remodeled into one of Granada's most glamorous addresses, and its mahogany accents, marble interior pool, and fabulously outfitted accommodations certainly have their charms. The less expensive rooms are small and dark; it's worth the money for something larger.

Even if you stay elsewhere, check out their recommended second-story bar, **El Balcón**, with its regal views and colorful past, or the elegant **El Arcángel Restaurant**, serving very good Latin fusion cuisine.

HOTEL GRANADA
Owner: Carlos Campos
2552-2178, 2552-2974
www.hotelgranadanicaragua.com
info@hotelgranadanicaragua.com
Calle La Calzada, frente Iglesia Guadalupe
Price: Moderate to Expensive
Credit Cards: Yes
Handicap Access: Yes
Wifi: Yes

With its splendid pool surrounded by a resort-style patio area, art galleries, fresh flowers, and fabulous fountains, the venerable Granada wins the "Most Improved Hotel" award, hands down. New rooms are flawless, with gleaming wood floors and ornate furnishings that create a polished tropical ambiance. All the usual amenities are accounted for, and junior suites add minibars and Jacuzzi tubs. The dingy old two-star rooms with their 1970s furnishings (but thankfully, new mattresses) have not yet been remodeled, and were available for about half the price at press time.

✪ **Restaurant Tratoría Garibaldi** (2552-2947; $$–$$$) serves Italian cuisine, including pizza and ravioli, as well as *guapote* (rainbow bass) and other Nica specialties. It's a refined spot for coffee on your way to or from the lake.

LA ISLITA BOUTIQUE HOTEL
Owner: Tim Payne
2552-7473, 8474-2257
www.laislita.com
info@laislita.com
Del alcaldía 2 cuadras al lago, 1.5 cuadras sur
Price: Moderate to Expensive
Credit Cards: Yes
Handicap Access: No
Wifi: Yes

This flawlessly executed boutique hotel has style to spare. It's Colonial, of course, but the hand-painted ceramic tiles are just a little bit more ornate than usual, elegantly accented with soothing greenery, relaxing fountains, and fine antiques.

There are eight rooms, all with air-conditioning, flat-screen TVs, excellent hot-water bathrooms, and great beds; two have private patios with views over the city. But artsy details like Far Eastern fabrics and artesanías, along with classic cane ceilings, set this great spot apart. The third-floor balcony beneath an enormous mango tree has wonderful cathedral and volcano views.

✪ JÍCARO ISLAND ECOLODGE
Owner: Karen Emanuel
2552-6353
www.jicarolodge.com
ecolodgeinfo@jicarolodge.com
Isletas de Granada, Lake Nicaragua
Price: Very Expensive
Credit Cards: Yes
Handicap Access: No
Wifi: Yes

On a private, lavishly landscaped volcanic island at the tip of the Asese Peninsula, this fantastic new ecolodge is poised become one of Nicaragua's premier resorts.

The setting is outrageous, with views from the polished cedar yoga deck and deeply inset swimming pool to regal Mombacho Volcano. The architecture, by Managua's own Simplemente Madera, is not only sustainable, but furnishes a tranquility that permeates the sophisticated gourmet restaurant, Zen-and-basalt spa, and exquisite villas. Each two-story bungalow, designed to echo the tropical terrain, is luxurious without air-conditioning or television; views over the tranquil water from your first-class room in the forest canopy should be enough.

Note that the rocky topography, opaque lake, deep swimming pool, and mirador tower make this a no-go for most children under 12 and a challenge for anyone with mobility issues. Though there are daily tours all over the region, the island's isolation isn't for everyone, either.

HOSTAL FAMILIAR EL MALTESE
Owner: María Luísa
2552-7641, 8893-4243
Plaza España, 50 metros sur, frente al lago
www.nicatour.net/en/elmaltese
elmaltese@nicatour.net
Price: Moderate
Credit Cards: Yes
Handicap Access: Yes
Wifi: Not yet

The real draw is Lake Nicaragua, so close that you can hear the waves crash. Here at the end of La Calzada, you're well away from the bustling city center—but the solitude may be exactly what you're looking for.

Rooms are large and clean, with high wooden ceilings and colorful artesanías on the walls; one sleeps five. All have good beds, private baths, and shared porches with lake views. The breezy **restaurant** (B, L, D; $–$$) serves guapote and traditional Nica dishes atop blue-and-white checkered tablecloths.

HOTEL PATIO DEL MALINCHE
2552-2235, 2552-4221
www.patiodelmalinche.com
info@patiodelmalinche.com
Calle El Caimito, del alcaldía 2.5 cuadras al lago
Price: Moderate to Expensive

Credit Cards: Yes
Handicap Access: Challenging
Wifi: Yes
Special: Rated sustainable by the Rainforest Alliance

This polished spot is flawless, not so much authentic as a modern homage to authenticity. Rather than arcaded construction, for instance, wooden doors and windows are arched, a stylish echo of classic Granada style.

Two floors of modern, air-conditioned rooms surround the clean pool and manicured patio gardens, and include cable TV, wifi, excellent new mattresses, tasteful lighting, and modern hot baths. There are plenty of places to relax around the grounds, and staff is attentive and knowledgeable.

✪ HOTEL PLAZA COLÓN
General Manager: María Isabel Cantón
2552-8489
www.hotelplazacolon.com
info@hotelplazacolon.com
parque central, costado oeste
Price: Expensive to Very Expensive
Credit Cards: Yes
Handicap Access: Challenging
Wifi: Yes

The finest hotel in Granada proper overlooks the central park's delightful hustle and bustle from its rambling porches, which is precisely why you should spring for a balcony room. Even without the wonderful view and horse-drawn carriages clip-clopping by, however, this would still be the city's most comfortable lodging.

The design is Colonial but the building is entirely remodeled, with a romantic lobby, gorgeous vigas and columns, and courtyard gardens transformed into one of the city's nicest pools. Rooms are huge and have lots of light gleaming on the hardwood floors and furnishings. All the amenities you'd expect at this price are in order, including

○ UCA TIERRA Y AGUA

Manager: Union of Agricultural Cooperatives
2552-0238
www.ucatierrayagua.org
turismo@ucatierrayagua.org
Granada office: de Shell Palmira 75 metros
oeste
Price: Inexpensive
Credit Cards: Yes
Handicap Access: No
Wifi: No
Special: Stays at rural hostels should be organized at the Granada office, open 8:30 AM–2 PM Mon., Wed., and Fri.

While Granada's warm beauty will satisfy most travelers, some of you may be curious about how the rest of this largely agricultural nation lives. You've seen the simple farmhouses and oxcarts, but with limited Spanish or experience in the developing world, perhaps you don't feel comfortable introducing yourself.

Welcome to UCA Tierra y Agua, representing nine agricultural cooperatives with more than 150 families who raise crops, produce *artesanías*, and welcome travelers like you to their chain of humble guesthouses, hiking trails, hot springs, and hammocks.

The cooperatives are located south of Granada, strung between Nandaime and Isla Zapatera; you can arrange to hike, ride horses, or take community boats between them. Facilities vary, but many, including **La Granadilla** (8876-7510), **Nicaragua Libre** (8880-5848), and **Sonzapote** (8899-2927) have simple wooden guest rooms with mosquito nets and cool baths, which can be rented as dorms or private accommodation for US$21.50 per person per night, including three meals and unlimited coffee. Others, such as **Cooperativa Claudia Chamorro,** still lack real housing but offer hammocks, food service, guided hikes, fishing expeditions, and other adventures.

In general, you should make reservations in advance with UCA in Granada, where they can discuss your comfort level and either arrange private transportation, or get schedules for public boats and buses. Guided hikes (US$8), horseback rides (US$10 per hour), farm tours, and other activities are available. Also ask about the sulfur hot springs, Lagunas de Macatepe, and Río Manares.

huge TVs, modern hot baths, hair dryers, and more.

CASA SAN FRANCISCO

Owners: Nancy Bergman and Terry Leary
2552-8235
www.csf-hotel-granada.com
csfgranada@yahoo.com
Convento San Francisco, Calle Corral #207
Price: Moderate to Expensive
Credit Cards: Yes
Handicap Access: Challenging
Wifi: Yes

This nine-room boutique beauty is well loved for its cheerful eclecticism and cute interior pool. All the accommodations are different, but quite comfortable with their creative beds, original art, oriental carpets, and fresh flowers—as well as modern amenities like cable TV, real hot water, and air-conditioning. The suite is great, with a fine four-poster bed and dramatic volcano views from the patio.

Their **Bar & Restaurant Los Chocoyos** (2552-8513; B, L, D; $$) gets high marks for its happy hour and Mexican fusion cuisine. Guests also enjoy special rates at Pure gym and spa.

HOTEL SPA GRANADA

2552-4678
www.hotelspagranada.com
Calle Atravesada, frente BanCentro

Price: Moderate to Expensive
Credit Cards: Yes
Handicap Access: No
Wifi: Yes
Special: Day passes US$5

This lavish, sprawling mansion dating from the late 1800s boasts acres of gleaming tile beneath elaborate wooden awnings, wrapped around multiple courtyard gardens. It's not quite a luxury property, but amenities include one of the best pools in town. Fresh juices and healthy cuisine are available in the poolside gardens, as are a variety of spa treatments including massages, facials, and pedicures.

Rooms and prices vary, but all have air-conditioning, cable TV, wifi, private hot baths, and creative, sculptural furnishings unlike anything else in the city. The least expensive are small, whitewashed, and close to the open-air shared kitchen; while second-story suites occupy airy, wooden rooms with spacious porches, fabulous bathrooms, and more. Long-term stays can be arranged.

✪ HOTEL TERRASOL

Owner: Victor and Katya Chamorro
2552-8825
www.hotelterrasol.com
info@hotelterrasol.com
Avenida Barricada
Price: Moderate
Credit cards: Yes
Handicap Access: No
Wifi: Yes
Special: One of the best ✪ restaurants in town

The best deal in town isn't as atmospheric as some of the more authentic Colonials, but the tidy rooms have lots of light, high cane ceilings, big closets, and original artwork with real Granadino character. All are well appointed, offering modern amenities including air-conditioning, cable TV, phones, and private cool baths. Rooms #3

and #6 have private balconies.

The big bonus, however, is the ✪ restaurant (open 11 AM–2 PM and 5 AM–9 PM Mon. through Sat.; $$), highly regarded for its innovative cuisine using fresh, local ingredients. Victor was a San Francisco chef and Katya a Bay Area baker before the couple decided to return to Granada, bringing with them fantastic recipes and a flair for presentation. The menu changes regularly, but look for pollo guayaba, chicken simmered with guava fruit, rum, and chilies; cerdo con tamarindo, roast pork in a tamarind-lime sauce; and chocolate terrine with mandarin orange.

CASA VIVALDI

Owner: Paolo Magnani
2552-7367, 2552-8422
www.casavivaldi.net
info@www.casavivaldi.net
Calle El Caimito, 4.5 cuadras al lago
Price: Moderate
Credit Cards: Yes
Handicap Access: Challenging
Wifi: Yes
Special: Day passes US$9 (US$3 redeemable at the restaurant)

Though best known for its enormous pool, complete with a waterfall and plenty of lounge chairs, Casa Vivaldi has rooms that creative types might love. Enormous and air-conditioned, they have fabulous beds, plenty of closet space, high ceilings, hot showers, modern paintings, glowing cactus lamps, and other wild details. It's a bit out of the city center, five blocks toward the lake on a quieter residential street.

Vacation Rentals

Granada is one of Central America's classic "slow tourism" destinations, with all sorts of enticements to relax right here for weeks—or years. There are several long-term vacation rentals online; **TripAdvisor** (www.tripadvisor.com) and **Vacation**

Rentals By Owner (www.vrbo.com) list scores. Several realtors offer upscale rentals, such as **Nicaragua Realty** (www.nicaraguarealty.com) and **Water's Edge** (www.realtornicaragua.com).

Auto Hotel Cocibolca (2552-2204; adm cocibolca@cablenet.com.ni; Calle El Caimito) Fan-cooled motel rooms with older furnishings and dingy private baths cost just US$150 per month (air-conditioned apartments with full kitchen run US$650), three blocks from the central park. The vibe is definitely love motel, but it seems safe and clean enough.

Granada Property Services (2552-7954, 8881-3758; www.gpsnicaragua.com) This site has apartment and house listings ranging from US$70 to US$300 per night.

Granada Vacation Rentals (granadahomerental.net) This Web site has listings for several rental homes around town.

Nicaragua Vacation Rentals (www.nicaraguavacationrentals.com) Has lots of listings for properties and lodges all over Southwest Nicaragua.

Xalteva Condominiums (2552-0982; 802-824-3055 (U.S.); www.hotelxalteva.com; info@hotelxalteva.com; Calle Obispo Ulloa; credit cards accepted; $$–$$$; wifi) Close to Iglesia Xalteva, this luxurious little oasis offers nine plush one- and two-bedroom condos with Masatepe-modern furnishings, solar-heated water, full kitchens, gated parking, and sweet volcano views from the balcony.

Bed and Breakfasts

CASA LA MERCED
Owner: Nicoletta De Voto
2552-2744
www.casalamerced.com
info@casalamerced.com
Calle Real Xalteva, frente Iglesia La Merced
Price: Moderate to Expensive
Credit Cards: Yes
Handicap Access: No
Wifi: Yes

This historic boutique hotel is housed in one of Granada's oldest buildings, which survived William Walker's fiery 1856 retreat intact. The current owners have carefully restored and furnished the tiled space with period antiques, with some of their finds—such as the old wooden doors refurbished as coffee tables—creatively re-envisioned.

Surrounding the courtyard gardens, a handful of spacious, sumptuously furnished rooms all have delicious bedding, fantastic bathrooms, wonderful furnishings, and atmospheric décor such as carved saints and Guatemalan fabrics. This is a true Colonial, so the rooms are a bit dark, but the gorgeous gardens make up for it. In addition to breakfast, there's an afternoon coffee break at 4:30 PM.

MISS MARGRITT'S B&B
General Manager: Rebecca Allodi
8941-2851
www.missmargrits.com
missmargrits@gmail.com
del Iglesia Xalteva, 2 cuadras norte
Price: Moderate
Credit Cards: No
Handicap Access: No
Wifi: Yes

You must have reservations to stay in one of the two palatial rooms in this sprawling B&B, a beautifully restored old home with wonderful woodwork, chandeliers, and even a small pool in the second courtyard garden. The rooms are both upstairs, with fantastic bathrooms, handmade furnishings, modern amenities including air-conditioning and hot water, and access to a gleaming lounge area—with wonderful Mombacho views to one side, and an incredible mural depicting the Isletas de Granada on the other.

Service is personalized, from fresh flowers and your choice of breakfast to organized tours and transportation.

HOTEL CASA SAN MARTÍN
Manager: Olga Marta Sánchez
2552-6185
javier_sanchez_a@yahoo.com
Calle La Calzada; catedral, 1 cuadra al lago
Price: Moderate
Credit Cards: Yes
Handicap Access: No
Wifi: Yes

Right on Calle La Calzada, this is another survivor of Walker's retreat, clocking in at just under three centuries for at least some of the authentically Colonial structure. The old adobe's thick walls and lush courtyard gardens muffle some of the street noise, but be sure to get interior accommodations. Spacious, cool, and a bit dark, these well-decorated rooms have high ceilings, excellent mattresses, wicker furnishings, and large hot-water bathrooms. Best of all, you're a two-minute stagger away from the bars.

CASA SILAS B&B
Owners: Rob Keddy
8904-9609, 905-228-3327 (Canada)
www.casasilas.com
casasilasbb@gmail.com
Calle La Concepción 206
Price: Moderate
Credit Cards: No
Handicap Access: No
Wifi: Yes

This quiet, Canadian-run B&B on the edge of the historic center has added a pretty pool to their interior gardens. Hammocks and hangout spots fill the patios, with the cane ceilings and tiled floors you'd expect in such a pretty Colonial.

But the walls are covered with wonderful reproduction murals of Picassos and Rothkos, and the two spacious rooms have modern amenities including air-conditioning and machine-heated showers. There's a kitchen that guests can use, and a big breakfast is included. Nice.

Other Hotels
There must be 30 other budget hostels within walking distance of Granada's Central Park. Look around.

Bearded Monkey (2552-4028; www.thebeardedmonkey.com; thebeardedmonkey@yahoo .com; Av 14 de Septiembre, costado oeste de los bomberos; credit cards accepted; $; wifi) Granada's most popular hostel has it all: cheap, acceptable dorms; basic private rooms; a recommended **restaurant** (B, L, D; $) with vegetarian options; hammocks, couches, DVDs, bicycle rentals, cheap tours, free coffee, free movies, computers for guests, and even a daily shuttle to Laguna de Apoyo. It's festive!

Hotel Casa La Luna (2552-7587; www.casalalunagranada.com; info@asalalunagranada.com; Calle Morazán, frente Casa Pellas; $–$$; wifi) Cute and clean, this family-run hostel has seven spotless rooms with private baths, tiled floors, and handmade furniture surrounding a tidy courtyard.

Hospedaje Cocibolca (2552-7223; hospedaje_cocibolca@yahoo.com; Calle La Calzada, de la catedral 3 cuadras al lago; $; wifi) Popular spot right on the Calzada has stayed awesome despite the hype, with loads of rocking chairs, computers for guests, a shared kitchen, great murals, hammock chairs, and more.

Hostal Dorado (2552-6932; www.hostaldorado.com; info@hostaldorado.com; Calle Real Xalteva, Calle 14 de Septiembre, y Calle Atravesado; credit cards accepted; $–$$; wifi) Look for the gorgeous hammocks hanging in the lobby, part of an initiative (www.tio

antonio.org) that provides milk, uniforms, and tutors to kids, and teaches young people (many of them deaf) to weave. The hostel, wrapped around shady gardens, is nice too. Fan-cooled rooms with private baths are comfortably furnished and fabulously decorated with murals, volcanic stone, and other crafty extras. There's free coffee and a shared kitchen for guests.

Hospedaje Esfinge (2552-4826, 2552-4826; esfingegra@yahoo.com; Mercado Municipal, costado oeste; cash only; $) Right across from the market, this bright yellow neocolonial cheapie is surprisingly peaceful. A delightful is patio lined with hammocks, and simple rooms with private baths are painted with flowers and lovingly decorated with mismatched furniture. There's a shared kitchen and excellent security.

Oasis (2552-8006, 2552-8006; nicaraguahostel.com; oasisgranada@yahoo.com; cash only; $–$$; wifi) This rather elegant hostel is a longtime favorite for the mellower crowd. It's got gardens surrounded with hammocks, dorms with sturdy beds and big lockers, chandeliers—and lots of clean, shared bathrooms. Private rooms are small and whitewashed with high ceilings; some have bathrooms and air-conditioning. There's even a small pool, and a bank of computers for guests.

La Pérgola (2552-4221; www.lapergola.com.ni; lapergolanic@yahoo.com; Calle El Caimito, alcaldía 3 cuadras al lago; credit cards accepted; $$; wifi) This popular mid-range option offers elegant Colonial style in a modern building, with fine rooms set up like a standard U.S. hotel. The orderly gardens are surrounded by a shady patio and two floors of rooms, with high cane ceilings, handmade furnishings, air conditioning, and hot bath.

Hostal Mochilas (2552-2803; www.hostalmochilas.com; hospedajemochilas@gmail.com; Calle Morazán 407, de Casa Pellas, 2.5 cuadras este; $; wifi) Above-average, Dutch-owned hostel is a deal, offering a shared kitchen, good dorms, bright colors, and clean and comfortable rooms with character.

Hostal San Ángel (2552-6373; mariacampos118@hotmail.com; parque central, 50 metros sur; credit cards accepted; $–$$) Attached to the Gran Francia (and probably just as historic) this family-run guesthouse has cluttered but clean common areas, free coffee, and eight clean, comfortable rooms with private baths, some with air-conditioning. Rates include a continental breakfast. They also rent bikes.

Viajero Clandestino (8675-5297; hewlet08@hotmail.com; De la Piedra Bocona, 50 meters al este; $; wifi) Cool hospedaje has clean rooms and dorms with excellent mattresses and clean shared baths, surrounding a courtyard presided over by Bob Marley, Jim Morrison, and Che Guevara. There's free coffee, the best *fritanga* in town shares the building, and the courtyard turns into a mellow bar scene beneath the stars.

RESTAURANTS AND FOOD PURVEYORS

Granada is fast becoming a foodie town, by Central American standards anyway, with a strollable collection of eclectic international cuisines and gourmet restaurants.

You can't leave the city without a moonlit meal on La Calzada, the pedestrian road lined with outdoor tables patrolled by mariachis, break-dancers, and a resourceful troupe of street kids who perform *La Gigantona* for tips. And you simply must spend a breezy afternoon by the lake, enjoying tasty *guapote*. It's just done.

Don't forget that most Granadino of treats, however, the humble *vigarón*. Mashed yucca is topped with a few fried

The place to be after dark is La Calzada, with a row of bistro restaurants and bars where you can mix and mingle beneath the stars.

pork skins and a tasty cabbage salad, and served cool and fresh on a banana leaf. The classic spot to enjoy this midday snack is at one of four kiosks that anchor the central park, with shaded wooden tables and premium prices.

But great *vigarón* is available all over town—my personal favorite is sold at the corner of Calle Atravesada and Calle Corrales, where the cook uses *puerco adobado* (barbecued pork) instead of traditional *chicharrones*.

Restaurant and Food Purveyor Price Code

The following prices are based on the cost of a dinner entrée with a nonalcoholic drink, not including Nicaragua's mandatory 13 percent restaurant tax and "suggested" 10 percent tip, which is usually included in the bill (so check).

Inexpensive ($)	Up to US$5
Moderate ($$)	US$5 to US$10
Expensive ($$$)	$10 to $20
Very Expensive ($$$$)	US$20 or more

Restaurants

CASA BOHEMIA
8387-6096
Calle Corrales, 4 cuadras del parque central
Price: Moderate
Cuisine: International
Serving: L, D (opens 6 PM Sat.)
Closed: Sun. through Mon.
Credit Cards: Yes

Child's Menu: No
Handicap Access: Challenging
Reservations: Yes

Creatively hip and romantically lit, this spot brings in new couples and old friends for a drink or something delicious off their short, ever-changing menu. The owner and chef, Heidi (locals refer to Casa Bohemia as "Heidi's"), finds what's fresh and tasty at area markets, then transforms the day's harvest into elegant entrees served in the old adobe's artsy interior gardens.

There's always something vegetarian, but if the chili con carne, shrimp gumbo, or ginger chicken are on the menu, omnivores could consider one of those. Heidi's also has a very full bar, cool scene, and sometimes live music.

LAS COLINAS DEL SUR

2552-3492
De Shell Palmira, 300 metros al lago
Price: Moderate to Expensive
Cuisine: Seafood
Serving: L, D (opens 4 PM Tues.)
Credit Cards: Yes
Child's Menu: No
Handicap Access: Yes
Reservations: Yes

It's worth the trip to this working class Granada neighborhood, for what's rumored to be the best guapote in Nicaragua. The setting is simple, with hard-packed sand floors and simple tables beneath the rustling palm fronds. So is the menu, with your choice of main dish—chicken, pork, or beef—served with the classic Nicaraguan trifecta of rice, beans, and plantains.

But go for the guapote, fresh from Lake Nicaragua and traditionally served whole—with the eyes, mouth, and tail—and topped with Las Colinas' signature salsa. They also do filets and churros de guapote (fish sticks), all of which go perfectly with a *servicio* of Flor de Caña rum.

BAR Y RESTAURANTE LOS ARTISTAS

8811-2442, 8461-3657
Calle La Calzada, 1.5 cuadras al lago
Price: Moderate
Cuisine: Fusion
Serving: D
Credit Cards: Yes
Child's Menu: No
Handicap Access: Yes
Reservations: Yes

Everyone's got their favorite place on La Calzada, and this just happens to be mine. The delightful restaurant and art gallery has fantastic paintings, soft jazz and twinkling lights in the courtyard garden, and beautifully presented fusion cuisine. Start with the gazpacho, salmon broschetta, or beef carpaccio, perhaps, before moving on to one of the rotating daily specials, perhaps fish in a ginger-soy sauce or vegetarian lasagna. There's also a very full bar with hard-to-find liquors like grappa, Jägermeister, and Campari.

Not for you? There are a dozen restaurants on the strip that deserved a great recommendation in this book, but wouldn't fit. Nectar, La Hacienda . . . there are too many great places to list. Pick the music, mood, and cuisine that are right for you, and enjoy.

CHARLY'S BAR Y RESTAURANTE

2552-2942
www.charlys-bar.com
de Petronic, 5 cuadras oeste
Price: Moderate to Expensive
Cuisine: German
Serving: L, D
Closed: Tues.
Credit Cards: Yes
Child's Menu: No
Handicap Access: No
Reservations: Yes

Popular for its pub-style atmosphere, unmatched selection of beers, and meaty cuisine, Charly's Bar is a Granada institution. Despite the Nicaraguan ambiance, this is a German outpost—serving dishes like maultaschen, spätzle, sauerbraten, and venison, as well as adult beverages from the old country to wash it all down. There's sometimes live music.

Charly's also has a **guesthouse** ($$) with three large, tiled rooms, private hot baths, and your choice of air-conditioning or fan.

✪ EL GARAJE

2651-7412
Calle Corrales 512, del Convento San Francisco, 2.5 cuadras al lago
Price: Moderate
Cuisine: International
Serving: L, D
Closed: Sat. through Sun.
Credit Cards: No
Child's Menu: No
Handicap Access: Yes
Reservations: No

Fresh and fantastic, El Garaje serves some of Granada's best bistro cuisine in a small, airy dining room with colorful art. Take your pick from two blackboard menus, one consistently offering delightful burritos, quesadillas, soups, and sandwiches. The other lists three daily specials, made with what was wonderful at the market that morning—the Thai noodle salad was divine. Everything is made fresh to order, with a real attention to flavor and presentation that you don't always find at this price. Beer and wine are served.

GARDEN CAFÉ

2552-8582
Calle La Libertad, del parque central, 1 cuadra al lago
Price: Moderate
Cuisine: International
Serving: B, L
Closed: Sun.
Credit Cards: Yes
Child's Menu: No

Handicap Access: Challenging
Reservations: Yes

Enjoy exceptional Granada architecture and absolutely exquisite gardens over light, beautifully prepared café cuisine. The interior patio has a handful of tables and thousands of flowers, as well as a fountain and, perhaps, doves. The menu is full of exceptional breakfasts and light lunches, with exotic salads and tasty sandwiches (try the pesto turkey sub) a great bet. The brownies are out of this world, hammocks comfortable, and there's even a book exchange.

IMAGINE RESTAURANT AND BAR

2552-4672, 8842-2587
www.imaginerestaurantandbar.com
Calle La Libertad, del parque central 1 cuadra al lago
Price: Very Expensive
Cuisine: International
Serving: D
Credit Cards: Yes
Child's Menu: No
Handicap Access: Challenging
Reservations: Yes

This is one of the priciest restaurants in town, and locals seem split as to whether it's worth it. (This may be proportional to their tolerance for the Beatles, which are usually playing.)

The setting is certainly stunning, in one of the city center's finest examples of "coffee-boom Colonial" architecture, and the menu features items you won't find elsewhere: lamb chops, imported steaks, duck en fuego, and mango bread—a dessert item that involves a great deal of chocolate. Many ingredients are organic. If your budget isn't too tight, it's worth a whirl.

✪ JIMMY THREE FINGERS
ALABAMA RIB SHACK

2552-8115
www.jimmythreefingers.com

Calle Consulado, del parque central 2.5 cuadras oeste
Price: Moderate to Expensive
Cuisine: Southern
Serving: L, D
Credit Cards: Yes
Child's Menu: No
Handicap Access: Challenging

There's not a lot of down home Southern cooking in Nicaragua, which makes Jimmy Three Fingers the site of some pilgrimage for anyone who has had to explain that, no, the term yanquí most emphatically does not refer to all U.S. citizens. Everyone in town loves Jimmy's country cooking, specializing in melt-in-your-mouth ribs, creamy mashed potatoes, and thick steaks, as well as specials like divine fried catfish.

It's not fancy, but there's a full bar with sports on the big screen, as well as a slightly scruffy courtyard for more romantic diners. Jimmy also has a good-value budget hotel, with a clean dorm and simple private **rooms** (www.hotelnuestracasa.com; $) with the option of air-conditioning and breakfast (recommended).

EL JARDÍN DE ORION
8429-6494
www.jardindorion.com
Calle El Caimito, parque central, 1 cuadra al lago
Price: Moderate to Very Expensive
Cuisine: French

The classic Granada midafternoon snack is vigarón, *served at the kiosks anchoring the central park.*

Serving: D
Credit Cards: Yes
Child's Menu: No
Handicap Access: Yes
Reservations: Yes

Lush gardens, romantic lighting, and the sound of classical guitar floating through this elegant space set the stage for what is arguably Nicaragua's finest French cuisine. The menu changes regularly, perhaps including beef medallions with blue cheese, tuna carpaccio with capers, or ricotta ravioli (there's always a vegetarian option). Be sure to try ice cream–filled profiteroles—in a dark, fresh, Nicaraguan chocolate sauce—off the menu. The wine list is predictably excellent.

✪ RESTAURANT MEDITERRANEO

2552-6764
Calle El Caimito
Price: Expensive to Very Expensive
Cuisine: Spanish
Serving: L, D
Closed: Mon.
Credit Cards: Yes
Child's Menu: No
Handicap Access: Yes
Reservations: Yes

Granada's oldest restaurant and still one of its best. Uniformed waiters swish through the romantic, candlelit courtyard, carrying trays of Spanish-inspired cuisine and renowned sangria. The specialty, of course, is paella—both a more affordable version made with chicken and vegetables, and the traditional dish featuring several types of seafood and sausage.

But there are plenty of other excellent offerings to enjoy while the roving mariachis play, including excellent steak and seafood dishes such as the zarzuela de mariscos, a type of Spanish seafood casserole; steak Roquefort; and camaron al ajillo, shrimp in garlic sauce.

PUERTO ASESE

2552-2269
info@aseselasisletas.com
Puerto Asese, Isletas de Granada
Price: Moderate to Expensive
Cuisine: Seafood, Nicaraguan
Serving: L (open 11 AM–5 PM)
Closed: Mon.
Credit Cards: Yes
Child's Menu: No
Handicap Access: No
Reservations: For groups

Since 1958, this lakeside restaurant overlooking the isletas has been serving some of the finest "spineless fish," or guapote, in Granada. The setting is stunning, surrounded by the clean, deep waters of the peninsula's far side—with islands and volcanoes rising from the lake for as far as you can see.

TERCER OJO

2552-6451
www.eltercerojo.com.ni
Calle El Arsenal, frente Convento San Francisco
Price: Moderate to Expensive
Cuisine: International
Serving: L, D
Credit Cards: Yes
Child's Menu: No
Handicap Access: No
Reservations: Yes

Get in touch with your metaphysical side amid the soothing colors and flowing designs of this longtime favorite. The menu is eclectic, to say the least—with Spanish tapas, pad Thai, sushi, Middle Eastern kebabs, and more than a dozen salads among the many vegetarian and organic options. The ambiance is mystical and laid back, and there's sometimes live music, usually mellow jazz or classical guitar.

☉ VILLAS MOMBACHO
2552-8552, 8873-0191
josesandino1@hotmail.com
Marina Cocibolca, 100 metros sur
Price: Moderate to Expensive
Cuisine: Seafood
Serving: B, L, D
Credit Cards: Yes
Child's Menu: No
Handicap Access: No
Reservations: Yes

At Puerto Cocibolca, overlooking a dozen unsullied lake isles, this wonderful restaurant's rustling rancheros cover heavy wooden tables and cheerfully uniformed waitstaff serve guapote to Granada's well-heeled upper crust. Or try the churrascos and chicken dinners served on sizzling metal plates, or stick to inexpensive bar food, like tasty tostones y queso (plantain medallions topped with fried cheese).

They also have two adorable brick-and-wood **cottages** ($$), with private cool baths, breezy porches, and tiled bedrooms with one soft double bed. During the day it might get loud, but the restaurant closes at 8 PM, and then it's just you, the stars, and the isletas.

ZAGÚAN
2552-2522
elzaguan@cablenet.com.ni
Catedral, costado este
Price: Expensive
Cuisine: Steakhouse
Serving: L, D
Credit Cards: Yes
Child's Menu: No
Handicap Access: Yes
Reservations: Recommended

This isn't just a fantastic place for authentic churrascos, grilled in an open kitchen with theatrical aplomb—though it's fun to watch chefs grilling your tasty corn on the cob, sausages, and fish. This is the consummate Granada dining experience. The décor is delightful, transforming a zagúan (garage) into a romantic, festive spot. The place gets packed on weekend evenings, when you should have reservations.

Food Purveyors

Asian
In addition to fusion restaurants like Tercer Ojo, with sushi and other Asian-influenced dishes, Granada has several eateries offering acceptable Chinese cuisine like *arroz chino* (fried rice), *chowming* (chow mien), *tacos chinos* (egg rolls), and *cerdo agridulce* (sweet and sour pork). All accept credit cards, offer vegetarian options, and deliver.

Restaurante y Bar Año Nuevo Chino (2552-8150; Calle El Martirio, Catedral 3 cuadras al lago, 25 varas norte; L, D; $$) Right off La Calzada.
Restaurante Min Nan Jiu Lou (2552-2667; Calle El Caimito, de la alcaldía 2 cuadras al lago; L, D; $$) Good chow mien.
Restaurante Yon Niy Ta (8746-4832; Calle Corrales; L, D; $$) Top-notch homemade tofu.

Bakeries
Vendors sell crusty butter loaves, braided cheese breads, and other pastries around the market and along Calle El Comercial (Atravesada), often showing up in late afternoon.

Panadería El Chele (2552-7667; Calle Inmaculada; B, L, D; $) Two blocks west of La Colonia supermarket, this big, basic bakery sells cheaper breads and pastries.

Panadería Estrella (Calle El Comercial; B, L, D; $) Half a block north of the market, close to Palí supermarket, this good bakery is convenient.

✪ **Panadería Luna Express** (2552-6699; Calle La Calzada, del parque central 50 metros al lago; open Mon. through Sat.; B, L, D) Fabulous French bakery offers fine pastries and excellent baguettes, which they also use to make sandwiches. The larger, more comfortable Calle Xalteva location (Iglesia Xalteva, 1.5 cuadras al lago) has a wider variety of sweets.

Breakfast

Café Isabella (2552-7654; 108 Calle Corrales y Calle Atravesada; B, L, D; $–$$) Serves omelets, pancakes, and other big breakfasts all day on its raised porch, plus other international meals. It turns into an expat bar in the afternoon.

Kathy's Waffle House (2552-7488; frente Convento San Francisco; credit cards accepted; B, L; $–$$) Serves great breakfasts, including many U.S.-style options, with one of the best views in town—the pale blue façade of Convento San Francisco.

Nica Buffet (8874-1555; Calle Vega, de parque central 100 metros sur, 50 metros oeste; cash only; B; $–$$) Between the central park and mercado, Nica Buffet (which is not a buffet) may not have the view, but great breakfasts are an excellent value.

Cafés

Café Don Simón (2552-8627 (central park), 2552-5899 (La Calzada); B, L, D; $) Enjoy great people-watching in two premium locations: the central park and La Calzada (closed Sun.), both with coffee, pastries, sandwiches, and more.

Café Latino (2552-3608; Plaza de los Leones; cash only; open 8 AM–6 PM; $) Nicaragua's answer to Starbucks serves espresso beverages and free wifi in poet Rubén Darío's old home.

Chocolate (2552-3400; www.hoteldario.com; Hotel Darío, Calle La Calzada; credit cards accepted; $$) You don't have to spend a fortune to enjoy fabulous Hotel Darío—grab a seat overlooking La Calzada and enjoy coffee, pastries, or a fancy cocktail.

✪ **Euro Café** (2552-2146; parque central, costado norte) Enjoy real iced coffee and other caffeinated beverages in a delightful courtyard right off the central park, or try the toasted paninis, tasty gelato, free wifi, table tennis, and Seeing Hands Blind Massage.

Mexican

Taquería La Jarochita (2552-8304; alcaldía, 2 cuadras al lago; credit cards accepted; $$$) Masaya's popular family-style restaurant has a second location in Granada.

✪ **La Mexicana** (2552-2413; Calle Real Xalteva 507 and Calle El Palenque; cash only; closed Sun.; B, L, D; $) Tiny, five-table café dishes up inexpensive tacos, burritos, tostadas, molletes, and other traditional Mexican dishes. Close to Iglesia Xalteva.

Tequila Vallarta (2552-8488; tequilavallarte@yahoo.com; Calle La Calzada; credit cards accepted; L, D; $$) Enjoy big burritos and strong margaritas on the Calzada. Their art gallery often shows very cool stuff.

Nicaraguan

There are dozens of spots serving cheap Nica cuisine around town, often with a steam table buffet (you point, and they'll serve) at lunch. If you're willing to try street food, *fritangas,* or outdoor barbecues, set up all over town around sunset. These usually offer your choice of grilled chicken or beef *churrasco,* served on a banana leaf with several sides—perhaps *gallo pinto* (rice and beans), *tejadas* (plantain chips), *maduros* (soft, sweet plantains), *papas* (fried balls of mashed potato with cheese), or other options—topped with vinegary cabbage salad for around US$3.

✪ **Comidas Típicas y Mas** (2552-4414; Calle La Calzada; L, D; $–$$) La Calzada favorite specializes in professionally prepared dishes you'd usually only find at the market, such as *baho* (pronounced "bow"), a layered beef, plantain, and yucca stew; *nacatamales,* oversized tamales; and much more. Wash it down with a traditional jícaro shell filled with *chicha* (a corn drink), *grama* (herbal tea), or *pinolillo*—the corn beverage that gives Nicaraguans one of their nicknames, *Pinoleros.*

El Palenque (2552-7519; Calle La Libertad and Calle El Palenque; B, L, D; $) Next to El Recodo (see Shopping), this petite place serves classic Nica cuisine such as *nacatamales, baho, repochetas,* and *tiste de cacao.*

✪ **Querube's Restaurant** (2552-7141; Calle El Comercio, frente al Tiangue; cash only; B, L, D; $) Quality steam-table buffet close to the market lets you choose which delicious dish you want (go for the chicken cannolis) with rice, beans, plantains, and salad.

Pizza

Don Luca (2552-7822; Calle La Calzada; credit cards accepted; L, D; $$) Serves wood-fired pizzas and pastas right on La Calzada, alongside something special from the full bar or wine list.

✪ **Tele Pizza** (2552-4219, 2552-7702; Calle El Arsenal, BanCentro 1.5 cuadras al lago; credit cards accepted; L, D; $–$$) Inexpensive, local joint has hefty pizzas by the pie or slice, serious salads, pastas, desserts, and amazing garlic bread. There's another Tele Pizza at Puerto Cocibolca.

Monna Lisa (2552-8187; pizz_monna_lisa@yahoo.com; Calle La Calzada, del Colegio Carlos Bravo, 30 varas al lago; credit cards accepted; closed Wed.; L, D; $$) With its elegant dining rooms, excellent service, and atmospheric brick oven, this popular Italian-owned pizza place is an upscale, romantic choice. Choose one of 24 types of pizza, or go for homemade pastas; the ravioli and lasagna get raves. Pair your favorite with one of 20 Italian wines.

CULTURE

Granada has always been one of the great cultural centers of Central America. Among the first European cities in the Americas, it was designed to awe with its architecture and artistry. Since the city's inception, the port has been a hub for shipping and trade, always staunchly conservative in its politics. It is also the site of Nicaragua's International Poetry Festival, an artistic beacon in the region. Though the past few decades of revolution and war might have temporarily dimmed Granada's charms, she has regained her rightful status as a highlight of any Central American trip, with good reason.

The Spanish Conquest

Granada was founded on the shores of Cocibolca by conquistador Francisco Fernández de Córdoba in 1524, and was one of the first Spanish cities in the Americas (Panama City and Veracruz, Mexico, are older).

Luis Enrique Mejia Godoy entertains the crowd at Granada's International Poetry Festival.

It was predated by perhaps nine hundred years by the neighboring indigenous town of Xalteva. Little is known about this lost city, though the location is marked by rather mysterious **Iglesia Xalteva** (Calle Xalteva, six blocks west of the central park), unmissable in its freshly painted 1898 neoclassical-federalist façade.

The retaining walls close to the church are part of Granada's original 1524 defenses, while **Parque Xalteva** has a whispered history of executions during the Walker era. It is likely both were once part of a fortress used to survey and control the original Xalteva. Granada itself is strategically placed between the older city and the gradually retreating lake.

As you wander through the historic center, take a moment to appreciate Spanish ingenuity. In times of war, each sturdy stucco mansion must be breached at great cost via house-to-house combat. Churches probably doubled as fortresses; the 1529 Inmaculada Concepción, today replaced by stunning **Convento San Francisco** (Calle El Arsenal), had a dual purpose—saving souls and controlling access to Cocibolca's fresh water, then much closer to the historic center. During peacetime, those same thick walls and high ceilings keep the streets shady and interiors cool, with the help of small windows, courtyard gardens, and cane (or wood) ceiling insulation.

The "oldest house in Granada" lies close to the old city wall, **El Recodo** (Calle Consulado and Corrales), a pricey antique shop that starred in the movie *Walker*. But many buildings have elements dating to the earliest days of settlement, such as the recently renovated **Hotel Gran Francia** (parque central), actually used by Walker, with interior walls scientifically dated to 1526.

The only truly Colonial church in town is **Iglesia de la Merced** (Calles Xalteva and 14 de Septiembre), considered one of Nicaragua's most beautiful for the elegant Mexican-style baroque façade. Come by during daylight hours, when tourists are welcome to ✪ **climb to the bell tower** (US$1) for the very best views over Granada, all the way to the lake.

The Age of Pirates

Before the Panama Canal was completed in 1903, Lake Nicaragua was the only waterway connecting the Caribbean and Pacific. Granada, as mistress of this international shipping bottleneck, grew wealthy with trade, attracting unwanted attention.

Most famously, the city's opulence caught the eye of buccaneer Henry Morgan. In 1655, the infamous captain became the first British pirate to make his way up the Río San Juan and across the lake, taking the city entirely by surprise. Morgan plundered Granada, and set her afire. He would twice repeat his conquest.

Morgan's exploits earned him an eternal and appropriately rum-soaked infamy, while Granada rebuilt to include several new fortresses. The most important was the 1624 **Iglesia Guadalupe** (Calle La Calzada, del parque central, 5 cuadras al lago) reinforced with stone and turrets to face east, a rarity among Spanish Catholic churches, and boon to early rising

Rebuilt during the economic boom of the late 1800s, Iglesia Xalteva is a monument to the ornate architectural style of the period.

Granada's most photogenic façade is Covento San Francisco, on the site of the city's first church.

photographers. Also built to defend Granada's honor were the 1751 **Fortaleza La Polvora**, near Xalteva; and the 1780 **Fortaleza San Pablo**, in the isletas.

Independence and Civil War

In 1821, Nicaragua won independence from Spain, and entered a period of turmoil. A short-lived confederation of the five neighboring nations, called the Central American Republic, fell apart in the late 1820s, leaving a power vacuum. The wealthy business families of Granada, the Conservative city, had long felt that their economic clout should translate into political power. The Liberal city of León, however, had been Nicaragua's administrative capital throughout the Spanish occupation.

The two cities began a destructive, low-intensity civil war that dragged on for decades, only pausing briefly after an 1852 peace agreement named the sleepy fishing town of Managua the capital. In 1855, however, León surreptitiously hired a group of U.S.-based private military contractors, led by Mexican-American War veteran William Walker. They called themselves *filibusteros*, a corruption of a Dutch term for pirates, and conquered Granada easily. Walker took control of the city—but did not turn it over to León.

Instead, he set up headquarters at what is now Gran Francia, declared himself president of Nicaragua and, funded by pro-slavery politicians in the U.S., made Granada the headquarters of his brief campaign to take over Central America.

Not quite two years later, Walker was defeated at the Battle of Rivas. As he retreated, Walker's men methodically burned Granada to the ground, leaving behind a plaque in the smoking remains of El Convento San Francisco that read: "Here Was Granada."

Rising from the Ashes

While Granada is considered a gem of "Colonial" architecture, most of the city was actually rebuilt in the late 1800s, after the fire. The floor plans and many walls date to the 1500s, but today's architecture is a delightfully lavish mix of authentic Colonial, neo-Colonial, neoclassical, and baroque styles, with random Art Deco and Porfiriano buildings thrown in for good measure.

Granada rebuilt quickly thanks to earnings from the "Nicaragua Route" between the Caribbean and Pacific. Steamships crossing the lake had continued to operate throughout the war, and traffic between New York City and the gold fields of California, along with the burgeoning coffee-shipping business, was booming.

There are fine buildings from this era all over town, including the 1886 **Train Station** (Calles Atravesada and La Inmaculada) and the 1890 **Mercado Municipal.** Creepier desti- nations include the allegedly haunted ruins of **San Juan de Dios Hospital** (Avenida Arel- lano), and **Granada Cemetery** (Avenida Arellano)—worth wandering for its remarkable

Relax with one of the best views in town at Forteleza La Polvora, in what was once the old indigenous city of Xalteva.

mausoleums, including those of six presidents. Most of the really flashy buildings, however, are on the **Central Park** and **Plaza de la Independencia**, originally called Plaza de los Leones.

Casa de los Leones (2552-4176; www.c3mundos.org; open 7 AM–6 PM daily; US$0.50/0.25 adult/child) is built around the oldest surviving structure in Granada, the Mudéjar-style stone archway of Portal del los Leones, flanked by roaring lions. The building was originally constructed in 1550, remodeled in 1720, and converted to a theater in 1889. In 1987, Austrian actor Dietmar Schönherr and Nicaraguan poet Ernesto Cardenal bought the splendid complex to house the **Fundación Casa de los Tres Mundos**, today a cultural center offering art galleries, classes, and regular public events.

Next door are the extravagantly columned **Episcopal Palace** and **Edificio Sandino**, used as military buildings throughout the civil war of the 1800s. A gunpowder explosion in 1897 destroyed both, but their graceful new façades have become symbols of the city. Granada's stately 1888–1910 **Catedral** (central park), with prim Ionic columns and four chapels, houses a far older Virgin—who may have once inhabited the original 1530 building.

Modern Granada

The 20th century was relatively kind to Granada, at least when compared to the turmoil suffered elsewhere in the country. Sandino's revolution, Somoza's oppression, and even the bloody wars of the 1970s and 1980s left the fair city more or less intact.

To be sure, the deprivation and degradation took its toll, as refugees poured into town. War atrocities fill a mass grave of several hundred somewhere out on the Asese Peninsula. And though this is one of Nicaragua's wealthiest cities, a short walk outside the historic center leads to *barrios* of dirt-floored homes made of corrugated tin. Here, however, unlike

The Palacio Episcopal and Casa de los Leones overlook Plaza de la Independencia, adjacent to Granada's Central Park.

Though most statues of the Zapatera Archipelago were spirited away by international antiquities thieves, these are displayed at El Convento San Francisco.

many cities that lay shattered after the 1988 peace accords, Granada's intact infrastructure was able to accommodate NGOs, missionaries, and even those first few curious tourists trickling over the border.

Today that has become a torrent, and business and investment (Granada's traditional pastimes) are currently focused on tourism. Freshly painted churches, recently stream-lined residency requirements, and Intur ads featuring the cathedral's iconic domes are finally returning Granada to the spotlight.

Museums

✪ CENTRO CULTURAL ANTIGÜO CONVENTO DE SAN FRANCISCO

2552-5535
www.inc.gob.ni
Calle El Arsenal
Admission: US$2/0.60 foreigners/Nicaraguans
Open: 8 AM–5 PM Mon. through Fri., 9 AM–4 PM Sat. and Sun.

Famed for its enormous sky-blue façade, El Convento San Francisco stands on the site of Granada's first church, the 1529 La Inmaculada Concepción. It was completely destroyed during William Walker's fiery 1856 exit; the current structure was completed in the late 1920s, hence the frilly Art Deco details.

The convent now houses a museum, most famous for the **Estatuaria de Zapatera**, a regiment of mysterious black basalt statues depicting men (gods?) that seem to be morphing into crocodiles and other creatures. They come from the Isla de los Muertos in the Zapatera Archipelago, a sacred place. Most experts date them to around 800 AD, but no one knows for sure.

There are other exhibitions worth seeing, including rooms full of pre-Columbian metates (stone corn grinders), pottery, and dioramas depicting indigenous life. An impressively detailed scale model of Granada takes up an entire room—fascinating. The museum also shows art exhibits, while the **Manolo Cuadra Library** has an 8,000-volume collection of Nicaraguan books that you can peruse Monday through Friday.

FORTELEZA LA POLVORA

Calle Xalteva, three blocks west of Iglesia Xalteva
Admission: US$0.50
Open: 8 AM–5 PM

This large, grassy fortress was constructed in 1751 to help defend against pirates, though it probably replaces an earlier military installation. Its thick walls and hexagonal guard towers could not stand against filibustero William Walker and his soldiers, and so it has been retired as a relaxed tourist attraction.

Knock on the gate, and they'll let you wander around the grounds and climb the various guard towers, with wonderful views across the city and lake. There are also some old cannons and the remains of the gunpowder room—La Polvora.

✪ MI MUSEO

2552-7614
www.mimuseo.org
Calle Atravesada 505
Admission: Free
Open: 8 AM–5 PM

Mi Museo is home to one of the most important collections in Nicaragua, some 6,000 pieces of pre-Columbian ceramics and stoneware gathered here by Peder Kolind, Granada's esteemed Danish patron and the benefactor behind Carita Feliz (www.caritafeliz.com).

The museum itself, an ethereally whitewashed old mansion, offers a flowing display space interrupted only by dark wood vigas and courtyard gardens. Though enormous, the museum can only display a fraction of the work at any one time; take a look at the expansive online catalog. Thus, the finest examples of pre-Columbian ceramics and stoneware are rotated every three months, and grouped by a theme. Pieces that could be interpreted as evidence of an indigenous matriarchy were being shown at press time.

MUSEO CASA NATAL SOR MARÍA ROMERO

2552-6069
www.sor-maria-romero.es.tl, www.sormariaromero.org
Iglesia de Xalteva, 1 cuadra al lago, 1 cuadra sur, Calle Estrada

One of the most important collections of pre-Columbian artifacts in Nicaragua is displayed at Granada's Mi Museo.

Admission: Free

Open: 8 AM–noon and 2 PM–5 PM Tues. through Sun.

Small museum honors the life of Sister María Romero, who despite her beauty and wealth, entered the monastic order of Don Bosco. As a nun, she went to (then) struggling Costa Rica, and set up a health clinic and other services.

Today, she is considered a saint by both Nicaraguans and Costa Ricans, and was venerated in 2002 by Pope John Paul II. Pilgrims visit her family home, where her childhood bedroom has been converted into a small chapel. Her personal effects are displayed throughout the house.

Nightlife

Granada has a great little nightlife scene, centered on the bars and restaurants lining **Calle La Calzada**. Tables spill out into the festively lit street, where locals and tourists enjoy everything from gourmet cuisine at some of the city's finest restaurants to cheap burritos at

Centralito. Different spots offer drink specials, party games, and even live music. Buskers offer all sorts of entertainment for a few córdoba, too.

There are many other bars scattered around the historic downtown, ask around to find out the current hot spots. For a more local vibe grab a cab to the lakefront ✪ **centro turístico**, with several nightspots, including **Kayak**, serving mellow tunes and cheap beer; the **Granada Beach Club**, with live salsa and merengue most nights; **Boricua**, the place to be on Sunday; or the ever-popular **César**, which gets going around 11 PM.

El Club (2552-4245; www.elclub-nicaragua.com; Calle La Libertad y Avenida Barricada; credit cards accepted; B, L, D; $–$$$) Stylish spot blasting techno and reggaeton attracts a young crowd, and also rents modern, minimalist ✪ **rooms** ($$).

Conchi's (formerly Café Nuit) (Calles La Libertad y 14 de Septiembre, 0.5 cuadras oeste; $$) Longtime favorite nightspot has good prices and live bands most nights.

Kelly's Bar (8493-7298; Calle El Caimito; 1 cuadra al lago; cash only; L, D; $$) Just off the strip, popular bar has sports TV and live music on Wednesday. Everyone loves the chicken enchiladas.

Mi Tierra (del parque central, 1 cuadra oeste; US$3 cover Fri. through Sun.) Second-story disco has salsa, merengue, reggaeton, and other Latin dance going late, with live music on Sunday.

O'Shea's Irish Pub Restaurant (8454-1140; Calle La Calzada 216; cash only; B, L, D; $$) Serves Irish beverages and cuisine, including Irish stew, shepherd's pie, fish and chips, and excellent smoothies with fresh tropical and imported fruits only, no water or sugar (though they will throw in liquor, try the piña colada). Wednesday is trivia night, which brings in a crowd. Nice folks.

Road House Drinks & Food (2552-8469; Calle La Calzada; credit cards accepted; L, D; $$–$$$) Friendly bar and grill has icy air-conditioning, huge TVs showing sports, sports memorabilia on the walls, and serious steaks and burgers made with imported USDA prime. Nachos, Del Mar crab sandwiches, and potato skins all go perfectly with a cold Toña and some NFL action.

Zoom Bar (2643-5655; www.zoombar.biz; B, L, D; $$) Granada's original gringo bar is still a favorite for big burgers, pitchers of sangria, and "Chicken Sh!t Bingo" (pick a number on the floor of the cage, and wait for the chicken to do its thing).

Spanish Schools

Granada has several competitive Spanish schools, as well as independent teachers who post flyers at local hotels. Schools generally offer 20 hours of instruction per week, individually or in small groups, as well as activities like volcano tours and salsa lessons. Most can arrange homestays with a local family for around US$85 per week, including three meals.

Ave Nicaragüita (2552-8538; www.avenicaraguita.com; Calle El Arsenal, del Convento San Francisco, 2.5 cuadras al lago) Volunteer opportunities, and partner schools in Managua, Masatepe, Ometepe, Juigalpa, Esteli, Matagalpa, and San Juan del Sur.

Casa Xalteva (2552-2436; www.casaxalteva.com; Calle Real Xalteva 103) Spanish and dance classes.

Cenac Spanish School (8454-1750; www.spanishschoolcenac.com; Avenida Guzmán, del parque central 4.5 cuadras norte) One-on-one classes.

Nicaragua Mia Spanish School (2552-8193, 8888-6567; www.nicaraguamiaspanish.com; Calle Caimito, de Gran Francia, 3.5 cuadras al lago) Arranges homestays and activities.

Spanish School Xpress (2552-8577, 8450-1722; www.nicaspanishschool.com; parque central, 2.5 cuadras norte) Sister schools in San Juan del Sur and León.

Other Classes

Casa de los Tres Mundos (2552-4176; www.c3mundos.org; Plaza de la Independencia; open 9 AM–6 PM daily) Renowned cultural center offers music, dance, and art classes, geared toward locals but open to foreigners.

La Calzada Centro de Arte (2552-1461, 8616-7322; Calle La Calzada) Offers mosaic tile and painting classes, plus other artsy activities, many for children. There are sometimes special events in the evenings, with wine tastings, games, and activities.

Alianza Français (8990-0885; af.granada@hotmail.com; Calle El Consulado 110) Offers French classes to Nicaraguans and foreigners.

Cinema and Theater

Most evenings throughout the dry season (and often in rainy season) there are free live performances or movies in the central park, usually sponsored by the **Casa de los Tres Mundos** (2552-4176; www.c3mundos.org).

Bearded Monkey (2552-4028; www.thebeardedmonkey.com; Av 14 de Septiembre) Popular hostel shows movies at 6 PM and 8 PM nightly, free for guests and a US$0.50 minimum purchase at their restaurant/bar for visitors. Shows primarily big English-language blockbusters.

Cine Karwala (2552-8974; Calle Atravesada) Granada's only real movie theater screens a different flick, usually a Hollywood blockbuster, every weekend.

On a clear day, the views of the Isletas de Granada from the top of Volcán Mombacho are spectacular.

The most popular way to see the Isletas de Granada is in a motorized panga, shown here with the sacred island of Zapatera rising in the background.

RECREATION

National Parks and Protected Areas

✪ ASESE PENINSULA AND THE ISLETAS DE GRANADA
Lake Nicaragua, just south of the centro turístico
Open: Daily
Admission: Free

Though not officially protected, the dark, rocky Asese Peninsula and its entourage of 365 tiny islands are Granada's signature natural attraction. Curling lush and green into the serene, silvery expanse of Lake Nicaragua, this peaceful place was torn from the Mombacho Volcano in an epic explosion some 12,000 years ago.

Some islets are so small that they barely break the surface with reeds, water lilies, and perhaps a white heron. Others are larger, several thousand square meters, topped with marvelous vacation homes, fragile fishing shacks, and even a few hotels and restaurants. More than 122 bird species flit through the impossibly beautiful landscape, with the ancient volcanoes of Mombacho, Zapatera, and smoking Concepción in the background.

There are several ways into the isletas, and every outfitter in Granada can arrange tours. There are a handful of restaurants on the islands, most very basic, as well as the 1781 **Forteleza San Pablo**, an old Spanish fortress. You can even spend the night. One of the best hotels in Nicaragua is off the tip of the peninsula, the fabulous **Jícaro Island Ecolodge** listed earlier. These are easier on the pocketbook:

Isleta El Roble (8894-6217; www.nicadescanso.com; nicadescanso@hotmail.com; $$–$$$) Four-bedroom house comes with a swimming pool, air-conditioning, kayaks, full kitchen, hammocks, and a motorboat and driver at your disposal.
Hotel Club Nautico La Ceiba (2266-1694, 2266-1018; www.nicaraolake.com; nir @nicaragolake.com; credit cards accepted; $$$) Nicarao Lake Tours operates this large private island, with a few basic cabins scattered around the pool.

✪ RESERVA NATURAL VOLCÁN MOMBACHO
2552-5858, 2248-8234
www.mombacho.org
10 km (6 miles) south of Granada
Open: Ecomobiles leave for the crater at 8:30 AM, 10 AM, 1 PM, and 3 PM Thur. through Sun.
Closed: Mon., open Tues. and Wed. to groups of ten or more with advance reservations
Admission: US$13/6 foreigner/Nicaraguan, including ecomobile transportation

Dominating the Granada skyline, the ragged crater of Volcán Mombacho is often wrapped in cool, glistening mists on an otherwise cloudless day. Beckoning from far above the sweltering city, these chill heights hold a unique and isolated cloud forest, home to beautiful endemics such as the bright orange Camaridium mombachoersis orchid and Bolitoglassa mombachoensis salamander, as well as 168 bird species, howler monkeys, red-eyed frogs, deer, foxes, and big cats.

Escaping into the clouds is easy, and every operator in Granada offers the trip, perhaps in conjunction with a canopy tour and visit to a coffee *finca* (plantation). Or have any Naindame bus drop you at the park entrance and walk the steep 2 km (1.2 miles) drive to the parking lot, where there's a *mariposario* (butterfly nursery) and orchid garden. There you'll wait for the ecomobile, a specially modified truck, to make the shockingly steep climb to the top.

There are two main hikes. The easy, 2-km **Sendero del Cráter**, suitable for families, offers incredible views over the Isletas de Granada while passing fumeroles, sulfur-laden geysers boiling to the surface, and "The Tunnel," a narrow canyon covered with bromeliads and mosses. Guides (US$5) are optional for the clearly marked trail.

The considerably more strenuous 4-km **Sendero La Puma** follows the crater rim up and down (and up, and down) on beautifully made, but slippery, trails. On a clear day, you'll see Zapatera and Ometepe. The other 80 percent of the time, you'll enjoy the misty forest scenery. Guides are mandatory—US$15 per group in Spanish, US$20 in English.

You can spend the night in their 14-bed dormitory for US$40, including thin mattresses, hot showers, breakfast and dinner, and a guided half-hour night hike in search of that endemic salamander. Camping can also be arranged. The cafeteria serves Nica cuisine for US$5–12.

PARQUE NACIONAL ARCHIPIELAGO ZAPATERA
8899-2927 (Cooperativa Sonzapote)
30 km (19 miles) south of Granada
Open: 24 hours
Admission: Free

Just south of the isletas, rising to a lush and lopsided volcanic cone, the sacred island of Zapatera is well off the beaten path. Few people visit the isle, and there is little infrastructure waiting once they arrive. But there is a mountain to climb, a fascinating community to explore, fish to catch, and an unparalleled wealth of archaeological treasures.

Zapatera and the neighboring, crescent shaped islets—actually the rims of even more ancient volcanoes—were the site of vast numbers of statues and petroglyphs, some of which are displayed at the Convento San Francisco in Granada. Most have, sadly, been stolen, and those that remain on the islands—such as the 350-square-meter petroglyph field that famously paves neighboring Isla del Muerto—are being rapidly degraded by increased traffic. Please tread lightly on what's left.

Several tour operators, including **Zapatera Tours** (www.zapateratours.com) and **Leo Tours Comunitarios** (www.leotours.blogspot.com) run trips to the archipelago. Or you can hire private captains yourself at Puerto Cocibolca. There's a US$8 community boat to the island, which leaves Tuesday, Friday, and Sunday mornings.

There are two places to stay on the island, and both offer meals. Other services are basic: Electricity and running water are unreliable, wifi and ATMs nonexistent. The hammocks, however, work just fine.

Albergüe Rural Sonzapote (8889-2927; www.sonzapote.blogspot.com; info@sonzapote .org; cash only; $) This community tourism project offers very simple rooms and dorms in a solar-powered ranchero, including all meals. Hammocks and campsites are even cheaper, but you'll pay for food (US$3–5). You can take the community boat, or they'll arrange transport for US$85 per boat (10 people), round-trip.

Hacienda Santa María (2266-9976; www.islazapatera.com; katiacordova9@gmail.com; cash only; $$$) For more than a century, this relaxed wooden ranch house has been the finest on the island, and is now spiffed up and attractively furnished for guests. The price includes meals, but private boat transport is extra, US$125 round-trip.

Other Parks and Natural Attractions

There are several parks in Granada itself, including the architecturally outstanding **Central Park** and attached **Plaza de la Independencia**, the heart of the city. Few travelers make it out to **Parque de los Poetas** (Calle Atravesada y Calle La Inmaculada), officially known as Parque Sandino, but it's worth the seven-block walk to see sculptures honoring Granada's wordsmiths, as well as the 1888 **Railway Station.**

Or catch some rays at the **centro turístico** (admission US$0.25), a long, gray, lakefront beach with wonderful views, fronted by a rambling collection of open-air restaurants, bars, playgrounds, and park benches that stretches from the Muelle de Granada, at the end of Calle La Calzada, to the Asese Peninsula. This obviously isn't the cleanest part of Lake Nicaragua, but families still swim here—it's absolutely packed on weekends. Boat tours of the isletas leave from the south side of the park.

Domitila Private Wildlife Reserve (8881-1786; www.domitila.org; Nandaime; open daily; admission US$5; rooms $$; dorm beds US$20 with student ID) Just south of Granada, this is a rustic escape into the dry tropical forest, with a riot of wildlife and several guided hikes (US$10). You can visit on a day trip, or spend the night in their simple, thatched-roof cabinas, surrounded with hammocks and nature. The restaurant serves Nica cuisine for US$10 per meal.

Tour Operators

More than a dozen tour operators, most located close to La Calzada, offer day trips around the region and multiday tours all over the country. Most tours have two- or three-person minimums, but solo travelers can usually find groups already booked; just ask around.

De Tours Viajes y Cultura (2552-0155, 8837-0559; www.detour-ameriquecentrale.com; Calle Caimito, alcaldía 50 metros al lago) French-owned operation offers the usual tours, plus adventurous treks to rural Chontales, active Telica Volcano, or mountain biking around Granada.

Leo Tours Comunitarios (8829-4372, 8422-7905; www.leotours.blogspot.com; leotoursgranada @gmail.com, Calle La Calzada) Tours to the isletas, Isla Zapatera, Mombacho, and more add a community twist—visiting rural families, picking coffee, or participating in traditional fishing.

Mombotour (2552-4548; www.mombotour.com; Avenida Barricada y Calle Real Xalteva) Specializes in Mombacho tours, perhaps combined with a trip to their private reserve, Hacienda Cutirre, with horseback rides and kayaking.

Opera Gioconda (2552-2876, 8436-9397; nicaguidesinger@yahoo.com; Calle Estrada, del Iglesia La Merced, 1 cuadra sur, 1 cuadra este) Gioconda, a trained opera singer, offers an amazing musical city tour. You can also find her through Hotel Darío.

Tierra Tour (2552-8723, 8862-9580; www.tierratour.com; Calle La Calzada, 2 cuadras al lago) Reputable, long-standing local operator has the widest variety of tours at good prices.

Va Pues Tours (2552-8291; www.vapues.com; parque central) Community-conscious operator offers unusual artsy and outdoorsy tours, and great packages to León.

Hacienda La Calera Private Reserve (2248-8234; www.mombacho.org) Just 15 minutes from Marina Cocibolca, amid the reed-filled wetlands that fringe Mombacho's undulating skirts, this private reserve is most famous for its hot springs, which you'll feel warming the lake as you draw close to shore. Before jumping in, enjoy a gentle hike or horseback ride through cacao, plantain, and coffee plantations, and past a pre-Columbian petroglyph. Then you'll appreciate a good soak.

Reserva Natural Lagunas de Mecatepe and Río Manares (Lagunas de Mombacho) (2552-4848, 8874-3039; KM 71.2 Panamericana; open daily) Formerly a private reserve, these five scenic crater lakes at the foot of Mombacho Volcano are now officially protected. Most travelers book a tour (try **UCA Tierra y Agua**) to enjoy horseback riding, hiking, fishing, or just paddling around in inflatable boats—looking for lagoon crocodiles.

Nicaragua Butterfly Reserva (8895-3012; 305-854-9444 (U.S.); www.backyardnature .net/nbr; 3 km (1.2 miles) from Granada; open daily; US$7) Just a few minutes from Granada by taxi (US$5) or a 45-minute, well-signed walk, this breezy *mariposario*, or butterfly garden, raises 20 spectacular species for sale and export. Tour their enclosure, then explore some 5 km of nature trails. They also rent basic **cabins** ($).

Boat Tours

Granada has three major ports on Lake Nicaragua. The **Muelle de Granada**, at the end of Calle La Calzada, is the disembarkation point for the twice-weekly ferry to Isla Ometepe and San Carlos; see the Getting Around section. The ferry Hilario Sánchez also leaves the muelle every Sunday at 11 AM and 3 PM for the **Cruceros Familiares Lago Cocibolca** (2552-

2966, 2552-6618; US$6/3 adult/child), a two-hour "Family Cruise of Lake Cocibolca."

The second, much less formal "port," called **Cabaña Amarilla,** is on the south end of the centro turístico, where Peninsula Asese begins. You can arrange isleta tours at the cabaña or on the beach close to Inuit Kayak, in covered, motorized *pangas* (boats) seating 10 for about US$20 per boat per hour. Unless you look Nicaraguan, you'll be approached by touts offering the tours as you enter the centro turístico.

On the other side ("the armpit") of the peninsula, **Marina Cocibolca** (2228-1223; www .marinacocibolca.net; open 8 AM–10 PM) is a more proper port. Covered pangas can be rented at either of two excellent restaurants, **Puerto Asese** (2552-2269; info@aseselas isletas.com) and **Villas Mombacho** (2552-8552, 8873-0191; josesandino1@hotmail.com) for around US$15 per boat per hour. Faster, pricier boats are available at the dock, which you can hire around the isletas or to Isla Zapatera, an hour away over choppy water.

The north side of the peninsula is more developed, and home to a 1781 Spanish fortress. The south side is deeper, cleaner, and wilder, with great volcano views. A panga around all Asese, between Casa Amarilla and Marina Cocibolca, would probably cost US$120 per boat. In addition to the regular pangas, there are a few specialty operators by the lake, including:

Inuit Kayak (2608-3646 (English), 2614-0813; centro turístico) Cocibolca is a great place for beginning kayakers, and you'll ease into a three-hour tour of eight islands and Fortress San Pablo for US$30, or enjoy 30 islands in 4.5 hours for US$5 more. They also have early morning birding tours and rent catamarans.

Nicaragua Dulce (2552-6351, 8913-6535, 8982-3906; www.nicaraguadulce.com; Marina Cocibolca) Innovative operator offers ecologically inspired vessels, including kayaks (US$8/hour), rowboats (US$15/hour), and silent electric *pangas* (US$25/hour) seating 10—perfect for an island tour. Or spend the day at their private island, Isleta Zopango; transportation and lunch are US$45 per person, two-person minimum. They also rent bikes and arrange hotel pickup.

Velago Nicaragua (8458-0175, 8459-4699; www.velagogranada.com; sailinglakenicaragua @gmail.com; Calle El Arsenal, contiguo Casa Capricho) Offers skippered sailboat tours around the isletas and to Zapatera (maximum of four people), sailing lessons, boat rentals (16-foot sailboats and a 14-foot Hobie Cat), kayaks, and even trips down the Río San Juan.

Canopy Tours

Canopy Tour Miravalle (8471-5516, 8872-2555; canopymiravalle@yahoo.com; US$29/19 foreigner/Nicaraguan) Often combined with a trip to Mombacho National Park, this is a solid 17-platform, 11-cable, 2-km (1.2-mile) canopy tour with a Tarzan swing. Visitors can also visit their *mariposario,* or butterfly garden, and hanging bridges.

Mombacho Canopy Tour (8997-5846, 8852-9483; canopy@cablenet.com.ni; 3.5 km de la entrada al parque; open 9 AM–5 PM) Closed for repairs at press time.

Fishing

While you'll see kids transporting strings of *guapote,* or rainbow bass (more properly known as "jaguar cichlid" or "Aztec cichlid") from their bicycle handles, this part of the lake is apparently poor for fishing. However, just about any boat captain can take you to richer waters; Marina Cocibolca is your best bet.

Horseback Riding

Any operator can arrange horseback tours; **UCA Tierra y Agua** (see Lodging) is the community-conscious choice. There are also two specialty operators, both offering transport to rural regions just outside town.

Ride a Painted Pony Horseback Tours (8881-3758) Four-hour tours above Laguna de Apoyo include lunch.

Volcano Ranch (8806-5123; www.nicaraguavolcanoranch.com) Located in Diriá, this ranch offers horseback tours and deluxe accommodation.

Spas and Gyms

✪ **CocoBerry Spa and Alternative Medicine** (8887-2856, 8962-8110, 2552-2888; Calle La Libertad, Hotel La Bocona; closed Sun.) One of the best spas in Nicaragua is located in one of the soothing courtyards of Hotel La Bocona. In addition to excellent massages—cupping, hot rocks, Swedish, etc.—for US$25 per hour, they also do acupuncture, facials, and other spa and holistic treatments. Therapists are certified in Canada and Costa Rica.

Seeing Hands Blind Massage (parque central; open 9 AM–6 PM daily; cash only) Drop by the Euro Café to make reservations with a blind massage therapist upstairs, ranging from a US$3, 15-minute neck rub to a US$15, full-body table massage, in makeshift "rooms" on a balcony above the central park.

Spa de Granada (2552-4678; Calle Atravesada, frente BanCentro) New Hotel Spa Granada (formerly the Mombacho Beach Club) offers spa services next to their exceptional pool.

Pure (8481-3264; www.purenica.com; Calle Corrales, del Convento San Francisco 1.5 cuadras al lago) Gym geared to expats has a decent selection of weights, several cardio machines, and for a few dollars more per month, yoga, dance, and kickboxing classes. They also offer massages, facials, wraps, and other spa treatments.

SHOPPING

Banks and ATMs

There are several banks with ATMs clustered just west of the central park; **Banco America Central** (BAC; corner Calle Atravesada and Calle La Libertad) is usually the easiest place for foreigners to withdraw money on their credit card.

Coyotes, or moneychangers, are usually honest in Granada, and may charge a lower exchange rate than the banks. They may also be willing to exchange other currencies, including euros, quetzales, colones, Canadian dollars, and pounds. Know how much to expect back, and be aware that they may count out the final few córdoba extra slooooowly, hoping you'll retract your hand early.

Groceries

Granada has two major grocery stores. **Palí** (Calle Atravesada, frente Mercado Municipal) is cheaper, crowded, and disorganized, while **La Colonia** (2266-7070; Calle Inmaculada, de Esso, 1.5 cuadras este) is pricier, cleaner, and calmer, with more foreign brands. There are dozens of small *pulperías* selling the basics around town. **Enoteca Vinos y Más** (2552-8514; enotecavinosymas.granada@gmail.com; parque central) has Granada's best wine selection.

Markets
✪ **Mercado Municipal** (Calle Atravesada; open 6 AM–6 PM) Granada's sprawling maze of none-too-tidy stalls, centered on the faded-green, neoclassical 1890 marketplace, can be a bit intimidating. It's worth the effort, however, to find fresh fruits and veggies, inexpensive clothing, homemade pastries, *nacatamales*, and *baho* on weekends. Food is generally safe to eat, though the butcher section might throw off more delicate stomachs.

Antiques
✪ **El Anticuario** (2552-4457, 8686-6787; anticuariofelicia@gmail.com; Calle Atravesada, del Parque Sandino, 0.5 cuadra sur) Amazing assortment of museum-quality antiques—paintings, instruments, furniture, saints, tiles—packed into an old home.

Casa Museo Harold (8982-0597; haroldsandino@hotmail.com; Calle 14 de Septiembre, de bombero, 50 metros norte) The antique store that furnished the sets for the movie *Walker* is still offering authentic antiques and elegant junque.

El Recodo (2552-0901; www.casaelrecodo.com; Calle La Libertad, parque central, 4 cuadras oeste) The "oldest house in Granada" is stocked with a cool collection of books, antiques, and handicrafts—all at premium prices.

Clothing and Accessories
The best place to find handmade hippie jewelry, some of it very high quality, is on the central park and first few blocks of La Calzada. The first price offered is rarely the lowest.

✪ **Exapiel** (2552-2003; de Enitel 100 metros al lago) Nicaraguan leather, Spanish metal-work, and Italian design come together thanks to a talented women's collective as a tempting collection of handbags, belts, and hats.

Spices & Sugar (8465-4335; spicessugar@hotmail.com; Calle La Calzada, de parque central 1.5 cuadras al lago) Creative, flattering designs by Mignon Vega and other Nica designers, with items suitable for a business meeting or date.

Tienda Olé (2552-1461, 8616-7322; olenicaragua@yahoo.com; Calle La Calzada; open 9 AM–1 PM and 5 PM–9 PM; closed Sun.) Good prices on locally made clothing, ceramics, and very creative handicrafts—check out the purses made with woven plastic bags.

Galleries
✪ **Arte Visual** (2552-4176; www.c3mundos.org; open 9 AM–6 PM daily) Kitty-corner from Convento San Francisco, this cooperative and workshop for six top local painters has a variety of fantastic canvases to peruse.

Casa Sacuanjoche Art Gallery (2552-6151; galeria.casasacuanjoche.com; Avenida La Sirena Casa 207, del Gran Francia, 1 cuadra al lago, 1.5 al sur) Artist Alvaro Berroteran displays his detailed ink drawings and realistic still lives and cityscapes.

L'atelier (www.jmcalvet.com; Calle Real Xalteva 416) Jean Marc Calvet's obsessively detailed, fiercely colored acid trips on canvas are well worth checking out.

Souvenirs
There are several good souvenir and cigar shops on the west side of the central park, and some vendors set up right on the plaza.

Watch cigars being rolled at Doña Elba, home of the award-winning Verdadero Organic.

✪ **Doña Elba Cigars** (8860-6715; elbacigars@yahoo.com.mx; Iglesia Xalteva, 0.5 cuadras este 515) Nicaragua is well known for its fine cigars, and Doña Elba's was responsible for one of the world's top five at press time, the Verdadero Organic. Watch award-winning stogies being rolled right here, or ask about plantation tours, geared to large groups (they cater to the cruise ship crowd).

Las Manos de Chepito (8457-8497; Calle La Calzada, de parque central 150 metros al lago) Tour office has a huge selection of inexpensive souvenirs.

✪ **El Parche Gift Shop** (8473-7700; Calle 14 de Septiembre) Top-notch cooperative works with 15 craftspeople who produce excellent leatherwork, silver jewelry, organic soaps, handmade paper, and much more.

Books

Book lovers can also check out **El Recodo** (with a selection of new books covering Nicaragua, including glossy photography tomes) and **Casa de los Tres Mundos,** with lots of left-wing reading. Many businesses, such as **Oasis,** the **Bearded Monkey,** and **Garden Café,** also have book "exchanges" (you may need to pay a couple of dollars to make the exchange).

A different float carries the Virgin Mary every night leading up to Granada's La Gritería, on December 8.

Gonper Librerías (2552-4489; Calle El Arsenal) Huge bookstore carries mostly Spanish-language titles.

Librería Hispamer (2552-2347; Calle El Arsenal, contiguo Tres Mundos) Mostly Spanish-language and academic books include a lot of classics.

Mockingbird Books (2552-2146; parque central, costado norte) Part of Euro Café, this has the best selection of used English-language books in town.

EVENTS

Casa de los Tres Mundos (2552-4176; www.c3mundos.org; Plaza de la Independencia) sponsors live theater, music, and movies on the central park throughout the year. Check the signboard in front of the Portal de los Leones for schedules.

February

✪ **Festival de Poesía Internacional de Granada** (third week in February; www.festival poesianicaragua.com) The International Poetry Festival brings in poets from more than

100 countries, who take over Granada's historic center with sidewalk slams, live music, parades, more berets than you'd ever expect in this heat, and a main stage featuring the best poetry in the world. Make hotel reservations in advance.

March or April

Semana Santa (March or April, week before Easter) While most of Granada is at the beach by Thursday or so, there are parades, fireworks, and special Masses throughout Semana Santa, notably **Víacrucis Acuatico de las Isletas,** when the Stations of the Cross are reenacted by small boats in the Isletas.

August

Hípicas Granada (mid-August) Granada goes country with horse parades, beauty contests, fireworks, live entertainment, and the running of the bulls.

December

Expo-Festival Navideña (December) Beginning with La Purísima and ending around New Year's, Granada's Christmas calendar is full of public performances and events.

6

SAN JUAN DEL SUR

Summertime, and the Living's Easy

Nicaragua's sunny southern Pacific coastline has been sculpted over the eons into a series of fantastic bays. Each glittering crescent is distinct, unique, and an even lovelier echo of those that lie just beyond.

Some are shallow and almost unprotected, others deeply carved into the slender isthmus, shaped by the same offshore winds that bring endless barreling waves, and the surfers who love them, to these shores. Today, travelers of every stripe are making their way to these beautiful beaches, some pure white above colorful coral reefs, others volcanic pearl gray, nestled into quiet coves.

The most beautiful of them all, a wide, soft beach luxuriantly cradled in a perfect horseshoe bay, is San Juan del Sur. Once a fishing village, it is today Nicaragua's own nascent resort town, the postcard-perfect *playa* lined with a festive collection of hotels, restaurants, bars, and little shops strung between two steep and forested headlands.

The northern bluff, encrusted with opulent mansions, was recently topped with a massive statue of Jesus that quite consciously echoes Rio de Janeiro. At the rocky tip of the headland, however, you'll still see the bay's older guardian—the *Cara del Indio,* Face of the Indian.

The southern promontory protects what has long been an important seaport, where pre-Columbian seafarers, Spanish conquistadors, and writer Mark Twain first appreciated Nicaragua's charms. The first cruise ships began returning a few years ago, their smiling

Online Resources

Del Sur News Online (delsurnewsonline.com) The local, bilingual free weekly runs its witty news items online as well.

San Juan del Sur Guide (www.sanjuandelsurguide.com) Somewhat helpful guide lists businesses, services, and vacation rentals. The ✪ **blog** has regularly updated events listings, including everything from yoga classes to live music.

San Juan del Sur Surf Sand Culture (www.sanjuandelsur.org.ni) Limited information about hotels, restaurants, activities, and more.

✪ **San Juan Surf** (www.sanjuansurf.com) Very complete, attractive site has a range of hotel recommendations, restaurant listings, maps, and volunteer opportunities, as well as a classified section (used surfboards, vacation rentals).

Even if you don't surf, you'll enjoy a day trip exploring the northern beaches, each lovelier than the last.

passengers reviving San Juan del Sur's long-standing reputation as a most hospitable port of call.

Day trippers can base themselves at one of the thatch-roofed seafood restaurants lining the broad beach, where you can enjoy a few beers between sunbathing sessions, or just gaze out over the yachts and fishing boats, patrolled by pelicans in the rolling sea. Longer-term visitors can take water taxis (or ground transportation) to cleaner, wilder shores north and south of town. Those willing to make the effort will find epic waves, sea turtle sanctuaries, unspoiled fishing villages, luxurious ecolodges, stylish condominiums, tumbledown surf shacks, and everything in between.

Though the town itself has attracted a few upscale developments and fine hotels in recent years, the village itself still has a laid-back endless summer feel, with legendary nightlife and a relaxed year-round surf scene. Small and strollable, it's got lodging and dining options for every budget inhabiting its cheerfully painted wooden buildings, some dating from the Gold Rush.

The boom years of the late 1800s were epic, economically. San Juan del Sur was an unavoidable stop on the fast, safe, steamboat-and-rail "Nicaragua Route" between New York City and San Francisco. Today's land rush, however, may eclipse even that heady era. This region boasts some of the least expensive beachfront property in the Americas, and not even the 2008 global economic collapse caused much of a bump in development.

Thus, San Juan del Sur and the surrounding beaches are changing, with a growing expat community, rising property prices, new high rises, and even appearances on television shows like *Survivor* and *House Hunters International*. Though almost everyone agrees that this is, overall, for the best, there's a certain nostalgia for the small town it may never be again.

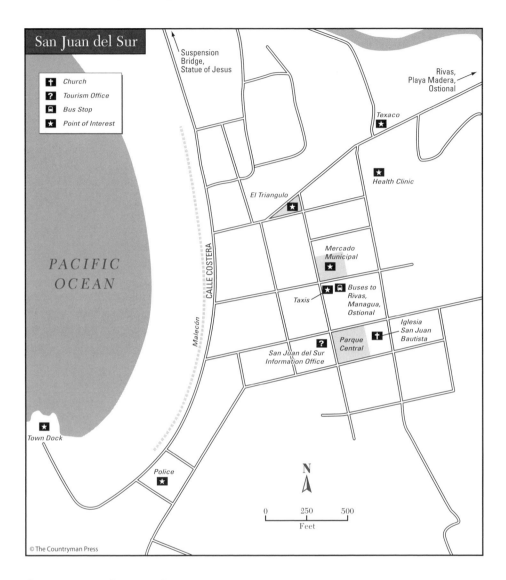

San Juan del Sur

- ✝ Church
- ? Tourism Office
- 🚌 Bus Stop
- ★ Point of Interest

Suspension Bridge, Statue of Jesus

Rivas, Playa Madera, Ostional

Texaco ★

Health Clinic ★

El Triangulo ★

PACIFIC OCEAN

CALLE COSTERA

Malecón

Mercado Municipal ★

★ 🚌 Buses to Rivas, Managua, Ostional

Taxis

Iglesia San Juan Bautista ✝

? Parque Central

San Juan del Sur Information Office

Town Dock ★

Police ★

N

0   250   500
Feet

© The Countryman Press

CRIME AND OTHER CONCERNS

San Juan del Sur is a party town, and has plenty of petty theft, illegal drug use, muggings, and occasionally violent crime. In general, it is safe for tourists, even into the wee hours, but be smart—walk in groups at night, avoid dark beaches, and leave valuables in the hotel.

If you are robbed, contact the **Police Department** (2568-2382; south end of the beach), which is better staffed and equipped than most thanks to **Amigos de la Policía** (Friends of the Police; www.amigosdelapolicia.com).

Party town rules apply: Never leave anything unguarded on the beach. Armed muggings have occurred on trails (even to groups), most notably on the path connecting San Juan del Sur and El Remanso. Take a shuttle or water taxi between beaches, or at least leave your camera at the hotel.

Charming hustlers of every sort mix and mingle, so please be a bit wary of new "friends."

They don't need to know where you're staying, they don't need to take you to a secluded beach under the stars, and they certainly don't need any money up front. If you ask a local to sit down to a beer, it is assumed that you are paying. If you are silly enough to let anyone—Nica or foreigner—into your room, make sure that all your valuables are secured.

TOURIST INFORMATION

The **SJDS Tourist Information Office** (parque central; open 8 AM–1 PM Mon. through Fri.), though it has a cool Sandino mural, didn't have its act together. Try private **Casa Oro Adventure Center** (2568-2415; www.casaeloro.com; de Hotel Colonial, 45 metros sur) in the big, yellow hostel around the corner, offering information, maps, tours, and shuttles. Look for the free weekly *Del Sur News*, with an excellent map.

GETTING AROUND

San Juan del Sur (SJDS) is at the end of an 18-km (11-mile) paved spur road off of the Panamerican Highway, which exits west at the tiny town of La Virgen, 12 km (8 miles) south of Rivas. There are direct buses from Managua, but most travelers will change buses (or grab a US$20 cab) in Rivas, with regular service to SJDS. Several tourist shuttles run between SJDS and both Granada and Managua.

If you are coming from the Costa Rican border, you can take any Rivas bus (US$1.25; every 15 minutes), and get off in La Virgen. There's a shady tree where you can wait for buses (US$0.75) or collective taxis (US$4) to SJDS. It's more convenient to grab a cab (US$20) at the border; find other travelers to share the ride. For information about crossing the Costa Rican border, see the Planning Your Trip chapter.

San Juan del Sur itself is small and easily explored on foot, with most hotels, bars, and restaurants located within three blocks of the beach. Taxis park next to the buses, on the south side of the Mercado Municipal.

The coastal road that connects SJDS to the beaches north and south of town is unpaved, and a four-wheel drive is necessary during the rainy season. Public transport can almost always get through, thanks to an Ostional bus that puts most military vehicles to shame, and cab drivers with special ninja skills.

If you're walking north, you can cross the river for the hike to the Jesus statue and Bahía Nacascolo on the graceful **pedestrian suspension bridge,** saving 2 km on La Chocolata (at low tide, people make the shortcut in cars, but sometimes get stuck).

To go farther north than Nacascolo, most people without rental cars or mountain bikes take private shuttles from SJDS. These are geared to surfers, and stop at Playa Madera (actually Playones), which is within walking distance of Playas Marsella, Majagual, and Arena Blanca—with snorkeling. Playa Ocotal is either a long walk or boat trip, unless you're a guest at plush Morgan's Rock. The coastal road does *not* continue to Playa Pie de Gigante; you'll either go by boat or backtrack through Rivas.

Fewer private shuttles regularly serve the beaches south of San Juan del Sur, except neighboring Remanso. Instead, three daily Bluebird buses make the run from the market all the way to Ostional, 30 km (18 miles) south of SJDS. Note that the bus drops you well away from some beaches, notably Playa Yankee, which requires a steep 25-minute hike (at least) back up to the main road.

The first beach heading south is Remanso, with decent waves and trail access to the surfing beaches of Tamarindo and Hermosa, to the south. This region has most of SJDS's reported muggings, so be smart and safe (or just pay for the water taxi).

Farther south is gorgeous but isolated Playa Yankee (Yanquí), with good waves and two amazing B&Bs; then broad, white Playa El Coco, 17 km (9 miles) south of SJDS, with more lodging options. La Flor Wildlife Reserve is 5 km farther south, and finally, you'll arrive in El Ostional, with charming but basic accommodations, at the end of the road.

Car

While the town of San Juan del Sur is connected to the main highway system by a recently improved, beautifully paved road, access to the beaches to the north and south is unpaved. These roads are passable to normal cars in dry season (December through mid-May) but it's nice to have a four-wheel drive anyway. It's four-wheel drive only in the rainy season. Never leave any valuables visible in your car.

Alamo (2277-1117; www.alamonicaragua.com) has rental cars on-site at Hotel Casa Blanca, and lets you cross the Costa Rican border for a fee. Other hotels and tour offices arrange rental cars, but many keep their vehicles in Managua. Allow two hours for them to drive your car down. **Hostal Beach Fun Casa 28** (2568-2441; marvincalde@hotmail.com; zona central), north of the market, rents motorcycles.

Buses

While international buses leave from Rivas, Granada, and Managua, you can buy your tickets right here in San Juan del Sur, at the Mundotel **Tica Bus office** (2568-2427; del Mercado, 1.5 cuadras oeste). Bring your passport.

Regular buses leave from the south side of the market. To get to the Costa Rican border (Peñas Blancas), have the Rivas bus drop you at **La Virgen** (US$0.75), then catch another bus to **Peñas Blancas** (US$1.25).

Rivas US$1; every 45 minutes 5 AM–5 PM (fewer on Sunday)
Managua US$3.25; 5 AM, 5:45 AM, 7 AM, 3:20 PM
Ostional (US$2.25) Buses leave Rivas at 11:30 AM, 3 PM, and 4 PM, and stop in San Juan del Sur at 1 PM, 4 PM, and 5 PM. Buses return from Ostional at 5 AM, 6:30 AM, and 3 PM, passing Playa El Coco at 6 AM, 7:30 AM, and 4 PM.

Private Shuttle

There are several private shuttles offering convenient transport to the beaches north and south of SJDS, as well as Granada, San Jorge (with ferries to Isla Ometepe), and Managua. Any of these companies can arrange private transport.

Adelante Express (8850-6070, 8850-6064, 2568-2390; www.adelanteexpress.com) Offers shuttles (US$35) to Granada at 7:15 AM, 9 AM, and 12:30 PM daily, returning at 10:45 AM, 1:15 PM, and 3:45 PM. Continuing service to Managua can be arranged. They have a "stop and shop" option for people who need a few hours in Managua.
Arena Caliente Surf Camp (8815-3247; www.arenacaliente.com; zona central) Arranges cheap shuttles to Playa Madera (US$6), Remanso (US$6), Yankee (US$12), and elsewhere, and one-way trips to the Costa Rican border (US$15) for groups of five or more.
Casa Oro Adventure Center (2568-2415; www.casaeloro.com; de Hotel Colonial, 45 met-

While the unpaved roads to beaches north and south of San Juan del Sur are well maintained in the dry season, drivers may run into other challenges.

ros sur) Three daily shuttles to Playas Madera, Majagual, Matilda, and Marsella; and two daily shuttles to Playa Remanso. There are often shuttles to Playa Yankee and Coco, so ask. This is also the SJDS office of **Paxeos** (2552-8291; www.paxeos.com), with daily shuttles to Granada and Managua.

Iskra Travel (8413-5510, 8425-5039; www.iskratravel.com; Gato Negro, 1.5 cuadras norte) Offers regular shuttle to Managua (US$40; MGA and Tica Bus) via Granada, at 7 AM, 9:30 AM, and noon.

Nicarao Lake Tours (2568-2244, 8808-1980 (Granada); www.nicaraolake.com; US$15–25) Full-service tour operator offers four daily shuttles to San Jorge and Granada at 8 AM, 10:30 AM, 2:30 PM, and 3:30 PM.

Taxi

Cabs line up next to the bus stop, on the south side of the market. It costs about US$1 anywhere around town. Designated *colectivo* taxis leave for Rivas (US$1.60 per person) when full, while private taxis for four to Rivas or San Jorge cost US$10.

You can also get taxis (prices change) to Remanso (US$7.50); Playa El Coco (US$40); Madera, Playones, and Majagual (US$10); the Costa Rican border (US$25); Granada (US$40); Managua (US$80); and beyond.

The friendly, strollable streets of San Juan del Sur are plied by all sorts of vehicles.

Water Taxis

In addition to the many fishing, sailing, and surf tours available, there are regular water taxis between the most popular beaches. You can also charter private boats to Playa Madera/Majagual (US$40), Gigante (US$70), Santana (US$90), Popoyo (US$100), Yankee (US$30), and El Coco (US$60).

Rana Tur (2568-2066; ranatours@gmail.com; Calle Costera) Look for the stand across from the BDF bank to book their daily US$10 shuttle to Majagual, leaving SJDS at 11 AM and returning at 5 PM. They also offer good-value tours.

Sailboat Shuttle (8747-4891; kassify@nicasur.com; US$25) You must have reservations for the Wednesday sailboat between SJDS and Playa Gigante.

LODGING

Lodging in this region really runs the gamut, from rickety surf shacks and tiny cement backpacker crash pads to fabulous handcrafted ecolodges, multimillion-dollar B&Bs, and plush vacation communities—with plenty of wonderful options in between.

Budget travelers will find my favorite cheapies in "Other Hotels," later in this chapter, but there are dozens more within five blocks of the bus stop. Pick one that looks good to you, and ask to see a room. There is plenty of competition in this town, and no reason to settle for grime.

Midrange and top-end travelers will find the widest variety of accommodations in Nicaragua, both in town and up and down the coast. There are several more upscale hotels slated for construction; if this is your category, check online for the latest listings.

Lodging Price Code

The cost of lodging is based on an average per-room, double occupancy rate during peak season (December through April). Nicaragua's 15 percent sales tax and gratuities are not included; note that paying cash sometimes results in taxes being waived. Prices are much higher during the Christmas holidays and Semana Santa (Easter Week), when just about every hotel in San Juan del Sur is booked weeks in advance. Plan ahead.

Inexpensive ($)	Up to US$25
Moderate ($$)	US$25 to US$60
Expensive ($$$)	US$60 to US$100
Very Expensive ($$$$)	US$100 and up

Hotels

San Juan del Sur

AVENTURA LODGE
Owner: Edwin Ruiz
8358-5924, 8903-7622
www.aventurasanjuan.com
aventura@surfzoneresorts.com
Salida por Playa Remanso
Price: Moderate to Expensive
Credit Cards: Not yet
Handicap Access: No
Wifi: Yes

On the outskirts of San Juan del Sur, at the turnoff to the southern beaches, this hidden little lodge is a shady, green sanctuary away from the city's endless summer. The gardens are centered on a gorgeous little pool and waterfall, surrounded by bamboo- and hardwood-accented rooms.

With the exception of the fan-cooled "tree house," a rather basic (but atmospheric) dorm made of bamboo and thatch, the rooms and apartments are modern and comfortable. All have air-conditioning, cable TV, tasteful original art, and wood furnishings. Family rooms have kitchenettes, and anyone can use the barbecue.

HOTEL AZUL PITAHAYA
Manager: Juan Tinoco
2568-2294
www.hotelazulsanjuan.com
Mercado, 1 cuadra oeste
Price: Moderate
Credit Cards: Yes
Handicap Access: Challenging
Wifi: Yes

The best deal in town is in this cute blue building. It looks simple from the outside, and it is, but good-sized rooms with polished wood accents are perfect, from the soothing paint schemes to the high-quality mattresses and great lighting. All include DirecTV, air-conditioning and fan, and modern private baths, as well as breakfast at the attached ✪ **Barrio Café.** They can sometimes arrange free transportation to area beaches, and provide all sorts of information about other offerings around town.

CASA BLANCA
2568-2568, 970-744-2082 (U.S.)
www.elhotelcasablanca.com
info@elhotelcasablanca.com
Calle Costera
Price: Expensive
Credit Cards: Yes
Handicap Access: Yes
Wifi: Yes

Though this good hotel has been eclipsed in recent years by newer luxury properties, it still has its five-star location and 14 polished doubles surrounding a flagstone courtyard with a small pool. The ample, attractive courtyards have plenty of hangout space, and there's even a shared kitchen—unusual in this price range. The suite is great, a hardwood, stand-alone structure with lighthouse-style details and a private porch overlooking the water.

CASA MARINA CONDOMINIUM HOTEL

Owner: Michael Jacovony
2568-2677, 925-353-1703 (U.S.)
www.casamarinacondos.com
info@casamarinacondos.com
Contiguo al BDF
Price: Expensive to Very Expensive
Credit Cards: Yes
Handicap Access: Challenging
Wifi: In restaurant only

Right on the malecón, this five-floor condo offers great views from huge two-bedroom, two-bathroom, two-TV apartments. They sleep six comfortably, with full (but small) kitchens, tastefully furnished living areas, hot water, balconies, and other amenities. They're sort of plain, but a good deal for families or groups. Try to get a unit as close to the top as possible—there's an elevator.

HOTEL COLONIAL

Administrator: Alvaro José Calderón
2568-2539
www.hotel-nicaragua.com
hotel.colonial@ibw.com.ni
Mercado Municipal, 1 cuadra al mar, 0.5 cuadra sur
Price: Moderate
Credit Cards: Yes
Handicap Access: Challenging
Wifi: Yes

Though you'd never know from the outside, this solid midrange choice has fantastic gardens, a gorgeous green space strewn with archways, and hidden spots to relax. Spacious rooms are great too, with all the modern amenities and local color, including Guatemalan fabrics, original art, and more. They also offer board rentals and surf tours.

IRISH HOUSE HOTEL AND PUB

Owners: Roberto and Elisha Ibáñez
8973-7855

irish.house2009@gmail.com
del Mercado, 2 cuadras norte
Price: Moderate
Credit Cards: Not yet
Handicap Access: No
Wifi: Yes

Look for the modern, whitewashed building with an Irish flag, to find Nicaragua's finest cuisine and adult beverages from the Emerald Isle. It's served by a friendly Irish-Nica couple that decided they preferred the sunshine of San Juan del Sur.

Upstairs, they offer huge, new rooms—a fantastic deal with stove, refrigerator, orthopedic beds, private baths, cable TVs, and balconies overlooking the street scene. It seems like things might get noisy if the pub downstairs is packed, but it closes at midnight.

✪ HOTEL VILLA ISABELLA

Owner: Jane C. Mirandette
2568-2568, 8877-7791
villaisabellasjds.com
janem101@aol.com
costado norte de la Iglesia Católica
Price: Moderate to Very Expensive
Credit Cards: Yes
Handicap Access: Yes
Wifi: Yes

This truly excellent hotel is built around a fine old wooden mansion polished to a modern level of comfort, filled with tasteful handmade furnishings, good art, and rooms for every budget. The least expensive rooms—there are two—share a spotless bathroom while still enjoying all the other amenities: excellent beds; TVs with DVD; free coffee and hot tea in the lobby; a big, delicious free breakfast; a small pool in the courtyard; and the wonderful porch out front, with rocking chairs.

More spacious rooms with private baths add art, hair dryers, nicer furnishings, and other amenities, while a newer building in the back has apartments with full kitchens, lots of light, great furnishings, and the same

Luxurious lodging options are cropping up all over the coast, though few can match Las Orquideas in Playa Yankee.

excellent service that guests in the hotel portion enjoy.

A portion of your very reasonable rate goes to operate SJDS's first public lending library, **Biblioteca Móvil** (www.sjds biblioteca.org), which accepts donations.

EL JARDÍN GARDEN HOTEL AND RESTAURANT

Owner: April Whann
2568-2677, 925-353-1703 (U.S.)
www.eljardinsanjuandelsur.com
awhann@hotmail.com
Nacascolo Bay
Price: Expensive to Very Expensive
Credit Cards: Yes
Handicap Access: Yes
Wifi: Yes

Perched high atop a bluff with magnificent views over San Juan del Sur and neighboring Nacascolo Bay, this Mexican-modern architectural marvel is one of the nicest boutique hotels in the country. The complex was designed by architect and co-owner Valerie Castillo, a symphony of geometric forms that connect and divide the 11 rooms. These are brightly painted and creatively laid out—with fans, fantastic showers, built-in nooks for privacy, and a complimentary breakfast at their renowned restaurant. Rates drop for longer stays.

The **restaurant** (D; open Thur. through Sun.; $$–$$$) changes its menu regularly, but features Asian-Mexican fusion dishes, such as the Thai green papaya salad, Aztec tortilla soup, and sweet-and-sour mahi

Even if you can't stay, it's worth dining at Pelican Eyes to appreciate the unparalleled view over San Juan del Sur's perfect bay.

mahi. It's all fresh and healthy, assuming you consider a Kahlua chocolate cheesecake healthy. Note that this spot is most easily accessible in a rental car or cab—it's a long, steep climb from the main road.

✪ PELICAN EYES HOTEL AND RESORT (PIEDRAS Y OLAS)

2563-7000, 866-350-0555 (toll free)
www.piedrasyolas.com
reservations@piedrasyolas.com
de la Parroquia, 1.5 cuadras al este
Price: Very Expensive
Credit Cards: Yes
Handicap Access: No
Wifi: Yes

The finest hotel in San Juan del Sur proper is also a beloved bastion of the community, with proceeds from its excellent rooms, villas, and two-story vacation homes going to various community projects.

There are several room configurations, composed of the hotel's signature flowing whitewashed stucco, with high cane ceilings, tropical landscaping, and environmental sustainability in mind. Larger cabinas are quite luxurious, with kitchenettes, marble sinks, hand-woven bedspreads, and huge satellite TVs; Ensueño, Dulce Vita, and Madroño are right next to the magnificent upper pool.

Full-sized casas, which are privately owned, include full gourmet kitchens and one or two bedrooms; some have private plunge pools. If you don't have a rental car, note that these are a steep ten-minute walk from the lobby.

Even if you don't stay here, stop by to enjoy views over the bay from either of their good **restaurants** (B, L, D; $$–$$$$) offering upscale international and Nica cuisine. For a US$10 day pass, you can use the fabulous pools as well, or drop by **Casa Tranquila** (2563-7000 ext 310) for a spa treatment. Locals come up the hill for the popular happy hour.

Pelican Eyes benefits the **Fundación A. Jean Brugger** (2568-2110; www.fundacion ajbrugger.org), an educational foundation, and **Stones and Waves Veterinary Clinic**, which cares for hurt and abandoned animals. If you need a cat, they've got plenty of vaccinated, fixed kitties to spare.

PARK AVENUE VILLAS
Owners: Ralph and Renda Hewitt
2837-0582
www.parkavenuevillas.com
info@parkavenuevillas.com
200 meters north of El Gato Negro; see their online map for directions
Price: Expensive to Very Expensive
Credit Cards: Yes
Handicap Access: Challenging
Wifi: Yes

With sweeping sunset views from fine wicker chairs on the expansive porch, this spot would be a winner even without all the extras offered by the thoughtful owners. Though it seems pricey, you get a lot more than elsewhere; the "very expensive" rooms are actually two-bedroom suites with full kitchens that sleep at least four.

All the rooms have restful color schemes, tasteful furnishings, great mattresses and bedspreads, air-conditioning, and TV/DVD players with a library of more than 200 movies. There's a big pool and on-site kitchen, plus one big bonus: The owners can take you out for a spin on their sailboat (www.nicasailing.com; US$50 per person, four-person minimum).

✪ LA POSADA AZUL
Manager: María Suárez
2568-2524, 8647-5244
www.laposadaazul.com
info@laposadaazul.com
BDF, 0.5 cuadras este
Price: Expensive to Very Expensive
Credit Cards: Yes
Handicap Access: No
Wifi: Yes

A work of art in and of itself, this flawlessly restored, century-old wooden mansion is both stylish and serene. Rooms are airy and elegant, with a touch of Santa Fe style (the owners are from New Mexico) evident in the atmospheric mix of period antiques and handmade Masatepe furnishings, arranged across the warm saltillo tiles. Thick European-style mattresses draped in colorful telas, piping hot water in the wonderful bathrooms, and icy cold air-conditioning guarantee a good sleep.

Wake up to a wonderful breakfast on the wooden porch overlooking palm-shaded gardens filled with flagstones, flowers, and a fine fountain—as well as a deep blue pool. It is an oasis of calm in the midst of an endless summer.

HOTEL ROYAL CHATEAU
Owners: Idalia Argentina Sevilla and Juan José Sevilla
2568-2551, 321-251-7405 (U.S.)
hotelroyalchateau.com
hotelroyalchateau@yahoo.com
Mercado Municipal, 1 cuadra este
Price: Moderate
Credit Cards: Yes
Handicap Access: No
Wifi: In most of the hotel

It's amazing how much farther your money goes three blocks from the beach. This three-story hotel offers value with large, freshly painted rooms, modern cool water baths, cable TV, great beds, and the option of air-conditioning. The shared porches

The End of the Road: Ostional

The tourists thin as you bump south along the unpaved coastal road, past Playa El Coco and La Flor Wildlife Reserve, to the sparsely populated southern beaches bordering Costa Rica. Few foreigners make it this far south, through the forests of howler monkeys and iguanas, to the millennia-old fishing village of Ostional.

The view from the powdery pearl gray beach is astounding, toward vast Santa Elena Peninsula, which protects Ostional's rich waters. The town is remote: phone service is spotty, Internet nonexistent, and services basic. However, there is regular bus service from San Juan del Sur, and locals operate a well-run and accessible community-tourism initiative.

Several unsigned guesthouses all offer the same deal: It's US$15 per person, cash only, for a spotlessly clean, fan-cooled room with orthopedic mattresses, kitchen access, purified water, and breakfast. All are part of collectively operated Turismo Comunitario (ostionalnica.blogspot.com), so while there are slight differences in quality, prices are set. Ask anyone to point you toward "hospedaje."

Local guides offer four-hour boat tours to a virgin beach for snorkeling, then up the Río Ostional to see birds and iguanas (US$10 per person, five-person minimum). You can also arrange night trips to see nesting turtles at La Flor, guided hikes, horseback rides, traditional fishing trips, or visits to inconsistent beach and reef breaks close by.

Hospedaje Glenda (8906-6436; green house with red fence) About 1 km away from the town and beach on the bus line, this four-room hostel is a couple of dollars cheaper and much more comfortable, with polished wood rooms, decent private baths, and mellow shared porches.

El Jícaro (506-8828-0437 (Costa Rica); behind the church) Look for the peach house with a wooden fence, behind the cinderblock church, to find this sunny spot with adorable rooms and frilly décor in the super-clean shared bath.

✪ **Hotel Manta Raya** (8366-7789; ospemanta@yahoo.es; 50 metros del mar) Sky-blue, wooden stand-alone cabin is right on the beach, with two simple rooms. Both have private cool baths, a shared porch, mosquito nets, and the best location in town.

El Modroño (no phone) Right by the bus stop, this yellow house with a black fence is a good choice for travelers with mobility issues, offering three clean, tiled rooms, one with a private bath on one level, and lots of rocking chairs.

Two buses per day go to Ostional (US$2.25), leaving Rivas at 11:30 AM, 3 PM, and 4 PM, and stopping in San Juan del Sur at 1 PM, 4 PM, and 5 PM. Buses return from Ostional at 5:30 AM, 7 AM, and 3 PM.

---

overlook appealing gardens, and there's a restaurant. But it's the little extras—great service, solid security, and towels rolled into little swans—that make the rather simple spot shine. Great for families.

VICTORIANO HOTEL

General Manager: Franzel Mairena
2568-2005, 2568-2006
www.hotelvictoriano.com.ni
info@hotelvictoriano.com.ni

Paseo Maritimo, costado norte Enitel
Price: Expensive to Very Expensive
Credit Cards: Yes
Handicap Access: Yes
Wifi: Yes

This gingerbread-trimmed 1902 Victorian mansion offers particularly fine bay views from the porch and pool, once enjoyed by the Somoza family. After the Revolution, the house was confiscated by the FSLN, which recently turned it into a hotel with profits going to benefit retired soldiers.

The 21-room boutique property does have a bit of that "government-run" sterility about it, but the common areas and rooms are light-filled and pretty, with amazing furnishings, chandeliers, air-conditioning, hot baths, and other amenities. The hotel is fully equipped for wheelchairs, and rates include a full breakfast.

South of San Juan del Sur

PLAYA REMANSO
REMANSO BEACH RESORT
Owner: Hector Sanchez
2568-2208, 2568-2259
www.remansobeach.com
remanso@ibw.com.ni
Playa Remanso, KM5 Camino Ostional
Price: Expensive
Credit Cards: Yes
Handicap Access: No
Wifi: Yes
Special: Day-trippers pay US$10, redeemable at the restaurant

There's only one hotel on this beach, known for a solid surf break, and better waves a short walk south to Playas Hermosa and Tamarindo. The aging, isolated lodge was closed for remodeling when I visited, which presumably means that their large, tiled, air-conditioned rooms—with partial kitchens and DirecTV—will be even nicer.

The grounds are on the weird side, filled with classically inspired statues and antiques from the Spanish and pre-Columbian periods. The beach certainly is nice. Several shuttle operators in town offer private round-trip transport to Remanso.

PLAYA YANKEE (YANQUÍ)
LATIN LATITUDES BED & BREAKFAST
Owners: Alan and Carolina
8671-9698 (messages only)
www.latinlatitudes.com
latinlatitudes@hotmail.com
Playa Yankee, KM11.5 Camino Ostional
Price: Moderate to Expensive

Credit Cards: No
Handicap Access: No
Wifi: Yes

Escape to this boutique B&B, high above Playa Yankee in the trees and deep blue sky. There are just three creatively designed rooms, with slate floors, sustainable hardwood furnishings from Simplemente Madera, and Guatemalan tapestries fluttering in the breeze. All have excellent beds and incredible views from the showers (two rooms share, while the suite has a private bath) and courtyard patio hammocks.

There is an emphasis on sustainability: There's no air-conditioning or hot water, and they've even a xeriscaped lawn with local cactus. Grounds are steep and it's quite a walk to the beach, so it's not for everyone. But it's beautiful, and there's a kitchen for guests. If you don't have a car, note that it's a 1-km walk from the bus stop (or US$20 cab ride from town).

ORQUIDEA DEL SUR
Owner: Robert Latham
www.orquideadelsur.com
info@orquideadelsur.com
Playa Yankee, KM11.5 Camino Ostional
Price: Very Expensive
Credit Cards: Not yet
Handicap Access: Challenging
Wifi: Yes

This regal bed & breakfast is easily among the most luxurious accommodations in Nicaragua, with world-class amenities and family-style attention. The main building's western face is a wall of glass, welcoming the wild, white-sand shore far below into an absolutely modern living space. The handmade furnishings contrast nicely with a high-end entertainment system and professional kitchen.

Every amenity seems an excuse to add more art, from the glittering mica in the concrete foundation, to the murals surrounding the honeymoon suite's hot tub.

Even the regular rooms are outfitted with colorful paintings, partial kitchens, and rainforest showers. The real masterpiece is the pool—a fancifully landscaped, multi-level creation with waterfalls, fountains, gardens, and hammocks that you'll never want to leave.

PLAYA EL COCO

✪ CASA DE DRAGONFLY

Manager: Heidi Henderson
8385-2032
jimcalifornia@gmail.com
Playa El Coco
Price: Inexpensive to Moderate
Credit Cards: Not yet
Handicap Access: No
Wifi: Yes

Brand-new at press time, this pretty boutique property offers Spanish style just steps from the sand. Wrapped around a stone patio and picturesque pool, the broad, shady porches provide ample respite from the sun, where you can enjoy your complimentary breakfast or something from the beachfront bar (with a pool table).

There are only three spacious, fan-cooled rooms, with high ceilings, dark wood furnishings, and private baths made with smooth river rocks. One can be rented as a dorm. There's a full kitchen that guests can usually use. The owners have boogie boards and can arrange horseback rides and other tours.

PARQUE MARÍTIMO EL COCO

General Manager: Rodolfo Chávez Vásquez
8999-8069
www.playaelcoco.com.ni
reservaciones@playaelcoco.com.ni
Playa El Coco
Price: Expensive
Credit Cards: Yes
Handicap Access: For some units
Wifi: Restaurant only

This older oceanfront community of privately owned vacation villas fronts one of the loveliest beaches in the country, broad white sands bookended by dramatically carved headlands.

The shady vacation village comprises independently designed houses made with elegantly crafted hardwoods, softly rounded stucco, and ceramic tiles. Some have a more traditional vibe, while others are more modern; all are air-conditioned, and most have full kitchens, hot water, and private porches. It's got a decidedly different vibe than newer developments, more local and laid back.

Be sure to check out their restaurant, **Puesto del Sol** (B, L, D; $$–$$$)—with incredible views, a pool that diners are free to use, quality Nicaraguan cuisine, and traditional German pastries.

North of San Juan del Sur

BUENA VISTA SURF CLUB

Owners: Marielle Mulder and Marc Krop
8863-4180, 8863-3312
www.buenavistasurfclub.com
info@buenavistasurfclub.com
Playa Madera
Price: Expensive to Very Expensive
Credit Cards: Yes
Handicap Access: No
Wifi: Yes

High above Madera's epic wave, this creatively constructed ecolodge brings to mind a more comfortable version of the Swiss Family Robinson. Suspended in the canopy, two hardwood tree houses with rustling palapa roofs have fine furnishings, great mattresses, and strategically hung hammocks on private porches. A master bedroom sleeps four comfortably.

This is an actual ecolodge, so there's no air-conditioning, TV, or reliable hot water (everything is solar), but the polished yoga platform has exceptional views and the family-style meals get raves.

Venerable vacation community Parque Marítimo El Coco is hidden in the forest fringing the isolated white sand beaches of Playa El Coco.

EMPALME DE LAS PLAYAS

Owners: Roy and Karen Goldman
8803-7280, 8994-9013
www.playamarsella.com
the_empalme@hotmail.com
Entrada Playa Marsella
Price: Moderate
Credit Cards: Not yet
Handicap Access: No
Wifi: Yes

This friendly hotel at the empalme, or turnoff, to Playa Marsella is also suspended in the forest canopy—four simple bamboo-and-thatch cabanas, connected by wooden decks and porches. The rooms are ecochic: not fancy but comfortable, with private baths, bamboo furniture, stone accents, and mosquito nets.

Subtle hippie touches—beaded curtains, exotic tapestries—add to the whole ambiance. Harmony with nature? You've got it [cue the howler monkeys just outside]. Breakfast is included, but be sure to arrange other delicious meals. There's a two-night minimum stay.

LAS MAÑANITAS

Owners: Elisabeth Trudeau and Alain Sanche
8803-8364
www.mananitas.net
lasmananitas@live.ca
camino a Playa Majagual
Price: Moderate
Credit Cards: No
Handicap Access: No
Wifi: No

Hidden in the forest, these two secluded bungalows with fine private porches share a shaded patch in the wilderness. The loft-style accommodations are decorated with clever built-in furnishings and richly hued Guatemalan tapestries. There's no air-conditioning, TV, or wifi, but each includes access to bicycles, three dogs, and a private kitchenette. They also offer gourmet meals ($$–$$$) on the porch, where you can watch the monkeys while you dine.

You're a half-hour walk from the beach on a tough unpaved road, making this a better choice for folks with four-wheel-drive transportation or a good pair of sneakers. The owners speak several languages and arrange any tour.

MANGO ROSA ADVENTURE TRAVEL AND SURF RESORT
Manager: Chad Unser
8477-3692, 8403-5326
www.mangorosanicaragua.com
greg@mangorosanicaragua.com
Playa Madera, KM6.5 Chocolate
Price: Expensive
Credit Cards: Yes
Handicap Access: Yes
Wifi: In the bar and some units

This welcoming spot isn't right on the beach, but eight houses scattered through the dry tropical forest grounds have relaxed private porches with hammocks, and access to an enormous pool. There are four stamped-concrete "small houses," sleeping four comfortably—with huge kitchens, SkyTV, air-conditioning, and one bedroom—while the "large houses" sleep eight. They're all very spacious, but sparsely decorated.

Staff can arrange fishing trips on their 30-foot panga (ask about night trips), booze cruises, horseback rides, surf lessons, or anything else. The **restaurant** (B, L, D; $–$$$) brings in local party people for the festive scene, good food, and very full bar.

✪ MORGAN'S ROCK
Owners: Eugenio and Claire Ponçon
2563-9005
www.morgansrock.com
info@morgansrock.com
Playa Ocotal
Price: Very Expensive
Credit Cards: Yes
Handicap Access: No
Wifi: Yes

This luxurious ecolodge overlooking serene Playa Ocotal is one of the best hotels in Nicaragua. Handcrafted from sustainably harvested hardwoods by Simplemente Madera (www.simplementemadera.com), each villa hidden throughout the dry tropical forest is a work of art. You can watch the howler monkeys swinging through the vines that cascade between you and the almost private gray crescent cove from your enormous bed, or descend the trails to delightful beachfront bungalows.

Tranquil and isolated, it would be easy to spend all day on your private porch's hanging bed, enjoying every thoughtful architectural detail. But don't miss breakfast at the traditional farm, offering a bit more insight into Nicaraguan culture than the average five-star experience.

PARQUE MADERA HOTEL
Director: Tyler Tibbs
8872-7310, 8872-7310
www.parquemadera.com
parquemadera@gmail.com
500 metros arriba Playones (Playa Madera)
Price: Inexpensive to Moderate
Credit Cards: No
Handicap Access: No
Wifi: Yes

This "Center for Art, Ecology, Natural Medicine, and Sustainable Living" sits atop a bluff a few hundred meters from the beach, wrapped in tropical rainforest and permaculture gardens with medicinal, herbal, and other local plants threaded through by hiking trails. The center itself is still a work in progress, but sometimes offers classes and retreats teaching herbology, ceramics, or yoga.

The dorms are great, offering only double beds (US$15/20 single/couple) with stone-inlaid, outdoor, shared baths. Three private rooms are whitewashed with shell accents and comfortable beds. They also allow camping for US$5 per night. Stop in for a mostly homegrown meal at their open-air **restaurant** (B, L, D; $$) with a la carte lunches and family-style dinners. Diners can use their hiking trails and wifi.

SURF ZONE

Managers: Gretchen and Thijs
8384-9834, 8408-4788
www.surfzonesanjuan.com
surfzonesanjuan@gmail.com
Playa Marsella and Madera, 6.5 km from SJDS on La Chocolata
Price: Moderate
Credit Cards: Yes
Handicap Access: No
Wifi: Yes

This new surf hotel gets points for the courtyard pool with a bridge, and the mani-

cured gardens with hammocks and bamboo lounge chairs. The palapa-topped buildings are freshly painted with colorful murals, and have a community kitchen and barbecue, TV room, and bar service.

Comfortable, fan-cooled rooms display a similarly cool combination of style and comfort, with lots of cane detailing and tropical-themed artwork. Book a surf package, or just rent the room with breakfast.

VILLA MAR MARSELLA BEACH

Owner: Urbana Cascante Herrera
2568-3008, 8663-0666
villamarmarsellabeach@gmail.com
Playa Marsella
Price: Moderate
Credit Cards: Yes
Handicap Access: No
Wifi: No

The only hotel right on stunning Playa Marsella is this very basic, Nica-owned cement lodge with a seafood restaurant (B, L, D; $$–$$$) on the front porch. Dark rooms have a bed, private baths, fluorescent lights, and some fake flowers for ambiance; four rooms also have air-conditioning. But it's clean, and what a beach!

Vacation Rentals

The rugged coastline is blooming with new "luxury developments," some of them successful communities of gorgeous vacation homes—others lonely, sunbleached entry gates in the middle of nowhere. Unless you're renting a villa right in town, such as one of the vacation homes at **Pelican Eyes** (listed earlier), you'll probably want a car.

These are just a few of your options. For many, many more listings, check **Vacation Rentals By Owner** (www.vrbo.com) and **Trip Advisor** (www.tripadvisor.com).

Aurora Beachfront Reality (www.aurorabeachfront.com) Lists rentals up and down the coast.

Bahía del Sol (2568-2828, 8421-7777; www.bahiadelsolnica.com; reservaciones@bahiadel solnica.com; La Chocolata, 2.2 km (1.3 miles) north of SJDS; credit cards accepted; $$$$; wifi US$7 per day) A half-hour walk north of SJDS proper, nine modern, luxurious, three-bedroom villas have amazing views, beautiful furnishings, full gourmet kitchens, and private porches.

Balcones de Majagual (2568-2498, 323-908-6730 (U.S.); www.balconesdemajagual.com; Playa Majagual; credit cards accepted; $$$–$$$$; wifi) Gorgeous, environmentally sustainable luxury development designed by the folks behind Morgan's Rock offers rentals north of SJDS.

Casa Marsella (8882-1134; www.marsellabeach.com; marthaobregon61@hotmail.com; Playa Marsella, 150 metros este; credit cards accepted; $$$–$$$$; wifi) Enjoy one of three deluxe vacation homes overlooking the unspoiled, white sand cove of Playa Marsella.

Finca Las Nubes (fincalasnubes.com) Sustainable, community-conscious development lists several luxurious vacation rentals.

Lobo Lira (8887-4167; www.lobolira.com; info@lobolira.com; credit cards accepted; $–$$; wifi) Need a long-term rental with a full kitchen, but the whole "gated-beachfront-community" thing isn't for you? Check out these eclectic, handmade, fan-cooled cabins with cable TV and private porches with hammocks, five blocks from central SJDS.

Local Treasure International (www.localtreasureinternational.com) Lists luxury rentals south of SJDS.

Nicaragua Surf Property (www.nicaraguasurfproperty.com) Real estate company offers rentals in and around SJDS, as well as the Tola beaches.

Nicaragua Vacation Rental and Property Management (2568-2498, 323-908-6730 (U.S.); www.vacationrentalsnicaragua.com) Rents properties around SJDS and Tola.

Playa Coco (8877-9590, 8864-0485; www.playacoco.com; billhays46@hotmail.com; Playa El Coco; credit cards accepted; $$$$; wifi) Modern luxury condos are arranged around a pool overlooking exquisite Playa El Coco. Units have three or four bedrooms, handmade wooden furnishings, huge windows, seashell-accented bathrooms, full gourmet kitchens, and third-floor terraces with wonderful views.

Villas de Palermo (8670-7283, 8672-0859, 800-613-2960 (U.S.); www.palermohoteland resort.com; hotel@villasdepalermo.com; credit cards accepted; $$$; wifi in some units) Just east of SJDS proper, fabulously outfitted stucco cottages offer luxurious accommodation, full gourmet kitchens, excellent views, and a great pool.

Other Hotels

San Juan del Sur

Casa Oro Adventure Center (2568-2415; www.casaeloro.com; de Hotel Colonial, 45 metros sur; credit cards accepted; $; wifi) Huge, yellow, wood-framed building houses the classic SJDS crash pad, catering to feral backpackers with decent dorms and private wifi, shared kitchen, budget tours, surf reports, and chaotic good times. Don't bother making reservations, as it's first come, first served.

Chale's House (8826-3549; delfinpizzi@hotmail.com; 15 metros sur del mercado; cash only; $) Tiny, family-run hostel with a fabulous chandelier has six clean, basic rooms with private cool baths and access to hammocks and a shared kitchen.

Hospedaje Nicaragua (de mercado, 50 metros norte; cash only; $) Airy, spotlessly clean rooms with private cool baths are gorgeous, a tad more expensive than most and worth it for pretty furnishings, top-notch mattresses, and great security. Reservations are emphatically not accepted.

Hotel Encanto del Sur (2568-2222, 8479-7606; www.hotelencantodelsur.co.cc; hotel encantodelsur@hotmail.com; del parque central, 75 metros sur; credit cards accepted; $$; wifi) It's a bit like staying in an atrium, but the small rooms have air-conditioning, cable TV, and a shared kitchen. Popular with vacationing Nicas.

Café Azul, next to Camping Matilda's, has simple yet exquisite seating.

Hotel Estrella (2568-2210; hotelestrella1929@hotmail.com; Calle Costera; cash only; $; wifi from 7 AM–7 PM) Since 1929, this graceful oceanfront hotel has offered breezy, very basic balcony rooms overlooking the sea. There's wifi during the day, a kitchen available in the evening, random power outages, shared bath, and not much else.

Guesthouse Eleonora (2568-2191; mercado, 1 cuadra este; cash only; $) Above-average surf shack on the budget strip has clean, fan-cooled rooms and a great second-story balcony.

Posada Puesta del Sol (8822-4393, 5568-2532; lalacaro98@yahoo.com; parque central, 25 metros oeste; cash only; $) Adorable five-room hostel is small but clean, with a tiny kitchen; some fan-cooled rooms have private baths.

Hotel Villas del Sol (2568-2002, 8439-2580; de la cabañita, 100 metros norte, 100 metros este; cash only; $) If you don't mind a steep, two-block climb, this hilltop hostel has grand views, fan-cooled dorms, good mattresses, and rooms with private baths and full kitchens (other guests can use the common kitchen). Worth the effort.

South Seas Hostal (2568-2084; www.thesouthseashostal.com; southseassjs@yahoo.com; credit cards accepted; $; wifi) In much nicer digs than the dedicated cheapies, South Seas offers exceptional value with new, freshly painted rooms with excellent beds and optional air-conditioning, all surrounding a well-kept courtyard garden and shared kitchen. The catch? All have shared bath.

Madera is not only Nicaragua's most popular wave, it has a great backdrop.

SOUTH OF SAN JUAN DEL SUR

Casa Canada (8877-9590; billhays46@hotmail.com; Playa El Coco; cash only; $; wifi) High atop a bluff across from the Parque Marítimo, this simple spot rents two very pretty rooms in what was once a pizza restaurant. Worth the climb.

Coco Cabañas (2276-5229, 305-898-7203 (U.S.); www.playacococabanas.com; contactus @playacococabanas.com; Playa El Coco; credit cards accepted; $$–$$$) Four grungy wooden cabins have full kitchens, air-conditioning, private cool baths, and porches. It wouldn't be bad if they scrubbed it down.

NORTH OF SAN JUAN DEL SUR

There are other surfer hostels hidden away in the hills, so ask around.

✪ **Camping Matilda's** (8456-3461; campingmatilda@gmail.com; Playa Majagual/Madera; cash only; $; wifi) The relaxed sprawl on the sand at this local institution centers on the "camping"—in pint-sized, US$6 cement "cabins" (more like large doghouses) right on the sand. Bring your own tent, and it's only US$4.50. Most folks opt for the US$10 dorm or US$35 room with private bath; prices drop for longer stays.

La Casa de Don Martín (8881-4727; talaquir@gmail.com; Playa Majagual, entrada; cash only; $–$$) Solid, cinderblock structure just off the beach has neatly tiled rooms and dorms with good beds, screens on the windows, fans, and private cool baths.

Madera Surf: Hostal de los Tres Hermanos (8670-3726; Playa Madera; cash only; $; wifi) Classic surf shack offers very basic rooms with sandy mattresses, jury-rigged fans, shared baths—and, of course, the best wave in Nicaragua, which you'll have all to yourself when the day trippers head back to SJDS. There's a restaurant, and they rent surfboards and boogie boards, and offer lessons.

RESTAURANTS AND FOOD PURVEYORS

The classic place to dine is at any of the fine beachfront ranchero restaurants, serving cold beer and fresh seafood with front row seats on the sunset. They'll let you stay all day on their shady porches for the price of a ceviche and Toña.

San Juan del Sur is developing into one of Nicaragua's best restaurant scenes, with international and gourmet options opening up. Check the Lodging listings for other options—don't miss **El Jardín's** and **Pelican Eyes'** excellent cuisine and bay views. Many of the bars also serve great meals.

Budget travelers (and everyone else) will enjoy the **Mercado Municipal** (open 6 AM–9 PM daily; cash only; $) with four tidy *comedores* serving inexpensive Nica cuisine. *Sodas* (simple restaurants) also dish up cheap set plates all over town.

Restaurant and Food Purveyor Price Code

The following prices are based on the cost of a dinner entrée with a nonalcoholic drink, not including Nicaragua's mandatory 13 percent restaurant tax and "suggested" 10 percent tip, which is usually included with the final bill (so check).

Inexpensive ($)	Up to US$5
Moderate ($$)	US$5 to US$10
Expensive ($$$)	$10 to $20
Very Expensive ($$$$)	US$20 or more

Restaurants

BAMBÚ BEACH CLUB
2568-2101
www.thebambubeachclub.com
Calle Costera, north end of town
Price: Moderate to Expensive
Cuisine: International
Serving: L, D
Closed: Tues.
Credit Cards: Yes

Child's Menu: No
Handicap Access: Challenging
Reservations: Yes

This sophisticated restaurant and bar offers unpretentious Zen ambiance, and complimentary towels after you've enjoyed their beachfront pool. The setting is serene and chic, and the food creatively tasty—from hearty plates like a bacon–blue cheese burger and pulled pork barbecue sandwich, to more delicate dishes such as a prosciutto and goat cheese appetizer.

The space twinkles with lights and candles after the sun slips into the sea, making this a rather romantic night out. The bar scene can be festive, however—particularly on Monday and Thursday, with pizza and free movies, while sushi is served Wednesday through Friday (but ask anytime).

BAR Y RESTAURANT INES
2568-2176
inesortega@yahoo.com
Calle Costera, Hotel Estrella, 20 varas este
Price: Moderate to Very Expensive
Cuisine: Seafood, Nicaraguan
Serving: B, L, D
Credit Cards: Yes
Child's Menu: No
Handicap Access: Challenging
Reservations: Yes

Everyone has a favorite beachfront restaurant, and this just happens to be mine. The open-air wooden dining room, with the palm thatch rustling overhead, offers flawless views over the beach, bay, boats, and endless parade of families, vendors, and bodyboarders though the brilliantly hued scene.

Ines offers approximately the same menu as its neighbors: fresh fish, shrimp, lobster, and calamari, served a la plancha (baked), al aljillo (in garlic sauce), al marinero (in a spicy tomato sauce), al vapor (steamed), or as a cocktail or ceviche. There are Nica set plates as well, and of course servicios of Flor de Caña (rum, Coke, ice cubes, and limes for several).

BARRIO CAFÉ

2568-2294
www.barriocafesanjuan.com
mercado, 1 cuadra oeste
Price: Inexpensive to Moderate
Cuisine: International
Serving: B, L, D
Credit Cards: Yes
Child's Menu: No
Handicap Access: Challenging
Reservations: No

Much loved café inside the Hotel Azul Pitahaya is well known for its healthy, creative menu offering ever-changing choices of inexpensive omelets, wraps, salads, kebabs, and sandwiches. There are always lots of vegetarian options, often with organic ingredients, or you can stick to their espresso beverages and tasty pastries. After dark, it becomes a fun little bar, sometimes with live music.

✪ BIG WAVE DAVE'S

2568-2203
bigwavedaves@turbonett.com.ni
de El Timón, 1 cuadra oeste
Price: Inexpensive to Moderate
Cuisine: International
Serving: B, L, D
Credit Cards: Yes
Child's Menu: No
Handicap Access: Challenging
Reservations: No

This local landmark and beacon of sociability has served the SJDS community for almost a decade, its relaxed atmosphere, very full bar, and kid-friendly scene always offering a hearty welcome to the shore. The food is great, with barbecued chicken burgers, meatloaf sandwiches, organic salads, and a Nicaraguan lunch special daily.

Dave operates the **Bed Head Shed** (two

blocks north of the church; cash only; $; wifi), a good hostel with shared kitchen, great beds, and private baths. He also offers shuttles to Managua (US$25) at 7 AM Tuesday and Friday.

✪ EL COLIBRÍ

8863-8612
Behind the Catholic church
Price: Moderate
Cuisine: International
Serving: D
Closed: Mon.
Credit Cards: No
Child's Menu: No
Handicap Access: No
Reservations: Yes

Take a seat on embroidered pillows, in gardens lit with candles and colorful lanterns, an exotic retreat from the rest of SJDS. This spot is usually lauded as the city's best restaurant, with a menu you'll find nowhere else.

Begin, perhaps, with their signature sangria and a brochette with olive tapanade and roasted peppers. The complicated curries, served with chicken or prepared for vegetarians, are divine, though the pollo en salsa de olivo, with dried fruits and other unusual ingredients, is apparently the local favorite. The bread is made fresh here, as is the coconut pistachio terrine, a fine choice for dessert if it's on the changing menu. A delight.

RESTAURANT-HOTEL DOLCE VITA

2568-2649, 8602-9321
www.dolcevitahotel.net
de Texaco, 1 cuadra oeste
Price: Expensive
Cuisine: Italian
Serving: D
Closed: Mon.
Credit Cards: Yes
Child's Menu: No

Handicap Access: No
Reservations: Yes

At the western tip of "The Triangle," at the entrance to town, this rather romantic Italian restaurant has red-and-white checkered tablecloths, courtyard gardens, flattering light, and deliberately distressed walls for ambiance. A short menu focuses on Italian-style seafood dishes, such as tuna carpaccio, dorado simmered in white wine and spices, and seafood marinara. Pizzas, fresh fettuccini, and wines from Italy, Chile, and Argentina are also on the menu.

They also rent six simple **rooms** ($$) with high ceilings, private baths, air-conditioning, cable TV, colorful mosaic tilework, and creative furnishings.

PIZZERÍA SAN JUAN
2568-2295, 8839-7201
Costado suroeste del Parque
Price: Inexpensive to Moderate
Cuisine: Pizza
Serving: D
Credit Cards: Yes
Child's Menu: No
Handicap Access: Yes
Reservations: No

"Maurizio's Place" has inspired an almost cultlike following among expats and travelers, who pack this pizzeria's tiny dining room and limited sidewalk seating every night. Get there early or prepare to wait.

It's worth it, with slices and pies of their creative thin-crust pizza loaded with an

San Juan del Sur's wide beach is lined with seafood restaurants that will let you hang out all day.

unusual array of toppings including atún (tuna, tomato, onion, and parsley) or Viennese (bacon and mushroom). There's also freshly made fettuccini, vegetarian options, and a few Northern Italian–style fish dishes. More than a dozen Italian wines are on offer as accompaniment, but be sure to save room for the vanilla or chocolate mousse.

EL POZO

8937-4935, 8495-7391
www.el-pozo.com
zona central
Price: Expensive
Cuisine: Latin Fusion
Serving: D
Credit Cards: Yes
Child's Menu: No
Handicap Access: Challenging
Reservations: Yes

This sleek spot looks like it would be more at home in San Francisco than San Juan del Sur, and adds a welcome sophistication to the scene. The food is also a cut above, putting a gourmet spin on international cuisines. The pipian cake appetizer has hints of indigenous El Salvador, while the gourmet bacon cheeseburger is an almost sculptural take on Americana.

The menu changes regularly, but keep an eye open for the achiote fried chicken breast with jalapeño honey, or perhaps the pork adobado, served with your choice of Colombian arepas or garlic mashed potatoes. Several people said that Pozo serves the best steak in town, and Sunday sushi night is tops. The full bar has good cocktails and a solid wine list.

LO STRADIVARI

8945-0261
andrea_camo@hotmail.com
Calle Costera, frente Hotel Casablanca
Price: Moderate to Expensive

Cuisine: Italian
Serving: L, D
Credit Cards: Yes
Child's Menu: No
Handicap Access: Challenging
Reservations: Yes

The newest eatery inhabiting the beachfront ranchero restaurants is the Pacific location of Managua's well-regarded Italian restaurant. Known in the capital for its upscale Italian dining, it duplicates those remarkable recipes right here, with fresh fettuccine, great Caesar salads, and Northern Italian–style seafood. The wine list is predictably very good, and the salmon ravioli was one the best dishes anywhere.

EL TIMÓN

2568-2243, 8966-7149
www.eltimonsjs.com
Calle Costera
Price: Expensive to Very Expensive
Cuisine: Seafood
Serving: B, L, D
Credit Cards: Yes
Child's Menu: No
Handicap Access: Yes
Reservations: No

This oceanfront rancho has long been the destination of choice for Nicaragua's vacationing bluebloods, who descend from their elegant mansions in the hills for El Timón's renowned lobster thermador, calamari al ajillo, and arroz con mariscos (Nicaraguan paella). Say what you will, these folks know quality, so why not take a seat between the patrician couples and soft-palmed politicians, and order something from the very full bar.

Thursday is "Noche de Verbenas," with traditional dances, marimba performances, and other cultural offerings explained in both Spanish and English. Classic Nicaraguan cuisine is on special.

Food Purveyors

Stock up on everything before heading to the much less developed beaches north and south of San Juan del Sur.

Bakeries

Pan de Vida (pandevidanicaragua@gmail.com; de Texaco, 50 varas oeste; cash only; open 8 AM–6 PM Thur. through Sat., noon–6 PM Wed., closed Sun. through Tue.; $$) Hearty, European-style loaves are pulled steaming hot from a brick oven at the center of this tiny store. Pricey, but a nice change from Nica pastries.

Panadería San Marcos (2568-2201; northwest corner of Iglesia; cash only; B, L, D; $) Typical Nicaraguan bakery sells mostly traditional sweet and savory breads, cheap, with a few items (donuts, sandwiches) for their international clients.

Pizza

Jerry's Pizza (8804-6640; frente mercado, costado sur; credit cards accepted; open Tues. through Sun.; B, L, D) Unassuming pizza place on surf-shack row gets packed with tourists ordering breakfasts, pastas, beer, grilled chicken, and of course pizza by the pie or slice. There's free wifi and a full bar, too, with several cocktails.

Rostí Pizza La Frigata (2568-3038; contiguo BanCentro; credit cards accepted; L, D; $) Cheap pizza, roast chicken, and other fast food is also delivered.

CULTURE

This is not generally considered one of San Juan del Sur's strong points, unless you count "surf culture" or "beach bum culture." One clever SJDS Web site has a section labeled "Traditional Food and Beverages," with just one entry: *cerveza.*

But there really is a bit of history here in this beautiful bay, with its old, colorfully painted houses. The perfectly protected harbor has been a fishing village and important port for millennia, perhaps providing safe anchorage for Nazca, Mayan, and even Chinese ships over the centuries. The Spanish arrived in 1522, when the bay became a convenient point for conquistadores and colonists to disembark before heading to cities inland.

After the Spanish discovery of the Río San Juan, which connects Lake Nicaragua to the Caribbean, San Juan del Sur became a point of transit for goods and people taking the "Nicaragua Route" between the two oceans. Just 18 km (11 miles) separate the lake from the Pacific, a half day's walk or a few hours on horseback. Travelers and merchants flowed through regularly.

In 1849, this became a flood. The U.S. conquest of northern Mexico had just opened the gold fields of California to East Coast prospectors and settlers. As anyone who has played the Oregon Trail game knows, the overland route took months, and was fraught with danger. Circumventing the snowy Rockies was a job for wily capitalists like Cornelius Vanderbilt—who offered safer, quicker passage between the coasts.

Passengers would leave New York City and other eastern ports in steamships bound for the Caribbean village of Greytown, today called San Juan de Nicaragua. There, they would catch smaller boats, capable of navigating the rapids, up the Río San Juan—then cruise across Lake Nicaragua to La Virgen. From there, they made their way along the same road as you will to San Juan del Sur, where ships to San Francisco were waiting.

Writer Mark Twain famously made the trip, expressing his awe of Isla Ometepe, appreciation of Nicaragua's lovely ladies, and a dreamy intention that a man might have to retire in a place described as "bright, fresh green on every hand, the delicious softness and coolness of the air." By 1851, the once sleepy port town had been named a city.

The boom ended when the Panama Canal was completed in 1903, closing the Nicaragua Route, though San Juan del Sur remained an important shipping port. The city saw some action during the Contra War, but continued operating and survived mostly intact. Transit business moved to the larger, more modern port of Corinto by the late 1990s, just as tourism was beginning to creep back into the area.

Though the surf scene helped put San Juan del Sur back on the map as a vacation destination after the turbulent 1980s, this has been a resort town much longer. For generations, the scenic bay has been a prime spot for the opulent vacation homes of the country's elite. Hotel Victoriano was once the Somozas' beachfront escape, while the Pellases once boasted the most impressive mansion on the bluffs above town. These have since been eclipsed by even more palatial escapes, many foreign-owned.

City officials have funneled tourism taxes into an impressive overhaul of downtown, fixing the roads, water mains, and central park. Investors, both public and private, have created cool projects that include a public library, pedestrian suspension bridge, and even a revamped police department.

San Juan del Sur's popular main beach brings in families from all over Southwest Nicaragua on weekends.

Most recently, Intur announced that the government will build a new pier, to receive increasing numbers of cruise ships. There's a bit of wistfulness about all this improvement, to be sure; one day, it seems, everyone's beloved little surf town and seaport may grow into a real resort community. It's not there yet, though, and the waves keep rolling in.

Nightlife

San Juan del Sur has one of Nicaragua's most enjoyable nightlife scenes, with relaxed bars offering live music, good food, and cool people—all within walking distance of your hotel. Muggings happen, so stay alert and bar hop in groups whenever possible.

In addition to the listings here, check out **Big Wave Dave's**, **Bambú Beach Club**, and **Barrio Café**, listed under Restaurants, or any of the beachfront restaurant-bars.

All of the developed beaches north and south of town have small bars, but it's worth hiring a taxi to the Playa Marsella turnoff for a brew at the **Mango Rosa** (8477-3692; www.mangorosanicaragua.com; Playa Madera, KM6.5 Chocolata), with sports on TV, Wednesday bingo nights, and air guitar competitions; and nearby **Restaurant Rancho Las Marías** (2948-8333; La Chocolata, Playa Marsella turnoff; L, D; $$), a ranchero-topped restaurant with live music, a local scene, and weekend dance parties.

The **San Juan del Sur Guide Blog** (www.sanjuandelsurguide.com/blog) has a regularly updated events schedule.

Bar Republika (www.r3publika.com; 300 metros Oeste Mercado Municipal) Groovy hookah bar has a variety of liquors and cocktails, plus a great pulled pork sandwich.

Coquito Beach (8640-7820; Calle Costera) Beachfront bar has live music on Saturday night and salsa lessons (US$5) on Thursday.

Crazy Crab Beach (Calle Costera, north end, next to the bridge; open 9 AM–8 PM daily, until 6 AM Thur. through Sun.) Serious party spot has 15-cord beer and rum, a huge dance floor, live DJs, Latin dance parties, and a US$3.50 cover on Saturday, when you should dress to impress. Drink your hangover away by the peaceful estuary the next morning.

❂ **Henry's Iguana Beach Bar** (8635-5204; www.iguanabeachbar.com; Calle Costera; credit cards accepted; B, L, D; $$) The hottest spot in town at press time, this beachfront bar has good music, hand-rolled cigars, tasty fish tacos, and late nights on their big breezy second floor. Wednesday is Ladies' Night, happy hours have 30-cord daiquiris, and there's a killer breakfast burrito and free coffee all morning.

Irish House Pub (8973-7855; del Mercado, 2 cuadras norte; D; $$) Serves shepherd's pie, Irish stew, and other items best washed down with a Guinness, or perhaps something from their whiskey collection: Jameson, Crested Ten, Tyrconnel, Paddy Powers, and Bunratty Poteheen, "illegal since 1661."

The Pier (8901-2202; sanjuanpier@gmail.com; Calle Costera, 113 staggers past Eskimo; L, D; $$) Effortlessly achieving levels of chill that other bars can only aspire to, the Pier has groovy murals, lots of hammocks, beach bonfires, and munchies—plus live music on Wednesdays and Fridays. Happy hour is fun.

Sport Bar M'Che (2568-2373; del Mercado, 1 cuadra norte) After-hours bar with low light, soft music, beer, rum, and snacks is open from 11 PM until 7 AM nightly.

Surf Casino (2568-2522; www.casinoscostarica.com; de la Cabañita 25 metros sur; open noon–4 PM daily) Players get free beer at this half-decent casino, with blackjack, roulette, and Texas Hold 'Em.

Watching the sun drop into the sea behind San Juan del Sur's protected harbor is one of life's great joys.

Spanish Schools

Most schools offer 20 hours of instruction per week, including dance lessons, cooking classes, and tours; surf lessons can be arranged, but usually cost extra. Homestays run US$95 per week, including meals. Some schools offer cheaper "just classes" packages—or look for independent instructors, who post their contact information on billboards around town.

Latin American Spanish School (8820-2252; www.spanishschoolsjds.com; parque central, 0.5 cuadras oeste) Arranges surf lessons.

Nica Spanish Language School (2568-2677; www.nicaspanish.com; parque central, 1 cuadra oeste) Nonprofit, teacher-owned school has special courses for missionaries, volunteers, and medical personnel.

San Juan del Sur Spanish School (2568-2432; www.sjdsspanish.com; frente BDF, Restaurant Lago Azul) Also has campuses in Granada and Isla Ometepe.

Spanish School House Rosa Silva (2649-8138; www.spanishsilva.com; mercado, 50 metros oeste) Lets you save money by skipping meals with your family, and offers classes on Isla Ometepe.

Spanish Ya (2568-3010, 8898-5036; www.learnspanishya.com; de la Texaco 100 metros norte) If you need "official certification," they offer pricier DELE (Diplomas of Spanish as a Foreign Language) classes, and can also arrange volunteer work.

RECREATION

Though very little of the Nicaraguan coast is officially protected, there are several private reserves worth visiting. You can also book a boat trip from Ostional or Playa El Coco to Costa Rica's **Bolaños Island National Wildlife Refuge,** a small, ancient island where many species of birds nest. No one seemed concerned with the legality of taking tours on foreign waters, but bring a copy of your passport, just in case.

National Parks and Protected Areas

LA FLOR WILDLIFE REFUGE
2563-4264
27 km (17 miles) south of SJDS
Open: 24 hours
Admission: US$10/5 foreigners/Nicaraguans; camping US$30 per tent

La Flor is the most visited sea turtle nesting area in Nicaragua, not just by the tortugas—some 170,000 arrived in 2009—but also travelers. The park's success has made it a model ecological project, proving to communities that have traditionally harvested the endangered animals and eggs that, with proper management, tourism is actually better business.

Although the egg trade is now illegal, you'll still see the musty things on menus and in markets all over Nicaragua, popular for their alleged aphrodisiac properties. Please refrain from ordering them; Viagra is widely available without a prescription.

Sea turtle populations have plummeted in recent decades, though they still frequent the Nicaraguan beaches. La Flor has been hosting the beauties for perhaps 30 million years, and today is used primarily by olive Ridleys (Lepidochelys olivacea), a smallish (45-kg/100-pound) species called paslama in Nicaragua; leatherbacks (Dermochelys coriacea), or toras, the largest of the world's reptiles; and the occasional, very rare lora (or hawksbill) turtle, hunted almost to extinction for its beautiful shell.

It is the olive Ridleys who arrive with the most pomp, in arribadas of thousands, and who will cover the sands for days at a time, laying nest after nest on top of each other. While paslamas arrive individually throughout the nesting months (July through January), these mass arrivals occur six or seven times a year at just a handful of beaches in Central America (including Chacocente, covered in the Rivas and the Tola Beaches chapter).

Arribadas usually begin with the evening high tide just after the first or last quarter of the moon. Usually. But the ladies come ashore when they feel like it, and local fishing captains (who communicate mass turtle sightings to park officials) are a better source of information.

Unless you are camping here, you'll probably be booking a night tour through your hotel or tour operator. Tours usually start around 6:30 PM, last five hours, and include a movie and a lot of waiting around while park rangers look for nesting turtles. There's no guarantee you'll see one—but if you do, it's something you'll never forget.

While La Flor is well organized and probably won't allow any such shenanigans, please do not touch the turtle, get in front of her, form a circle around her, shine a flashlight anywhere on her, or use flash photography without the express permission of the guide (even this is controversial). All of these things can stress the lady out right when she needs to be focused, and disrupt the egg-laying process.

Tiny baby sea turtles push their delicate little noses up out of the sand about 45 days after an arribada, in a celebration called a nacimiento. This usually begins just before day-light, so you'll either need to arrange a special tour, or spend the night.

Other Parks and Natural Attractions

Toro Mixcal Private Wildlife Preserve (2266-9004, 2278-7140; www.redrspnica.com; Comunidad Las Marías, 5 km (3 miles) north of SJDS; admission by reservation) Book a tour through local operators to this oceanfront property, with trails through the dry tropical forest, views over Bahía Nacascolo, and wildlife.

✪ **Finca La Primavera Private Agricultural-Forest Preserve** (2265-8626, 8867-4684; betben@ibw.com.ni; Comunidad San Antonio) Tucked away in a traditional inland com-munity northeast of Playa Madera, this 35-hectare demonstration *finca* offers the expe-rience of visiting an old-fashioned working farm. Day trips, organized by area hotels and operators, involve a big breakfast and the opportunity to milk cows, feed *pueybueys* (short-haired tropical sheep), and do other farm chores. Or you can stay overnight in their farmhouse or campsite (US$15 per person).

Ostional Private Wildlife Reserve (opwr.org; Ostional) This 26-manzana (48-acre) pri-vate reserve just outside Ostional will officially open December 12, 2012, but already has two hours' worth of hiking trails. Ask at your guesthouse in Ostional about arranging a visit.

ATV Tours

Beach Front Rentals (2586-2030; www.nicabeachfrontrentals.com; Calle Costado, frente Eskimo) On the north end of town, this place rents ATVs (US$20 per hour), motorbikes, and Jet Skis. They also offers several guided ATV treks, which could be combined with a canopy tour or hiking.

Hostal Beach Fun Casa 28 (2568-2441; javieralara@hotmail.com; SJDS centro; $; wifi) Fun hostel in the center of town also rents ATVs and motorcycles, and organizes tours.

Boat Tours

Booze-Sunset Cruise (2568-2022; www.sanjuandelsursurf.com; del Mercado Municipal, 20 metros oeste, mano derecha) San Juan del Sur Surf and Sport Nicaragua runs a sunset booze cruise (US$16 per person) every evening from 3:30 PM to 6 PM.

Ferry Isadora Minicrucero (2525-3782, 8888-8855, 8888-8851 (ferry); 10 AM–5 PM Fri. through Sun) Miniature cruise ship from Norway now offers all-inclusive tours (US$60)—including beer, rum, and even a cold buffet—to nearby beaches, where you can swim ashore.

Gypsy Sailing Adventures (8608-9498; www.sailgypsy.com) Offers half-day (US$30 per person) and full-day (US$40 per person) treks on their sleek 30-foot sailing vessel for "fun and debauchery," snacks and beverages included.

Nica Sailing (2837-0582, 8837-0582; www.nicasailing.com; nicaralph@gmail.com; US$50 per person, four person minimum) Spend the day with the "Sea Scouts," local kids who captain Ralph Hewitt (owner of Park Avenue Villas) has been showing the ropes on his yacht. Tours of the beaches and bays, snorkeling Playa Blanca, and then heading south to Coco for lunch run from about 9:30 AM–5 PM. **Exploradoras Marinos Thirsty Thursday**

Sailing Cruise takes the first 12 people to sign up on the special liquor-soaked version, Thursday only.

Pastora Tours (8910-0241, 8841-5146; www.pastoratours.com) Outfitter offers fishing trips, surf tours, and pleasure cruises in their 27-foot covered pangas for up to six people. They'll pick you up anywhere between SJDS and Punta Teonoste.

Pelican Eyes (2563-7000, 866-350-0555 (toll free); www.piedrasyolas.com) Gorgeous 42-foot wooden sailing sloop operated by Piedras y Olas is the classic way to explore the coast, either on a day trip or sunset champagne cruise.

Rana Tur (8871-6562, 8877-9255; 100 metros este Mercado municipal) Offers regular water taxis, and good prices on snorkel, surf, and fishing tours. They have a booth on the malecón.

Canopy Tours

Da' Flying Frog Nicaragua (8613-4460, 8465-6781; daflyingfrog@hotmail.com; La Chocolata; US$30) Nicaragua's longest canopy tour—16 cables and 2.5 km—is just north of SJDS. This is a very professional operation with the highest safety standards. They also rent horses (US$12 per hour), which you can ride to see a very impressive pre-Columbian petroglyph.

Fishing

You can arrange *artesanal*, or traditional, fishing (using nets and simple lines) with local captains anywhere, but San Juan del Sur is home to the largest professional fleet of serious sport-fishing yachts.

From May through November, the catch of the day is likely to be sailfish, grouper, dolphin fish, kingfish, barracuda, mackerel, roosterfish, and tasty yellowfin tuna. From December through April, you'll be trolling for black and yellowfin tuna, jackfish, mackerel, and roosterfish. Cooler water in late January and February can bring in big grouper.

Also check out the boat tour operators (mentioned earlier) and surf operators (mentioned later), who also arrange fishing trips.

There are even hotels that cater to the fishing crowd, such as **Gran Océano** (2568-2219, 2568-2428; www.hotelgranoceano.com.ni; hgoceano@ibw.com.ni; credit cards accepted; $$–$$$; wifi), offering half- and full-day tours (US$300/600) including all fishing equipment, snorkel gear, and Flor de Caña rum.

Nicovale (2568-2240, 8845-8690; www.nicovale.com; del Timón 1 cuadra al este; $$; wifi) is another fishing-focused option with 10 cabins equipped with full kitchens, private hot baths, satellite TV, and great views.

San Juan del Sur Surf and Sport (2568-2022; sanjuandelsurs_s@yahoo.com; mercado municipal, 20 metros oeste) Professional operation runs three-hour fishing tours on their yacht, the *Gabriela V*, for US$95, and even door-to-door transport from your hotel in Managua or Granada.

Sancho Sport Fishing (fishingnicaragua.com; San Juan del Sur) Offers full- and half-day trips, as well as multiday fishing packages.

Sport Fishing Nicaragua (www.nicaraguafishingtrips.com; San Juan del Sur) Fishing outfit does big game trolling and organizes many other tours.

Surfing San Juan del Sur

The Southwest Nicaraguan Pacific is blessed with consistent, offshore winds some 330 days of the year, a trick of climatology caused by Lake Nicaragua. This is called the "Papagayo Effect," and is why this region has some of the best surfing in Central America.

San Juan del Sur, though it lacks really good waves right in the bay, is the unofficial surf capital of the country. This is the best spot to hook up surfboards before heading out into the hinterlands, and is home base for many established surf camps and tour operators.

There are several Web sites with surfing information, including Surfer's Guide Southwest Nicaragua (www.thesurfersguides.com), created by the publishers of Mike Parise's ✪ *Surfer's Guide to Costa Rica and Southwest Nicaragua*. Also consider *The Essential Surfing Nicaragua Guide & Surf Map Set* (US$18.95), a slim 70-page volume published by Blue Planet Surf Maps.

WAVES

These are just a few of the best-known breaks near San Juan del Sur, which does have some mellow, inconsistent surf on the north end of the beach. Keep in mind that surfers are notoriously secretive about their waves (hence the confusion between "Playones" and "Playa Madera" beaches), particularly with guidebook writers.

Playa Madera (5 km/3 miles north of S|DS) The most popular wave in Nicaragua is this consistent, sandy-bottomed beach break, with a peeling right and short, fast left—plus a few other good breaks close by. There are a handful of hotels nearby, plus daily shuttles from S|DS, so this wave gets crowded.

Remanso (3 km/1.8 miles south of S|DS) Medium and small waves are good for beginners, and you're within walking distance to better breaks at Playas Tamarindo and Hermosa.

Yankee (9 km/5 miles south of S|DS) Beautiful, white-sand beach has lefts with fast, hollow barrels when conditions are right.

Playa Escama (11 km/7 miles south of S|DS) Medium-sized break has good (if inconsistent) lefts and rights.

Ostional (40 km/25 miles south of S|DS) Tranquil fishing village close to the border has an inconsistent reef break.

SURF SHOPS, CAMPS, AND OUTFITTERS

There are dozens of businesses renting boards, usually around US$10 per day for shortboards, US$15 for longboards, and US$5 for bodyboards. Just about anyone can arrange lessons, which usually cost around US$50 for two hours, including the use of your board all day. Quality (and language skills) vary; ask around or look online for recommendations.

If you're planning to buy or rent a board to use during your vacation, start here—this is the best selection in the country. These are just some of the surf-oriented businesses around town.

Arena Caliente Surf Camp (8815-3247; www.arenacaliente.com; S|DS center; cash only; $) Budget surf camp with staying power offers inexpensive surf packages, predictably basic US$6 rooms with shared baths and kitchen—and great prices on lessons, board rentals, sales, ding repair, and more.

Chica Brava (8894-2842, 832-519-0253 (U.S.); www.chicabrava.com; Edificio Chica Brava, malecón) Nicaragua's first all-woman surf operator offers two packages. If you're feeling flush, enjoy their luxurious hilltop surf camp, "The Cloud Farm," a chic all-inclusive with gourmet meals, massages, yoga, and airport transfer—your bridesmaids may even forgive you for that dress. If your budget is as tight as a surfgirl's abs, go for the Casa Chica Brava package, with simple, air-conditioned lodging in down-

The rocky points that bookend the bays make for some excellent waves.

town S|DS, transportation to the airport and area beaches, and two hours of yoga per week.

Good Times Surf Shop (8675-1621, 8662-8295; www.goodtimessurfshop.com; outerreefsa@gmail .com) Top-notch surf shop rents and sells new and used surfboards, and offers lessons for US$30 including board and transportation. They also run day trips and overnights to the Tola beaches.

Madera Surf: Hostal de los Tres Hermanos (8670-3726; Playa Madera; cash only; $) The famous surf camp at Playa Madera rents surfboards, boogie boards, and offers lessons to hostel guests and daytrippers.

Mope's Surf Shop (8676-9657; Malecón, frente Restaurant Inés) Sells new and used boards, offers ding repair, lessons with local experts, beach transport, and more.

NSR (8451-1618, 8879-7197; www.nicaraguasurfreport.com) The Nicaragua Surf Report is a great, useful Web site with all sorts of listings, a fabulous blog, a surf camp and classes for adults and kids, and much more. They can rent boards, four-wheel-drive cars, and vacation homes right on-site. Their roving photographers capture the best surfers and waves daily, so be sure to check and see if you've made the grade.

Ocean Green (5278-1478; www.oceangreen.org) Company specializes in ecologically friendly boards.

San Juan del Sur Surf and Sport Nicaragua (2568-2022, 954-557-4933 (U.S.); www.sanjuandelsur surf.com; del Mercado Municipal, 20 metros oeste, mano derecha) Solid tour company offers surfing and fishing packages with all the trimmings, and also offers lessons and rents surfboards, beach umbrellas, boogie boards, fishing poles, and more.

Surfari Nicaragua Tours (8887-6255; www.surfarinicaragua.com) Offers all-inclusive surf packages up and down the Nica Pacific.

Baloy Surf Shop (8405-9471; luisbaloy@hotmail.com; de la farmacia communal, 20 varas oeste) Small surf shop also rents and sells boards, offers lessons, and claims to be the local distributor for leashes, wax, and other items.

Hiking

There are several hikes around San Juan del Sur, but some of them cross private property and can't be recommended here, while others—such as Las Delicias to El Remanso—are known for armed muggings. Ask around.

The most popular hike is safe and legal, however—the paved, 45-minute climb to see the **giant fiberglass Jesus**, constructed atop the bay's northern escarpment to commemorate Semana Santa 2009. "But it wasn't finished on time," sighed one hotel manager. "We celebrated Easter with a headless savior."

The statue is complete, and while it's not exactly Rio de Janeiro, the whole effect of Jesus above the bay looks pretty cool, and marks one of the best spots in town to watch the sunset.

To get here, head north along the beach toward the tip of the point, to the *Cara del Indio* (Indian's Face), the evocative stone formation that seems to depict a warrior looking out at the sea. Close by, you'll see a yellow house, where signed steps mark the journey up to the statue. There's a US$1 entry fee.

Horseback Riding

Just about any hotel or tour operator can arrange horseback tours, or try **Guillermo Mena** (8618-9724; cabalgatahorsebacktour@hotmail.com), offering three-hour guided trips for US$20 per person.

Rancho Chilamate (8755-6475, 8995-7025; www.ranchochilamate.com; Playa Yankee) Vancouver natives and seasoned world travelers have gone quite comfortably off the grid, with wifi, modern bathrooms, and a pool. They offer several different horseback tours, as well as meals and lodging, at their solar ranch. They also arrange visits to a private preserve maintained by NicDev (nicadev.com), a local ecodeveloper, which you probably won't see any other way.

San Juan del Sur Horses (2673-3127; www.sjdshorse.com; southeast of SJDS) Finca Caballo Pinto raises fine horses, and offers two-hour rides for US$30 through their forested countryside, including hotel pickup in town. They also operate **The Iguana Project**, a nursery that aims to repopulate the area with native green and black iguanas.

Other Activities

Marsella Valley Frisbee Golf (La Chocolata to Playa Madera, just before Marsella exit; open daily; US$3) No vacation is complete without Frisbee golf, and this shady 12-hole course is convenient to a cluster of hotels. Frisbees, which you can use throughout the day, are included in the fee.

San Juan del Sur Beach Camp (8998-7739; www.sanjuandelsurbeachcamp.com; north of the footbridge; open 1 PM–5 PM Mon. through Sat., closed Sun.; US$20) Offers four hours of fun, games, and supervision daily for "children of all ages."

Snorkeling and Scuba Diving

Most snorkel tours are headed to Playa Arena Blanca, just north of Playa Majagual, with the region's only easily accessible coral reef.

Neptune Diving (2568-2752, 8903-1122; www.neptunenicadiving.com; mercado, 20 metros sur) This is the Nicaraguan Pacific Coast's only PADI (Professional Association of Diving Instructors)-certified operation, run by bilingual, experienced instructor Fidel

López Briceño. There are two primary dive sites hidden in SJDS's volcanic, rocky seascape, where you can explore steep pinnacles, a sunken Russian shrimp boat, 12 species of eel, angelfish, butterfly fish, dolphins, octopus, anemones, urchins, and shovelnose guitarfish that you can pet.

Both sites, La Flor and La Paloma, are within 40 minutes of SJDS, have an average temperature of 28°C (81°F), and are fairly shallow, 16 meters (52 feet) and 18 meters (60 feet), respectively. A 3mm wetsuit is recommended. A two-tank dive with all gear is US$85. López can also take you diving in Xiloá and Apoyo crater lakes.

Spas and Gyms

San Juan del Sur is becoming a wellness-oriented destination, with several businesses offering massages, yoga classes, water aerobics, and spa services. This scene is growing, so ask around about new offerings.

Bonnie Lassie Luxury Spa (8903-7080; contiguo BDF) Offers a variety of massages, facials, and more unusual treatments—such as the apple cider body glow.

Buena Vida Fitness Centre (www.buenavidafitness.com; between Gato Negro and The Barrio Café; open 7 AM–11 AM and 3 PM–7 PM Mon. through Fri., 8 AM–11 AM Sat.) Fine spot for a workout has a few machines and weights, plus yoga, salsa, Pilates, self-defense, and other classes.

Casa Tranquila (2563-7000 ext 310; Pelican Eyes) Pelican Eyes Hotel and Resort has a full-service spa that offers massages, facials, pedicures, waxing, and hair care, most using natural ingredients.

Gaby Massage Studio (2568-2654; estrelladeluna@hotmail.com; del mercado, 1 cuadra este) Gaby offers massages for US$25 per hour.

Nica Yoga (8400-0255, 678-500-9199 (U.S.); www.nicayoga.com; info@nicayoga.com; 5 km from SJDS) Yoga classes, retreats, and rather plush lodging at tranquil **El Camino del Sol** (www.elcaminodelsol.com; credit cards accepted; $$), a yoga community in the hills above town. They offer shuttles from Buena Vida.

SHOPPING

Banks and ATMs

There are several banks with ATMs in San Juan del Sur proper, but none at the surrounding beaches, so stock up. All ATMs are located within half a block of the malecón, a **BAC** at Hotel Casa Blanca, **BanCentro** right around the corner; and **BDF** on the south end of the malecón.

Groceries

The only full-sized grocery store in the region is **Palí**, located 1 km east of SJDS on the main entrance road, just east of the turnoff to Ostional. There are several well-stocked pulperías in downtown San Juan del Sur, clustered around the **Mercado Municipal**, with all your fruits and veggies.

Pick up groceries before heading to the northern or southern beaches. To the south, there is a small, pricey convenience store at **Playa El Coco** (22 km/13 miles south of SJSD), and a very basic pulpería behind the church in **Ostional** (40 km/25 miles south of SJSD).

Markets

✪ **San Juan del Sur Mercado Municipal** (open 6 AM–9 PM daily; cash only; $) This tidy, tiny little market is easy to navigate and has several stands selling fruits, vegetables, swimwear, and other items. There are also four great little *comedores*, serving delicious breakfasts and set plates for around US$3, more expensive seafood dishes for US$5–8, about half what you'd pay at the beach.

Shops

✪ **El Gato Negro** (8970-9466; www.elgatonegronica.com; de BanCentro 0.5 cuadras al este; open 7 AM–3 PM daily) This pleasant spot is the largest English-language bookstore in Nicaragua, with more than 3,500 well-chosen volumes. The impressive Latin American collection is excellent by any standard, and the general fiction and nonfiction selections also very good. There are a few titles in French, German, and other languages, too. It's also a relaxed, artsy **café**, with its own homegrown and roasted coffee, light meals (organic salads, bagels with Norwegian salmon), and a four-chocolate espresso fudge brownie that will power you through a novel or two.

Galería del Sur (2568-2110; www.galeriadelsur.org; del Mercado Municipal, 0.5 cuadras al sur) Pelican Eyes sponsors part of this gallery, exhibiting work by local fine artists.

K Gallery Art (2568-2400; miguelsjs62@hotmail.com; de Texaco, 50 varas oeste) Original modern art in bright, beautiful color.

Nica Designs T-Shirts (8897-2711; next to Big Wave Dave's; open "as soon as I can get here—as long as I can stand it") Stop in to say hello to delightful designer Cathye Aley, and check out her cool cotton T-shirts, just US$10 each.

✪ **La Posada Azul** (2568-2524, 8647-5244; www.laposadaazul.com; BDF, 0.5 cuadras este) Artsy, upscale B&B has the best handicrafts shop in town, with fine primitivist paintings from Solentiname, pine-needle basketry from the Segovias, ceramics and embroidered clothing from throughout the country, antique wooden saints, and much more. Quality is high, but some pieces are quite affordable.

Salomon Tattoo (8895-6335; del Mercado, 0.5 cuadras; open 4 PM–8 PM Wed. through Fri., 2 PM–6 PM Sat., or by appointment) Looking for the perfect memento of your Nicaraguan adventure, one that won't get stolen, pickpocketed, or left behind on the bus? Consider a tattoo by Salomon Nägeli, who posts photos on his Salomon Tattoo Facebook page.

Vastu (8906-3690; vastu99@gmail.com; de la cabanita, 25 varas sur) Great prices on imported Italian fashions—pants, blouses, dresses—plus artsy jewelry.

EVENTS

San Juan del Sur often celebrates major national holidays with a seaborne component, such as taking the Virgin María for a spin around the bay. Area beaches participate in the **National Surf Circuit** (www.circuitosurfnica.com).

February

Howler Mountain Bike Race (mid-February; www.sanjuanhowler.com) The big race has 17-, 28-, and 40-km competitions.

March

✪ **Semana Santa** (March or April, week before Easter) Despite the heartfelt religious sentiment, every Nicaraguan with two córdobas to rub together celebrates Easter Week by
heading to the beach for several days of drinking, dancing, passing out on the sand, random fireworks, snare drums, and other epic debauchery—with San Juan del Sur the top
party *playa* in the country. Make hotel reservations well in advance, expect to pay top
dollar everywhere, and be ready to get your fiesta on. Not for amateurs.

June

Xterra Off-Road Triathlon (mid-June; www.sanjuanhowler.com) If you've got it, flaunt it
at this tough triathlon.

July

Homenaje a la Virgen de Carmen (July 15–16) Boat captains carry an image of the Virgin of
Carmen, Patron Saint of Fishermen, around the bay.

7

Rivas and the Tola Beaches

Pristine Bays, Empty Waves

Just north of the San Juan del Sur coast, for decades isolated by poor access roads, are a series of serene and sandy bays known as the Tola beaches. They remain little known—save to surfers, fishing families, and luxury developers—but that seems set to change. The roads, while still unpaved, are now open to regular cars almost year-round. The beaches, while still unspoiled, are now home to luxury developments, surf lodges, and traditional fishing villages quite consciously gearing up for tourism.

Though the small town of Tola gives this rolling coast its name, the region's major city and travel hub is the decidedly Spanish Colonial town of Rivas—perhaps more authentically so than Granada. Despite its colorful, kitschy central plaza fronting the 1607 Iglesia San Pedro y San Pablo (one of Central America's oldest surviving churches), this pleasant, pretty working city has never really developed into a destination.

It is perhaps best known for the dusty, chaotic bus lot, where you change buses for Granada, San Juan del Sur, San Jorge (Isla Ometepe), and the Peñas Blancas border with Costa Rica. Thus, Rivas makes a great base for exploring the region, particularly if you're one of those rare travelers who eschews popular tourist destinations in lieu of a more authentic experience.

The Tola beaches have also been ignored by international travelers, most of whom head

Online Resources

En Linea (www.enlineacon.com) Spanish-language site covers Costa Rica, but also has the best online hotel, restaurant, and business listings for Rivas.

Playa Gigante (www.playagigante.com) Thorough and personable online guide offers a great English-language overview of this groovy beach town.

Popoyo Surf Report (www.popoyosurfreport.com) More than just a surf report, it's also got photos, videos, accommodation listings, and other local information—in English.

Popoyo.com (www.popoyo.com) English-language site offers listings and activities around Playa Popoyo and Guasacate, but rather than give direct contact information, you have to book everything through them.

The departmental capital of Rivas, with its expansive central park and impressive 1607 church, is the economic, political, and transportation hub of the isthmus.

south to San Juan del Sur. Tola's windswept bays of wildlife-rich forest and soft sand, however, are longer, broader, and perhaps more beautiful. Since the unpaved coastal road opened in 2002, more people have been discovering (and coveting) this for themselves.

Just west of Tola is Playa Pie de Gigante, "Giant's Foot Beach," named for the slipper-shaped headland. While it is a classic surf town and fishing village—colorful, friendly, and unpretentious—it is surrounded by more upscale spots, including the much-anticipated Guacalito de la Isla luxury community, being developed by Nicaragua's wealthy Pellas family.

Continuing north, you'll pass two of Nicaragua's best known upscale developments, geared to U.S. and Canadian investors looking for an inexpensive piece of paradise where they might retire. With world-class surfing, beautiful beaches, a golf course, and a variety of comfortable vacation villas for rent, they are an excellent option for a family escape.

As the road bumps north, it passes small Nicaraguan villages and all sorts of surf lodges before arriving in Las Salinas de Nahualapa, a salt-producing town with access to Nicaragua's most famous wave, Popoyo (along with several other good breaks).

More perfect beaches scallop the shoreline, some with lovely hotels, as you approach the end of the road. The working fishing village of El Astillero has a few good waves and hotels, plus access to Refugio De Vida Silvestre Río Escalante-Chacocente, a new sea turtle preserve.

CRIME AND OTHER CONCERNS

While violent crime is rare, the Tola beaches are poor, rural areas where it would be foolish to walk alone with valuables, particularly at night. Be smart, and stay alert. Never leave anything unguarded on the beach or around the hot springs.

TOURIST INFORMATION

Intur (2563-4914; rivas@intur.gob.ni; de Texaco 0.5 cuadras este; open 8 AM–1 PM Mon.
through Sat.) Small Rivas office has free brochures and limited information about Rivas,
Ometepe, San Juan del Sur, and the Tola beaches.

GETTING AROUND

Rivas is the regional transportation hub, with direct buses to the Tola beaches, San Juan del
Sur, Granada, Managua, the Costa Rican border at Peñas Blancas, and San Jorge—where you
catch ferries to Isla Ometepe.

Note that all the beaches, except El Astillero, lie at least 1 km from the bus stop on the
main road; Playa Gigante is 5 km (3 mi) from the bus stop. Taxis do not generally meet the
buses; you'll either need to walk, hitchhike, or arrange transport with your hotel in
advance. It's often much easier to take a taxi from Rivas.

Taxis (along with pedicabs and horse-drawn carriages) swarm around the edges of the
Rivas bus lot, waiting to compete for your business. The small town of Tola is not a good
place to arrange taxis, and has little tourist infrastructure. Once you are at the beaches,
return taxis should be arranged in advance, and may be more expensive.

Car

Rivas lies on the Panamerican Highway, a beautifully paved, well-signed road with plenty of
gas stations. The coastal road is another story.

From Tola to Salinas, the coastal road is unpaved, but generally passable to regular cars
in dry season, and usually four-wheel drives in rainy season (which coincides with surfing
season). But even the coastal road can devolve into a swampy, muddy mess after several
days of rain, so be safe and ask about road conditions before setting out in stormy weather.
There are no gas stations, so fill up in Rivas.

In dry season, there are two shorter routes from the Panamerican Highway to the Tola
beaches. The unpaved road from the Ochomogo Bridge (a well-known speed trap just south
of Nandaime) to Las Salinas is usually passable to normal four-wheel-drive cars in dry season, though you do need to ford a fairly deep stream. The road from Jinotepe to El Astillero
is only for full-sized, four-wheel-drive vehicles and only recommended in dry season.
Both are marked with yellow signs to Punta Teonoste.

International Buses

Rivas has two international bus offices. Both are clearly signed on the Panamerican Highway, just south of the Texaco station. You must purchase tickets in advance, in person, with
your passport—you can do this several days beforehand, before you head out to the Tola
beaches. For information on crossing the border to Costa Rica, see the Planning Your Trip
chapter.

Tica Bus (8877-1407, 2453-4301; www.ticabus.com) Three buses to Liberia and San José,
Costa Rica (US$14.)
Transnica (2453-6619) Three buses to Liberia and San José, Costa Rica (US$14.)

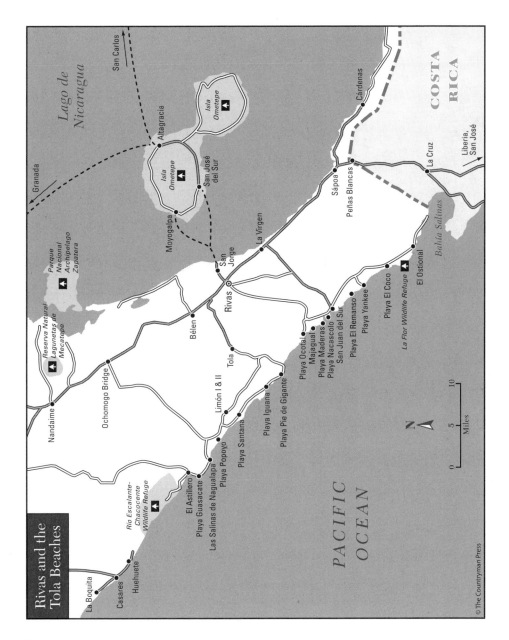

Buses

Rivas offers direct bus connections to the Tola beaches as well as San Juan del Sur, San Jorge (ferries to Isla Ometepe), the Costa Rican border, Granada, and Managua. All leave from the rather disorganized and chaotic public bus lot.

Don't panic! There's a kiosk with bus schedules, and the guys yelling out destinations can point you toward your bus. Taxis, horse-drawn carriages, and pedicabs wait on the fringes of the lot. If you have time between buses, the Rivas Museum of Anthropology is only four blocks away; pedicabs charge US$0.50 if you can't find it yourself.

Horse-drawn taxis in Rivas may not have all the ribbons and pretty paint, but they'll get you around town.

El Astillero US$4; 5 AM and 4 PM

Granada US$1.50; 5:45 AM, 6:30 AM, 7:55 AM, 10:30 AM, 11:20 AM, 12:15 PM, 1:55 PM, 3:20 PM, 4:20 PM

Managua Mercado Huembes US$4.25; 5 AM, 5:45 AM, 7 AM, 3:20 PM

Ostional US$3; 9:30 AM and 4 PM. Stops at San Juan del Sur, Playa Yanquí, and Playa El Coco en route.

Sapoá–Peñas Blancas (Costa Rica) US$1.50, every 30 minutes. Buses marked "Cárdenas" first go to **Cárdenas**, on the southern shore of Lake Nicaragua, before stopping at the border.

Las Salinas de Nahualapa US$3; 5:30 AM, 9:15 AM, 11 AM, 12:45 PM, 2:45 PM, 4:20 PM, and 4:45 PM. En route, the bus passes the entrance to **Playa Gigante** (5 km from the beach), **Playa Santana (Limon #2)**, and **Playa Guasacate (Popoyo)** (1 km from the beach). Buses return from Salinas at 5:00 AM, 6:00 AM, 6:45 AM, 8:15 AM, noon, 2 PM, and 2:30 PM, and pass the Guasacate empalme about half an hour later. Ask at your hotel about when to meet the bus.

San Jorge US$0.25; every hour

San Juan del Sur US$1; every 45 minutes

El Astillero

This fishing village in the far north of Tola isn't accessible on the same bus line as more southerly destinations, but you can change buses in Salinas (US$0.50).

Rivas US$2.25; 7 AM and 10 AM, returning from Rivas at 5 AM and 4 PM.
Nandaime US$2; 5:40 AM and 1 PM, returning from Nandaime at 9 AM and 2:30 PM.

Taxi

Rivas is packed with taxis. If you're staying in town, consider grabbing a pedicab or horse-drawn carriage (actually a cart rolling on old car tires, as opposed to the gussied up Granada version) and doing a little tour.

While you can take bus to the Tola beaches, it's often more convenient in a taxi. Rates are reasonable for four people to Playa Gigante (US$20), Playa Santana (US$25), and Playa Popoyo (US$35). Make arrangements for them to pick you up.

If it's been raining for more than three days, normal four-wheel drive vehicles will not be able to make the trip to Playa Pie de Gigante, so call **Hell or High Water 4WD Taxi Service** (8924-7301; hombligobueno@yahoo.com).

Boat

There is irregular boat taxi service between Playa Gigante and San Juan del Sur; see the San Juan del Sur chapter for more information. You can also arrange private boat transportation up and down along the coast; see Boat Tours.

LODGING

You're well off the tourist trail, which means fewer hotel choices, especially in the midrange category. There are plenty of basic hostels geared to Nicaraguan travelers and budget surfers, as well as really spendy, all-inclusive surf camps and pricey vacation rentals in opulent gated communities.

Peak surf season for the Tola beaches is April through September, when rates rise and it's best to book surf hotels in advance. Many surf camps rent rooms to walk-ins during off-season for a fraction of what they charge the all-inclusive crowd.

Lodging Price Code

Cost of lodging is based on an average per-room, double occupancy rate during peak season (December through April). Nicaragua's 15 percent sales tax and gratuities are not included; note that paying cash sometimes results in taxes being waived. Prices are much higher during the Christmas holidays and, to a lesser extent, Semana Santa (Easter Week), when you should have reservations.

Inexpensive ($)	Up to US$25
Moderate ($$)	US$25 to US$60
Expensive ($$$)	US$60 to US$100
Very Expensive ($$$$)	US$100 and up

Hotels

RIVAS

At press time, a new option called **Hotel Brisas del Sur** was under construction on the Panamerican, just south of Texaco, and looked like it would be a great midrange option (something Rivas needs).

There are a dozen very basic budget spots located on the Panamerican Highway. Always ask to see a room before committing.

LA MAR LAKE RESORT

Owner: Dennis Martinez
2563-0021, 8856-7235
www.lamarlakeresort.com
info@lamarlakeresort.com
KM123 Panamerican Highway, La Virgen
(12 km south of Rivas)
Price: Moderate
Credit Cards: Yes
Handicap Access: Challenging
Wifi: Yes

This unusual entry, right off the Panamerican Highway, offers inspiring views of Isla Ometepe from the thatch-roofed restaurant, playground, and palm-shaded swimming pools. Once a breezy prison, this rather upmarket spot was remodeled by Baseball Hall of Famer Dennis Martinez, and is now one of the most comfortable hotels on the lake.

Sizeable rooms are creatively (and geometrically) partitioned, with cheerful bedspreads and sturdy furnishings, clearly designed with families in mind. All are air-conditioned, with cable TVs, refrigerators, machine-heated showers, and other comforts. The **restaurant** (B, L, D; $$–$$$) specializes in guapote (rainbow bass), but serves other well-prepared Nicaraguan cuisine, and is a great place to decompress after crossing the border. La Mar is a US$1 cab ride (12 km) south from Rivas.

✪ HOTEL NICARAO INN

General Manager: Roberto Torres
2563-3234, 2563-3836
www.hotelnicaraoinn.com.ni
nicaraoinn@turbonett.com.ni
Del BAC, 0.5 cuadra este
Price: Moderate
Credit Cards: Yes
Handicap Access: Yes
Wifi: Yes

The finest hotel in Rivas gives a tantalizing hint of what this city's stately Colonial architecture could be with Granada-level investment. It's not particularly authentic, but the modern, whitewashed rooms are very comfortable, with spotless hot baths, icy cold air-conditioning, huge TVs, and wifi.

The rather fancy lobby and street-side patio boast the only "gourmet" **restaurant** (B, L, D; $$–$$$) in town, specializing in steak and seafood. Your money goes a long way in Rivas, and if you really just need a night of developed-world comforts in a quiet Colonial town, this is a great choice.

PLAYA PIE DE GIGANTE

This small community of surfers and fishing families is cradled in one of Nicaragua's prettiest bays.

AQUA YOGA AND WELLNESS RETREAT

2278-8823, 509-456-7737 (U.S., Spokane, WA)
www.aquanicaragua.com
info@aquanicaragua.com
Playa Redondo
Price: Expensive
Credit Cards: Yes
Handicap Access: No
Wifi: Yes

New ecochic retreat on the Tola coast offers all the luxury of the other top-end developments, but a wholly different vibe. Named Nicaragua's Model Ecotourism Project by MARENA (Ministry of Environment and Natural Resources), Aqua sits on 202 hectares (500 acres) of recovering dry tropical forest, most of which will remain wilderness, and fronts 5 km (3 miles) of stunning coastline on a more private bay just over the "foot" from Playa Pie de Gigante.

The theme is green—each of the tree houses, surrounded with forest canopy, is designed for sustainability. Handcrafted from teak and mahogany—with luxury accents like slate floors and Balinese showers—these one-, two-, and three-bedroom vacation rentals are just beautiful. Plunge pools, beach views, a wellness spa, and a recommended natural foods restaurant complete the scene.

DALE DAGGER SURF TOURS
Owner: Dale Dagger
8921-8694
www.nicasurf.com
dale@nicasurf.com
Entrada 100 metros sur
Price: Very Expensive
Credit Cards: Yes
Handicap Access: Challenging
Wifi: Yes

The original Playa Gigante surf camp is still the plushest surf pad on the beach, in a thoroughly modern house with air-conditioning, hot showers, private bathrooms, wifi, DirecTV, and a relaxed living room with huge windows overlooking the beach. You're here for the waves, of course, and Dale includes unlimited boat trips for fishing or surfing—with the best captains and local knowledge around.

The Web site has regularly updated surfing pics, if you need something to get you through another day at the office. If there's space, they may accommodate walk-ins.

GIANT'S FOOT HOTEL SURF
Owners: Bryce and Lisa Kluclock
8924-7301
www.giantsfoot.com
reservations@giantsfoot.com
Entrada 250 metros sur
Price: Inexpensive to Very Expensive
Credit Cards: Yes
Handicap Access: No
Wifi: Yes

Make a left at the Pacific to find this relaxed surf lodge. It's not outrageously plush, but they've invested where it counts: good mattresses, comfortable air-conditioned rooms, cool bamboo furnishings, loads of hammocks for wave-weary bodies, table tennis, surf tours, and unlimited beer and rum if you've booked a surf package.

From October to March, this is an inexpensive hostel, but during surf season it becomes an exclusive, all-inclusive surf camp. Either way, they also have kayaks, bikes and snorkel gear, and can arrange massages and Spanish classes. The owners are great, and may be able to offer transport from Rivas.

HOTEL BRIO
Owner: Robert Dull
2433-9737
www.hotelbrio.com
info@hotelbrio.com
500 meters east of Playa Gigante
Price: Moderate
Credit Cards: Yes
Handicap Access: No
Wifi: Yes

This is a solid midrange option for the Tola coast, a sweet spread with beach views from the dry tropical forest. The **restaurant** (B, L, D; $$–$$$) gets recommendations for its creative, international cuisine, and the five spacious, whitewashed rooms are great—with polished wood, glass brick, and stainless steel accents; hot showers and air-conditioning.

The hotel also offers Spanish and yoga classes, and access to owner Robert Dull's private protected area (generally visited by students and scientists), Reserva Ecológica Zacatán.

MOMO SURF CAMP
Owner: Vincent Thaubaunguet
8990-1531
www.surfcamp-nicaragua.com
Playa Gigante de Gigante
Price: Expensive to Very Expensive
Credit Cards: Yes
Handicap Access: No
Wifi: No

French-operated surf camp offers two packages: an "economic" all-inclusive in their

Another perfect sunset at Playa Pie de Gigante

clean, acceptable surf shack right on the beach, with fan-cooled rooms, great beds, and shared baths; and the pricier "executive" choice, with much nicer accommodation, better cuisine, snorkeling, sport fishing, and more. They offer boat transport, surfing, and fishing tours for guests and nonguests alike anywhere on the Tola coast.

BETWEEN PLAYA GIGANTE AND PLAYA GUASACATE (POPOYO)

Strung between the surfing and fishing communities of Playas Gigante and Popoyo are several upscale vacation communities, seemingly plucked whole from Southern California and dropped like picturesque oxymorons onto the rural Nicaraguan *campo.* These are geared to North American and European retirees and investors.

In addition to the glamorous gated communities, there are plenty of smaller, independent hotels and surf camps along Playa Santana, the unimproved shore just north of Rancho Santana, accessible via the blue-collar Nicaraguan towns of Limon #1 and Limon #2.

✪ BUENA ONDA BEACH RESORT

Owners: Sarah Ruf and Philip Bienz
8973-0101
www.buenaondaresort.com
info@buenaondaresort.com
Playa Santana
Price: Inexpensive to Moderate
Credit Cards: Not yet
Handicap Access: No
Wifi: US$10 for your entire stay

Stylish and sophisticated, this surf-oriented hotel rises with a colorful geometry from an otherwise undeveloped stretch of Playa Santana. Rooms and dorms are well thought out and comfortable, with handmade Masatepe furnishings, pretty painted tiles and glass brick accents, and primitivist art that contrasts fabulously with the modern sensibilities. There's even a two-story house with full kitchen.

The Swiss owners (who speak German, English, French, and Spanish) opted against an all-inclusive, as they wanted to cater to both surfers and their spouses (and anyone who wants to enjoy this pretty beach). Thus, they offer very reasonable room rates and separate charges for boat excursions, surf lessons, horseback rides, and family-style meals in their beachfront ranchero. The hotel is 1.5 km (1 mile) from a sign on the coastal road; they can send someone to pick you up at the bus stop.

HACIENDA IGUANA

Owners: Various
8855-7906, 269-912-5929 (U.S.)
www.haciendaiguana.com
info@haciendaiguana.com
Playa Colorado
Price: Very Expensive
Credit Cards: Yes
Handicap Access: Yes (for condos and some villas)
Wifi: Some units (may cost extra)
Special: Access to Nicaragua's best surf breaks

They say that the developers of this upscale, 162-hectare (400-acre) vacation community didn't even realize that its powdery white-sand beaches overlook two of Nicaragua's best surfing waves, Panga Drops and Colorado. They actually chose the rolling property because it would be excellent for golfing, a judgment the nine-hole, Neils Oldenburg–designed course has proven true.

The best part about the view over Hacienda Iguana's golf course and perfect beach? It's from the balcony of your luxury condo.

Regardless, the oceanfront greens and big breaks have helped make this plush community one of Nicaragua's most popular, where luxurious homes and condominiums can be rented short- or long-term. (It's often cheaper to rent independently than through the offices; check online.)

Two-bedroom condominiums are luxuriously outfitted with marble floors, fabulous furnishings, full gourmet kitchens, SkyTV, and a complimentary golf cart. Houses are unique, but all are modern and pretty darned plush.

HOTEL LAS TORTUGAS

Owner: Orlando Amador
8993-4898
www.hotellastortugas.com
hotel.tortugas@gmail.com
Playa Santana (Limón #2)
Price: Inexpensive to Expensive
Credit Cards: Yes (not for walk-ins)
Handicap Access: No
Wifi: No

The least expensive surf camp close to Playa Santana is actually closer to the Nica town of Limón #2 than the beach. The basic two-story structure has seven small, clean, fan-cooled rooms with private baths and good beds. All-inclusive prices are the best in the region, and walk-ins pay US$15 per person. There's an on-site restaurant.

JIQUILITE SURF

Owners: José Ángel and Joselina Granado
8884-1467, 8670-9261
www.villajiquelite.com
villajiquelite@gmail.com
Playa Santana
Price: Inexpensive to Moderate
Credit Cards: No
Handicap Access: No
Wifi: No

Right on the volcanic gray sands of Playa Santana, in sight of Rancho Santana's cliff-top mansions, this is quite literally a million-dollar location. The Granados, however, offer Santana's three perfect peaks and simple brick rooms packed with beds, for a much lower price. Air-conditioning is an extra US$15. The mellow restaurant (B, L, D; $–$$) has Nica cuisine and fresh seafood; the owners know local captains who'll help you catch your own. They also organize surf tours and horses.

Next door on the beach a probably pricier place, **Paraiso de Los Bendaña**, was under construction; check it out.

RANCHO SANTANA

Owners: Various
8877-6164
www.ranchosantana.com
marcb@ranchosantana.com
Playa Santana
Price: Very Expensive
Credit Cards: Yes
Handicap Access: Yes
Wifi: Some units

Draped across the windswept Pacific bluffs, Rancho Santana's dazzling collection of luxury homes and condominiums is one of Nicaragua's premier oceanfront communities. The 1,093-hectare (2,700-acre) development (including a 600-acre wildlife preserve) has several sizes and styles of privately owned villas.

The least expensive are two-bedroom casitas (small houses) with air-conditioning, full kitchens, sofa beds, cable TV, and perhaps wifi, running US$150–200 per night. Spend US$300-plus per night, and you'll get a sprawling mansion with an infinity pool, fabulous furnishings, private beach access, and other amenities too extravagant to list. Vista del Mar, which will have hotel rooms, was under construction at press time.

Guests at Rancho Santana have beach access to three of the best waves on the coast; **Surf Santana** (surfsantana.com) has information. They also offer horseback riding packages; **Rancho Santana Equestrian Dreams** (www.ranchosantanaequestrian.com) has information.

THE SURF SANCTUARY
Owners: Tony and Nancy Longobucco
8894-6260, 904-219-3864 (U.S.)
www.thesurfsanctuary.com
info@thesurfsanctuary.com
Playa Santana (Limón #2)
Price: Moderate to Very Expensive
Credit Cards: Yes
Handicap Access: Challenging
Wifi: Yes

Relaxed, popular, family-run surf camp has all-inclusive options and regular rentals, with your choice of hotel-style rooms or spacious two- and three-bedroom casitas with full kitchens. These are scattered throughout the manicured gardens and around the recommended **restaurant** and a huge, deep, fish-shaped pool with a swim-up bar that's popular with a local crowd. Boats, boards, and other beach necessities are all available on-site.

The friendly owners also offer a poolside sunset happy hour, perfect after a long day riding waves. The attractive compound is about five minutes on foot from Playa Santana.

LAS SALINAS DE NAHUALAPA AND PLAYA GUASACATE (POPOYO)
The major town on this stretch of the Tola coast is Las Salinas de Nahualapa, named for the massive salt evaporation ponds that have been its livelihood for generations. Close by are two of Nicaragua's most famous waves, Popoyo and the Outer Reef. These are most easily accessible from the strip of hotels and restaurants on Playa Guasacate, which most people refer to as Playa Popoyo.

There are a handful of better options on Guasacate's north end, while "the point" is home to low-budget surf shacks.

CASA MAUR
Owner: Maritza Urbina
8378-3822, 8887-3393
www.popoyocasamaur.com
Between Playa Santana and Playa Popoyo
Price: Inexpensive to Moderate
Credit Cards: Yes
Handicap Access: No
Wifi: Yes

Casa Maur isn't expensive—dorms are just US$10, though the US$80 suite does have a fine private porch overlooking the ocean. But it's much nicer and cleaner than the serious budget places, in a rambling house with seashell décor, boards for rent, and a beachfront patio area with a pool, hammocks, cold beer, and spectacular sunsets.

✪ HOTEL POPOYO
Owners: Diego Blatt and Paloma Andrés Urrutia
8885-3334
www.hotelpopoyo.com
info@hotelpopoyo.com
Playa Guasacate
Price: Inexpensive to Moderate
Credit Cards: Yes
Handicap Access: Challenging
Wifi: Yes

A big step up from the crash pads on the point, Hotel Popoyo offers clean, air-conditioned accommodation, ranging from third-floor dorm beds to "lujo" rooms with handmade wooden furnishings, high cane ceilings, great bathrooms, and gorgeous bamboo beds. There's also an apartment with a full kitchen.

All include access to the big pool surrounded with hammock chairs, and breakfast in the excellent restaurant, **El Toro** (B, L, D; $$) worth stopping by even if you're not a guest; diners can use the hotel's wifi for US$2 per hour. The usual surfing amenities—boat tours, instruction, board rental—are happily arranged.

To disguise the location of their favorite wave, surfers deliberately confused Playa Popoyo and Guasacate; this is (probably) the real Popoyo.

POPOYO SURF LODGE

Owners: JJ and Kimberly Yemma
321-735-0322 (U.S.)
www.surfnicaragua.com
Entrance to Playa Guasacate
Price: Expensive to Very Expensive
Credit Cards: Yes
Handicap Access: No
Wifi: Yes

The original Popoyo surf camp (apparently the reason why everyone calls Playa Guasacate "Popoyo") has only improved with age, offering some of the plushest accommodation in the area. Great accommodation, big pools, and gorgeous grounds are matched with exceptional regional knowledge and great service. Most people book through Wavehunters (www.wavehunters.com).

TWO BROTHERS SURF

Owners: Robert and Susan Gregory
8877-7501, 904-808-0524 (U.S.)
www.twobrotherssurf.com
info@twobrotherssurf.com
Salinas, near entrance to Playa Guasacate (Popoyo)
Price: Expensive to Very Expensive
Credit Cards: Yes
Handicap Access: No
Wifi: Yes

High atop a bluff with astounding views over the entire Tola coast is the most luxurious surf camp in the region. Inspired by architect Antonio Gaudi, it is an architectural achievement, accented with mosaic tilework and organic lines that almost rival the magnificent backdrop.

The villas are well designed, with tiled full kitchens and modern bathrooms, great bedding, air-conditioners, amazing views from your private porch, and what may be Nicaragua's best pool. Two Brothers doesn't do surf packages, so you pay for excursions, board rentals, and other items separately. Note that the prices are per villa, which sleep up to six.

BAHÍA EL ASTILLERO

At the end of the road, this picturesque fishing village is close to the entrance of Chacocente Wildlife Refuge, and far from everything else. Several local fishermen offer surf tours; look for signs. There is currently no Internet café in El Astillero.

BAHÍA PARAÍSO

Administrator: Guillermo Maradiaga
8353-7191
El Astillero
Price: Inexpensive
Credit Cards: Not yet
Handicap Access: Yes
Wifi: No

This brand-new, locally owned, budget spot on the beach is a great deal, with simple wooden rooms (go for the second floor) just steps from the shore, painted a cool blue. All have fans, good beds, and shared cool baths. The **restaurant** (B, L, D; $–$$) next door is considered the best in town, and you can get a package deal with meals when you rent your room.

Communities like El Astillero, where turtle eggs have traditionally been harvested, are now protecting the fragile nests; stop by and show your support.

HOSTAL HAMACAS

Owner: Joaquín Talavera
8810-4144
www.hostalhamacas.com
info@hostalhamacas.com
El Astillero, de la cancha, 50 metros norte
Price: Moderate
Credit Cards: Yes
Handicap Access: No
Wifi: No

The best hotel in El Astillero proper, this Pacific outpost of San Jorge's relaxed establishment is right on the beach (with a chain-link fence separating the shore from the property). Nine large, cement rooms, some with flagstone floors and air-conditioning, are decorated with artesanías from San Juan del Oriente and quite comfortable. There are lots of hammocks on the shared front porch and rancho, with wind chimes and an outdoor grill. Breakfast is included.

LAS PLUMERÍAS

Owners: Emeline Lopez and Etienne
8979-7782, 8379-7366
www.lasplumerias.com
infos@lasplumerias.com
Playa Gavilán, El Astillero
Price: Expensive to Very Expensive
Credit Cards: Yes
Handicap Access: No
Wifi: Yes

In between El Astillero and Playa Guasacate/Popoyo, this ecologically minded, French-owned surf lodge lies 300 meters from a white sand beach known for its uncrowded waves. The circular, thatch-roofed casitas, made with local materials, look great against the jungle mountain backdrop. Inside, they are appealingly simple, with fans, pedestal beds, and modern private baths, as well as private porches with a view.

The main ranchero, where you'll enjoy three French-accented meals with your rooms, has plenty of hammocks. Surf packages are available, but they rent boards and offer instruction separately.

PUNTA TEONOSTE
NATURE LODGE AND SPA

Owner: Walter Bühler
2267-3008, 2563-9001, 786-345-5195 (U.S.)
www.puntateonoste.com
info@puntateonoste.com
Between Salinas and El Astillero
Price: Very Expensive
Credit Cards: Yes
Handicap Access: No
Wifi: Yes

This glamorous ecoresort, with its luxuriously outfitted villas, enjoys a privileged position on one of the most beautiful beaches on the Tola coast. Enjoy views of that otherwise empty swath of soft white sand over your complimentary welcome cocktail.

Sixteen circular cabins are tranquil and elegant, hewn from tropical hardwoods and paved with stones and parquet in a spiral motif. Each has two stories, outdoor showers, and wonderful décor—but no air-conditioning or TV. Rates include a full breakfast, surfboards and boogie boards, a small pool, horseback rides, and 3 km (2 miles) of trails to the mirador.

If you visit between August and January, you may see paslama (olive Ridley) and torita (leatherback) sea turtles laying eggs on the beach. Come 45 days later, and you'll watch the babies hatch in their private vivero, where they protect the nests from poachers.

There's an on-site spa with massages, facials, and an "ozone room," and a very pricey French **restaurant** (B, L, D; $$$$).

Vacation Rentals

The most popular spots for long-term rentals are the community developments of Rancho Santana and Hacienda Iguana, listed above. Also check Vacation Rentals in the San Juan del Sur chapter; many of those sites also have listings for the Tola beaches.

Honey Ox (www.honeyox.com) Small site has a number of luxury listings.

Nicaragua Surf Report (www.nicaraguasurfreport.com) This one specializes in plush properties on the Tola coast and around San Juan del Sur.

Nicasurfing.com (www.nicasurfing.com) Surf tours and information, plus a good selection of Tola rentals.

Other Hotels

None of these hotels has wifi, easy handicap access, or accepts credit cards unless specifically noted.

RIVAS

Bar-Hospedaje Español (2563-0006; del parque central, 1 cuadra este; $) Spanish-owned spot close to the central park offers five fan-cooled rooms with very clean, shared bath and saggy single beds.

Hospedaje Hilmor (8830-8175; del parque central, 1 cuadra este; $) Large but very basic rooms in a two-story building have fans and private baths; for US$10 more, you get TV. There's a shared kitchen.

Hospedaje Lydia (2453-3477; de Texaco, 1 cuadra oeste; $) Basic but reliably clean cheapie right off the Panamerican Highway has fan-cooled rooms with shared bath, good breakfasts, and excellent service.

Hotel y Restaurante Gaury #2 (8865-9082; Entrada Principal del Hospital, 50m arriba de Panamericana; $) Just north of Rivas proper, at the turnoff to Tola and the beaches, this hotel offers small but spotless, freshly painted budget rooms with fans, decent beds, and private cool baths. It's popular with Nica travelers, so make reservations.

Hotel Río Lago (8887-2842, 8888-7667; hotelriolago@gmail.com; KM11.5 Panamericana; credit cards accepted; $$) The blue-collar version of La Mar Lake Resort, a few hundred meters north, this lakeside hotel has air-conditioned cabins with private baths—some with kitchenettes, a big pool, boats for rent, and those same great views of Ometepe.

NANDAIME

Hotel Brisas de Mombacho (2301-1080; Panamerican Highway, 1 km south of the Granada exit; $–$$) If you get stuck in Nandaime, this family-run guesthouse is adorable, offering seven clean, fan-cooled rooms (air-conditioning is US$5 extra) with cable TV, lots of sunlight, private cool baths, knick-knacks, and other homey touches.

PLAYA PIE DE GIGANTE

Acopio Beach House (8360-7508; kassidy@nicasurf.com; north end of town; $–$$; wifi) Housed in a totally remodeled, colorfully muralled *acopio*, or fish-processing plant, this cute cottage has a comfy dorm and immaculate private room—or rent the whole house (sleeps six) for just US$60. They're planning to build a tree house and another cottage.

✪ **Chele Palmado's BareFoot Bar and Grill** (8912-8918; lowe.w.david@gmail.com; L,

D; $$), the sandy-floored onsite restaurant, serves gourmet burritos, fancy sandwiches, and creative cocktails from their very full bar.

✪ **The Swell Beach Hostel** (8904-0187; theswellgigante@hotmail.com; south end of town; $; wifi) This well-run budget option offers clean, simple, fan-cooled rooms in a breezy beach home, offering a shared kitchen, free potable water, hammocks on the rambling wooden deck, and a few second-floor rooms with shared baths that are worth reserving.

Blue Sol Hotel Restaurant (8906-6018; entrada Playa Gigante, 10 metros norte; $) This locally owned crash pad is the cheapest in town, with grimy cement rooms and very basic shared bath, next to a popular local bar.

SALINAS AND GUASACATE (POPOYO)
Budget travelers head straight to "the point," at the end of the access road, with a cluster of basic cheapies.

✪ **Cabina Tica #2** (8375-1620; the point; $) Bright blue hotel has two stories of fan-cooled rooms with surprisingly good beds; US$3 more gets you a private bathroom. The restaurant, right on the estuary, has pizza Tuesday and a barbecue on Friday.

Hotel Restaurant Bocona Surf (8370-5643; on the point; $) This cinderblock hotel, sometimes called the "Tiltin' Hilton," has simple, clean, fan-cooled rooms with private baths, and a second-story hangout area with rocking chairs.

Magnificent Rock (8888-5550; between Playas Santana and Popoyo; $) This weird wooden Victorian, far from all other hotels, tops a slab-slate point separating Santana and Popoyo's vast and untamed bays, a truly magnificent view. Rooms aren't terrible, just musty, with decent beds, private baths, and a few cobwebbed pieces of furniture—including a minifridge, which you should keep full, as the restaurant wasn't working and it's 4 km (2.5 miles) from the coastal highway. The view is worth it.

Nicawaves (8980-0485, 843-222-3114 (U.S.); nicawaves.com; info@nicawaves.com; $–$$) On the other side of the point, overlooking Popoyo proper rather than Playa Guasacate, Nicawaves rents several basic, breezy houses, some with air-conditioning, on a forested hillside. To get here, take the turnoff toward Magnificent Rock, just south of Salinas, until you see a small sign for Nicawaves. They also rent boards, do photography, and arrange all-inclusive packages.

Popoyo Loco (8322-9933; scrinzi.santiago@gmail.com; 100m from the point; $) Dark, cleanish rooms are so close to the waves that you won't even be able to finish your joint walking out there. There's a shared kitchen and on-site surf instructors—who will probably help you with that joint, if need be.

RESTAURANTS AND FOOD PURVEYORS

It's certainly not Granada, but Rivas has a fair selection of restaurants, with Chinese food and pizza places close to the central park, as well as typical Nicaraguan fare around town.

Once you're out on the Tola beaches, however, you generally have two choices: hotel restaurants, or basic beachfront spots selling seafood and chicken with the usual rice, beans, plantains, and cabbage salad. Get groceries in Rivas.

Restaurant and Food Purveyor Price Code

The following prices are based on the cost of a dinner entrée with a nonalcoholic drink, not including Nicaragua's mandatory

13 percent restaurant tax and "suggested" 10 percent tip, which is usually included with the final bill (so check).

Inexpensive ($)	Up to US$5
Moderate ($$)	US$5 to US$10
Expensive ($$$)	$10 to $20
Very Expensive ($$$$)	US$20 or more

Restaurants

RIVAS

COCTELERÍA EL MARISCAZO

2563-1077
del Estadio, 800 metros sur
Price: Moderate to Expensive
Cuisine: Seafood, Nicaraguan
Serving: L, D
Credit Cards: Yes
Child's Menu: No
Handicap Access: Yes
Reservations: No

The best restaurant in town is beneath this big thatched ranchero right off the highway, serving spectacular ceviche and seafood cocktails, often enjoyed over a beer or several. Pricier entrees include cambute (a type of conch), red snapper, shrimp dishes, and classic Nica platters with chicken or beef. Kids love the grassy garden, with playground equipment, but come after dark for a more romantic ambiance.

EL PRÍNCIPE II

2563-0338
Contiguo al Estadio
Price: Inexpensive to Moderate
Cuisine: Nicaraguan, International
Serving: L, D
Credit Cards: Yes
Child's Menu: No
Handicap Access: Yes
Reservations: No

With a full bar and dance floor, this place brings in party people (with kids in tow) for good music and a big menu. Budget travelers can try the comida rapida, including

burgers and sandwiches, or go for the Chinese food. There are also plenty of Nica typical dishes on offer.

✪ SUPER POLLO

2563-0109
del museo, 0.5 cuadras este
Price: Moderate to Expensive
Cuisine: Nicaraguan
Serving: L, D
Credit Cards: Yes
Child's Menu: Yes
Handicap Access: No
Reservations: No

This centuries-old building is convenient to both the museum and bus lot, and is well worth seeking out for some of the best food in town. Grab a table on the rather fabulous (though fragile-looking) second-floor terrace before choosing your chicken filet: a la naranja (orange glaze), salsa de piña (pineapple sauce), salsa de hongos (mushroom sauce), or jalapeña (creamy, spicy chili sauce). There are also burgers, sandwiches, ceviche, and a very full bar offering wines and international liquors.

PLAYA PIE DE GIGANTE
This tiny town has a surprising number of good restaurants, ranging from absolutely authentic to international surfer cuisine.

LA GAVIOTA RESTAURANT

8643-2844, 8921-8918
Playa Gigante
Price: Inexpensive to Expensive
Cuisine: Seafood, Nicaraguan
Serving: B, L, D
Credit Cards: Yes
Child's Menu: No
Handicap Access: Yes
Reservations: Yes

A handful of locally owned restaurants clustered right on the beach offer fresh pargo (red snapper), langosta (lobster), and camarones (shrimp) with a view and a brew.

Relax and have a brew or two at La Gaviota, and contemplate the "Giant's Foot" of Playa Pie de Gigante.

The best of the bunch is La Gaviota, with wonderful vistas from the newly remodeled front porch, and a few international and vegetarian dishes to compliment their classic Nicaraguan recipes.

Next door, **Bar y Comedor Mary Mar** (8694-3722; cash only; L, D; $–$$), serves tasty seafood and cold beer, but no beach views; while **El Mirador Margarita** (8948-2042; cash only; B, L, D; $–$$) has a second-story view of the bay as well as big breakfasts (including international items such as yogurt and omelets), inexpensive seafood, and a few vegetarian items.

Any of these can arrange boat captains for fishing and surfing trips, while La Gaviota plans to build a guesthouse.

✪ PIE DE GIGANTE RESTAURANT
8904-0187

www.piedegigante.net
Playa Pie de Gigante, south of entrance
Price: Moderate
Cuisine: International
Serving: B, D (and L in high season)
Credit Cards: No
Child's Menu: No
Handicap Access: Challenging
Reservations: No

Not just an excellent restaurant, this is the friendly social hub of the fishing and surfing community, where dreadlocked travelers teach local kids how to fire dance in the gardens, and well-heeled surfers duck out of their all-inclusive packages for the evening to enjoy healthy, international dishes prepared by the restaurant's French-Basque chef. There's even wifi.

Ingredients are fresh, and whenever

possible organic or locally sourced. Everything is washed in purified water and prepared to developed-world standards. A three-course, prix fixe dinner always showcases what's in season, or go for something a la carte, perhaps the lobster flambé or fresh pesto pasta (vegetarian items are creative and plentiful). Go ahead and finish up with the to-die-for cheesecake—surfing burns a lot of calories. There are sometimes parties or events, so drop by to see what's on.

Playa Guasacate (Popoyo)
Other good restaurants, such as ✪ **El Toro** at Popoyo Surf Lodge, are at area hotels.

RESTAURANT DISCO-BAR AMORES DEL SOL
8847-9950
On the point
Price: Moderate
Cuisine: Seafood, Nicaraguan
Serving: B, L, D
Credit Cards: No
Child's Menu: No
Handicap Access: Challenging
Reservations: No

Enjoy Popoyo's remarkable sunsets at this restaurant, sprawling from beneath its pretty palapa-topped ranchero and out into the soft sand. The specialty is good vibes, served with a side of rum or beer, pargo, or tostones con queso—all perfect as you watch the stars lit like candles against the velvet blue sky.

Note that the leashed monkey hates women, likes beer, and will occasionally masturbate on passersby.

RESTAURANT KATHEERE
8460-1535
300 meters from the point
Price: Moderate
Cuisine: Seafood, Nicaraguan
Serving: B, L, D
Credit Cards: No
Child's Menu: No
Handicap Access: Challenging
Reservations: No

A short walk from the main cluster of beach hotels, this surfer favorite serves large portions of pescado a la plancha (grilled fish), jalapeño chicken (in a creamy, spicy sauce), and a few vegetarian options at simple wooden tables in the sand, surrounded by palm trees.

CAFÉ BAR PIZZERÍA RANA ROJA
8478-8893
www.ranarojanicaragua.com
500 meters from the point
Price: Moderate to Expensive
Cuisine: Italian
Serving: D
Closed: Mon.
Credit Cards: No
Child's Menu: No
Handicap Access: Challenging
Reservations: No

The most elegant option in Popoyo is this Italian-owned and -operated restaurant that specializes in wood-fired pizzas and homemade pastas served in a romantic, candlelit courtyard with lots of bamboo. Choose from a variety of creative pies and classic sauces, as well as the good wine and cocktail list.

Food Purveyors

Cafés
Holy Grounds Bakery (8999-8368; Salinas; cash only; B, L; $) Just south of the turnoff to Guasacate (Popoyo), this bakery and café also serves Mexican food.
Julieta's Café Casa Cerámica (8826-7312; www.nicaraguaovercoffee.com; Rivas, frente BDF; B, L, D; closed Sun.; $–$$) Café and handicrafts shop in downtown Rivas serves

cheesecakes, smoothies, coffee, and traditional Nica snacks such as *tiste*—a popular (but gritty) corn beverage—quesillos, and *repochetas* (cheese-stuffed tortillas).

Paradise Bakery and Café (8955-4313; gkattyroxana@yahoo.com; Escuela Limón #1, 900 varas abajo; B, L; open Mon. through Fri.) In the tiny town of Limón #1, cool little café has big breakfasts, espresso beverages, and lots of tasty baked goods. It's right on the main road.

Pizza

Rivas has a competitive pizza scene.

Pizza Hot (2563-4662; parque central; credit cards accepted; L, D; $–$$) Great people watching on the kitschy central park, good pizza, and fried chicken.
Pizza Hotter (2563-0927; www.hotterpizza.com; Texaco costado oeste; credit cards accepted; $–$$) Serves presumably hotter pizza, as well as pasta dishes and beer, close to the Panamerican Highway's budget hotels and buses.
Villa's Rosti Pizza (2563-0712; parque central; L, D; $$) In a Colonial-era arcaded building, Villa's serves pizza and fried chicken in more upscale environs.

Mexican

Mama's Fish Tacos (www.mamasfishtacos.com; Limón #1; cash only; open daily; $) Family-run stand cooks fresh fish tacos to order—and yes, they have a Web site, but it's just a tiny local place with plastic chairs in the dirt. It's well signed from the coastal road.

CULTURE

Rivas

Though they don't brag about it in the tourism literature, Rivas and neighboring San Jorge were almost certainly founded one year before Granada, in 1523. Prior to that, this was the important city-state of Nicarao Callí, which dated from at least 600 AD. For centuries, this capital controlled the Rivas Isthmus and sacred Ometepe Island, just offshore.

Spanish Conquistador Gil González Dávila first met Cacique, or Chief, Nicarao (in Spanish chronicles, the chief often shared his or her name with the nation) in 1522. The spot is now marked by **La Cruz de España**, suspended above the road to San Jorge and flanked by statues of the two men. The Spanish offered to spare Nicarao's people if they converted to Christianity within three days. The Cacique had presumably already heard what happened to those who refused the Spaniards' offer, and commanded 1,000 warriors to convert on the spot.

The Spanish destroyed the Nicarao anyway, but preserved their name in the name of their new colony, Nicaragua. They built their major isthmus city, Rivas, close to the fallen Nicarao capital. It is easy to navigate, built on a classic Colonial grid, with a huge central park (now with painted cement animals and playground equipment) fronted by the 1607 **Iglesia San Pedro y San Pablo.**

The pretty, pale church with interesting saints on display is only open in the early morning (from 6 AM–8 AM) and evening (5 PM–7 PM). A secret underground tunnel supposedly connects the ancient edifice with the 1776 **Iglesia San Francisco,** four blocks west. You can also visit **Cemetery Hill,** with views over Rivas and Ometepe.

The Cruz de España marks the spot where Cacique Nicarao and Conquistador Gil González first met.

Just outside the city center, close to the bus lot, the **Rivas Museum of Anthropology and History** occupies a beautiful old estate house that was once the headquarters of U.S. mercenary William Walker. From here, he won the First Battle of Rivas in 1855, occupying the city. The Second Battle of Rivas, in 1856, did not go so well for him.

The war had proven more expensive than Walker had planned, so he declared himself president of Nicaragua to try and leverage some funding. In order to curry favor with Southern U.S. politicians he had legalized slavery; in order to repay his war debt he decreed that his former benefactor Cornelius Vanderbilt's Accessory Transit Company be "given" to competitors, Garrison and Morgan.

The old robber baron promised to ruin the conspirators, then went to every neighboring country and offered to train and arm their troops, free of charge. When Walker made his move into Costa Rica, its President Juan Mora surprised the small, overconfident contingent with 3,000 men at Hacienda Santa Rosa, just over the border. After a 14-minute fight, Mora chased Walker's retreating troops back to Rivas, where the final, brutal battle was won by combined Nicaraguan and Costa Rican forces.

Today, Rivas is a relatively prosperous city of 40,000, a department capital, and the political and market hub of the isthmus.

The Tola beaches are made up of deep, sandy bays separated by dramatic slate points that stretch out into the barreling Pacific.

Tola

While this tiny town, perhaps named for the Toltecs (*toltec* is the Nahuatl word for "artisan") is pleasant enough, its most enduring contribution to Nicaraguan culture is probably the idiom, "You left me waiting like the bride of Tola."

In the most sordid scandal of 1876, young Hilaria Ruiz was left at the altar, jilted by a playboy fiancé who ran off with his mistress, Juanita Gazo. There's even a statue of the poor girl in front of the church.

The Tola Beaches

Neither the Spanish nor indigenous inhabitants of Central America built large, permanent settlements along the pretty Pacific. This puzzled some historians, until a 1992 tsunami destroyed much of the Nicaraguan coast. The Tola beaches were particularly hard hit, with entire villages and hundreds of people simply washed away.

This disaster, coming on the heels of the wars and Hurricane Mitch, dissuaded settlement for a decade. The coast wasn't even electrified until 2000 (most Nicaraguans still go without), while the coastal road reopened only in 2002. While the majority of the coast was until recently occupied only by small fishing villages and a smattering of surf camps, that is changing.

Huge tracts of land purchased cheaply in the last decade are now being developed into luxurious oceanfront communities, divided into lots sold primarily to North American investors and retirees. The politics of these places is, unsurprisingly, not quite as pretty as the view, but they undeniably bring money and stability to a country sorely in need of both. Check out the documentary *Land* for more insights.

Museums

If you're interested in a city tour, drop by Julieta's Café, also home to **Nicaragua Over Coffee Tours** (8914-8487; www.nicaraguaovercoffee.com; mikeviaemail@aol.com; frente BDF), which offers Rivas city tours and longer custom trips. Owner Mike King wrote a cool little self-published guidebook, *Foot Prints in History: Do-It-Yourself Tours of Rivas* (US$4), available here and around the isthmus.

RIVAS MUSEUM OF ANTHROPOLOGY AND HISTORY
2563-3708
Escuela Internacional de Agricultura, 1 cuadra este, 1.5 cuadra norte
Admission: US$2/0.50 foreigners/Nicaraguans
Open: 9 AM–noon and 2 PM–5 PM Mon. through Sat.

Probably the most interesting part of this museum is the proud old plantation mansion itself, collapsing into dilapidation with a regal stoicism. It was most famously William Walker's headquarters during the battles of Rivas, but was also home to the newspaper El Termómetro, best remembered for publishing Rubén Darío's first poem.

It's not the Smithsonian, but if you enjoy supporting small, underfunded local museums, stop by—it's just four blocks from the Rivas bus lot. You'll enjoy a handful of pre-Colombian ceramics and stone metates (corn grinders) from Isla Ometepe, some mammoth bones, a few rusty old guns, and lots of moth-eaten taxidermy. Most signage is in Spanish, as is your guided tour.

Nightlife

There's not a lot going on along the Tola beaches, other than the usual beachfront bars. Don't miss **Restaurant Pie de Gigante** in Playa Gigante for dinner and drinks, and **Amores del Sol** in Popoyo at sunset.

Rivas's tiny expat population gathers at **Whiskey Bar** (8698-5731; Enitel, 200 metros sur; L, D), with inexpensive beer, good liquor, and surprisingly healthy snacks, including organic salads and popcorn with oregano and chili.

Cosmos (2563-4442; sanio1@abv.bg), right on the central park, is sort of like walking into a Day-Glo cave from an old Star Trek episode, and has beer, rum, air-conditioning, and *comida típica* with astronomical names (*carne de res en salsa Júpiter,* anyone?).

On the highway, **El Príncipe II** (see Restaurants and Food Purveyors) and a few other festive ranchero restaurants both have a good scene in the evening. **Bar Mi Barra** (De Gymnasio Humberto Méndez, 0.5 cuadras este) has a friendly scene and gaming machines.

Spanish Schools

Escuela Big Foot (2433-9737, 512-377-9808 (U.S.); escuelabigfoot.com; 300 meters east of Playa Gigante) Tola's only Spanish school is operated by Hotel Brio. Packages can include room, board, and/or surfing lessons.

RECREATION

National Parks and Protected Areas

REFUGIO DE VIDA SILVESTRE RÍO ESCALANTE-CHACOCENTE
8927-7679 (field station), 8920-0089 (MARENA)
www.chacocente.com
chacotur@yahoo.es
Open: 24 hours
Admission: US$5/2.50 foreigners/Nicaraguans

Protecting an absolutely undeveloped 11.6-km (7.2-mile) beach stretching between El Astillero and Huehuete, Chacocente is isolated. Nesting sea turtles love it, and some return here annually—mostly paslamas (olive Ridleys), which famously arrive by the thousands in arribadas (mass nestings), and endangered toras (leatherbacks), who swim from beneath the polar ice caps to lay their eggs here.

Triggered, perhaps, by the moon, arribadas happen half a dozen times during the July to January nesting season. Call the field station for their best guess. If you go on a daytrip from El Astillero, fishermen will know when the turtles arrive offshore.

Chacocente staff collect all the eggs that they can find and place them in nests close to their headquarters—guarded by the Nicaraguan military. There they mature for 45–53 days, when hatchlings begin digging their way out of the sand. This usually happens in the very early morning, while the mothers arrive to nest between the evening high tide and around 2 AM.

Several operators offer evening trips and overnights at the park. It's possible, but confusing, to arrange lodging on your own. You must call ahead (in Spanish) to reserve hot group tents with cots, bedding, and the option of meals (US$3–5)—all offered by COSERTUCHACO (Cooperative Servicios Turisticos Chacocente; 8481-1202). This local tourism cooperative, which is not part of the park, also offers all the guided hikes, horseback and oxcart rides, and other tours.

However, if you have your own tent, you'll be staying at the unimproved campsite, which is managed by the field station (8927-7679). They do not offer tours or food service, so consider giving COSERTUCHACO a call anyway.

The park is only accessible with private transportation, and in rainy season (also most of nesting season), you'll need a four-wheel-drive vehicle. Taxis can be arranged from El Astillero, as can guided tours.

Other Parks and Natural Attractions

Rivas offers access to the lakeshore, most famously the popular, restaurant-lined beach in **San Jorge** (covered in the Isla Ometepe chapter)—just grab a US$1.50 shared taxi from the bus lot. There are other, less-developed beaches, too, including **Playa La Virgen**, 10 km (6 miles) south of Rivas. Ask about hiring a boat to **Laguna de Nocarime**, a lake lagoon that apparently has great birding.

Estancia del Congo Wildlife Reserve (2228-1206; www.redrspnica.com; Buenos Aires, KM85 Panamerican Highway) This 42-hectare (104-acre) private reserve lies on the lakeshore, with great views of Mombacho, Concepción, and Maderas Volcanoes. It was founded in 1997 by economist Freddy Cruz Cortez to protect an isolated family of howler

Well off the beaten path, the lakefront town of Cárdenas offers the rare opportunity to experience Cocibolca's quieter coast.

Cárdenas: Cocibolca's Quieter Shore

The southern coast of Lake Nicaragua, most easily accessible from Rivas, has a hidden treasure. The tiny town of Cárdenas is a fishing village, but thanks to increasing popularity with Costa Rican tourists eager to see the neighbor's big lake, has a handful of hotels and restaurants, plus a delightful *malecón*. From here, you'll enjoy the southern view of Isla Ometepe.

The best hotel in town is **Hospedaje Pulpería y Panadería Fiorella** (2563-0911; central park; cash only; $), fronted by a bakery and convenience store. The modest entrance hides fan-cooled rooms with TVs and private baths, all surrounding tidy gardens and patios with rocking chairs, murals, and an outdoor kitchen for guests.

A close second is right on the beach, at **Marisco Bar** (8604-4685; 200m de parque central; cash only; $), also considered Cárdenas's best restaurant. Clean, cement, fan-cooled rooms have good beds, plastic furnishings, and private baths—plus breezy lake views from the second floor.

The **restaurant** (B, L, D; $–$$) serves seafood from both Cocibolca and the Pacific, and less expensive Nica plates. Across the street, palapa topped **El Ranchón** (cash only; B, L, D; $) serves similar dishes (but no Pacific seafood) a bit more cheaply. Other simple eateries are scattered around town.

There are also several other small *hospedajes*. Ask around or contact the very helpful **Cárdenas Alcaldía** (8825-7867, 8737-5948; aravanegas4@yahoo.es, rodolfo_privera@yahoo.com; 200 meters del parque central; open 9 AM–noon and 2 PM–5 PM Mon. through Fri., sometimes Sat.), or mayor's office, which currently acts as the town's tour operator (but no one speaks English).

In addition to providing hotel and restaurant information, the *alcaldía* can arrange awesome four-hour lake tours for up to 15 people in a really cool old *panga*. You'll explore the lake's southern coastline, the fishing village of Colón, several caves, and rarely visited Isla Zanate.

Note that there is no gas station or ATM in Cárdenas, though there is Internet access at the library, right at the entrance to town. There are also lots of beautiful pearl-gray beaches with simple restaurants on the coastal road, and even a volcano-themed miniature golf course, **Blue Morpho** (8608-3272; 8 km/5 miles west of Cárdenas), set to open before this book hits the shelves.

Cárdenas is easy to reach—buses run from both Rivas and the border (US$0.60; every 30–45 minutes). The route is well signed for drivers; look for the exit just north of the Peñas Blancas border.

monkeys (*monos congos*). Today, there are five healthy howler troupes in the trees, as well as sloths, anteaters, raccoons, deer, foxes, squirrels, coyotes, boa constrictors, and dozens of bird species. Though they don't get many tourists, you can visit with reservations; it's easiest to work with a tour operator in Granada or San Juan del Sur.

El Astillero Vivero de Tortugas (tortugasoluble@ideay.net.ni; El Astillero Beach) The Tola beaches are patrolled every night by bicyclists with headlamps, who are looking for nesting sea turtles. They hope to harvest the eggs illegally, and sell them for a pittance to support their own families. In El Astillero, however, the community has just completed a new *vivero*, or "nursery," to protect at least some of the nests—if one of their employees finds a sea turtle first, the eggs are quickly moved here. At press time, they had a small bamboo information center with hatching schedules, and planned to offer tours. This is exactly the type of grassroots community project that tourists can support just by showing an interest in conservation, so drop by.

Salinas Hot Springs (5 km (3 miles) from Guasacate/Popoyo; open 24 hours; free) A few hundred meters from the Salinas police station, these deep, glistening thermal pools in the forest are a fine way to end a hard day of surfing. They are public, so don't bring any valuables, particularly at night. (You could bring your laundry, however, as there are several *pilas* set up for washing.) The EU apparently plans to improve the springs, but they will remain free and open to the public.

Reserva Ecológica Zacatán (2433-9737; www.zacatan.org; Playa Pie de Gigante) This private reserve, operated by Robert Dull of the excellent Hotel Brio (see Lodging) in Playa Pie de Gigante, protects a 12-hectare (29-acre) plot of endangered dry tropical rainforest. Easily adapted for pasture, farmland, and beachfront developments, these last remaining stands are an important home for all three Nicaraguan monkeys, scores of bird species, guatusos, pizotes, iguanas, and many other creatures. Most visitors to the reserve are students and scientists, but Hotel Brio can arrange regular guided hikes.

Boat Tours

The Tola beaches are both fishing communities and surfing destinations, so boats are easy to come by. This isn't San Juan del Sur, and there aren't dozens of English-speaking operators with top-of-the-line equipment. The Tola beaches are wilder, so you'll have to be a bit more resourceful.

If you speak Spanish, it's cheaper to talk directly to boat captains, who can certainly take you fishing and usually know surf breaks and snorkel spots. For more organized tours, your best bet is one of the outfitters below or any well-organized surf lodge.

Captain Max (info@playagigante.com) Offers half-day and full-day sailing trips (US$100/150 for six people) and sailing lessons from Playa Gigante, and provides passenger service to San Juan del Sur every Wednesday at 7 AM, returning at 12 noon.

Costa Nica Expeditions (2433-9737, 512-377-9808 (U.S.); www.costanica.com) In Playa Pie de Gigante, Hotel Brio operates boat charters anywhere on the coast between Playa El Coco and El Astillero, as well as snorkel tours, fishing trips, and more.

Kayaking Playa Pie de Gigante (8743-5699; hombligobueno@yahoo.com; Giant's Foot Surf Camp; kayaks US$15/20 single/double) Ask around for John, who rents kayaks and runs guided trips around the point and into Arenas Bay, where you can opt to climb an 11-meter (35-foot) rock and jump into the ocean.

Sportfishing Charters (8978-5710, 8980-0243; pescanicaragua@yahoo.com) Fully equipped sport fishing trips along the Tola beaches.

Golf

At press time, Hacienda Iguana had the only operating public golf course, but several more were set to open.

Hacienda Iguana (8855-7906, 269-912-5929 (U.S.); www.haciendaiguana.com) Tola's first golf course was designed by Neils Oldenburg, with nine challenging holes right along the beach. There are interesting hazards, beautiful views, and occasionally howler monkeys. Nonmembers can reserve a game for US$130–140.

Montecristo Beach (www.montecristobeach.com) From the same fine folks behind famous Hacienda Pinilla in Costa Rica, this development will feature an 18-hole, Mike Young–designed, 7,060-yard, par-71 course with a more than 100 meters (300 feet) of elevation change. *Golf Digest* has already named it one of the world's best new courses.

Seaside Mariana (888-484-4425 (U.S.); www.seasidemariana.com) Luxury oceanfront development was planning to open a world-class, 18-hole Jack Nicklaus Signature golf course—as well as a beach club, spa, golf villas, and condominiums.

Snorkeling

There aren't many well-known snorkel spots along the Tola beaches, though you should certainly ask around. In **Playa Gigante**, there's good snorkeling at the tip of the point (the "Giant's Foot") separating Gigante from Arenas Bay, recommended for strong swimmers only. There's also snorkeling near Pelican Island, at Playa Guacalito, with boat access. Both Casa Amarilla and Giant's Foot Surf Camp rent snorkel gear.

There are also apparently protected coves with good snorkel sites between **Playa Popoyo** and **El Astillero**.

Surfing

The Tola beaches have some of the best waves in Central America, crashing into an as-yet almost undeveloped coastline. Stone reefs, *boconas* (river mouths), and a wave-sculpting offshore wind conspire to create some of the best, most varied breaks in Central America. They say there are more than 40 surf spots along the Tola coast.

Tola can be surfed almost year round, but April through September is high season, when southern swells roll through. Make reservations at surf lodges in advance. For more general information about surfing Nicaragua and a list of national tour operators, see the San Juan del Sur Surfing sidebar. These waves are listed south to north.

Manzanilla Hire a boat to almost guaranteed surfing on large and medium waves.

El Arco Gigante doesn't usually have good surfing, but this beginner's wave close to Acopio Beach House in Gigante can sometimes get big.

Amarillo A 10-minute walk from Playa Gigante, this beach break has reliable surf for beginners.

Colorado In front of Hacienda Iguana, about an hour's walk from Gigante, this river mouth beach break is considered one of Central America's best—a very consistent, hollow, fast, powerful wave with both rights and lefts.

Playa Rosada Just south of Playa Santana, this pretty pink beach has a fast, hollow, left point break with a shallow takeoff, for experienced surfers. Just south, **Perfect Peak** is a fast, left reef break that works on the incoming tide.

Playa Santana This fun, reliable beach break has three defined peaks, an A-frame and two that will barrel right and left on the high tide.

Popoyo Experienced surfers loves this famous, reliable, A-frame wave with a long left and some good rights. Just a 15-minute walk from the Guasacate surf shacks, this is also one of Tola's few potentially crowded waves.

Outer Reef Past Popoyo, this is a very big, very hollow, very serious pipeline, a truly epic big wave. For strong surfers only.

Guasacate North of Popoyo, this mellow beach break is convenient and sometimes works pretty well.

Panga Drops Slab-rock river break can hold a big swell.

Playa Gavilán In front of Las Plumerias Lodge, this right point break works on big swells.

El Astillero Experienced surfers will enjoy this empty, fairly reliable point break with right and left peaks, as well as the beach breaks nearby and at Chacocente Wildlife Reserve. El Astillero is a fishing village, but some captains specialize in surf tours.

Chacocente Few surfers get to this hollow, fast, reliable beach break with rights and lefts. Also ask about **Lance's Left** and **Playgrounds**. These are off-limits during *arribadas,* when nesting sea turtles get first dibs.

Spas and Gyms

Businesses in both Playa Pie de Gigante and Playa Guasacate had flyers advertising yoga and massage, while **Aqua Yoga and Wellness Retreat** (2278-8823; www.aquanicaragua.com) can arrange spa treatments. Playa Gigante Online (www.playagigante.com) has more information.

Shopping

Banks and ATMs

Rivas has a handful of banks and ATMs in the city center, several blocks from the bus station—hire a pedicab. Stock up on cash here, as there are no ATMs on the Tola beaches, and only the upscale spots accept credit cards.

Groceries and Markets

The Tola beaches have a few simple stores where you can pick up the basics, but it's worth stocking up in Rivas. The enormous ✪ **Mercado Municipal** is conveniently located next to the bus lot, about 1 km from the city center, with acres of fruit, vegetables, and other groceries—as well as clothing, leather shoes, and souvenirs, plus small eateries and stands selling prepared foods. Downtown, there's a good-sized **Palí** (two blocks east of the central park) offering a less chaotic shopping experience. **Texaco** (Panamerican Highway) has a 24-hour convenience store.

In Playa Pie de Gigante, **Pulpería Mena**, in the center of town, has the basics; knock on the window. Close by, **El Acopio** sells very fresh fish. If you can swing it, drop by the **Gigante Farmer's Market** (Saturday from 2 PM–5:30 PM), on the north end of town, for local produce and homemade marmalades, ceviche, and more.

The tiny towns of Limón #1 and Limón #2, between Rancho Santana and Playa Popoyo, have very basic pulperías; the best is in Limón #2, **Gustavo's Convenience.** Salinas also has basic pulperías and vegetable stands.

Surf Shops

Most surfers rent boards in San Juan del Sur, where there's a much larger selection. However, you can also rent, buy, or repair boards through the various surf camps and shops in Playas Gigante, Santana, and Guasacate (Popoyo).

There are a handful of small surf shops that rent, sell, and repair boards in Playa Popoyo, including **Maximo Ding Repair** (8988-2390; maximriv@hotmail.com), across from the Rana Roja, and French-owned **Popoyo Ding Repair** (www.popoyodingrepair.com).

Nica Surf Shop (8880-4318; 610-624-3204 (U.S.); www.surfaricharters.com), at the entrance to town, is a more upmarket place with boards, rods, and fishing tours, plus wifi in their outdoor restaurant.

EVENTS

Both Tola and Salinas have modest celebrations for Semana Santa (Easter Week) and la Purísima (December), but the best place to enjoy big national holidays is in Rivas, with processions and events on par with any major Nicaraguan city. During Semana Santa, the Tola beaches are absolutely packed. Make reservations in advance.

March

Carretas Peregrinas (Semana Santa) (March or April, week before Easter) In addition to the usual church and beach festivities, Easter is celebrated with a parade of traditionally decorated oxcarts rolling slowly from Nandaime to the Popoyupa Sanctuary in Rivas. San Jorge has similar events.

June

✪ **Hipica Rivas** (mid-June) Rivas prides itself on *sabanero*-style cowboy culture, on display during this festival. Horse parades, or *hípicas,* are held, along with bull "fights" (the bull is never killed, though human participants are sometimes hurt as they run around the bullring, trying to touch the animal's horns), live music, and heavy drinking.

Fiestas Cívicas Rivas (June 29) Rivas honors its patrons, San Pedro and San Pablo.

8

Isla Ometepe and Lake Nicaragua

Isle of Myth and Magic

Rising like a legend from Lake Nicaragua, Isla Ometepe seems a mystic's vision. Meditate for a moment, as you arrive at the tiny, pre-Columbian port of San Jorge on the wind-churned waters of Cocibolca, the "Sweet Sea." It stretches away like a forgotten ocean into a hazy horizon, pierced only by this sacred island's two epic volcanoes. There is no other view like this in the world.

Bound together by a windswept isthmus for the whole of human history, these mythic, fire-wrought peaks form a tranquil isle, its soft gray sands and lush green jungles protected by its scenic moat from the frantic globalization of human endeavor. This peace is an illusion of the petty human timescale, and regularly interrupted by ash-and-lava upheavals. Yet even the island's impermanence makes it alluring.

Take your place on one of the ferries, perhaps the swaying, sun-drenched upper deck where you can watch Ometepe emerge unimpeded. The dark, elegant cone of active Volcán Concepción reveals its deep and dangerous chasms as you sail ever closer. Just beyond, views of the fertile farms and misty forests of dormant Volcán Maderas sharpen to dramatic tropical color. This is no pale mirage of paradise. It is real.

Step off the boat onto this voluptuous hourglass of an island, loosely bound by a partially paved coastal road, and consider your forebears. Ometepe has been considered a holy place

---

Online Resources

Bainbridge–Ometepe Sister Islands Association (www.bosia.org) English-language site has information, news, and links.

⊗ **Isla Ometepe: Touring Around** (www.visitaometepe.com) Basically an online, English-language guidebook to the island, it lists hotels, restaurants, transportation information, and more.

Ometepe-Projekt Nicaragua (www.ometepe-projekt-nicaragua.de) German-language site has information and links.

Ometepe Turistica (www.ometepeturistica.com) The Spanish counterpart to the Touring Around site has more detailed background information.

There are 1,700 known petroglyphs scattered across the island, with a remarkable collection displayed in situ at Finca El Porvenir.

for millennia, where trails you'll take to the fuming peak of active Concepción, and the cool cloud-forested crater lake of Maderas, were originally opened to accommodate sacred processions.

Their fertile skirts are still marked with the handiwork of the divine, the thick forests scattered with basalt petroglyphs, images chiseled at some unknown date into the dark volcanic boulders. No one knows, exactly, who carved them or why, but they also left behind stone statues, perhaps of deities, caught for all eternity between animal and man.

Today, the volcanoes and their isthmus are fringed with small hotels, where you can escape the world for a while, and swim, hike, bicycle, ride horses, or kayak out to even smaller, attendant isles. It is possible to indulge in a simple vacation here, but most will instinctively understand that this ancient place is truly special.

CRIME AND OTHER CONCERNS

In general, Isla Ometepe is very safe, although opportunistic crime does occur. If your hotel has poor security, leave valuables with the front desk, or at least secured in the room.

More of a concern is Ometepe's infrastructure, which is shaky. Avoid the tap water; bottled and purified water is widely available. Because streetlights are rare and electricity flickers out regularly, keep flashlights and candles handy. Most roads are unpaved, and bus service can be irregular; factor in extra time to tight travel schedules.

Moyogalpa has the only **Police Station** (2 blocks up and 0.5 blocks south of the pier) and

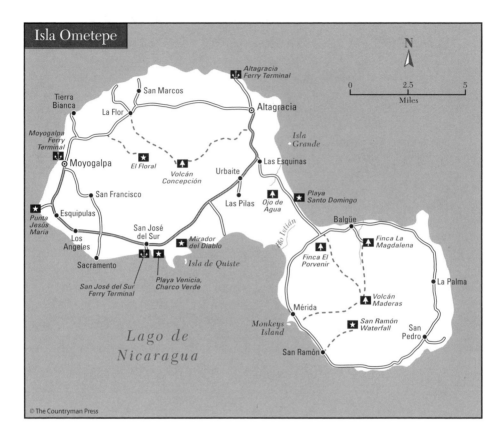

Isla Ometepe

Tierra Bianca

San Marcos

La Flor

Altagracia Ferry Terminal

Altagracia

Isla Grande

Moyogalpa Ferry Terminal

Moyogalpa

El Floral

Volcán Concepción

Urbaite

Las Esquinas

San Francisco

Las Pilas

Ojo de Agua

Playa Santo Domingo

Punta Jesús Maria

Esquipulas

San José del Sur

Balgüe

Finca La Magdalena

Los Angeles

Sacramento

Mirador del Diablo

Isla de Quiste

Finca El Porvenir

La Palma

San José del Sur Ferry Terminal

Playa Venicia, Charco Verde

Volcán Maderas

Mérida

San Ramón Waterfall

San Pedro

Monkeys Island

San Ramón

Lago de Nicaragua

0   2.5   5
Miles

N

© The Countryman Press

post office (one block north of the church). It is also home to the island's only ATM, but it is apparently unreliable—be smart and bring all the cash you'll need. Both Moyogalpa and Altagracia have very basic health clinics and pharmacies, as well as the only reliable Internet on the island (though this was set to improve).

Lake Nicaragua is home to tiny flying insects called *sayules* (or *chayules*) which swarm in huge short-lived clouds several times a year. Though related to mosquitoes, they don't bite or sting—but they can be annoying. Keep windows tightly shut and head inland.

GETTING AROUND

The only way to Isla Ometepe is by boat. The most convenient ferries run almost hourly between Ometepe and **San Jorge**, 8 km (5 miles) east of the major mainland city of **Rivas**, with direct bus connections to San Juan del Sur, Granada, Managua, and San José, Costa Rica. (See the Rivas and the Tola Beaches chapter.) Buses (US$0.50) make a 8-km (5-mile) run between San Jorge and Rivas hourly; convenient *colectivo* taxis cost US$1.50.

There are also two weekly ferries from **Granada** (four hours), with continuing service to the far side of the lake and **San Carlos** (seven hours)—which has daily boat service to the Río San Juan, Solentiname Archipelago, and Los Chiles border with Costa Rica.

You will arrive to Ometepe at one of the three main ferry terminals, all on the Concepción side of the island: **Moyogalpa**, Ometepe's major "city," receives most convenient San

Jorge ferries; **Altagracia**, a stop on the Granada–San Carlos line; or **San José del Sur**, with a brand-new ferry terminal. Buses and taxis meet the Moyogalpa ferries, taxis the others. Buses run between all three towns on the island's one paved road.

This hourglass of an island has one main *carretera*, or road, which circumnavigates both volcanoes and connects them along the isthmus. Only the southwestern portion between Moyogalpa and Altagracia is paved, and plied by almost hourly buses. Other roads that are unpaved have fewer available buses—with no service at all between San Ramón and La Palma on the southwest side of Maderas.

Fewer buses and ferries run on Sunday, making that an inconvenient day to meet tight travel schedules. Some hotels—notably Finca Magdalena, Totoco, and Tesoro de Pirata—are more than 1 km above the bus stop, which can be challenging with lots of luggage. Taxis meet all the ferries, but should otherwise be arranged one day in advance.

Throughout the chapter, I have divided the island into three main regions, primarily for convenience. The **Concepción side** of the island surrounds the active volcano, and is home to Ometepe's two major cities, Moyogalpa and Altagracia, as well as Charco Verde. The **Isthmus** (Istiam) refers to the low, sandy saddle connecting the two volcanoes, including popular Playa Santo Domingo, lined with hotels. The southern shore is a wetlands area, and accessible on kayak tours.

The **Maderas side** surrounds dormant, thickly forested Maderas volcano, and is even less developed than Concepción. The main population centers are Balgüe, home to hippie magnets like Finca Magdalena and Project Bonafide; Santa Cruz, with a major petroglyph field; Mérida, the old Somoza-era coffee port; and San Ramón, famous for its beautiful waterfall and yacht mooring.

Car

If you are driving from Rivas to the San Jorge ferry terminal, note that the main road jogs confusingly (and with no signs!) in the town center: When the road comes to a T-intersection in front of the church, make a left, drive three blocks, then make a right, asking everyone you see, "*¿Donde esta el puerto?*" ("Where is the port?")

You can pay to park at the terminal, or take your car with you on one of the large car ferries that run between San Jorge and Moyogalpa: **Ometepe** (2278-8190 (Managua), 2569-4224 (San Jorge)), **Che Guevara** (2563-4779, 8694-1819; ferryometepequiroga@yahoo.es), and **Estrella del Sur** (2563-4779, 2563-0665; karlissetjimenez@yahoo.es, ometepetours 2007@yahoo.es). **El Rey de Cocibolca** (8691-3669, 2552-8745; alcaldiaaltagracia@yahoo .com) runs from San Jorge to San José del Sur.

You should make reservations for your car in advance (Spanish only), and confirm on the day of travel. Unless it's a peak period, however, you can usually just show up—they recently added three car ferries, so you no longer need reservations weeks in advance. The fee situation remains mysterious, however, with the US$18 fee augmented by surprise bonus charges that may include US$2.50 for a "manifesto," US$2 to enter the city of Moyogalpa, and whatever else they can think of.

You can rent cars and motorcycles on the island through **Hotel Ometepetl** (2569-4276; ometepetling@hotmail.com) or any of the tour operators in Moyogalpa. There are gas stations in both Moyogalpa and Altagracia, which charge about 25 percent more than on the mainland.

A single main road circumnavigates both volcanoes, connected through the isthmus. Only the road southwest from Altagracia to Moyogalpa is paved, and you will be sharing it

San Jorge, Gateway to Isla Ometepe

Few international tourists even stop in San Jorge proper. They grab a cab in Rivas and zip right through the small town of *tejas* kilns and banana plantations, straight to the faux Spanish castle guarding the ferry terminal. The driver may point out **La Cruz de España** suspended above the ancient road, marking the spot where Spanish conquistador Gil González Dávila first met Cacique Nicarao, and changed the destiny of a continent.

San Jorge is actually a few months older than Granada, and its quaint downtown boasts venerable architectural treasures, the most important of which is the **Iglesia Las Mercedes**. This wood and stucco structure was built around 1590 and remains intact, which makes it one of the oldest surviving European buildings in the Americas. It's rarely open to the public, but ask around and someone can open it for you.

The lake has receded since San Jorge was founded, so you'll need to continue 800 meters (0.5 mile) from the city center to one of Cocibolca's finest beaches. The long swath of hard-packed sand is lined with restaurants serving *guapote* (rainbow bass) and a few hotels.

Lodging

Azteca Hotel (2563-0759, 2563-1088; de Iglesia Mercedes, 2 cuadras este, hacia el lago y I calle al norte; credit cards accepted; $; wifi) Backpacker shack has a huge, cheap dorm, air-conditioned private rooms, and a big pool—all in downtown San Jorge.

Hotel California (8856-1495, 8804-6699; myhotelcalifornia@yahoo.com; 400 metros del muelle; credit cards accepted; $$; wifi) In a rather pastoral spot five minutes from the pier, this pleasant hotel offers a row of 14 good-sized, very clean rooms, tastefully decorated and air-conditioned, with private hot baths, and a long covered porch.

Hotel Dalinky (2563-4990, 8912-1205; hoteldalinky.com; muelle, 200 metros oeste; credit cards accepted; $$; wifi) The closest hotel to the port does not get good recommendations. The modern, air-conditioned rooms looked fine, however.

Hotel Hamacas (8810-4144; www.hostalhamacas.com; info@hostalhamacas.com; San Jorge, 300 metros del muelle; credit cards accepted; $$; wifi) Tranquil and shady, this gem of a hotel is strung with comfortable Masaya hammocks. Pretty brick rooms are spacious and clean, with good beds, handmade furniture, cable TV, and modern hot baths. For US$10 more, you get air-conditioning. It's three blocks to the beach.

Dining

The sleepy central park, presided over by **Iglesia Nuestro Señor de Rescate** and its images of Saint George, has several food stands and *fritangas* that start up at sunset. Restaurants line the breezy beach, with awesome Ometepe views.

Bar-Restaurante El Navegante (8333-3898; entrada al muelle; credit cards accepted; B, L, D; $–$$) Right on the pier, this spot specializes in big sandwiches and pricier Italian pastas and fish dishes. They

with oxcarts, bicycles, piglets, motorcycles towing ice cream carts with children riding them, and so on. Stay alert. All other roads are unpaved, and a four-wheel-drive vehicle is highly recommended, particularly during rainy season.

Buses

Most people take the ferry to Isla Ometepe from **San Jorge**, with hourly buses (US$0.30) and frequent *colectivo* taxis (US$1.50) to **Rivas**, a department capital with regular bus con-

Pressed for time, but you still want to enjoy a beach with Ometepe views? Stay in San Jorge, with hotels and easy access to Rivas buses.

also sell imported Italian wines, pastas, sauces, and other items that you can take to Ometepe.

Centro Recreativo El Gran Diamante (8886-0384; Iglesia Católica 3 cuadras al sur; credit cards accepted; L, D; $$–$$$) The best restaurant in town specializes in *guapote*, or rainbow bass, and *pueybuey*, a type of short-haired tropical sheep. The open-air ranchero also has a playground for kids, fabulous lake views, and live music on weekends.

Restaurant El Refugio (2563-4631, 8851-0267; beachfront; credit cards accepted; L, D; $–$$) Just south of the pier, this is a good option for Nica cuisine and cold beer.

nections to Granada, Masaya, Managua, San Juan del Sur, the Tola beaches, and Costa Rica. See the Rivas and the Tola Beaches chapter for schedules.

Bus service on the island is more relaxed than the mainland. While buses making the smooth, paved, one-hour run between Moyogalpa and Altagracia are fairly reliable, others may show up late, or just decide not to work that day. On Sunday, the Maderas side can only count on one or two buses, though you just never know. It's always best to ask at your hotel about the latest schedules.

MOYOGALPA

Buses meet all ferries before heading to **Altagracia** (US$1; one hour), passing Punta de Jesús María (Los Angeles), Charco Verde, San José del Sur, and Las Esquinas, the turnoff to Playa Santo Domingo. All Moyogalpa buses headed to the Maderas side of the island stop in Altagracia first, adding an hour to the trip—so consider getting of in Las Esquinas, then taking a 2-km (1.2-mile) downhill walk to most Playa Santo Domingo hotels.

Three buses (US$1; two hours) take the unpaved northern route to Altagracia, via La Flor (the main trail summiting Concepción) and the increasingly developed town of San Marcos.

ALTAGRACIA

Note that the Altagracia ferry terminal is more than a kilometer (almost a mile) from the town and all buses. Taxis and colectivo pickup trucks meet the ferry.

Balgüe (US$1.25, 2 hours) 4:15 AM (continues to La Palma), 9 AM, 10:15 AM, 11 AM, 1:30 PM (continues to La Palma), 2 PM, 3:15 PM, 6 PM.

Moyogalpa (US$1; 1 hour) Hourly buses on the paved southern route; three buses take the two-hour, unpaved northern route via San Marcos and La Flor.

Mérida (US$1.25; 2.5 hours) 7 AM (continues to San Ramón), 10 AM (continues to San Ramón), 2 PM, 4 PM, and 5:30 PM.

PLAYA SANTO DOMINGO AND SANTA CRUZ

Santa Cruz lies at the crossroads between Playa Santo Domingo, Balgüe, and Mérida, making the handful of hotels close by very convenient.

Altagracia (US$1; 1.5 hours) and **Moyogalpa** (US$1.25; 2.5 hours) 4:30 AM, 5 AM (Altagracia only), 7:30 AM (Altagracia only), 8:10 AM, 9 AM, 11 AM, 11:30 AM, 1:15 PM, 2 PM, 4 PM, and 5:30 PM. On Sundays, buses run "reliably" at 5 AM, 7:45 AM, and 9 AM, all with service to both Altagracia and Moyogalpa.

Mérida (US$0.50; 1.5 hours) and **San Ramón** (US$0.50; 1.5 hours) 8:15 AM, 11 AM, 4:30 PM (Mérida only), and 6 PM (Mérida only). On Sunday, buses run reliably at 4:15 PM only.

Balgüe (US$0.50; 1 hour) at 5:30 AM (continuing service to La Palma), 10 AM, 11:30 AM, 12:15 PM, 2:30 PM (continuing service to La Palma), 3 PM, 4:30 PM, 5:30 PM, 7 PM. On Sunday, only the 5:30 PM bus is reliable.

MÉRIDA

Altagracia via Santa Cruz and Playa Santo Domingo (US$1.25; 2.5 hours) 4 AM (continues to Moyogalpa), 5:45 AM, 8:30 AM (continues to Moyogalpa), 10:15 AM (continues to Moyogalpa), and 3:30 PM. On Sunday, only the 8:30 AM bus runs reliably.

BALGÜE

Altagracia via Santa Cruz and Playa Santo Domingo (US$1.25; 2 hours) Eight times daily, fewer buses run on Sunday.

Taxi

Taxis are expensive and uncommon on Ometepe. They meet every ferry, but should otherwise be arranged in advance. Hotels can find private transport as well. From Moyogalpa, taxis and minivans run to Altagracia (US$15), Playa Santo Domingo (US$25), Balgüe (US$30), Mérida (US$30), and San Ramón (US$40).

You can also rent taxis by the day for between US$60 and US$100. Try the **Cooperativa**

Two new car ferries were recently added between San Jorge and Ometepe, making it much more convenient to bring your four-wheel-drive to the island.

de **Transporte Turístico de Ometepe** (COOSTRATO; 2485-6076, 8845-3227; coostrato ometepe@yahoo.es) or **Transporte Isla Ometepe** (2563-4675, 8657-0588).

Boat

While it is possible to arrange private boats to Isla Ometepe, this is expensive and potentially dangerous. Most people take car ferries or *lanchas* (passenger ferries) to the island. The most convenient are hourly car and passenger ferries that make the one-hour trip from San Jorge to either Moyogalpa or San José del Sur, though you can also take the twice-weekly passenger ferries from Granada (four hours). Hacienda Mérida (see Lodging; US$30 for one or two people) operates a speedboat between Mérida, on the Maderas side, and the new ferry terminal in San José del Sur.

Hotels can arrange boat transportation to the smaller surrounding isletas, such as Isla Quiste, close to Charco Verde, with unimproved camping. Hacienda Mérida, Los Caballitos de Mar, and Hotel Charco Verde rent kayaks; see the Recreation section for more information.

GRANADA–ALTAGRACIA–SAN CARLOS FERRY

A passenger ferry crosses Lake Nicaragua twice weekly, leaving Granada, stopping in the town of Altagracia on Ometepe, then continuing across the lake to San Miguelito and San

Carlos, the Río San Juan, the Solentiname Islands, and the Costa Rican border (at Los Chiles). There is a cheaper lower deck, but it's worth a few dollars for the upper level, with padded chairs and less sway (folks prone to seasickness should probably bring Dramamine anyway). Between Granada and Altagracia, tickets cost US$3/6; it's US$5/10 to go all the way to San Carlos.

The ferry leaves Granada at 2 PM Monday and Thursday, arriving in Altagracia at 6 PM. The same ferry leaves Altagracia at 7:30 PM for San Miguelito and San Carlos, arriving the following morning. Ferries leave San Carlos for the return trip at 3 PM Tuesday and Friday, arriving in Altagracia at 11 PM, then continuing to Granada at 12:30 AM (no typo) Wednesday and Saturday, arriving in Granada at 6:30 AM.

From San Jorge

It's almost always more convenient to leave from San Jorge, a small port town near the city of Rivas. Private shuttle companies in San Juan del Sur and Granada offer direct connections geared to foreign tourists; check those chapters for details. Direct buses from Granada, San Juan del Sur, Managua, and the Costa Rican border serve nearby Rivas, where it's easy to grab a bus (US$0.50, hourly) or collective taxi (US$1.50) from the bus lot.

Lanchas (US$1.25) or passenger ferries, are smaller, cheaper, and run more often. If you are prone to seasickness, or it's a particularly choppy day, it's worth waiting on a larger, more stable car ferry (US$1.75 per passenger; US$18 per car).

Until recently, all boats were operated by **Transporte Turístico Milton Arcía** (2278-8190 (Managua), 2569-4224 (Moyogalpa); gerencia@transportelacustre.com), which still runs lanchas and ferries from San Jorge at 7:45 AM (ferry), 9 AM (lancha; doesn't run on Sunday), 9:30 AM (lancha), 10:30 AM (ferry), 11:30 AM (lancha; doesn't run on Sunday), 1:30 AM (lancha), 2:30 PM (ferry; doesn't run on Sunday), 3:30 PM (lancha), 4:30 PM (lancha; doesn't run on Sunday), and 5:40 PM.

Lanchas and ferries leave Moyogalpa at 5:30 AM (lancha; doesn't run on Sunday); 6 AM (ferry), 6:30 AM (lancha), 7 AM (lancha), 9 AM (ferry), 11 AM (lancha; doesn't run on Sunday), 11:30 AM (lancha), 12:30 PM (ferry), 1:30 PM (lancha), and 4 PM (ferry).

However, they've recently added three new ferries:

Ferry Che Guevara (2563-4779, 8694-1819; ferryometepequiroga@yahoo.es) Car ferry leaves San Jorge at 7 AM and 4 PM, returning from Moyogalpa at 11 AM and 5:30 PM.

Estrella del Sur (2563-4779, 2563-0665; karlissetjimenez@yahoo.es, ometepetours2007 @yahoo.es) Passenger ferry leaves San Jorge at 11 AM and 3:30 PM, returning from Moyogalpa at 7 AM and 1 PM.

El Rey de Cocibolca (8691-3669, 2552-8745; alcaldiaaltagracia@yahoo.com) This community-owned vessel leaves San José at 5:40 AM, 7:30 AM, 1:30 PM, and 3:20 PM, returning from the new terminal at San José del Sur (not Moyogalpa!) at 9:30 AM, 10 AM, 4:30 PM, and 5 PM.

Tourist Information

There is no official tourism office, but handful of private tour operators close to the San Jorge and Moyogalpa piers have information and fliers.

If Ometepe isn't remote enough for you, escape to one of the smaller islets—such as Isla Quiste, where solitude seekers can camp.

Lodging

Ometepe is inexpensive, a boon to budget and midrange travelers. There are only a few hotels geared toward higher-end visitors (and these are not luxury hotels), including Villa Paraíso, Totoco Ecolodge, Hotel Charco Verde, and brand new Finca San Juan de la Isla. Others are slated to open while this book is on the shelves, so do some online research if this is your category.

No matter how nice your hotel, keep a flashlight or candles handy in the room, as electricity is shaky. Internet access in hotels is currently rare and expensive, though this will change.

Lodging Price Code

The cost of lodging is based on an average per-room, double occupancy rate during peak season (December through April). Nicaragua's 15 percent sales tax and gratuities are not included; note that paying cash sometimes results in taxes being waived. Prices are much higher during the Christmas holidays and Semana Santa (Easter Week), when you should make reservations.

Inexpensive ($)	Up to US$25
Moderate ($$)	US$25 to US$60
Expensive ($$$)	US$60 to US$100
Very Expensive ($$$$)	US$100 and up

Hotels

Moyogalpa

The most popular ferry terminal is also Ometepe's big city, with "eighteen hotels, twenty-two restaurants, five discos, five tour operators, four Internet cafes, two banks, and one ATM," according to the sign. Most accommodations are in the budget category. I've listed a few in "Other Hotels," but you'll find many more.

✪ AMERICAN CAFÉ AND HOTEL

Owners: Robert and Simone Santelli

8645-7193, 8650-4069
simonesantelli14@gmail.com
Muelle, 100 metros arriba
Price: Inexpensive to Moderate
Credit Cards: No
Handicap Access: No
Wifi: Not yet

Ignore the overly modern façade and step inside amazing American Café, by far and away the best hotel in Moyogalpa. Hidden behind the good restaurant are five enormous, immaculate, flawlessly crafted casitas with high ceilings, two ceiling fans, wonderful handmade Masatepe furnishings, and spacious bathrooms with real hot water. There's no air-conditioning or TV, but you can (the owners are deservedly proud of this) flush your toilet paper.

The **café** (B, L; $–$$), with seats overlooking the mellow Moyogalpa street scene, is also great, with lovingly prepared U.S. and Italian dishes that you won't find anywhere else, such as corned beef hash; clam chowder; pasta with real, fresh pesto; and tasty chili con carne. Whatever you get, order home fries on the side and chocolate cake for dessert.

HOTELITO OMETEPETL
Owner: Nora Gómez
2569-4276, 8887-9891
ometepetlng@hotmail.com
Frente al puerto de Moyogalpa
Price: Inexpensive to Moderate
Credit Cards: Yes
Handicap Access: No
Wifi: No

Founded more than 30 years ago, this was once Ometepe's best hotel. Though its star has dimmed, aging cement rooms are comfortable, with private baths, cable TV, decent beds, and the option of air-conditioning. The porches, filled with rocking chairs overlooking the magnificently arcaded gardens, are exceptional. They arrange all the tours, rent cars, and offer transportation to their property on Playa Santo Domingo, Casa Hotel Istiam.

Charco Verde and San José del Sur
Surrounding the emerald green interior lake of Charco Verde, with fine beaches and hiking trails to Mirador del Diablo, are several hotels. Close by, the new ferry port at San José del Sur promises even more development.

✪ CHARCO VERDE INN
Owner: Ruben Rivera
2569-4276, 8887-9891
www.charcoverdeinn.com.ni
nicaraguacharcoverde22@yahoo.es
San José del Sur
Price: Moderate
Credit Cards: Yes
Handicap Access: Challenging
Wifi: In the restaurant

Wrapped around a jungle-shrouded, pearl-gray beach at the entrance to Charco Verde Ecological Preserve, this hotel is one of the island's finest. Though moderately priced (and lacking hot showers), 19 spacious, spotless bungalows are designed with the discriminating traveler in mind, boasting polished wooden ceilings, attractive handmade furnishings, good mattresses, soft lighting, and excellent modern bathrooms.

Your private terrace, surrounded by tropical gardens, is the perfect place to lounge after kayaking out to Isla Quiste (they can arrange camping as well), horseback riding, or hiking. The sandy-floored, open-air ✪ **restaurant** (B, L, D; $$–$$$) is consistently recommended as one of Ometepe's best. Enjoy a short menu of Nicaraguan and international cuisine, from ceviche and sandwiches to more creative entrees such as guapote broiled with anise and parsley butter.

HOTEL PLAYA SANTA MARTHA
Owner: Luz Marina Obregón
8820-4648, 8479-7296

hotelplayasantamartha.com
info@playasantamartha.com
San José del Sur
Price: Inexpensive
Credit Cards: No
Handicap Access: No
Wifi: No

Convenient to the new San José del Sur ferry terminal, this family-run hotel right on a sweet little beach is a great deal. Rooms are fine, packed a bit tightly with bunk beds, but clean and fan cooled—with a private, modern cool bath. One room is right on the water, with views from the porch to Ferry El Rey de Cocibolca, while the other terrazas overlook colorful botanical gardens and playground equipment. There's a very local bar and restaurant with Latin music and a mellow vibe.

TESORO DEL PIRATA
Owners: Douglas and Auxilieth Céspedes R.
8927-2831, 8747-7799, 8820-2259
KM15 Carretera Moyogalpa–Altagracia
Price: Inexpensive to Moderate
Credit Cards: No
Handicap Access: No
Wifi: No

Nestled into an impossibly scenic little cove close to Isla Quiste, this popular hotel has simple, sweet cement cabins with good beds and private cool baths; there's an inexpensive dorm as well. They have a dock and organize boat excursions as well as the usual tours, and the restaurant—with a wine list and notable fish dishes—gets high marks. A small playground on the grassy lawn keeps kids happy, too.

The hotel is almost 1 km downhill from where the bus drops you off.

HOTEL FINCA PLAYA VENECIA
Owners: Duvall Briseño and Alicia Rivera
2409-1486, 8887-0191, 8872-7668
www.hotelfincavenecia.com.ni
hotelfincavenecia@yahoo.com

San José del Sur
Price: Moderate
Credit Cards: Yes
Handicap Access: No
Wifi: No

Wonderful rooms for every budget (including a pretty five-bed dorm) and a relaxed atmosphere are all right on a grassy shore. Older fan-cooled cement rooms with private baths are more affordable. Or spring for a newer, lovelier brick room right on the beach, with views over the gardens and water and the option of air-conditioning. Some are spacious, and sleep four.

The open-air restaurant, surrounded by manicured gardens that contain an excellent collection of pre-Columbian pottery and stonework, gets recommendations. Groups can ask about having a barbecue (or bonfire) right on the beach. The friendly staff, some of whom speak excellent English, can arrange horseback rides, scooter rental, and all the usual tours. They also operate **Hotel Casa Moreno** (2357-7349; casamoreno@fincavenecia.com; credit cards accepted; $) in Moyogalpa, and arrange transport between the two.

ALTAGRACIA
Any hotel in town will let guests hang out in their hammocks until taxis leave for the 12:30 AM Granada ferry.

✪ HOTEL CENTRAL
Owner: Oscar Danilo Flores Guttierez
2552-8770, 2552-8782
del parque, 2 cuadras al Sur
Price: Inexpensive
Credit Cards: Yes
Handicap Access: No
Wifi: No

Operated by the same folks as fabulous Finca El Porvenir, this hotel is sweet, with a rambling green courtyard and pretty fan-cooled rooms. The least expensive are small, with good beds and cleanly tiled shared baths. A couple dollars more gets you a larger brick cabañita, with private porches and bath; some are hexagonal. Hammocks and kiosks are strewn throughout the shady grounds, and there's a good **restaurant** (B, L, D; $$).

HOTEL EL CASTILLO

Owner: Julio Castillo Monge
2552-8744, 8856-8003
www.elhotelcastillo.com
info@hotcastillo.com
Iglesia Católica, 1 cuadra al Sur, 0.5 cuadra al Oeste
Price: Inexpensive to Moderate
Credit Cards: Yes
Handicap Access: Challenging
Wifi: Yes

This relaxed hotel just off the main drag is a solid choice, with an excellent ✪ **restaurant** (B, L, D; $–$$), shady courtyard with hammocks, and an on-site Internet café. Rooms are simple and very clean, offering high ceilings, soft beds, and private cool baths. Pay a few dollars more and you'll enjoy air-conditioning, cable TV, and a nicer bathroom.

Playa Santo Domingo

Ometepe's best beach is draped across the breezy northern shore of the isthmus, shrinking in rainy season to a narrow, volcanic gray stretch of sand—and revealing some 30 glorious meters of beach during summer. The shore is lined with half a dozen hotels and restaurants, and even has a canopy tour, making this the closest thing Ometepe's got to a resort town. It's still really low-key.

FINCA SAN JUAN DE LA ISLA

Owners: Various
8886-0734, 2277-3791
www.sanjuandelaisla.com
info@sanjuandelaisla.com
Empalme El Quino, 200 meters norte, 2.3 km este

Price: Moderate to Expensive
Credit Cards: Yes
Handicap Access: Challenging
Wifi: Yes

This brand-new, upscale development is offering lake-view lots, charmingly Colonial sensibilities, and modern infrastructure with foreigners in mind. They will eventually offer vacation homes and rental units, and have faithfully restored an old adobe hacienda dating from the 1800s as part of a future hotel.

HOTEL FINCA SANTO DOMINGO

Owners: Alcides Flores and Melida Luna
8927-2019
hotel_santo_domingo@yahoo.com
Playa Santo Domingo
Price: Moderate
Credit Cards: Yes
Handicap Access: No
Wifi: No

This relaxed midrange option offers a variety of well-maintained, comfortable rooms, a few right on the water. At the time of research, some were decorated with an unfortunate penchant for Day-Glo, but all have good beds, clean private baths, and fans (two rooms have air-conditioning). Ask to see a couple of rooms if the first is too bright for you. The beachfront **restaurant** (B, L, D; $$–$$$) is excellent.

CASA HOTEL ISTIAM

Owner: Nora Gómez
2569-4276, 8887-9891
ometepetlng@hotmail.com
Playa Santo Domingo, south end
Price: Inexpensive
Credit Cards: Yes
Handicap Access: Yes
Wifi: No

Well away from the Santo Domingo strip, and popular with vacationing Nicaraguans perhaps for that reason, this quiet wooden hotel has awesome views over the Río Istiam wetlands and a very private, pale stretch of sandy shore. Accommodations range from clean, US$5 fan-cooled rooms with shared bath to much larger, nicer, air-conditioned rooms with flagstone floors and private baths for US$45, still a great deal for groups. They arrange inexpensive transport from Hotel Ompeteptl in Moyogalpa.

✪ HOTEL VILLA PARAÍSO
Owners: Carlos Flores and Sonya Koffler
2563-4675, 2657-0588
www.villaparaiso.com.ni
ometepe@villaparaiso.com.ni
Playa Santo Domingo
Price: Moderate
Credit Cards: Yes
Handicap Access: Challenging
Wifi: Guests can use an on-site computer for US$4 per hour

Among the first, and still one of the nicest, hotels on the island, Villa Paraíso has long been the choice of discriminating travelers. Thirteen attractive rooms and suites (more in neighboring Las Kabañas, with the same management and plush circular bungalows) are ensconced in lush, terraced jungle above the island's loveliest stretch of sand, best appreciated from the hammock slung across your private porch.

Rooms aren't luxurious by international standards (neither are rates), but boast gleaming hand-carved furnishings, cool tiled floors, soothing color schemes, rich hardwoods, and dark stone. All are equipped with optional air-conditioning, satellite TV, and private hot baths. Service is excellent, and the **restaurant** (B, L, D; $$–$$$) is considered one of Ometepe's best.

VOLCÁN MADERAS
The Maderas side of Ometepe is much less developed, with unpaved roads and less reliable buses and infrastructure.

SANTA CRUZ
Santa Cruz is convenient, with regular

buses to Balgüe, Mérida, and Altagracia, its own trail (via El Porvenir) to the top of the volcano, and a 20-minute walk to Playa Santo Domingo.

EL ENCANTO
Owner: Carlos Espino
8867-7128
www.goelencanto.com
cespino@goelencanto.com
Santa Cruz
Price: Inexpensive to Moderate
Credit Cards: No
Handicap Access: No
Wifi: No

Some 300 meters from the main road, this pretty place is surrounded by farmland and flowers. Cheerfully painted brick rooms have good beds, relaxing porches, and artsy touches such as hammered-tin lamps and local ceramics. The English-speaking owner leads several tours and offers **international cuisine** (B, L, D; $–$$) such as mole, cashew pesto chicken, chicken in lemongrass, and other dishes—many made with local ingredients. Great spot.

FINCA ECOLÓGICA EL ZOPILOTE
Owners: Bruno and Cristiano
8369-0644
www.ometepezopilote.com; zopiloteorganicfarm.blogspot.com
zopiloteorganicfarm@gmail.com
300m past Santa Cruz toward Balgüe
Price: Inexpensive
Credit Cards: No (you can use Paypal)
Handicap Access: No
Wifi: No

Sustainability through simplicity is the key to this excellent, truly ecological granola getaway on an organic permaculture farm. It's not for everyone: Cabanas and dorms are sustainably constructed using only hand tools from palm thatch, fallen wood, and stones, and shared bathrooms have outdoor showers and composting toilets. It is an operating farm, and lets some independent travelers and **Wwoof** (www.wwoof.org) members volunteer in exchange for a 20 percent discount.

There's no restaurant, but a community kitchen lets you cook your own meals, perhaps using some of the farm's products available at the excellent ✪ shop, including chocolate, bread, tahini, honey, yogurt, flavored rums, and more. Wood-fired pizza is served at 6:30 PM on Tuesday, Thursday, and Friday; make reservations.

✪ ALBERGÜE ECOLÓGICO EL PORVENIR

Owner: Oscar Flores Gutierrez
8447-9466, 2552-8770
Santa Cruz
Price: Inexpensive
Credit Cards: No
Handicap Access: No
Wifi: No

It's well worth a day trip (US$1), at least, for 2 km (1.2 miles) of trails through these tropical botanical gardens that hold the most important collection of petroglyphs on the island. This is also one of the trailheads for the Maderas hike. Enjoy lunch at the **restaurant** (B, L, D; $$), with sublime views and recommended pescado en salsa Ometepe—guapote served in a sauce made with tomato, onion, garlic, sweet pepper, sugar, and rum.

Or stay right here, in one of ten spacious, spotless, fan-cooled rooms, offering excellent beds, fine porches, and private cool baths with smooth natural stone accents. It's a great deal, but note that it's 600 meters uphill from the bus stop.

✪ TOTOCO

Owners: Roslyn Winstanley, Jonathan Rogiest, and Martijn Priester
8425-2027, 8659-8558
www.totoco.com.ni
ecolodge@totoco.com.ni

between Santa Cruz and Balgüe
Price: Inexpensive to Very Expensive
Credit Cards: Not yet
Handicap Access: No
Wifi: Not yet

High above the lake, with flower-filled views across the isthmus to Volcán Concepción, this handcrafted lodge is truly ecosensible, yet offers some of the most comfortable villas on the island. Don't expect TV or air-conditioning. Instead, you'll enjoy graceful little details such as hand-carved furnishings, stone floors, cane ceilings, delightful outdoor showers, private porches, and guaranteed odor-free composting toilets.

The gardens are a work of art, as is their recommended international cuisine; full- and half-board options (cheaper for vegetarians) are a great deal. Flashpackers should check out the airy, awesome dorm.

Note that Totoco is a serious 3-km (1.8-mile) climb from the main road. Drivers should look for the Totoco sign on your right, 250 meters past the high school.

BALGÜE

This relaxed little town definitely has a bit of a hippie vibe. It's centered on a successful Sandinista coffee commune at Finca Magdalena, and is also an international permaculture center.

Project Bona Fide (8901-5782; www .projectbonafide.com) is the best known of permaculture initiatives, promoting an agricultural management system that works with natural processes to increase crop yields while reducing the use of pesticides, fertilizers, and other chemical inputs. It has a well-run volunteer program and 2.5-hour guided tours of their solar and wind energy production, composting techniques, water catchments, and other sustainable agricultural tools. They now produce so much food that they've begun providing nutritious meals to area children.

Other area hotels are also involved in the

Though Isla Ometepe is often considered something of a hippie haven, ecolodges like Totoco are now offering sustainability with style.

permaculture scene, particularly **Finca Ecológica El Zopilote** (earlier), with its own volunteer program.

ASÍ ES MI TIERRA

8924-9059, 8943-1997
www.mitierraometepe.com
herrera_ometepe@yahoo.com
Balgüe
Price: Inexpensive
Credit Cards: No
Handicap Access: Challenging
Wifi: No, but guests can use a dial-up line for US$5 per hour

The best budget rooms in Balgüe are in this attractive old home, with cool tilework, pleasant décor, and tangled courtyard gardens. Rooms are simple and clean, with lots of light, mosquito nets over acceptable beds, newish fans, and shared clean baths. Cheapskates can even rent hammocks for US$2 a night. It's popular with volunteers and NGOs, thus the English-speaking owners offer transport, meals, tours, bicycle and motorcycle rental, and so on with group rates.

FINCA MAGDALENA

Owner: Cooperativa Carlos Diaz Cajina
8498-1683
www.fincamagdalena.com
info@fincamagdalena.com
Balgüe
Price: Inexpensive to Moderate
Credit Cards: No
Handicap Access: No

Wifi: Computers available for US$3 per hour

This working organic coffee farm, operated by a 1980s-era Sandinista cooperative, was once the place to stay on Ometepe, and by that I mean the only place to stay. A steady stream of adventurous souls, undeterred by the civil war, came here to climb Volcán Madera. By the time peace treaties were signed, the cooperative had transformed part of the old hacienda into a very basic guesthouse and restaurant.

It's historic, and the rooms are too—which isn't necessarily a good thing. Rows of tiny wooden boxes with fans are furnished with thin foam mattresses or folding cots, and the shared bathroom is, um, rustic. There are two much nicer cabins with better furnishings and private baths, but neither is a great deal.

But . . . but it's Finca Magdalena, and it's beautiful and magical and cheap, with inspiring views, fantastic coffee, and constant breezes that sway all those hammocks filled with dreadlocked dreamers and feral revolutionaries. The ancient trail to the crater lake begins here, heralded by petroglyphs and coffee fields. You should at least stop in for a beer or fresh fish dinner after descending the volcano. Note that it's a steep, 1.5-km (1-mile) climb from the bus stop.

MÉRIDA AND SAN RAMÓN
On the least developed part of the island (save for the yacht moorings and a few upscale vacation homes), either town is a great choice for folks who want to kayak, hike to the waterfall, and escape from it all.

✪ CABALLITO'S MAR
8451-2093, 8961-7296
www.caballitosmar.com
fernando@caballitosmar.com
Mérida
Price: Inexpensive

Credit Cards: No
Handicap Access: No
Wifi: Guests enjoy 25 free minutes per day on the hotel computer

This sturdy, simple brick hostel on its own banana-shaded crescent beach has good dorms that can be rented as private rooms. All had tidy shared baths, but larger rooms with private baths were in the works. All have fans and excellent mattresses, a fine shared ranchero, plus a couple of outstanding amenities.

The **restaurant** (B, L, D; $) has a basic Nica menu spiced up with Spanish favorites like paella de mariscos, honey chicken, and ceviche, with live local music some nights. And, it has kayaks—most hotels book their Río Istiam trips through Caballitos, but you'll be relaxing right here on the water.

HACIENDA MÉRIDA
Owner: Alvaro Molina
8868-8973, 8894-2551
www.hmerida.com
haciendamerida@gmail.com
Mérida
Price: Inexpensive to Moderate
Credit Cards: Yes
Handicap Access: Challenging
Wifi: No

Popular backpacker destination in the small town of Mérida has a lot to recommend it: a great dock, used to ship coffee during the Somoza era; lots of hammocks; good (if pricey) buffet meals; easy access to Volcán Maderas and San Ramón Waterfall; and kayaking to Monkeys Island or the Río Istiam. They also rent mountain bikes and have several types of boat excursions. Dorm rooms are crowded but clean, while private rooms—particularly the pretty wooden upstairs accommodations—are quite nice, if a bit pricey for what you get.

It's not for everyone, however. The 10 PM "silence rule" is strictly enforced, and there's a steep US$5 corkage fee, among other restrictions. As the Web site says, "if you want a place to party, this is not it."

LA OMAJA
Owner: Jaime David Carson
8885-1124
www.laomaja.com
laomaja@hotmail.com
300m up the road from Mérida, on the left
Price: Moderate
Credit Cards: Yes
Handicap Access: No
Wifi: Yes

The most comfortable accommodations in the region are at this hilltop hotel, with great views over the western side of the island. It's isolated, away from either town, and a steep 150 meters from the main road, where there's a small beach and dock.

Five spacious, cement cabins are connected to one another and the **restaurant** (B, L, D; $$) by rough paths through the manicured grounds. They aren't fancy, but are big enough for families, with good beds, attractive cane roofs, fans, mosquito nets, and private, machine-heated baths with river-rock accents. Rooms furnished with air-conditioning and cable TV run US$10 more, but even then you'll probably spend most of the evening enjoying the cool lake breeze and lovely views from your private porch.

OMETEPE BIOLOGICAL FIELD STATION
Owner: Molina family
305-666-9932 (U.S.)
www.lasuerte.org
info@lasuerte.org
San Ramón
Price: Inexpensive to Moderate
Credit Cards: Yes
Handicap Access: No
Wifi: No

Most famously the trailhead for the 3-km (1.8-mile) hike to 35-meter (115-foot) San Ramón Waterfall (as well as an alternate trail up Volcán Maderas), this is also a biological field station, offering hands-on courses covering primate behavior, tropical ecology, and other subjects accredited by some U.S. universities.

Accommodations are geared to groups and students, but anyone can stay in the spacious, air-conditioned dorms with lots of light and hot baths, which can be rented as private rooms. The manicured gardens and pier across the street make for a nice view from the **restaurant** (B, L, D; $$).

Other Hotels
None of these hotels has wireless Internet, handicap access, or accepts credit cards unless specifically noted.

MOYOGALPA
Budget travelers have many more options within four blocks of the *muelle,* or pier. Look around if these don't appeal.

Hotelito Aly (2569-4196, 8686-0830; hotelitoaly@yahoo.com; del muelle, 150 metros arriba; $) I like this unassuming hotel, with its courtyard hangout areas, rocking chairs and hammocks—and good, cheap food. Rooms are clean with OK beds and private cool baths; a few have air-conditioning.

Hospedaje Casa Familiar (2569-4240; islacasafamiliar@hotmail.com; 2 blocks up, 20 meters south of the dock; $) Comfortable budget choice has good rooms with metal bunk beds (double on the bottom, single on top) and private cool baths; air-conditioning costs a few dollars extra. The restaurant is outstanding.

Hospedaje Central (2569-4262; 3 blocks up, one block south of the dock; $) Classic crash pad is covered with murals, has a deer and some cats in the garden, a book exchange and hammocks in the courtyards, and cheap dorm beds and private rooms (two with air-conditioning) that shouldn't scare off experienced budget travelers. The **restaurant** (B, L, D; $) is actually very good.

Hotel Escuela Teosintal (2569-4105; teosintalometepe09@yahoo.com; de Curacao, 125 metros sur; $) Clean airy rooms and dorms are geared to students, but anyone can rent one of their very clean rooms with excellent bunk beds, fans, and cable TVs.

Soma (2569-4310; www.hospedajesoma.com; info@hospedajesoma.com; frente del Instituto R. Smith; $–$$; wifi) European-owned flashpacker joint offers clean, airy, tiled cabinas scattered around manicured gardens. A few dollars more gets you air-conditioning, and rates drop for longer stays.

Altagracia

Posada Cabrera (8664-2788; anamariacabrera@yahoo.com; Altagracia Parque Central; $) Not great, but very basic cement rooms with plastic ceilings, overgrown gardens, and shared baths are clean and cheap.

✪ **Hospedaje Ortiz** (2552-8763, 8698-8459; aquiles1ortiz@yahoo.com; parque central, 200 m sur, 100 m east, 50 m sur; $) Perfect local budget spot run by Mario Alcides Ortiz has clean private rooms with thin mattresses and shared baths, plus murals, rocking chairs, nice gardens, a small book exchange, bicycle rental, lots of local information, and guide service.

San José del Sur and Charco Verde

Posada Chico Largo (8886-4069, 2473-7210; chicolargo.net; chicolargo@yahoo.com; Charco Verde, San José del Sur; Visa only; $–$$) Hammock-strewn budget spot shares the fine cove beach with upmarket Finca Venecia, but its cramped, cleanish, fan-cooled dorms are much cheaper. Private rooms have the option of air-conditioning. They also offer camping atop Mirador del Diablo.

Soda Sinai (8664-2362, 2485-6390; christian_fam@yahoo.com; $) Right on the main road close to the new ferry terminal, this very basic, family-run hostel has charm to spare thanks to English-speaking owner Danny Jossiel Navoa. Comfortable whitewashed cement rooms in the old family home have fans, good beds with thin mattresses, and immaculate shared baths. Serious budget travelers can rent hammocks. The on-site *soda* (basic café) serves inexpensive meals, and there's a guest kitchen you can use for the price of propane.

Playa Santo Domingo

Hospedaje Buena Vista (Playa Santo Domingo; $) You can't make reservations for this popular budget hotel, offering clean, cramped, brick rooms with fans, some with private cool baths, right on the beach. The sandy patio has the lowest guest to hammock ratio on the island.

Hotel Costa Azul (2958-4943, 8855-1410; Playa Santo Domingo; $$) This midrange option right on the beach was still being renovated, but a few of the enormous rooms were finished, with elegant handmade furnishings, large TVs, and optional air-conditioning.

Villa Aller (8479-9847; allegrapr1@yahoo.com; Playa Santo Domingo; $$–$$$) This gem offers just three polished wooden cabins with elegant artisanal furnishings and décor, SkyTV, private hot baths, refrigerators, and microwaves. Go for cabin #1, right on the beach.

SANTA CRUZ

Hostel and Restaurant Santa Cruz (8884-9894; santacruzometepe@gmail.com; Santa Cruz; $) Conveniently located at the Santa Cruz crossroads, this little guesthouse offers seven clean, inexpensive cement rooms in all different shapes and sizes. All have private modern baths (one is external) and a few basic furnishings. The rancho-style ✪ **restaurant** (B, L, D; $–$$) offers vegetarian options in addition to the standard Nicaraguan menu, as well as hammocks. Camping is allowed.

Hotel Finca del Sol (8364-6394; hotelfincadelsol.blinkweb.com; hotelfincadelsol@gmail .com; Santa Cruz, 300 meters from crossroads, toward Balgüe; $$) Very comfortable spot on a sustainable farm and orchard offers three charming, ecologically friendly bungalows elegantly constructed with dark flagstone floors and thatched roofs. They're simple and circular, with TV, purified drinking water, solar panels, and private baths with composting toilets; the hexagonal Orchid Loft has fantastic volcano views from the rocking chairs. Meals are available and recommended.

Little Morgan's Lakeside Resort (8949-7074; www.littlemorgans.com; crowemorgan @yahoo.com; Santa Cruz; $–$$) About 200 meters past the Santa Cruz turnoff toward Balgüe, this festive spot on a quiet cove beach offers dorm beds and hammocks in open-air (read: use the luggage lockers) ranchos with shared composting toilets. Private rooms are sturdier, and some have air-conditioning. The bar and **restaurant** (B, L, D; $–$$) get recommendations, particularly the curry.

BALGÜE

Hospedaje Maderas (8432-9969; Balgüe; $) Right at the entrance to Finca Magdalena, this basic, family-run hotel has good-sized, second-story wooden rooms with fans, foam mattresses, shared baths, and not much else. The two rooms overlooking the street get more light. The on-site restaurant serves good-value Nica cuisine.

MÉRIDA AND SAN RAMÓN

✪ **Hospedaje La Cascada** (8942-4297, 8365-2763; San Ramón; $) Delightful family-run hostel at the end of the bus line offers five simple, slightly lopsided, but very clean rooms with private cool baths. They provide meals, served on the shared porch alongside the hammocks, and are right across the road from the water—though the closest sandy beach is a short walk away.

Hostal Pescaditos (8435-4799; Mérida; $) Right outside famous Hacienda Mérida, Anselmo Carrillo's basic cement guesthouse offers two fan-cooled rooms (more to come!) with shared cool bath and a *comedor* serving inexpensive Nica and vegetarian food—perfect if you get kicked out for disobeying "silence time" next door.

Monkeys Island Hotel (8844-1529, 8659-8961; www.freewebs.com/monkeysisland; monkeysislandjacinto1@hotmail.com; Mérida; credit cards accepted; $) The Hurtado family runs a great hostel just past Mérida, with simple, fan-cooled cement rooms, lots of hammocks, and a small, sandy cove beach. For US$5 more, you get a private bath and better mattress. They also offer good food, guided hikes, mountain bikes, and dorms.

RESTAURANTS AND FOOD PURVEYORS

Isla Ometepe's fertile volcanic soil is carpeted with luxuriant farmland, growing top-quality plantains, papayas, rice, beans, and more—a variety of vegetables that follow the cooling climate up into chill coffee-growing altitudes. Add pastoral tribes of cattle, pigs, chickens, *pueybuey* (a short-haired tropical sheep), and the renowned *guapote* (rainbow bass) of Cocibolca, and you've got all the fixings of a great meal.

While you'll enjoy wholesome and delicious dining during your time on the island, most of Ometepe's eateries are quite simple, combining the ingredients above into wonderful soups, big set plates, and hearty breakfasts. Those craving more variety can head to the hotels, some of which are known for their quality cuisine.

In Moyogalpa, don't miss **Casa Familiar**'s *pescado al vapor,* **Hospedaje Central**'s cheap international dishes, or **American Hotel**'s Italian-accented home cooking. Enjoy upscale environs, well prepared cuisine, and serene beach views at **Inn Charco Verde**, **Villa Paraíso**, and **Hotel Santo Domingo** on the isthmus. Finally, you could make reservations to dine in the skirts of Volcán Maderas at either upscale **Totoco** or rustic **Finca Ecológica El Zopilote**, offering wood-fired pizza and organic products from their farm.

Restaurant and Food Purveyor Price Code

The following prices are based on the cost of a dinner entrée with a nonalcoholic drink, not including Nicaragua's mandatory 13 percent restaurant tax and "suggested" 10 percent tip, which is usually included with the final bill (so check).

Inexpensive ($)	Up to US$5
Moderate ($$)	US$5 to US$10
Expensive ($$$)	$10 to $20
Very Expensive ($$$$)	US$20 or more

The classic way to enjoy Ometepe's guapote, or rainbow bass: served whole—smothered with tomatoes, onions, and herbs.

Restaurants

CAFÉ CAMPESTRE
8695-2071
sites.google.com/site/fincacampestre,
www.ometepe.info
Balgüe, 500 meters past the bus stop
Price: Moderate
Cuisine: Healthy International
Serving: B, L, D
Credit Cards: Yes
Child's Menu: No
Handicap Access: No
Reservations: No

Just past the bus stop, this family-run organic farm has started serving creative, healthy meals that are easily the best in Balgüe. Many of the ingredients are raised right here, including plantains, organic vegetables, ducks, turkeys, and more. The short menu varies, but always includes fresh homemade pastas, bread baked in their outdoor clay oven, and their own ham.

They also have a fully equipped **campsite** ($) and self-service **hospedaje** ($–$$), which share a full, outdoor kitchen and rancho for relaxing. Great views.

CHIDO'S PIZZA

2414-8735
Moyogalpa, Comercial Arcia, 50 metros norte
Price: Inexpensive to Moderate
Cuisine: Pizza
Serving: L, D
Credit Cards: No
Child's Menu: No
Handicap Access: No
Reservations: No

Chido's has been serving up tasty pizzas and Nica dishes on their pretty, plant-filled terrace dining area for years. Order by the slice (they're huge) or pie, and enjoy.

COMEDOR NICARAO

8425-5062
Altagracia, parque central
Price: Inexpensive
Cuisine: Nicaraguan
Serving: B, L, D
Closed: Sun.
Credit Cards: No
Child's Menu: No
Handicap Access: Challenging
Reservations: No

Reliably good, inexpensive *comida casera* (set plates) are your best bet, though there are daily specials and pricier seafood. These are all served with a cold beer or fruit juice and five-star people-watching from the front tables.

☻ LAS MANOS MÁGÍCAS

8747-7767
Alcaldía Municipal, two cuadras al norte,

0.5 al oeste
Price: Moderate to Expensive
Cuisine: Italian
Serving: D
Closed: Wed. and Thur.
Credit Cards: No
Child's Menu: No
Handicap Access: Challenging
Reservations: No

Two blocks north of the alcaldía, this Italian-owned restaurant offers exceptional, creatively topped pizzas and homemade pastas in a quiet little home. It's simple but elegant, with plastic tables and white tablecloths, candles, and pleasant outdoor seating.

Owner and chef Michele Pavanello prepares several types of pizzas, or you may select one of three handmade pastas—fettuccini, stringue, and trofie—and match it with your favorite sauce. Beer and wine are also served, making this Altagracia's most romantic date night.

HOTEL-RESTAURANT TAGÜIZAPA

8855-1388, 8606-6237
asguillenr@hotmail.com
Altagracia, 1.3 km toward the lake
Price: Inexpensive to Moderate
Cuisine: Nicaraguan
Serving: L, D
Credit Cards: No
Child's Menu: No
Handicap Access: Challenging
Wifi: No

It's worth strolling through the platanos down to the lakeshore to enjoy this beachfront, rancho restaurant. The specialties are guapote, churrasco, and cold beer, which you'll enjoy (if you're lucky) watching owner and noted musician Julio Guillén playing a few of his hits from the 1970s and 1980s.

There are also a handful of small brick cabins scattered through the banana trees. They're simple, with fans, private baths, and fine porches, all packed with thin-mattressed beds. It's a neat spot, but call ahead—it's not always open.

BAR EL TIBURÓN
8929-3573
tyroneometepe@hotmail.com
Moyogalpa, del muelle, 100 metros arriba
Price: Moderate
Cuisine: Nicaraguan
Serving: B, L, D
Credit Cards: No
Child's Menu: No
Handicap Access: Challenging
Reservations: No

There are a handful of small, inexpensive restaurants close to the Moyogalpa port, where you can enjoy cold beer, fish dishes, and perhaps your last bowl of real Ometepe-style chicken-and-vegetable soup—while making absolutely sure that the ferry doesn't leave without you. The colorfully painted Shark Bar has great service, cold beer, and cheap and tasty comida corriente, everything you need.

✪ RESTAURANTE LOS RANCHITOS
2569-4112, 8332-4495
www.losranchitos.com.ni
Moyogalpa muelle, 200 metros arriba, 50 metros sur
Price: Moderate
Cuisine: Nicaraguan, Italian
Serving: B, L, D
Credit Cards: Yes
Child's Menu: Yes
Handicap Access: Challenging
Reservations: Yes

Beneath a relaxed thatched-roof ranchero, rather elegant despite an earthen floor and simple hand-hewn wooden tables draped in royal purple, is what many consider Moyogalpa's (and perhaps the island's) best restaurant. Music is mellow, lighting is romantic, and the uniformed waiters offer all sorts of tasty meals: beef medallions a la plancha, grilled guapote, and vegetarian pastas.

Pair your choice with something off the best wine list on the island—which isn't saying much, but there are some good Chilean and Italian vintages. Los Ranchitos also has acceptable, fan-cooled **rooms** ($) with private baths.

YOGI'S CAFÉ
8403-6961
yogisbar@gmail.com
Hospedaje Central, 50 metros sur
Price: Moderate
Cuisine: International
Serving: B, L, D
Credit Cards: Yes
Child's Menu: No
Handicap Access: Challenging
Reservations: No

Named for the owner's friendly black dog, Yogi's is a cool spot to relax with sandwiches, hamburgers, pasta, and big American-style breakfasts, served with excellent smoothies and coffee. Desserts get special mention. There's often sports on TV and a full bar, giving this spot a convivial atmosphere.

CULTURE

Unique on the planet, Ometepe is the world's largest lake island, composed of two fantastic volcanoes. The almost perfect cone of active **Volcán Concepción** (1,610 meters/5,280 feet) still regularly erupts quiet ashfalls as it grows ever skyward, while dormant **Volcán Maderas** (1,395 meters/4,576 feet) is capped with cool cloud forests and an emerald crater lake, held sacred for untold centuries.

Geologists hypothesize that Ometepe arose from the shallow, spreading tectonic graben

Volcán Concepción is still active, and hikes can be cancelled at the last minute due to minor eruptions like this one.

beneath Lake Nicaragua sometime during the Holocene Era, perhaps 12,000 years ago. An indigenous tale, in a more Shakespearian vein, suggest that both the island and lake formed within the human timescale.

According to legend, the land beneath the lake was once a vast and fertile valley, populated by many rival nations. Two young lovers from enemy tribes, Princess Ometepetl and the warrior Nagrandanos, were discovered in an illicit embrace by her parents. They forbade the youths to ever see each other again, but the lovers could not bear to be apart, and instead committed suicide. The tragedy so saddened the gods that they racked the valley with their sobs and flooded it with tears, transforming the princess into Isla Ometepe, and her lover into nearby Isla Zapatera. It is hypothesized that an eruption or massive earthquake led to the sudden flooding of Lake Nicaragua.

At any rate, the mythmakers held the islands sacred, and left behind a wealth of petroglyphs and stone statues, most of which cannot be accurately dated. These have, for the most part, gone unstudied, which has certainly left room for other colorful explanations (flying saucers, anyone?). Most people think they date to between 300 and 800 AD, but no one really knows.

From 1995 to 1999, the **Ometepe Petroglyph Project** (culturelink.info/petro) surveyed 73 petroglyph fields on the Maderas side of the island, recording some 1,700 petroglyphs over five seasons. Carvings most commonly depict spirals that seem to represent the island, geometric shapes, anthropomorphic figures (often people morphing into animals), and symbols that could represent a sort of primitive writing.

Pre-Columbian Ometepe

Archaeologists believe that the first humans visited the island around 11,000 years ago, probably Chibcha-speaking hunter-gatherers originally from the Amazonian rainforests. A few thousand years later, their descendents built the island's first permanent settlements in San José del Sur and Los Angeles. Simple stone utensils, including flat burial plaques, may date to this period.

Nahuatl-speaking Chorotegas from southern Mexico arrived in two distinct waves, one around 300 AD and another in 600 AD, and gave the island its Nahuatl name—*ome* (two) *tepetl* (hills). Their priests had seen the island in a vision, and led their people to its peaceful shores, perhaps to flee the bloody oppression that preceded the Classic Mayan collapse.

Little is known about these people, who may have carved the basalt statues, and planted loquat trees throughout the island to feed their sacred red macaws. Around 900 AD, another migration arrived from the north, this time of the equally mysterious Nahuas. They hailed from mythical cities of Ticomega and Mahuatega (perhaps Tula, Mexico), and worked with jade and gold, still found around Esquipulus. They declared Ometepe entirely sacred.

They may have been the first to call Maderas *Coatlán*, "Place of the Sun," and give Concepción the name *Choncoteciguatepe*, "Place of the Moon" (she was also called *Mestliltepl*, the "Menstruating Mountain," perhaps for her regular cycle of lava flows). The Nahuas had complex religious ceremonies atop the volcanoes, as well as on Mirador del Diablo, Río Buen Suceso, and elsewhere on Ometepe. They built their capital close by, on the mainland: Nicarao, between what are now Rivas and San Jorge.

Modern Ometepe

After occupying Nicarao in 1523, Spanish conquistador Gil González Dávila sent up-and-coming conquistadors Francisco Hernández de Córdoba and Hernando de Soto out to explore Lake Nicaragua and its islands. Franciscan monks arrived at Ometepe in 1613, and left behind intriguing, if incomplete, chronicles. They noted that the language spoken on Ometepe was very different than the Nicaraguan mainland, or anywhere else in New Spain—and a group of tall, light-skinned people occupied the Maderas side.

They evidently spent more time chronicling than converting, as it was not until 1835 that the first Christian indigenous cemeteries were founded. Heck, the original Altagracia (a corruption of *Aztagalpa*, "Nest of Herons") church grounds still display ancient stone idols depicting the old deities.

Their tardiness may have been due to pirates who settled on Ometepe from the late 1600s through the mid-1700s, and used the island as a base to attack Granada and merchant vessels plying the lake. They raped and pillaged Ometepe's indigenous population as well, driving them up into the hills, where many traditional communities still stand. Urbaite and Las Pilas, on the Concepción side, are now the hubs of the seven-village Comunidad Indígena, which still uses traditional government structures and offers tours.

On December 8, 1880, Concepción erupted for the first time since the European occupation, followed by major events in 1883, 1889, 1907, 1924, 1948, and most recently 1957. Though the government sent every boat available to Ometepe, almost no one evacuated. Subsequent rumblings, including a serious 2005 blast accompanied by a 6.2-magnitude earthquake, are generally met with the same stubborn impulse to stay on the island.

All Ometepe was declared a natural reserve in 1995, but some 42,000 people live here. The vast majority are farmers and fishing families, though tourism is certainly an important and growing part of the Ometepe economy. Increasing numbers of foreigners are also settling on the island, building more organic farms and ecologically conscious properties than the usual modern luxury developments. Perhaps some things really are still sacred.

Museums

Almost every hotel and restaurant displays a private collection of ceramic and stone artifacts of mysterious origin, while others offer tours through their petroglyphs, most impressively at Finca El Porvenir (see the Lodging section).

IGLESIA SAN DIEGO DE ALCALÁ
Altagracia Parque Central
Admission: free (but may start charging US$1)
Open: Daily

Altagracia's modest Colonial church is the oldest on the island, and almost certainly sits on ground hallowed far earlier. While most Christians destroyed indigenous temples and idols, often incorporating such sacred stones into their own churches, these relaxed Franciscans actually left several statues intact in the courtyard—including a fearsomely artistic anthropomorphized eagle.

This is also the site of the famed Dance of the Zompopo (leaf-cutter ant), traditionally performed on November 17th—a date sacred to Xolotl, God of the Harvest. Dancers emulate the industrious ants by carrying "leaves" home.

✪ MUSEOS EL CEIBO
8874-8076, 8823-9515
www.elceibomuseos.com
8 km from Moyogalpa
Admission: US$4/6 foreigners, US$3/4 Nicaraguans, for one/two museums
Open: 8 AM–5 PM daily

Though relatively expensive and difficult to visit, El Ceibo is well worth the effort. There are two separate museums, and I recommend them both.

Begin with the **Museo Numismático,** an impressive collection of Nicaraguan currency, but also a history museum that uses money as a motif. For instance, the fact that the Somozas put their sister, a beauty pageant queen, on the C$1 bill, gives you a feel for their very personal use of power. A C$1,000,000 bill from the 1980s, emblazoned with an image of Sandino, offers insight into the explosive inflation of the civil war era. Exhibits take you back in time, through U.S. dollars, Spanish galleons, and finally Nicarao's cacao beans.

The **Museo Precolombino** picks up where the chocolate left off, displaying a truly splendid collection of pottery, petroglyphs, metates (corn grinders), knives, scalpels, and jewelry. There's even a reconstructed tomb (the original was found only 100 meters from here) that shows how wealthier folks were buried, with gold, jade, and other treasures. The collection is displayed according to epoch and style. The oldest piece, a 5,600-year-old gold statue, depicts a female shaman. There's a map of where everything was found.

The museum also organizes "rooster boxing," or cockfighting light. Rather than letting

Luna pottery displayed at Museos El Ceibo dates to the 1400s, perhaps supporting Gavin Menzies's hypothesis that China "discovered" the Americas in 1421.

the roosters battle to the death, the birds have tiny "boxing gloves" covering their business talons, allowing tourists to gamble without too much guilt. The museum can usually arrange a match the same day for US$3 per person.

Any Moyogalpa–Altagracia bus can drop you off at the entrance, a 2-km walk to the museums themselves.

ARCHAEOLOGICAL MUSEUM OF OMETEPE

8691-4034, 8905-3744
manuelhamilton2000@yahoo.com
Altagracia, del parque central, 50 metros oeste
Admission: US$1.50 (an additional US$1.20 to take photos)
Open: 8 AM–noon and 1 PM–4:30 PM Mon. through Sat., 9 AM–2 PM Sun.

This small museum in Altagracia is educational if not outstanding. The impressive topographical map of the island is surrounded by yellowing scientific maps outlining lava flows, potential danger zones, soil types, and other data. Other aging exhibits include photos of Concepción's crater and displays about the Dance of the Zompopo. There's a moth-eaten taxidermy collection of the island's wildlife, a very cool painting of Chico Largo, and a solid collection of ceramics, petroglyphs, and basalt statues, the finest displayed in the overgrown central courtyard.

MUSEO ARQUEOLÓGICA AND CYBER OMETEPE
2569-4225
cibercafeomepete@yahoo.com
Moyogalpa muelle, 300 metros arriba
Admission: US$1
Open: 8 AM–8 PM daily, may open later on Sunday

Small, family-operated museum and cybercafe occupies a modest Moyogalpa home and its statue-studded courtyard gardens, conveniently close to the ferry terminal. It's absolutely jam-packed with pre-Columbian metates (corn grinders), cooking vessels, petroglyphs, stone tools, and—most impressively—a fantastic collection of the womb-shaped ceramic funeral urns for which Ometepe is so well known.

These still-mysterious ceramic vessels were anachronistically emblazoned with Olmec-style bats, snakes, and jaguars (the Olmec Empire, based in Veracruz, Mexico, fell a thousand years before the ceramics were fired), and could not possibly hold a human body. Most islanders were actually buried twice: First, immediately after death, the bodies were interred in the earth, then exhumed after their burden of flesh had returned to the volcanic soil. Their bones were then encased in the graceful pots, and buried close to the family home. The owner's kids offer Spanish-language tours.

Nightlife
Ometepe isn't exactly a nightlife center, but Moyogalpa has several watering holes, from all-night dance parties at **Flor de Angel** (8853-8953; muelle, 150 metros arriba; open Fri. through Sun.), with chrome and disco balls, to the cozier environs of **Bar y Restaurant Timbo al Tambo** (muelle, 200 metros arriba; open 2 PM–whenever), with inexpensive Nica food. **Los Caballitos** in Mérida sometimes has live music, while **Finca Ecológica El Zopilote** and **Mirador del Diablo** both host the occasional Full Moon Party, perhaps with fire dancers and live music.

Spanish Schools
Asociación Puesta del Sol (2619-0219, 8617-1405; www.puestadelsol.org; info@puestadelsol.org; La Paloma) Part of the Comunidad Indígena, this school offers Spanish classes and homestays as part of all-inclusive guided treks that combine traditional tourist activities with real community interaction.

Chuku-Chukú (8363-5757; www.chuku-chuku.com; chuku.spanishschool@gmail.com; Balgüe) The catchy name means "teaching culture" in Nahuatl, and offers two hours of group classes a day for just US$6, homestays US$10 per night including meals. Cheap!

Ometepe Spanish School (8844-0555; www.ometepenicaraguaspanish.net; info@ometepenicaraguaspanish.com) Make advance reservations to take classes at this school, with campuses in Granada, León, Juigalpa, and elsewhere.

RECREATION
Isla Ometepe is an explorer's paradise, with remarkable hikes, relaxed horseback rides, hidden beaches, lush wetlands, deserted islets, and much more. Some spots can be easily visited on your own, including **San Ramón Waterfall**, **Ojo de Agua**, and **Punta de Jesús María**. Other trails require guides, including the hikes up **Volcán Concepción** (10–12

hours) and **Volcán Maderas** (8 hours). Guides are inexpensive, easy to find, and could save your life.

Currently, all of Ometepe's guides are part of **Unión Guías de Ometepe** (8827-7714; www.ugometepe.com), which theoretically arranges tours and packages. In practice, it's usually easier to work with your hotel or established tour operators directly. These are just some local outfitters:

Cacique Tours (8497-1440 (English), 8653-0820 (Spanish); caciquetour@gmail; Moyo-galpa, del Puerto 2 cuadras arriba)

Island Tours (8825-4402; island_tours@hotmail.com; island_tours@hotmail.es; Moyo-galpa)

Ometepe Expeditions (8933-4796, 8363-5783; oneisland@hotmail.es, discovering ometepe@hotmail.es; Moyogalpa)

Ometepe Tours (2563-4779, 2563-0665; ometepetours2007@yahoo.es; Port of San Jorge)

National Parks and Protected Areas

Ometepe is a natural wonder, wholly declared a Natural Reserve in 1995 by Nicaragua, and recognized in 2010 as a UNESCO Biosphere Reserve. It is unique, at 276 square km (107 square miles), the Earth's largest lake island, and the only one with such a striking silhouette.

Historically, Ometepe has been a "paper park," officially preserved but not well protected. Underfunded, understaffed MARENA offices do their best to rescue lost hikers, but have not been able to control poachers and squatters on the poor, densely populated isle. This is changing.

As infrastructure improves, fees have gone up across the board, with previously free attractions now charging a few dollars. Soon, there may be a US$5 entry fee to the island itself. Funds are being used to hire and train more rangers, enforce environmental protection laws, and even build a welcome center at Finca Magdalena. The new program has already started training rangers, who have added 40 new species to Ometepe's bird list.

CHARCO VERDE ECOLOGICAL RESERVE
2569-4276, 8887-9891 (Charco Verde Inn)
www.charcoverdeinn.com.ni
San José del Sur
Open: daily
Admission: US$1

The centerpiece of this 20-hectare (50-acre) lowland tropical forest preserve is the "Green Pond," a serene, emerald lake rich with life and myth. Threading the guanacastes, hawthorns, and freshwater mangroves are several short but beautiful hiking trails, including a stunning 1.7-km loop to Punta Gorda and a viewpoint over Isla Quiste. This is also the trailhead for Mirador del Diablo.

According to ✪ **Charco Verde Inn**, which administrates the park, this was originally called Xistleteot, "Place where the Gods Pee." There are several legends associated with the pond, including a cigar-smoking ghost, a lost enchanted city, a beautiful woman who appears on Good Friday. But the most famous is that of Chico Largo, "Long Boy."

There are several versions of the tale, all involving a tall, pale man who lurks around the lake. He may be the spirit of Francisco Rodríguez, a shape-shifting *nagual*, or Nicaraguan warlock, who lived here in the 1800s. Though he was killed by hunters while disguised as a deer, his body disappeared before burial.

If you come upon old Chico Largo, note that he may offer you wealth, servants, and other earthly delights for seven full years. If you accept, he will arrive right on schedule to collect your soul, then transform you into a cow here on Ometepe. And indeed, there have been reports on this island of butchered cattle with gold teeth.

VOLCÁN CONCEPCIÓN NATURAL RESERVE
www.ineter.gob.ni/geofisica/vol/concepcion/concepcion.html
Isla Ometepe
Open: daily
Admission: Free, but a guide is mandatory

The symmetrical, smoking cone of Volcán Concepción (1,610 meters/5,280 feet . . . and growing) is a tempting climb, but serious. Be in good physical condition and wear real shoes. This is a classic volcanic ascent, with crumbling rock and grades approaching 50 degrees toward the cone. Most hikes begin at around 6 AM from either La Flor, just north of Moyogalpa via a short bus ride, or from a trailhead within walking distance from Altagracia. You can hike from La Flor about midway up the mountain to fine viewpoints, lava flows, and other settings enfolded into the volcano's skirts; all guides offer the trip. Even less ambitious volcano lovers could also do the short half-hour hike from San Marcos to Peña La Chirca, with old lava flows and good birding.

Note that Concepción is very active, and has had more than 25 major eruptions, and still has minor gas and ash releases almost monthly. If vulcanologists detect danger, they'll close the park.

VOLCÁN MADERAS NATURAL RESERVE
www.ineter.gob.ni/geofisica/vol/maderas/maderas.html
Isla Ometepe
Open: daily
Admission: Free, but a guide is mandatory

Swathed in cool cloud forests, Maderas lies in chill repose, lush and calm unlike its active, graying sister. The 1,394-meter (4,572-foot) volcano seems small only next to Concepción, and the popular (and muddy) five- to seven-hour hike to the top will remind you that this massive stratovolcano is indeed a giant.

Maderas pierces several distinct ecosystems as you climb toward its hidden crater—including dry, montane, elfin, premontane, and cloud forests, each with its own interesting plant and animal species, including a handful of endemics.

Maderas's last major eruption probably occurred around 3,000 years ago, allowing the jungle to cover the rich volcanic soils unmolested. The steeply walled, 800-meter-wide crater (your guide should bring ropes, to help assist you in the descent), has long been a sacred place—where a cool, soft-bottomed crater lake gleams in the mist.

Three trails go to the top, beginning at Finca Magdalena (considered the easiest), Finca El Porvenir, and San Ramón Biological Station. Trails are muddy and steep, and you should bring snacks (perhaps something to share with your guide). MARENA evidently plans to build a welcome center at Finca Magdalena and charge an entrance fee.

Though Maderas Volcano is a bit smaller than Concepción, it is still a tough (and slippery) climb to the cool crater lake on top.

Other Parks and Natural Attractions

At the time of research, a new waterfall hike from Balgüe was in the works, a two-hour roundtrip to the 25-meter (75-foot) waterfall **Cascadas Jerusalén**, with petroglyphs and the opportunity for a swim.

El Apante (1 km north of Moyogalpa; open daily; free) This wetlands area, which may start charging an entrance fee, offers an easy, fairly flat, circular walking trail that takes about two hours to complete. Birders will have good luck in the morning.

Finca Mirador del Diablo (8886-4069, 2473-7210; chicolargo.net; chicolargo@yahoo.com; Charco Verde, San José del Sur) Ometepe actually has a third, rarely noticed volcano that rises from the foot of Concepción, close to Charco Verde. More properly known as El Mogote Hill, it earned its curious popular name, "The Devil's Lookout," because it once belonged to old Chico Largo himself. Today, it is a plantation operated by the owners of **Posada Chico Largo** (see Lodging), which arranges day trips and camping, if you don't mind vampires (real, toe-biting vampire bats, not sparkling teenage heartthrobs). They sometimes hold Full Moon Parties, with bonfires and ghost stories, at the top.

✪ **Ojo de Agua** (8820-4499; www.ojodeaguaometepe.com; Finca Tilgüe, Playa Santo Domingo; open 7 AM–6 PM daily; US$2) The isthmus is well watered by this sparkling artesian spring, surrounded by gardens and plantains, that is carved into deep, inviting pools. Take a dip with their rope swing, hike 45 minutes of mellow nature trails, or just ease into a hammock in one of their thatched poolside ranchos. Meals are available, and you can arrange camping and horseback tours. It's on the north end of Playa Santo Domingo, with two well-signed entrances close to the Buen Suceso Bridge.

Punta de Jesús María (Los Angeles; open daily; free) This particularly photogenic natural wonder is a sandbar, hypothetically made of accumulated volcanic ash, that stretches some 2 km into the lake toward San Jorge. During the pre-Columbian and pirate eras, it was a natural port. Today, it is a relaxed tourist destination with a few simple food stands (usually open), a friendly monkey, and a couple of ranchos where you can relax. In dry season, you can stroll well out into the lake to fantastic volcano views, as well as the obligatory "walking on water" photo. In rainy season, lake levels rise, but you can still walk a few hundred meters out into the sea. The point is 3 km (2 miles) from Moyogalpa; a well-signed, shady dirt road runs the final kilometer from the bus stop.

Roca Inculta (Playa Santo Domingo; open daily; US$1) This new, uneven but easy 1.5-km trail leads through dry tropical forest to a large rock, with opportunities for rappelling. It's a good walk for birders and nature lovers as it's home to thousands of parakeets, yellow-throated parrots, howler monkeys, and other critters.

Punta Jesús María is a unique "sandbar" stretching 2 km from Ometepe toward the mainland.

Ruta de las Fincas Verdes, "Route of the Green Plantations"

Ometepe Island is at the epicenter of a sustainable agricultural movement. Because of the island's isolation and poverty, Ometepe's family farms were still mostly organic in the 1990s, when the whole-foods movement began sweeping the developed world and raising prices for local products. It was easy to adapt.

Permaculture farms such as **Project Bona Fide** (www.projectbonafide.com) and **Finca Ecológica El Zopilote** (www.ometepezopilote.com) provide tours and volunteer programs, while **Fundación Entre Volcanes** (2569-4118, 8849-5420; www.fundacionentrevolcanes.org) offers an indigenous women's perspective (as well as an inexpensive hostel).

Ometepe is also home to **Fincas Verdes** (www.fincasverdes.com), a cooperative of 11 plantations geared toward sustainability. These each have a variety of different offerings, including agricultural tours, the opportunity to do some farm work, and a range of lodging.

Finca Charco Verde (www.charcoverde.com.ni) and **Finca Venecia** (www.hotelfincavenecia .com.ni) both have recommended hotels, while simpler accommodation can be found at the famous **Finca Magdalena** (www.fincamagdalena.com), with an organic coffee plantation; **Hacienda Mérida** (www.hmerida.com), with kayaking and the Somozas' old dock; **Finca La Florida** (isiamador@yahoo .com), a tobacco plantation; and **Finca Samaria** (2451-5228, 8824-2210; Los Angeles, 5 km south of Moyogalpa), with dairy cattle.

Others may not have lodging, but do offer activities. **Finca Tilgüe** (www.ojodeaguaometepe.com; www.posadacabrera.com) is home to **Ojo de Agua; Finca María Andrea** (2569-4276, 2659-8964; ometepetlng@hotmail.com; La Concepción, 3 km north of Moyogalpa) has farm tours and guided hikes; **Finca La Esperanza** (2563-1007, 8876-9970; Las Cruces, 13 km de Moyogalpa) has a honey-production farm and three-hour horseback rides to Cerro La Pelona; and **Finca Agroturistica Tel Aviv** (8874-8076, 8823-9515; moisesghitis@hotmail.com; Sacramento, 10 km from Moyogalpa), part of Museos El Ceibo, has dairy cattle, cheese production, oxcart rides, and "rooster boxing."

✪ **San Ramón Waterfall** (305-666-9932 (U.S.); www.lasuerte.org; open daily; US$3) The Ometepe Biological Field Station (see Lodging) in San Ramón is the starting point for this popular 3-km hike to a 35-meter (115-foot) waterfall. There's water all year round, but it is more powerful and impressive in rainy season. The path is steep but nontechnical, with great lake views, a small hydroelectric plant, and plenty of birds and other wildlife en route. This is also the trailhead for the steepest, most challenging hike up Volcán Maderas, but you'll need to hire a guide.

Biking

Mountain bikes are available for rent all over the island; your hotel probably has a few. They usually cost US$1 per hour, aren't nearly as nice as your bike back home, but are an absolute joy as you explore the island. The loop around Volcán Maderas is a classic.

Canopy Tours

Canopy Sendero Los Monos (8927-2019; rportocarrero@natuwa.com; Playa Santo Domingo; US$8 per person.) Smallish six-platform, four-cable canopy tour is still a great flight through the jungle with amazing isthmus views. They can also arrange rappelling trips.

Fishing

It seems that every seaside family has a tiny dugout canoe, taken out in the morning and evening by teenage boys who always seem to return with a string of smallish *guapote*. The official story, however, is that fishing isn't that great around Ometepe. Regardless, if you want to go out on the lake with your line, ask your hotel or tour operator to hook something up.

Horseback Riding

Isla Ometepe is one of Nicaragua's easiest, cheapest, and most enjoyable places to arrange horseback rides. Just about every hotel can organize the treks for around US$5 per hour, with the option of a Spanish-speaking guide for US$10, but prices vary widely. More expensive operators may have English-speaking guides and larger horses.

Kayaking

Near Mérida, both **Caballito's Mar** and **Hacienda Mérida** rent kayaks for a visit to Monkeys Island, where you can be bitten by frustrated spider monkeys; or, much better, a tranquil, three-hour paddle up the **Río Istiam**. Really more of a wetlands area that consumes most of the isthmus in rainy season, it is home to owls, kingfishers, herons, and many other birds. You might also see turtles, coral snakes, iguanas, boa constrictors, *guajipal* (caimans), and howler monkeys. The wetlands shrink in dry season (December through March), when this trip might not be available.

    Charco Verde Inn, on the Concepción side, also rents kayaks, which you can use to visit undeveloped little **Isla Quiste**. Any hotel can arrange these trips.

Kite Surfing

Pro-Kiting (8886-0173; www.jamisonsmith.com; Lake Nicaragua) Experienced kite-surfing instructor teaches you to soar across Lake Nicaragua between November and February, when winds are at their best. Lessons run US$60–165 per day, or try an all-inclusive camp.

Spas

Better hotels can arrange massages, or try **Healing Hands** (8496-2453; manos.curativas .balgue@gmail.com), offering "Indian head massages" in Balgüe for US$10.

SHOPPING

Ometepe is not exactly a shopping mecca.

Banks and ATMs

At the time of research there was one Visa/Plus ATM machine in Moyogalpa, **Banco Pro-Credit,** 300 meters uphill from the pier. It is apparently unreliable, so be smart and get all the cash you need in Rivas or Granada.

Groceries and Markets

It's best to stock up on groceries in Rivas or Granada before catching the ferry. Everything that isn't grown here has to be expensively shipped, and costs about 20 percent more than on the mainland.

Both Moyogalpa and Altagracia have fairly well-stocked pulperías and fruit stands, but no major markets. Smaller towns, including Balgüe, Mérida, San José del Sur, Santa Cruz, and San Ramón, also have tiny shops. **Finca Ecológica El Zopilote** (see Lodging) is worth the climb for fresh-baked bread, homemade jams, hummus, and other wholesome products.

Shops

✪ **Galería de Arte Museo Carlos A. Vargas** (2569-4207, 8923-9117; galleriacarlosvargas @hotmail.com; Esquipulas; usually open 9 AM–7 PM daily, or knock) Around 4 km south of Moyogalpa, you'll see this small gallery signed from the main road. Carlos Vargas is part of a family well known for their primitivist art, the brightly colored, naïve style of painting for which the islands of Solentiname, on the other side of the lake, are famed. These take Ometepe as their subject, and are beautiful; Vargas (who trained with Ernesto Cardenal) has exhibited and sold them all over the world. Here, they are scattered around the humble wooden home, and cost between US$25 and US$1,200. Just looking is free.

Sala Arqueológica Ometepe (2569-4225; cibercafeomepete@yahoo.com; Moyogalpa, del muelle 300 metros arriba) This tiny museum and Internet café also has a great selection of traditional *artesanías*.

"Primativist" painter Carlos Vargas has all Ometepe for his muse.

Tienda de Artesanías Luna (2569-4132; ometeptl@hotmail.com; Hotel Ometepetl) Conveniently located right on the Moyogalpa dock, this souvenir shop has local handicrafts, clever kitsch, and a fine selection of Ometepe T-shirts.

EVENTS

Major national holidays, such as Semana Santa and La Purísima, are celebrated with decidedly indigenous flair—flower carpets, traditional dances—in both Moyogalpa and Altagracia.

March

Semana Santa (March or April, week before Easter) Though not quite as crowded as the Pacific beaches, both Ometepe and San Jorge are packed during Semana Santa. Make hotel reservations well in advance, particularly on Playa Santo Domingo. An oxcart parade from Nandaime arrives at San Jorge's Iglesia El Señor de Rescate during Semana Santa.

April

San Jorge Civic Fiestas (April 19–23) San Jorge honors its patron with processions, marimba, traditional dances, and special dishes such as *chicha* and tamales.

✪ **Danza del Zompopo** (last full moon of April and first full moon of May) The ancient Leaf-Cutter Ant Dance is performed with full religious pomp twice a year in the port town of Altagracia, once known as *Aztagalpa*, "Nest of Herons." In addition to the amazing costumes, they play music using pre-Columbian percussion instruments such as *tunkules* and *tepnastles*.

San Ramón Fishing Tournament (end of April) Famous fishing competition is serious business.

May

Urbaite Civic Fiestas (May 11–15) The famously indigenous town of Urbaite honors its patron, San Pío.

July

Moyogalpa Civic Fiestas (July 23–27) Moyogalpa honors its patron, the Virgin of Santa Ana, with processions, *topes* (horse parades), bull riding, fireworks, live music, and the *Baile de las Inditas* (Dance of the Indian Maidens), an ancient performance in which young ladies wear traditional embroidered Nicaraguan *hüipiles* and fresh flowers. There's a procession to Punta Jesús María.

Tagüizapa Civic Fiestas (July 16–26) Lakeside village close to Altagracia has its municipal festivities.

August

Fiestas Patronales San Diego Alcalá (August 2) All of Isla Ometepe honors its patron with religious events, traditional dances, beauty queens, and heavy drinking.

Altagracia's rich folkloric traditions often add an indigenous flavor to national festivals, such as La Gritería.

November

✪ **Altagracia Civic Fiestas** (November 12–18) The ancient port town of Altagracia honors its patron, with feast days that coincide with a much more ancient festival, honoring the Aztec God of the Harvest—another excuse to perform the Dance of the *Zompopo*.

December

Balgüe Civic Fiestas (December) Balgüe honors the Sacred Heart of Jesus with festivities that go on throughout December.

9

SUGGESTED READING

"Every Nicaraguan is considered a poet until proven otherwise."

—José Coronel Urtecho

Nicaragua is a nation of poets, with wordsmiths dominating the popular consciousness in the way actors, sports stars, and war heroes do elsewhere—even President Daniel Ortega has published a few verses. If you speak Spanish, there is an entire universe of Nicaraguan writers to explore, but at least three have been widely translated.

Rubén Darío (1867–1916) was a literary prodigy, ambassador, world-class drinker, "Father of Modernism," and the greatest writer in Latin American history, not to mention Nicaragua's least controversial national hero. **Ernesto Cardenal** (1925–), Nicaragua's first minister of culture, founder of Solentiname's primitivist art movement, and a faithful but irreverent Sandinista and Catholic priest, is the *de facto* poet laureate despite his witty critiques of the current government. **Gioconda Belli** (1948–) was both a revolutionary Sandinista operative and the sexual revolutionary who gave a literary voice to the passions of women, war, and her native land.

ADVENTURE

Belt, Thomas. *The Naturalist in Nicaragua.* 1874. US$29.99. Insightful book is half ecosystems ecology, half travelogue, and considered one of the greatest natural history books ever written. Republished in 2010.

Bubenik, Jenifer. *Thoughts From the Chicken Bus.* 2009. US$15. Chick lit meets Central America: After quitting her job and breaking up with her man, Jenifer hits the road on a backpacker budget, trekking across Central America by bus. Fun, inspiring beach read.

Rushdie, Salman. *The Jaguar Smile: A Nicaraguan Journey.* 1987. US$17.95. On break from writing *The Satanic Verses,* noted British novelist Salman Rushdie decided to take a lyrical and investigative vacation in wartime Nicaragua. The result is a well-written travelogue that reserves its harshest critiques for Reagan and his proxies, but turns a satirical eye toward Rushdie's welcoming Sandinista hosts as well.

Squier, Ephraim. *Nicaragua: Its People, Scenery, Monuments, Resources, Condition and Proposed Canal.* 1854. Out of Print. Packed with maps and illustrations, this is the masterwork of an observant and influential author, anthropologist, and U.S. ambassador who also wrote the 1860 *Travels in Central America, Particularly in Nicaragua.*

COFFEE TABLE BOOKS

Aguirre Sacasa, Francisco. *Nicaragua: An Historical Atlas.* 2003. US$40. Nicaragua's former foreign minister himself compiled and published this massive collection of beautifully reproduced maps, dating from the colonial period through the 20th century.

Banco America Central. *Nicaragua: Paraíso de Oportunidades.* 2009. The Pellas family (Nicaragua's wealthiest) publishes this interesting photography tome that shows the business-friendly side of the country.

✪ Correa Oquel, César. *The Nicaraguans.* 2008. US$40. Work from 50 of Nicaragua's finest photographers is showcased in this elegant, oversized collection.

Lacayo, Rossana. *Granada: La Sultana del Gran Lago de Nicaragua.* 2009. US$20. In its second edition, this collection captures Granada's beauty and history in more than 200 full-color photos.

HISTORY

Bolaños-Geyer, Alejandro. *William Walker, the Gray-Eyed Man of Destiny.* 1988. Out of Print. This five-volume, encyclopedic tale is considered the definitive study of William Walker.

Colburn, Forrest D. *My Car in Managua.* 1991. US$17.95. Ostensibly a collection of interesting anecdotes about trying to maintain a car in wartime Managua, this slim, easy read has adorable illustrations and powerful insights into the culture, society, and on-the-ground economics of Nicaragua's 1980s. The author has also written such serious-sounding tomes as *Post-Revolutionary Nicaragua: State, Class, and the Dilemmas of Agrarian Policy* (1987, out of print).

Cruz, Consuelo. *Political Culture and Institutional Development in Costa Rica and Nicaragua: World Making in the Tropics.* 2009. US$34.99. Armchair anthropologists and boozy expats have spent years discussing the markedly different paths of historical development undertaken by Nicaragua and Costa Rica. Cruz, however, has addressed this issue using facts, evidence, statistics, and historical context, guaranteed to make you sound like the smartest person at the bar next time some newbie real estate investor uses the usual third-person anecdotes as debate points.

Dando-Collins, Stephen. *Tycoon's War: How Cornelius Vanderbilt Invaded a Country to Overthrow America's Most Famous Military Adventurer.* 2009. US$17.75. This tale of William Walker's misadventure in Southwest Nicaragua cheers the filibusterer on even as the Commodore, Cornelius Vanderbilt, pulls out all the stops to destroy him.

Glasgow, Michael. *The Bridge: The Eric Volz Story; Murder, Intrigue, and a Struggle for Justice in Nicaragua.* 2008. US$17.95. True crime thriller explores the brutal 2006 murder of San Juan del Sur businesswoman Doris Jímenez. Eric Volz, a U.S. expat and her exboyfriend, was arrested and hastily convicted of the murder. Volz was suddenly released from prison in 2007, 29 years early, and deported under unusual circumstances. He was about to publish his memoir at press time, *Gringo Nightmare: A Young American Framed for Murder in Nicaragua* (2010, US$25.99).

Healy, Paul F.; Pohl, Mary. *Archaeology of the Rivas Region, Nicaragua.* 1980. Out of Print. The only real archaeological study of Southwest Nicaragua's rich pre-Columbian heritage studies seven excavations in the old Nicarao polity, undertaken between 1959 and 1961. It almost accidentally established the ceramics-based, pre-Columbian chronology of

Gran Nicoya that is considered canonical in most modern museums (and referred to as factual throughout this book). Even Pohl pointed out, however, that this small sample size and lack of reliable dates needed a great deal more study.

MacAulay, Neil. *Sandino Affair*. 1971. US$24.95. Written by a former U.S. Army officer who had fought in the Cuban Revolution, this is considered the definitive English-language history of Sandino's six-year war against the U.S. Marines, focusing on military and political strategies rather than the general's mythic significance.

REVOLUTION AND CONTRA WAR

The vast majority of English-language books about Nicaragua are set in the turbulent 1970s and 1980s, and were written just afterward.

◆ Belli, Gioconda. *The Country Under My Skin: A Memoir of Love and War*. 2003. US$16. Arguably Nicaragua's greatest living poet, and certainly its sexiest, Belli was an upper-crust Managua debutante, undercover Sandinista operative, and successful business-woman in the age of blood and disco. Her passionate memoir is a must for anyone interested in the Revolution or Nicaraguan sexual politics, or who just needs an epic "girl power" beach book.

Kinzer, Stephen. *Blood of Brothers: Life and War in Nicaragua*. 2007. US$18.95. This critically acclaimed account was written by the former *New York Times* Managua bureau chief, who examines the causes, courses, and major mistakes of the Revolution and Contra War. It includes several interviews with major players.

Walker, Thomas W. *Nicaragua: Living in the Shadow of the Eagle*. 2003. US$12.95. Lefty view of the Revolution and Contra War is an informed foil to the official version. Well researched and written.

LONG-TERM VISITORS

ACHAM. *Doing Business in Nicaragua*. 2010. US$10. The Nicaraguan-American Chamber of Commerce publishes this guide to living, working, and investing in Nicaragua for free online (www.acham.org.ni) or US$10 bound. Contact their Managua offices (2266-2758; publicrelations@acham.org.ni) for more information.

Berman, Joshua; Woods, Randall. *Living Abroad Nicaragua*. 2006. US$17.95. The authors of the Moon Nicaragua guidebook have geared this very useful and well-written guide for expatriates and investors.

Rogers, Tim. *Christopher Howard's Living & Investing in the New Nicaragua*. 2005. US$19.95. Longtime resident, *Time* magazine correspondent, and *Nica Times* editor Tim Rogers offers advice on surviving and thriving in Nicaragua.

MOVIES

There are dozens of documentaries about the Revolution and Contra War, many of them free online.

◆ Cox, Alex. *Walker*. 1987. The director of *Sid and Nancy* adds a hallucinogenic spin and Joe Strummer soundtrack to the tale of William Walker. The filibustero's attempt to overthrow Central America is consciously anachronistic, with helicopters and stock market tickers that draw heavy-handed parallels with the Contra War, but it was also shot on-site in Granada using authentic costumes and set pieces.

Raymont, Peter. *The World Stopped Watching.* 2003. The sequel to the hard-hitting 1987 documentary *The World is Watching* is more about Nicaragua's postwar trials and tribulations than the original, which was more of a media critique comparing stories submitted by ABC Managua correspondent John Quinones to those reported by anchor Peter Jennings.

Spottiswoode, Roger. *Under Fire.* 1983. Nick Nolte stars as a hard-boiled war journalist who doesn't "take sides," he "takes pictures." After meeting an amoral American mercenary, a wise Nicaraguan priest, and even Anastasio Somoza, Nolte has a change of heart.

SURFING

Blue Planet Surf Maps. *The Essential Surfing Nicaragua Guide & Surf Map Set.* 2010. US$18.95. Slim 70-page volume covers Nicaragua's best waves.

✪ Parise, Mike; Towner, Robert. *The Surfer's Guide to Costa Rica & Southwest Nicaragua.* 2010. US$17.95 The essential guide to surfing Southwest Nicaragua, with information about the neighbors as well.

WILDLIFE

While there aren't many wildlife guides written specifically for the region, Southwest Nicaragua shares flora, fauna, and ecosystems with Guanacaste, Costa Rica, which has been exhaustively covered.

Garrigues, Richard. *The Birds of Costa Rica: A Field Guide.* 2007. US$29.95. Popular guide has the photos and information you need without weighing you down in the field.

Pickering, Helen. *Wildflowers of Mombacho.* 2006. US$15.95. Informative, photo-rich guide has English and Spanish descriptions of more than 200 flowers native to Mombacho Volcano.

Reid, Fiona A. *A Field Guide to the Mammals of Central America and Southeast Mexico.* 2009. US$45. Comprehensive field guide includes 47 color plates and information about various habitats.

Van Perlo, Ber. *Birds of Mexico and Central America.* 2006. US$29.95. Definitive guide for birders lists some 1,500 species.

Index

A

accommodations: about, 34–35; price codes, 11; Carazo, 87, 91–95; Cárdenas, 227; Granada, 125–35; Isla Ometepe, 241–44; Managua, 55–62; Masaya, 87–89, 93; Playa Ostional, 176; Pueblos Blancos, 87, 89–91, 94; Rivas, 207–8, 217; San Jorge, 236; San Juan del Sur, 170–84; Tola beaches, 207, 208–18. *See also specific accommodations*
Acopio Beach House (Playa Gigante), 217
addresses, locating, 41
Adelante Express, 39, 168
adventure books, recommended, 269
Aeropuerto Granada, 122
Aeropuerto Internacional Augusto C. Sandino (Managua), 38, 53; car rentals, 54
air travel (airlines), 38, 39
airports, 38–39; Costa Rica, 39; Granada, 122; Managua, 38, 53
AK47 Tattoo (Managua), 79
Al Di La (Managua), 67
Alamo Car Rentals, 40, 54, 122, 168
Albergüe Ecológico El Porvenir (Ometepe), 246
Albergüe Rural Sonzapote, 131, 156
Alcaldía Cárdenas, 227
Alcaldía Catarina, 84
Alcaldía Managua, 51
Alcaldía Masatepe, 84
Alcaldía Masaya, 84
Alcaldía Niquinohomo, 84
Alcaldía San Juan de Oriente, 84
Aley, Cathye, 200
Alianza Français (Granada), 153
Alianza para Las Areas Silvestres (ALAS), 13
Altagracia: boat travel, 235, 239–40; buses, 238; church, 257; events, 267–68; groceries, 266; lodging, 243–44, 250; museums, 258
Altagracia Civic Fiestas, 268
Altamira (Managua), 51; food purveyors, 66–67; lodging, 57–59, 61–62; shopping, 78–79
Alter Eco (Managua), 79
American Café and Hotel (Moyogalpa), 241–42, 252
Ananda (Managua), 67
ANDEN (Huehuete), 94
Anniversary of the Revolution, 49, 79
antiques, shopping for, 160, 200
Apoyo Beach, 108
Apoyo Camp, 109

Apoyo Lagoon. *See* Laguna de Apoyo
Apoyo Lagoon Natural Reserve, 107–9
Aqua Yoga and Wellness Retreat (Playa Gigante), 208–9, 230
Aquiler de Equinos (Catarina), 112
Arboretum Nacional Dr. Juan Bautista Salas Estrada (Managua), 74
archaeological museums, 70–71, 258–59
architecture, 23; Managua, 68–69
Arena Blanca: snorkeling, 198–99
Arena Caliente Surf Camp (San Juan del Sur), 168, 196
art galleries: Granada, 160; Managua, 78–79; Moyogalpa, 266; San Juan del Sur, 200
Arte Visual (Granada), 160
arts and crafts. *See* handicrafts
Asese Peninsula, 154–55
Así Es Mi Tierra (Balgüe), 247
Asociación Puesta del Sol (La Paloma), 259
ATM machines. *See* banks
ATV tours, 194
Aurora Beachfront Reality (San Juan del Sur), 181
Auto Express, 54
Auto Hotel Cocibolca (Granada), 133
Ave Maria University (San Marcos), 104
Ave Nicaragüita (Granada), 152
Aventura Lodge (San Juan del Sur), 171
Azteca Hotel (San Jorge), 236

B

Bahía del Sol (La Chocolata), 181
Bahía El Astillero. *See* El Astillero
Bahía Paraíso (El Astillero), 215
Baile de Chinegros (Nindirí), 116
Baile de los Diablitos (Masaya), 117
Bainbridge-Ometepe Sister Islands Association, 232
bakeries: Catarina, 99; Granada, 141–42; Managua, 66; Masatepe, 99; Masaya, 99; San Juan del Sur, 189; San Marcos, 99
Balcones de Majagual (Playa Majagual), 181–82
Balgüe, 235; buses, 238; events, 268; hiking, 262; lodging, 246–48, 251; restaurants, 252–53; Spanish schools, 259; spas, 265
Balgüe Civic Fiestas, 268
Ballet Folklórico Nicaragüense (Managua), 73
Baloy Surf Shop (San Juan del Sur), 197
Bambú Beach Club (San Juan del Sur), 185, 191

Banco America Central, 47; Granada, 159
banks, 47; Diriamba, 113–14; Granada, 159;
  Isla Ometepe, 265; Managua, 77; Masaya,
  113–14; Rivas, 230; San Juan del Sur, 199
Bar El Muellecito (Managua), 72
Bar El Tiburón (Moyogalpa), 254
Bar Mi Barra (Rivas), 225
Bar Republika (San Juan del Sur), 191
Bar y Comedor Mary Mar (Playa Gigante), 220
Bar y Restaurant Ines (San Juan del Sur),
  185–86
Bar y Restaurant Los Chocoyos (Granada), 131
Bar y Restaurant Timbo al Tambo
  (Moyogalpa), 259
Bar y Restaurante Los Artistas (Granada), 137
Barceló Montelimar (Managua), 59–60
Bar-Hospedaje Español (Rivas), 217
Bar-Restaurante El Navegante (San Jorge),
  236–37
Bar-Restaurante Eliath (La Boquita), 98
Barrio Café (San Juan del Sur), 171, 186, 191
bars. See nightlife
Base Camp International (Jinotepe), 94
Basílica Menor de San Sebastián (Diriamba),
  103–4
Batalla de San Jacinto, 49
bathrooms, 43
Beach Front Rentals (San Juan del Sur), 194
beaches. See Carazo; Tola; and entries begin-
  ning with "Playa"
Bearded Monkey (Granada), 134, 153, 161
Bed Head Shed (San Juan del Sur), 186
Belli, Gioconda, 269, 271
Bello Horizonte (Managua): nightlife, 71
Best Western Las Mercedes (Managua), 59
Between the Waves, 29
Biblioteca Móvil (San Juan del Sur), 173
Biblioteca Roberto Incer Barquero
  (Managua), 69, 78
bicycling, 43; Granada, 124; Isla Ometepe,
  264
Big Wave Dave's (San Juan del Sur), 186, 191,
  200
birds (birding), 12–13; books, 272;
  Chacocente Wildlife Reserve, 226; Granada,
  154, 155, 158; Isla Ometepe, 261–63; Laguna
  de Nocarime, 226; Managua, 73; Tisma
  Lagoon System, 110–11
Bisou Bisou (Managua), 66
Bistró Layha (Jinotepe), 97
Blue Morpho (Cárdenas), 227
Blue Sol Hotel Restaurant (Playa Gigante), 218
boat travel, 43; Altagracia, 235, 239–40;
  Granada, 125, 157–58; Isla Ometepe, 125,
  157, 234–35, 239–40; Laguna de Apoyo, 112;
  Managua, 76–77; Moyogalpa, 234–35,

239–40; Playa Gigante, 207, 228; Rivas, 207;
  San José del Sur, 239–40; San Juan del Sur,
  194–95
Bohdin Adventure Services, 31
Bohemian Paradise (Granada), 126
Bolaños Island National Wildlife Refuge, 193
Bolonia (Managua): food purveyors, 66–67;
  lodging, 56–57, 61; nightlife, 72; safety, 53;
  shopping, 78
Bonnie Lassie Luxury Spa (San Juan del Sur),
  199
books, suggested, 269–72
bookstores: Granada, 161–62; Managua,
  78–79; San Juan del Sur, 200
Booze-Sunset Cruise (San Juan del Sur), 194
Boquita beach. See La Boquita
border crossings, Costa Rica, 40
Boricua (Granada), 152
Bosawas Maps, 37
Budget Car Rentals, 54, 122
Buen Gusto (Jinotepe), 99
Buena Onda Beach Resort (Playa Santana),
  210–11
Buena Vida Fitness Centre (San Juan del Sur),
  199
Buena Vista Surf Club (Playa Madera), 178
bull sharks, 13
buses, 39, 42; Carazo, 85; Catarina, 85–86;
  Diriamba, 86; El Astillero, 207; Granada,
  122, 124; Isla Ometepe, 236–38; Jinotepe,
  86; Laguna de Apoyo, 86; Managua, 54–55;
  Masatepe, 86; Masaya, 84–85; Rivas, 204–7;
  San Juan de Oriente, 85–86; San Juan del
  Sur, 168–69; San Marcos, 86–87

C

Caballito's Mar (Mérida), 248
Cabaña Amarilla, 125, 158
Cabina Tica #2 (Guasacate), 218
cabs. See taxis
Cacique Tours (Isla Ometepe), 260
cafés: Granada, 142; Jinotepe, 99; Managua,
  66; Masaya, 99; Playa Popoyo, 221; Rivas,
  221–22; San Marcos, 99
Café Bar Pizzería Rana Roja (Popoyo), 221
Café Campestre (Balgüe), 252–53
Café Don Simón (Granada), 142
Café Isabella (Granada), 142
Café Latino (Granada), 142
Café Le Poeta (Managua), 66
Café Mama Quilla (Managua), 66
Café Negro (San Marcos), 99
Calle La Calzada (Granada), 119; nightlife,
  151–52
Camino Real (Managua), 59
camping: Balgüe, 253; Laguna de Apoyo, 109;

Managua, 73; Masaya, 105; Playa Majagual, 184; San Juan del Sur, 196–98; Sonzapote, 156
Camping Matilda's (Playa Majagual), 184
Canopy Sendero Los Monos (Playa Santo Domingo), 264
Canopy Tour Miravalle (Granada), 158
canopy tours: Granada, 158; Isla Ometepe, 264; Managua, 75–76; San Juan del Sur, 195
Canopy Tours Nicaragua (Managua), 75–76
Captain Max (Playa Gigante), 228
car rentals: Granada, 122; Isla Ometepe, 235; Managua, 54
car travel, 42; Granada, 121; Isla Ometepe, 235; Managua, 53–54; Masaya, 83; Rivas, 204; San Juan del Sur, 167–68
Carazo (Carazo beaches), 10, 28, 80–115; culture, 103–6; food purveyors, 98–99; information, 82, 87; lodging, 87, 91–95; map, 82; recreational activities, 107–13; restaurants, 95, 97–98; safety, 81; transportation, 81–87
Cardenal, Ernesto, 148, 269
Cárdenas, 227
Carita Feliz (Granada), 121, 126, 150
Carnival (Masaya), 116
Casa Bohemia (Granada), 136–37
Casa Canada (Playa El Coco), 184
Casa Catarina (Catarina), 89–90
Casa Concepción Navarro (San Marcos), 94
Casa de Cajetas (Diriomo), 99
Casa de Cultura Alejandro Martinez (Tisma), 111
Casa de Dragonfly (Playa El Coco), 178
Casa de Huespedes Santos (Managua), 61
Casa de los Leones (Granada), 148
Casa de los Mejía Godoy (Managua), 72
Casa de los Tres Mundos (Granada), 148, 153, 161, 162
Casa del Sol Hotel Boutique (Managua), 59
Casa El Güegüense (Diriamba), 87, 106, 112
Casa Hotel Istiam (Playa Santo Domingo), 244–45
Casa La Merced (Granada), 133
Casa Marina Condominium Hotel (San Juan del Sur), 172
Casa Marsella (Playa Marsella), 182
Casa Maur (Playa Popoyo), 213
Casa Museo Harold (Granada), 160
Casa Naranja (Managua), 57
Casa Oro Adventure Center (San Juan del Sur), 167, 168–69, 182
Casa Sacuanjoche Art Gallery (Granada), 160
Casa San Francisco (Granada), 131
Casa Silas B&B (Granada), 134
Casa Tranquila (San Juan del Sur), 175, 199
Casa Vanegas (Managua), 61

Casa Vivaldi (Granada), 132
Casa Xalteva (Granada), 152
Casa-Museo Comandante Camilo Ortega Saavedra (Masaya), 105
Casares: buses, 85, 86; events, 116; lodging, 92–93; restaurants, 98
Cascadas Jerusalén, 262
Catarina, 101–2; buses, 85–86; culture, 101–2; events, 116; horseback riding, 112; information, 84; lodging, 89, 94, 95; restaurants, 96–97, 99; Spanish schools, 107
Catarina Mirador, 95, 96, 111–12
Catarina Spanish School, 107
Catedral de Santiago (Managua), 68
Catedral Inmaculada Concepción de María (Managua), 69
cell phones, 44
Cemetery Hill (Rivas), 222
Cenac Spanish School (Granada), 152
Central Line, 39, 122
Central Park (Granada), 148, 156
Centro Cultural Antigüo Convento de San Francisco (Granada), 149–50
Centro Nicaragüense de Escritores (Managua), 78
Centro Recreativo El Gran Diamante (San Jorge), 237
Centroamerica, 29
Centros Turísticos, 34. See also specific destinations
ceramics, in San Juan de Oriente, 102, 114, 116
César (Granada), 152
Chacocente Wildlife Reserve, 226, 230
Chale's House (San Juan del Sur), 182
Chamorro, Violetta, 18–19, 44, 69, 118
Charco Verde, 260–61; lodging, 242–43, 250
Charco Verde Ecological Reserve, 260–61
Charco Verde Inn, 242, 260, 265
Charly's Bar y Restaurante (Granada), 137–38
Chele Palmado (Playa Gigante), 217–18
Chica Brava (San Juan del Sur), 196–97
Chido's Pizza (Moyogalpa), 253
Chocolate (Granada), 142
Chocoyero-El Brujo Natural Reserve, 73
Christmas, 49
Chuku-Chukú (Balgüe), 259
cigars, 79, 160–61
Cigars Zone (Managua), 72
Cine Karwala (Granada), 153
cinemas: Granada, 153; Managua, 73
Civil War, 15–16, 146
Click Managua, 51, 71
climate, 32
clothing, 23; Granada, 160
Cocina de Doña Haydée (Managua), 67

cockfighting, 257–58
Coco Cabañas (Playa El Coco), 184
CocoBerry Spa (Granada), 126, 159
Cocopeli Tours, 31
Cocos (Managua), 79
Coctelería el Mariscazo (Rivas), 219
Coctelería Vuelve de Vida (Managua), 67
coffee. *See* cafés
coffee plantations, 75, 103, 112, 155, 157, 225, 264
coffee table books, 270
Comedor Nicarao (Altagracia), 253
Comida Buffet (Masaya), 99
Comidas Típicas y Mas (Granada), 143
communications, 44
Conchi's (Granada), 152
consulates, 44
Contra War, 18–19, 190; books, 271
Convento de San Francisco (Granada), 144, 149–50
Cooperativa Claudia Chamorro, 131
Cooperativa de Transporte Turístico de Ometepe, 239
Coquito Beach (San Juan del Sur), 191
Cosmos (Rivas), 225
Costa Nica Expeditions (Playa Gigante), 228
Costa Rica: airports, 39; border crossings, 40; websites, 40
crafts. *See* handicrafts
Crater's Edge (Laguna de Apoyo), 109
Crazy Crab Beach (San Juan del Sur), 191
credit cards, 47
crime, 31–32; Carazo, 81; Granada, 119, 121; Isla Ometepe, 233–34; Managua, 53; Masaya, 81; Pueblos Blancos, 81; Rivas, 203; San Juan del Sur, 166–67; Tola beaches, 203
crossing the Costa Rican border, 40
Crowne Plaza Hotel Managua, 56, 66
Cruceros del Golfo, 39
Cruceros Familiares Lago Cocibolca (Granada), 125, 157–58
Cruz de España, 222, 236
cuisine, 24–25
culture, 23; Carazo, 103–6; Granada, 143–51; Isla Ometepe, 254–59; Managua, 68–71; Masaya, 100–106; Pueblos Blancos, 101–6; Rivas, 222–23, 225; San Juan del Sur, 189–91; Tola beaches, 222, 224–25
currency and exchange, 47. *See also* banks
Cyber Ometepe (Moyogalpa), 259

D

Da' Flying Frog Nicaragua (San Juan del Sur), 195
Dale Dagger Surf Tours (Playa Gigante), 209
dance, 25–26, 106, 107, 117, 257, 258, 267

dance classes, 152–53, 192
Dance of the Chinegros, 116, 117
Dance of the Zompopo, 257, 258, 267
Darío, Rubén, 68, 100, 118, 142, 225, 269
debit cards, 47
Del Sur News, 164, 167
dengue fever, 46
DeTours Viajes y Cultura (Granada), 124, 157
Día de la Cruz, 49
Día de la Raza, 49
Día de los Difuntos, 49
Diriá, 15, 100, 102; events, 116; horseback riding, 112; nightlife, 106; restaurants, 95, 97, 99
Diriamba, 100, 103–4; buses, 86; culture, 103–4; *El Güegüense*, 18, 25, 103, 107; events, 103, 116, 117; groceries, 114; lodging, 91–92, 94; museums, 106; parks, 112; restaurants, 99
Diriamba Online, 84
Diriangén, 15, 80, 100
Diriomo, 100, 102; events, 116; restaurants, 99
disabled travelers, 45
Discover Granada, 118
Dollar Car Rentals, 54, 122
Domingo de Trinidad (Masatepe), 116
Domitila Private Wildlife Reserve, 156
Don Luca (Granada), 143
Don Pepe (Masaya), 96
Doña Elba Cigars (Granada), 160–61
driving. *See* car travel
drugstores: about, 46

E

eating. *See* bakeries; cafés; food purveyors; groceries; pizza; restaurants
Eco-albergue Oropendola (Managua), 75
Ecoposada el Jardín Tortuga Verde (Diriamba), 91
Edificio Sandino (Granada), 148
El Anticuario (Granada), 160
El Apante, 262
El Arcángel Restaurant (Granada), 129
El Arco: surfing, 229
El Astillero, 203, 226, 228; boat tours, 228; buses, 206, 207; lodging, 215–16; surfing, 230; snorkeling, 229
El Astillero Vivero de Tortugas, 228
El Balcón (Granada), 129
El Brujo Waterfall, 73
El Bucanero (Masaya), 95
El Buen Gusto (La Boquita), 95
El Camino del Sol (San Juan del Sur), 199
El Caramanchel (Managua), 72

El Chocoyero-El Brujo Natural Reserve, 73
El Club (Granada), 152
El Colibrí (San Juan del Sur), 186
El Convento San Francisco (Granada), 144, 149–50
El Encanto (Santa Cruz), 245
El Garabato (Managua), 63
El Garaje (Granada), 138
El Gato Negro (San Juan del Sur), 200
El Güegüense (Diriamba), 87, 112
El Güegüense (play), 18, 25, 103, 107
El Jardín de los Olivos (Jinotepe), 92
El Jardín de Orion (Granada), 139–40
El Jardín Garden Hotel and Restaurant (San Juan del Sur), 173–74, 185
El Jícaro (Ostional), 176
El Libro Café (Catarina), 96
El Mirador Margarita (Playa Gigante), 220
El Modroño (Ostional), 176
El Palenque (Granada), 143
El Parche Gift Shop (Granada), 161
El Pozo (San Juan del Sur), 188
El Príncipe II (Rivas), 219, 225
El Quesillazo (Managua), 67
El Ranchón (Cárdenas), 227
El Recodo (Granada), 144, 160, 161
El Rey de Cocibolca (San José), 240
El Tercer Ojo (Managua), 66
El Timón (San Juan del Sur), 188
El Tranvía (Granada), 127
embassies, 44
emergencies, 46–47
Empalme de las Playas (Playa Marsella), 179
En Linea, 202
Enoteca Vinos y Más (Granada), 159
Enoteca Vinos y Más (Managua), 78
Escuela Big Foot (Tola), 225
Escuela Hoteleria y Turismo Masachapa (Managua), 62
Estación Biológica FUNDECI/GAIA (Laguna de Apoyo), 107
Estadio Nacional Dennis Martínez (Managua), 27, 69
Estancia del Congo Wildlife Reserve, 226, 228
Estatuaria de Zapatera (Granada), 150
Estrella del Sur (San José), 240
Euro Café (Granada), 142
events, 48–49; Altagracia, 267–68; Granada, 162–63; Isla Ometepe, 267–68; Managua, 79; Masaya, 115–17; Rivas, 231; San Juan del Sur, 200–201; Tola beaches, 231. *See also specific events*
Exapiel (Granada), 160
Expo-Festival Navideña (Granada), 163

F
Fabríca de Chocolate Momotombo (Managua), 78
Fabrica de Hamacas (Masaya), 114–15
Feria Navideña de Artesanos de Carazo (Diriamba), 117
Ferry Che Guevara (San José), 240
Ferry Isadora Minicrucero (San Juan del Sur), 194
Ferry La Novia de Xolotlán, 76
Festival de Poesía Internacional de Granada, 162–63
Festival Folklórico (Masaya), 117
festivals. *See* events; *and specific festivals*
Fiesta Cerámica (San Juan de Oriente), 116
Fiesta de la Virgen de la Asunción (Masaya), 116
Fiesta San Juan Bautista (Catarina), 116
Fiesta San Lázaro (Masaya), 116
Fiestas Diriá, 116
Fiestas María Magdalena (Masaya), 116
Fiestas Niquinohomo, 116
Fiestas Patronales de San Jerónimo (Masaya), 117
Fiestas Patronales de San Sebastián (Diriamba), 103, 116
Fiestas Patronales San Diego Alcalá (Isla Ometepe), 267
Fiestas Virgen de Guadalupe (Jinotepe), 117
Finca Agroturistica Tel Aviv, 264
Finca Charco Verde, 264
Finca Ecológica El Zopilote, 245–47, 252, 259, 264, 266
Finca La Esperanza, 264
Finca La Florida, 264
Finca La Primavera Private Agricultural-Forest Preserve, 194
Finca Las Nubes, 182
Finca Magdalena (Balgüe), 247–48, 264
Finca María Andrea, 264
Finca Mirador del Diablo, 259, 262
Finca Playa Venecia, 243, 264
Finca Samaria, 264
Finca San Juan de la Isla (Playa Santo Domingo), 244
Finca Tilgüe, 264
Fincas Verdes, 264
Find It Granada, 118
fishing: El Astillero, 228; Granada, 154, 158; Isla Ometepe, 265, 267; Laguna de Apoyo, 112; San Juan del Sur, 195–97; Tola beaches, 228–29
Flor de Angel (Moyogalpa), 259
Flor de Pochote (Masatepe), 90
Fonseca, Carlos, 68
food: overview, 24–25. *See also* bakeries;

cafés; food purveyors; groceries; markets; pizza; restaurants
food purveyors, 35–36; Carazo, 98–99; Granada, 141–43; Managua, 66–67; Masaya, 98–99; Pueblos Blancos, 98–99; Rivas, 221–22; San Juan del Sur, 189
Fortaleza El Coyotepe (Masaya), 101, 105
Fortaleza La Polvora (Granada), 146, 150
Fortaleza San Pablo (Granada), 146, 154–55
French classes, 153
Frisbee golf, 198
Frontera Books (Managua), 78–79
Fruti Fruti Smoothies (Masaya), 99
Fundación A. Jean Brugger (San Juan del Sur), 175
Fundación Casa de los Tres Mundos (Granada), 148
Fundación Entre Volcanes, 264
Futuro Mejor Spanish School (near Jinotepe), 107

G

Gaby Massage Studio (San Juan del Sur), 199
Galería de Arte Museo Carlos A. Vargas (Moyogalpa), 266
Galería del Sur (San Juan del Sur), 200
Galerías Santo Domingo Mall (Managua), 72, 73, 77, 78
Garden Café (Granada), 138, 161
gay and lesbian travelers, 44–45; Managua, 44, 72–73
Gay Nicaragua, 44
Giant's Foot Hotel Surf (Playa Gigante), 209
Gigante Farmer's Market (Playa Gigante), 230
Global Gayz, 44
Go To Nicaragua, 29
Go Visit Costa Rica, 40
Golden Pizza (Diriá), 99
golf: Managua, 60, 77; Tola, 229
Gonper Librerías (Granada), 161; (Managua), 79
González Dávila, Gil, 15, 100, 222, 236, 256
Good Times Surf Shop (San Juan del Sur), 197
GPS Travel Maps, 37
Gran Francia (Granada), 128–29, 144
Gran Océano (San Juan del Sur), 195
Gran Pacifica Beach and Golf Resort (Managua), 60, 77
Granada, 11, 28, 118–63; banks, 159; cinema, 153; culture, 143–51; events, 162–63; food purveyors, 141–43; history of, 143–49; hospitals, 47; information, 118, 121; lodging, 125–35; map, 120; museums, 149–51; nightlife, 151–52; recreational activities, 154–59; restaurants, 135–43; safety, 119, 121; shopping, 159–62; Spanish schools, 152–53;

theater, 153; tours, 157; transportation, 121–25
Granada Beach Club, 152
Granada Blog, 118
Granada Catedral, 148
Granada Cemetery, 147–48
Granada Mercado Municipal, 160
Granada Property Services, 133
Granada Spa, 159
Granada Vacation Rentals, 133
Granada-Altagracia-San Carlos Ferry, 239–40
Gray Line Tours Nicaragua, 31
Grill 50 (Managua), 67
groceries: Diriamba, 114; Granada, 159; Isla Ometepe, 265–66; Jinotepe, 114; Limón, 231; Managua, 77–78; Masatepe, 114; Masaya, 114; Rivas, 230; San Juan del Sur, 199
Guesthouse Eleonora (San Juan del Sur), 183
Guía Nicaragua Médica, 46
Guía Turística Nicaragua, 29
guitars, 115
Gustavo's Convenience (Limón), 231
Gutierrez, Helio, 114
gyms. See spas
Gypsy Sailing Adventures (San Juan del Sur), 194

H

Hacienda Iguana (Playa Colorado), 211–12, 229
Hacienda La Calera Private Reserve, 157
Hacienda Mérida, 248–49, 264, 265
Hacienda Puerta del Cielo (Masatepe), 90–91
Hacienda San Pedro Hotel Boutique (San Marcos), 92
Hacienda Santa María (Zapatera), 156
Hamacas Vicente Sauzo (Masaya), 115
hammocks, 114–15
handicrafts, 36–37; Granada, 160–61; Isla Ometepe, 266–67; Managua, 79; Masaya, 114–15; San Juan del Sur, 200
Healing Hands (Balgüe), 265
health care, 46–47
Hecho Magazine, 30, 71
Hell or High Water 4WD Taxi Service (Playa Gigante), 207
Henry's Iguana Beach Bar (San Juan del Sur), 191
Hertylandia (Jinotepe), 112
Hijuela, 31
hiking: Granada, 155, 157; Isla Ometepe, 259–60; Laguna de Apoyo, 107–8; Managua, 73, 75; San Juan del Sur, 198; Volcán Masaya, 110
Hilton Princess Managua, 57

Hipa Hipa (Managua), 72
Hípica Casares, 116
Hípica Diriá, 116
Hípica Diriamba, 117
Hípica Granada, 163
Hípica Jinotepe, 116
Hípica Masatepe, 116
Hípica Rivas, 231
Hípica Tisma, 116
history, 12–20; books, 270–71
Holy Grounds Bakery (Playa Popoyo), 221
Holy Week. *See* Semana Santa
Homenaje a La Santa Cruz (La Boquita), 116
Homenaje a la Virgen de Carmen (San Juan del Sur), 201
Honey Ox, 217
horseback riding: Granada, 159; Isla Ometepe, 265; Managua, 76; San Juan del Sur, 198
horse-drawn carriages, in Granada, 124
Hospedaje Buena Vista (Playa Santo Domingo), 250
Hospedaje Casa Familiar (Moyogalpa), 249, 252
Hospedaje Central (Moyogalpa), 250, 252
Hospedaje Cocibolca (Granada), 134
Hospedaje El Cangrejo (Managua), 62
Hospedaje Esfinge (Granada), 135
Hospedaje Euros (Catarina), 94
Hospedaje Glenda (Ostional), 176
Hospedaje Hilmor (Rivas), 217
Hospedaje La Cascada (Mérida), 251
Hospedaje Lydia (Rivas), 217
Hospedaje Maderas (Balgüe), 251
Hospedaje Nicaragua (San Juan del Sur), 182
Hospedaje Ortiz (Altagracia), 250
Hospedaje Pulpería y Panadería Fiorella (Cárdenas), 227
hospitals, 46–47
Hostal Beach Fun Casa 28 (San Juan del Sur), 168, 194
Hostal de los Tres Hermanos (Playa Madera), 184, 197
Hostal Dorado (Granada), 134–35
Hostal Dulce Sueño (Managua), 61
Hostal Familiar el Maltese (Granada), 130
Hostal Hamacas (El Astillero), 216
Hostal Mi Casa (Masaya), 93
Hostal Mochilas (Granada), 135
Hostal Pescaditos (Mérida), 251
Hostal Real (Managua), 62
Hostal San Angel (Granada), 124, 135
Hostal San Felipe (Managua), 61
Hostal Santa María (Masaya), 93
hotels. *See* lodging; *and specific hotels*
Hotel Alhambra (Granada), 125–26
Hotel Azul Pitahaya (San Juan del Sur), 171, 186
Hotel Besa-Flor (Masaya), 87–88
Hotel Brio (Playa Gigante), 209, 225, 228
Hotel Brisas de Mombacho (Nandaime), 217
Hotel Brisas del Sur (Rivas), 207
Hotel Cailagua (Masaya), 93
Hotel California (Masaya), 93
Hotel Casa Blanca (San Juan del Sur), 171–72
Hotel Casa Blanca (San Marcos), 91
Hotel Casa La Luna (Granada), 134
Hotel Casa Mateo (Jinotepe), 92
Hotel Casa Moreno (San José), 243
Hotel Casa San Martín (Granada), 134
Hotel Central (Altagracia), 243–44
Hotel Club Nautico La Ceiba (Granada), 155
Hotel Colonial (Granada), 126–27
Hotel Colonial (San Juan del Sur), 172, 182
Hotel Con Corazón (Granada), 127
Hotel Costa Azul (Playa Santo Domingo), 250
Hotel Dalinky (San Jorge), 236
Hotel Darío (Granada), 127, 142
Hotel Ejecutivo (Managua), 61
Hotel el Casino de Casares, 92–93
Hotel El Castillo (Altagracia), 244
Hotel El Conquistador (Managua), 56
Hotel El Gran Marquez Bed and Breakfast (Managua), 61–62
Hotel Encanto del Sur (San Juan del Sur), 182
Hotel Escuela Teosintal (Moyogalpa), 250
Hotel Estrella (San Juan del Sur), 183
Hotel Faleiros (Masatepe), 94
Hotel Finca del Sol (Santa Cruz), 251
Hotel Finca Playa Venecia (San José), 243, 264
Hotel Finca Santo Domingo, 244
Hotel Granada, 129
Hotel Hacienda Puerta del Cielo (Masatepe), 90–91
Hotel Hamacas (San Jorge), 236
Hotel Ivania (Masaya), 88
Hotel Jaaris (Catarina), 94
Hotel La Bocona (Granada), 126, 159
Hotel La Pyrámide (Managua), 62
Hotel Las Tortugas (Playa Santana), 212
Hotel Los Cisneros (Managua), 61
Hotel Los Robles (Managua), 57–58
Hotel Lupita (Casares), 93
Hotel Manta Raya (Ostional), 176
Hotel Masaya, 88
Hotel Monimbó (Masaya), 88
Hotel Mozonte (Managua), 56–57
Hotel Nicarao Inn (Rivas), 208
Hotel Ometepetl (Isla Ometepe), 235, 242
Hotel Patio del Malinche (Granada), 130
Hotel Playa Santa Martha (San José), 242–43
Hotel Plaza Colón (Granada), 130–31

Hotel Popoyo (Playa Guasacate), 213
Hotel Regis (Masaya), 93
Hotel Restaurant Bocona Surf (Guasacate), 218
Hotel Río Lago (Rivas), 217
Hotel Royal Chateau (San Juan del Sur), 175–76
Hotel Sol y Luna B&B (Managua), 62
Hotel Spa Granada, 131–32, 159
Hotel Summer (Managua), 60
Hotel Terrasol (Granada), 132
Hotel Villa Isabella (San Juan del Sur), 172–73
Hotel Villa Ordoñez (Managua), 62
Hotel Villa Paraíso (Playa Santo Domingo), 245
Hotel Villas del Sol (San Juan del Sur), 183
Hotel Vista al Mar (Managua), 62
Hotel Vistamar (Managua), 60–61
Hotel Volcán Masaya (Masaya), 110
Hotel y Restaurant Suleyka (La Boquita), 93
Hotel y Restaurante Gaury #2 (Rivas), 217
Hotel y Spa Mi Bohio (Diriamba), 91–92
Hotelito Aly (Moyogalpa), 249
Hotel-Restaurant Tagüizapa (Altagracia), 253–54
Howler Mountain Bike Race (San Juan del Sur), 200
Huehuete: buses, 85, 86; lodging, 92, 94; restaurants, 98; surfing, 112

I

I Do! Bodas, 31
IBW Internet Gateway, 30
Iglesia de la Merced (Granada), 145
Iglesia El Calvario (Nindirí), 106
Iglesia Guadalupe (Granada), 145–46
Iglesia Las Mercedes (San Jorge), 236
Iglesia Maria Magdalena (Masaya), 101
Iglesia Nuestra Señor de Rescate (San Jorge), 236
Iglesia Nuestra Señora de la Asuncion (Masaya), 100–101
Iglesia Nuestra Señora de la Candelaria (Diriomo), 102
Iglesia Nuestro Señor de Rescate (San Jorge), 236
Iglesia San Diego de Alcalá (Altagracia), 257
Iglesia San Francisco (Rivas), 222
Iglesia San Jerónimo (Masaya), 101
Iglesia San Juan Bautista (Masatepe), 102
Iglesia San Juan Bautista (Masaya), 101
Iglesia San Pedro y San Pablo (Diriá), 102
Iglesia San Pedro y San Pablo (Rivas), 222
Iglesia San Sebastián (Masaya), 101
Iglesia Santa Ana (Nindirí), 106
Iglesia Santa Ana (Niquinohomo), 102

Iglesia Santiago Xilotepetl (Jinotepe), 104
Iglesia Xalteva (Granada), 144
Iguana Project, 198
Imagine Restaurant and Bar (Granada), 138
Independence Day, 49
INETER, 38
infrastructure issues, 32, 34
Inspiration Tours (Managua), 75
Intermezzo del Bosque (Managua), 63
Internet access, 44. See also specific destinations
Intur, 28–29; Granada, 121; Managua, 53; maps, 37; Masaya, 87; Rivas, 204
Inuit Kayak (Granada), 158
Irish House Hotel and Pub (San Juan del Sur), 172, 191
Iskra Travel, 169
Isla del Amor, 76
Isla Ometepe, 11, 28, 232–68; banks, 265; boat travel, 125, 157, 234–35, 239–40; culture, 254–59; events, 267–68; history of, 15, 255–57; information, 232, 240; lodging, 241–44; map, 234; museums, 257–59; nightlife, 259; recreational activities, 259–65; restaurants, 252–54; safety, 233–34; shopping, 265–67; Spanish schools, 259; transportation, 234–40
Isla Ometepe: Touring Around, 232
Isla Quiste, 265
Island Tours (Isla Ometepe), 260
Isleta El Roble (Granada), 155
Isletas de Granada, 154–55
ITMB Nicaragua, 37

J

Jardín de Orion (Granada), 139–40
Jerry's Pizza (San Juan del Sur), 189
Jícaro Island Ecolodge (Granada), 129–30, 155
Jiloa Lagoon, 75
Jimmy Three Fingers Alabama Rib Shack (Granada), 138–39
Jinotepe, 104; buses, 83, 86; culture, 104; events, 116–17; groceries, 114; information, 87; lodging, 92, 94; restaurants, 97–99; water park, 112
Jiquilite Surf (Playa Santana), 212
Joya de Nicaragua (Managua), 79
Jueves de Verbena (Masaya), 107
Jui Fook Restaurant (Managua), 66
Julieta's Café Casa Cerámica (Rivas), 221–22, 225

K

K Gallery Art (San Juan del Sur), 200
Kathy's Waffle House (Granada), 142
Kayak (bar, Granada), 152

kayaking, 43, 112, 158, 228, 265
Kelly's Bar (Granada), 152
King Quality, 39
kite surfing, 265

L

La Boquita, 98; boat tours, 112; buses, 85, 86; events, 116; horseback riding, 112; lodging, 92, 93, 95; restaurants, 98; surfing, 112
La Calera Private Reserve, 157
La Calzada Centro de Arte (Granada), 153
La Casa de Don Martín (Playa Majagual), 184
La Casa de los Nogueras (Managua), 63
La Casona Coffee Shop (San Marcos), 97–98
La Chocolata: canopy tours, 195; lodging, 181; nightlife, 191
La Colonia (Granada), 159; (Managua), 77
La Concha Acustica (Managua), 68
La Costeña Airlines, 38
La Cruz de España, 222, 236
La Cueva de la Sirena (Managua), 62
La Flor Wildlife Refuge, 193–94
La Gaviota Restaurant (Playa Gigante), 219–20
La Granadilla, 131
La Islita Boutique Hotel (Granada), 129
La Maquina, 112
La Mar Lake Resort (La Virgen), 208
La Mariposa Spanish School and Ecohotel (San Juan de la Concepción), 107
La Marseilles (Managua), 64
La Mexicana (Granada), 142
La Olla de Barro (Masatepe), 97
La Omaja (Mérida), 249
La Orquidea Casa de Huésped (Laguna de Apoyo), 109
La Pagoda de Oro (Jinotepe), 98
La Pérgola (Granada), 135
La Pirata (Managua), 72
La Posada Azul (San Juan del Sur), 175, 200
La Posada del Sol (Granada), 127–28
La Posada Ecológica Abuela (Laguna de Apoyo), 109
La Purísima, 49
La Ronda Bar Restaurant (Masaya), 106
La Terraza Peruana (Managua), 65
La Virgen. See Playa La Virgen
Labor Day, 49
Laguna de Apoyo, 107–9; boat tours, 112; buses, 86; Catarina Mirador, 95, 96, 111–12; horseback riding, 159; information, 84; lodging, 109; nightlife, 106; restaurants, 95, 96–97
Laguna de Nocarime, 226
Laguna de Tiscapa, 73–74
Lagunas de Mecatepe, 157

Lagunas de Mombacho, 157
Lance's Left, 230
language, 48
Las Cabañas Encantadas (Nindirí), 94
Las Colinas del Sur (Granada), 137
Las Mañanitas (Playa Majagual), 179–80
Las Manos de Chepito (Granada), 161
Las Manos Mágicas (Altagracia), 253
Las Perlas (Managua), 60
Las Plumerías (El Astillero), 216
Las Salinas de Nahualapa, 203; lodging, 213–14
L'Atelier (Granada), 160
Latin American Network Information Center, 30
Latin American Spanish School (San Juan del Sur), 192
Latin Latitudes Bed & Breakfast (Playa Yankee), 177
Leo Tours Comunitarios (Granada), 156, 157
Liberia, Costa Rica Info, 40
Librería Hispamer (Granada), 162; (Managua), 79
Likun Payasca (Managua), 63–64
Little Morgan's Lakeside Resort (Santa Cruz), 251
live music. See music
Lo Stradivari (San Juan del Sur), 188
Lobo Lira (San Juan del Sur), 182
lodging: about, 34–35; price codes, 11; Carazo, 87, 91–95; Cárdenas, 227; Granada, 125–35; Isla Ometepe, 241–44; Managua, 55–62; Masaya, 87–89, 93; Playa Ostional, 176; Pueblos Blancos, 87, 89–91, 94; Rivas, 207–8, 217; San Jorge, 236; San Juan del Sur, 170–84; Tola beaches, 207, 208–18. See also specific lodgings
Loma Tiscapa National Historical Park, 73–76
long-term visitors, books for, 271
Los Caballitos (Mérida), 259
Los Cardones Surf Lodge (Managua), 77
Los Chorredores Fritanga and Grill (Masaya), 95–96
Los Petroglifos del Cailagua, 112
Los Robles (Managua), 51; lodging, 57–59, 61–62; nightlife, 72; restaurants, 63–64, 66–67

M

Madera's Inn Hotel (Masaya), 83, 88–89
Maderas Volcano. See Volcán Maderas Natural Reserve
Magnificent Rock (Popoyo), 218
mail, 44
Mama Delfina (Managua), 79
Mama's Fish Tacos (Rivas), 222

Managua, 10, 28, 50–79; banks, 77; cinemas, 73; culture, 68–71; events, 79; food purveyors, 66–67; hospitals, 46–47; information, 51, 53; lodging, 55–62; maps, 51, 52; museums, 69–71; nightlife, 71–72; recreational activities, 73–77; restaurants, 63–67; safety, 53; shopping, 77–79; Spanish schools, 72–73; theater, 73; transportation, 53–55. *See also specific neighborhoods*
Managua, Lake, 50, 68; boat tours, 76–77
Managua New Cathedral, 69
Managua Old Cathedral, 68
Managua Zoo, 75
Manfut, 30
Mango Rosa Adventure Travel and Surf Resort (Playa Madera), 180, 191
Manolo Cuadra Library (Granada), 150
Mansión Teodolinda (Managua), 57
Mapas Naturismo, 37
maps: to buy, 37–38. *See also specific destinations*
March for Sexual Diversity, 44
Marea Alta (Managua), 64
MARENA (Ministry of Environment and Natural Resources), 13
Marhaba Hookah House (Managua), 64
marimbas, 26, 100, 107, 113
Marina Cocibolca, 125, 158
Marisco Bar (Cárdenas), 227
markets, 36; Granada, 160; Isla Ometepe, 265–66; Managua, 78; Masatepe, 114; Masaya, 114; Playa Gigante, 230; Rivas, 230; San Juan del Sur, 185, 199, 200
Marsella Valley Frisbee Golf, 198
Masatepe, 100, 102; buses, 86; events, 116; groceries, 114; information, 84; lodging, 90–91, 94; markets, 114; restaurants, 97, 99
Masatepe Online, 84
Masaya, 10, 28, 80–115; banks, 113–14; culture, 100–106; events, 115–17; food purveyors, 98–99; groceries, 114; handicrafts, 114–15; information, 82, 87; lodging, 87–89, 93; maps, 82, 83; markets, 114; museums, 105; nightlife, 106; recreational activities, 107–12; restaurants, 95–96; safety, 81; shopping, 113–15; Spanish schools, 107; theater, 107; transportation, 81–87. *See also specific neighborhoods*
Masaya Civic Fiestas, 117
Masaya New Market, 114
Masaya Old Market, 36, 101, 107, 113, 114
Masaya Spanish School, 107
Masaya Viva, 84
Maximo Ding Repair (Playa Popoyo), 231
Mena, Guillermo, 198
Mercado de Artesanías Mazatepelth

(Masatepe), 114
Mercado Huembes (Managua), 78; buses, 54
Mercado Israel Lewites (Managua), 78; buses, 54–55
Mercado Mayoreo (Managua), 78; buses, 54
Mercado Oriental (Managua), 78; buses, 55
Mérida, 235; buses, 238; kayaking, 265; lodging, 248–49, 251; nightlife, 259
Mesón Español (Managua), 67
MetroCentro (Managua), 73, 78
Mi Museo (Granada), 150
Mi Tierra (Granada), 152
Mirador El Boquete (Diría), 95, 102
Mirador El Pollo (San Juan del Oriente), 97
Mirador Tiscapa (Managua), 72
Miss Margritt's B&B (Granada), 133–34
Mockingbird Books (Granada), 162
Mombacho Canopy Tour (Granada), 158
Mombacho Volcano, 154, 155
Mombotour (Granada), 157
Momentos Café (Jinotepe), 99
Momo Surf Camp (Playa Gigante), 209–10
money, 47–48. *See also* banks
Monimbó (Masaya), 101; events, 116; information, 87; lodging, 88; museum, 105; shopping, 113
Monimbó Insurrection, 18, 100, 105
Monkey Hut (Laguna de Apoyo), 109
Monkeys Island Hotel (Mérida), 251
Monna Lisa (Granada), 143
Montecristo Beach, 229
Montelimar Cave, 75
Montibelli Private Wildlife Reserve, 75
Monument to the Nicaraguan Worker (Managua), 69
Monumento Rubén Darío (Managua), 68
Moods (Managua), 72
Moon River Burritos (Managua), 67
Mope's Surf Shop (San Juan del Sur), 197
Morgan, Henry, 145
Morgan's Rock (Playa Ocotal), 180
Movie Review, 73
movie theaters (cinemas): Granada, 153; Managua, 73
movies, suggested, 271–72
Moyogalpa, 262; banks, 265; boat travel, 234–35, 239–40; buses, 238; events, 267; groceries, 266; lodging, 241–42, 249–50; museums, 257–59; nightlife, 259; police, 233–34; restaurants, 252–54; shopping, 266–67
Moyogalpa Civic Fiestas, 267
Mr. Lorch's Bar & Grill (Masaya), 106
Muelle de Granada (Granada), 125, 157
Multicentro Las Americas (Managua), 78
Museo Arqueológica (Moyogalpa), 259

Museo Casa Natal Sor María Romero (Granada), 150–51
Museo Comunitario Etnógrafico de Monimbó (Masaya), 105
Museo de Nindirí Cacique Tenderí (Nindirí), 106
Museo del Departamento de Malacología Ciencias Naturales (Managua), 69–70
Museo Ecológico de Trópico Seco (Diriamba), 106
Museo Nacional de Nicaragua Dioclesiano Cháves (Managua), 70
Museo Numismático (Moyogalpa), 257
Museo Precolombino (Moyogalpa), 257
Museo Sitio Huellas de Acahualinca (Managua), 70–71
Museo y Galería de Heroes y Martires (Masaya), 105
Museos El Ceibo (Moyogalpa), 257–58
museums: Diriamba, 106; Granada, 149–51; Isla Ometepe, 257–59; Managua, 69–71; Masaya, 105; Nindirí, 106; Rivas, 225. See also specific museums
music, 25–26; Granada, 151–52; Isla Ometepe, 259; Managua, 71–72; Masaya, 106; Rivas, 225; San Juan del Sur, 191; San Marcos, 106; Tola beaches, 225
MVP Sports Bar (Managua), 72

N

Nahual Tours (Granada), 124
Nandaime, 131, 156; buses, 207; events, 267; lodging, 217
National Day of the Nicaraguan Entrepreneur, 49
National Surf Circuit, 200
natural history, 12–13; books, 272
natural history museums, 69–70, 106, 150
Nejapa Country Club (Managua), 77
Neptune Diving (San Juan del Sur), 198–99
New Year's Day, 48
Nica Buffet (Granada), 142
Nica Designs T-Shirts (San Juan del Sur), 200
Nica Express, 39, 124
Nica Living, 30
Nica Sailing (San Juan del Sur), 194–95
Nica Spanish Language School (San Juan del Sur), 192
Nica Surf Shop (Playa Popoyo), 231
Nica Times, 31
Nica Yoga (San Juan del Sur), 199
Nicán Park Peréz Nogüera, 77
Nicaragua, Lake, 118, 154–56, 232; boat travel, 125, 157–58, 228, 234–35, 239–40; fishing, 158; lodging, 241–51; map, 234; recreational activities, 259–65; southern coast, 227. See

also Isla Ometepe
Nicaragua Art Gallery (Managua), 79
Nicaragua Butterfly Reserva, 157
Nicaragua Dulce (Granada), 124, 158
Nicaragua Guide, 31
Nicaragua Libre (Granada), 131
Nicaragua Mia Spanish School (Granada), 152
Nicaragua Over Coffee Tours (Rivas), 225
Nicaragua Realty, 133
Nicaragua Surf Property, 182
Nicaragua Surf Report, 197, 217
Nicaragua Vacation Rental and Property Management, 182
Nicaragua Vacation Rentals, 133
Nicarao Lake Tours, 124, 169
Nicasurfing.com, 217
Nicawaves (Popoyo), 218
Nicovale (San Juan del Sur), 195
Nicoya Peninsula, 40
nightlife: Granada, 151–52; Isla Ometepe, 259; Managua, 71–72; Masaya, 106; Rivas, 225; San Juan del Sur, 191; San Marcos, 106; Tola beaches, 225
Nindirí: events, 116; lodging, 87–88, 94; museum, 106; petroglyphs, 112
Niquinohomo, 100, 102; events, 116; information, 84; restaurants, 96–97
Norome Resort (Laguna de Apoyo), 109
Nuestra Señora de la Asuncion (Masaya), 100–101

O

Oasis (Granada), 135, 161
Ocean Green (San Juan del Sur), 197
Ojo de Agua, 262–64
Ola Verde (Managua), 64–65, 79
Olas Escondidas (La Boquita), 95, 112
Old Cathedral of Managua, 68
Ometepe Archaeological Museum (Altagracia), 258
Ometepe Biological Field Station, 249
Ometepe Expeditions (Moyogalpa), 260
Ometepe Petroglyph Project, 255–56
Ometepe Spanish School (Balgüe), 259
Ometepe Tours (San Jorge), 260
Ometepe Turistica, 232
Ometepe-Projekt Nicaragua, 232
online resources. See websites
Opera Gioconda (Granada), 157
Orquidea del Sur (Playa Yankee), 177–78
Ortega, Camilo Saavedra, 105
Ortega, Daniel, 20–21, 78, 269
O'Shea's Irish Pub Restaurant (Granada), 152
Ostional. See Playa Ostional
Ostional Private Wildlife Reserve, 194

P

Paintball Las Colinas (Managua), 76
Palace of Korea (Managua), 66
Palacio de los Pueblos de America Latina (Managua), 68
Palacio Nacional de la Cultura (Managua), 68, 70
Palí (Granada), 159; (Masaya), 114; (Rivas), 230; (San Juan del Sur), 199; (San Rafael del Sur), 78
Pan de Vida (San Juan del Sur), 189
Panadería Brenes (Masatepe), 99
Panadería Central Quintanilla (Catarina), 99
Panadería El Chele (Granada), 141
Panadería Estrella (Granada), 142
Panadería Luna Express (Granada), 142
Panadería Norma (Masaya), 99
Panadería San Marcos (San Juan del Sur), 189
Panamerican Highway, 42, 204; lodging, 207–9, 217
Pane y Vino (Managua), 67
Panga Drops, 211, 230
Paradise Bakery and Café (Rivas), 222
Paraiso de los Bendaña (Playa Santana), 212
Park Avenue Villas (San Juan del Sur), 175
Parque 17 de Octubre (Masaya), 101
Parque de la Paz (Managua), 69
Parque de los Poetas (Granada), 156
Parque Histórico Nacional Loma de Tiscapa, 73–76
Parque Madera Hotel (Playa Madera), 180–81
Parque Marítimo el Coco (Playa El Coco), 178
Parque Nacional Archipielago Zapatera, 155–56
Parque Nacional Volcán Masaya, 80, 110
Parque Xalteva (Granada), 144
Parroquia Nuestra Señora de la Asuncion (Masaya), 100–101
Parroquia San Jerónimo (Masaya), 101
passports, 48
Pastelería Sampson (Managua), 66
Pastora Tours (San Juan del Sur), 195
Paxeos, 39, 124, 169
Pelican Eyes Hotel and Resort (San Juan del Sur), 174–75, 181; sailing, 195; spa, 199
Perfect Peak, 230
petroglyphs, 75, 106, 112, 156, 157, 246, 255–59
pharmacies: about, 46
Pie de Gigante Restaurant (Playa Gigante), 220–21, 225
Piedras y Olas (San Juan del Sur), 174–75, 195
Pier, The (San Juan del Sur), 191
pizza (pizzerías): Diriá, 99; Granada, 143; Managua, 67; Masaya, 99; Rivas, 222; San Juan del Sur, 189; San Marcos, 99

Pizza Hot (Rivas), 222
Pizza Hotter (Rivas), 222
Pizzeria Amigos (San Marcos), 99
Pizzería Coliseo (Jinotepe), 98
Pizzería Los Idolos (Managua), 71
Pizzería Rock Munchies (Managua), 67
Pizzería San Juan (San Juan del Sur), 187–88
Playa Amarillo: surfing, 229
Playa Arena Blanca: snorkeling, 198–99
Playa Boquita. See La Boquita
Playa Colorado, 229; lodging, 211–12
Playa de los Romanticos (Managua), 72
Playa El Coco, 168; groceries, 199; lodging, 178, 182, 184
Playa Escama, surfing, 196
Playa Gavilán, 230; lodging, 216
Playa Gigante, 203, 228; boat tours, 207, 228; groceries, 230; information, 202, 230; kayaking, 228; lodging, 208–10, 217–18; restaurants, 219–21; snorkeling, 229; surfing, 229, 231; transportation, 204, 206, 207
Playa Gigante Online, 230
Playa Guasacate: buses, 206; lodging, 210–15, 218; restaurants, 221; surfing, 230, 231
Playa La Virgen, 226; lodging, 208; transportation, 167, 168
Playa Madera: buses, 167, 168–69; lodging, 178, 180–81, 184; nightlife, 191; surfing, 196, 197
Playa Majagual: lodging, 179–82, 184
Playa Manzanilla: surfing, 229
Playa Marsella: lodging, 179, 181, 182; nightlife, 191
Playa Masachapa, 50; golf, 77; lodging, 60, 62
Playa Montelimar: lodging, 59–60; surfing, 77
Playa Ocotal: lodging, 180
Playa Ostional, 168, 176; groceries, 199; lodging, 176; surfing, 196
Playa Pochomil, 50; buses, 55; horseback riding, 76; lodging, 60–62
Playa Popoyo, 203; lodging, 210–15, 218; nightlife, 225; restaurants, 221; snorkeling, 229; surfing, 202, 230, 231
Playa Remanso, 168; lodging, 177; surfing, 196
Playa Rosada: surfing, 230
Playa Santana: buses, 206; lodging, 210–13, 218; surfing, 230, 231
Playa Santo Domingo, 262–63; buses, 238; canopy tours, 264; lodging, 244–45, 250–51
Playa Yankee, 168; lodging, 177–78; surfing, 196
Plaza de la Fé Juan Pablo II (Managua), 68
Plaza de la Independencia (Granada), 148, 156
Plaza de la República (Managua), 68
Plaza de la Revolución (Managua), 68, 79
Plaza Inter (Managua), 73, 78

Popoyo. *See* Playa Popoyo
Popoyo Ding Repair (Playa Popoyo), 231
Popoyo Loco, 218
Popoyo Surf Lodge (Playa Popoyo), 214
Popoyo Surf Report, 202
Popoyo.com, 202
Posada Cabrera (Altagracia), 250
Posada Chico Largo (San José del Sur), 250, 262
Posada Ecológica Abuela (Laguna de Apoyo), 109
Posada La Viña (Diriamba), 94
Posada Puesta del Sol (San Juan del Sur), 183
post offices, 44. *See also specific destinations*
PriceSmart (Managua), 77
Procesión de los Ahüizotes (Masaya), 117
Procesión de Torovenado (Masaya), 117
Project Bona Fide (Balgüe), 246, 264
Pro-Kiting (Lake Nicaragua), 265
protests, 34
Proyecto Mosaico (Granada), 121
Proyecto Parque Nacional Ecológico del Café, 112
Pueblos Blancos, 10, 28, 80–115; culture, 101–6; food purveyors, 98–99; information, 87; lodging, 87, 89–91, 94; map, 82; recreational activities, 107–12; restaurants, 95, 96–97; safety, 81; shopping, 113, 114–15; transportation, 81–87
Puerto Asese (Granada), 140, 158
Puerto Carlos Fonseca, 76–77
Puerto Salvador Allende, 68, 76
Puerto Turístico Rúben Darío (Managua), 72
Puesto del Sol (Playa El Coco), 178
Pulpería Mena (Playa Gigante), 230
Punta de Jesús María, 263
Punta Teonoste Nature Lodge and Spa (El Astillero), 216
Pure (Granada), 159
Purple Roofs, 44

Q
Querube's Restaurant (Granada), 143
Quinta Lupita (near Diriamba), 94

R
Rana Tur (San Juan del Sur), 170, 195
Rancho Brava Mar (La Boquita), 95, 112
Rancho Chilamate (San Juan del Sur), 198
Rancho Santana (Playa Santana), 212–13
reading, suggested, 269–72
Reagan, Ronald, 18
Real Intercontinental Metrocentro Managua, 58–59
recreational activities: Carazo, 107–13; Granada, 154–59; Isla Ometepe, 259–65;

Managua, 73–77; Masaya, 107–12; Pueblos Blancos, 107–12; Rivas, 226–30; San Juan del Sur, 193–99; Tola beaches, 226–30. *See also specific activities*
Red de Reservas Silvestres Privadas Nicaragua, 13
Refugio de Vida Silvestre Río Escalante-Chacocente, 226, 230
Remanso Beach Resort, 177
rental properties. *See* vacation rentals
Reposteria Adelita (San Marcos), 99
Reserva Ecólogica Charco Verde, 260–61
Reserva Ecólogica La Maquina, 112
Reserva Ecológica Zacatán, 228
Reserva Natural Apante, 262
Reserva Natural Chocoyero-El Brujo, 73
Reserva Natural Laguna de Apoyo, 107–9
Reserva Natural Lagunas de Mecatepe, 157
Reserva Natural Río Manares, 157
Reserva Natural Volcán Concepción, 254, 259–61
Reserva Natural Volcán Maderas, 254, 261
Reserva Natural Volcán Mombacho, 155
restaurants: about, 35–36; food, 24–25; price codes, 11; Carazo, 95, 97–98; Cárdenas, 227; Granada, 135–43; Isla Ometepe, 252–54; Managua, 63–67; Masaya, 95–96; Pueblos Blancos, 95, 96–97; Rivas, 218–19; San Jorge, 236–37; San Juan del Sur, 185–89; Tola beaches, 218–21. *See also specific restaurants*
Restaurant Casa Blanca (Jinotepe), 98
Restaurant Disco-Bar Amores del Sol (Popoyo), 221, 225
Restaurant El Refugio (San Jorge), 237
Restaurant Katheere (Popoyo), 221
Restaurant Los Faroles (Catarina), 96
Restaurant Los Jicaritos (La Boquita), 98
Restaurant Mediterraneo (Granada), 140
Restaurant Paraíso (San Marcos), 99
Restaurant Rancho Las Marías (La Chocolata), 191
Restaurant Tratoría Garibaldi (Granada), 129
Restaurant-Bar Don Segundo Cruz (Huehuete), 94, 98
Restaurante Brumas de Apoyo (Catarina), 96
Restaurante Intermezzo del Bosque (Managua), 63
Restaurante Los Ranchitos (Moyogalpa), 254
Restaurante Min Nan Jiu Lou (Granada), 141
Restaurante Monteverde (Laguna de Apoyo), 108
Restaurante y Bar Año Nuevo Chino (Granada), 141
Restaurante Yon Niy Ta (Granada), 141
Restaurante Yuan-Lin (Jinotepe), 98

Restaurant-Hotel Dolce Vita (San Juan del Sur), 186–87
restrooms, 43
Revolution, 17–18; Anniversary of the, 49, 79; books, 271
Ride a Painted Pony Horseback Tours (Granada), 159
Rincón Romántico (Masaya), 106
Río Istiam, 265
Río Manares Natural Reserve, 157
Río San Juan, 189
Rivas, 11, 28, 202–31; banks, 230; culture, 222–23, 225; events, 231; food purveyors, 221–22; information, 202, 204; lodging, 207–8, 217; map, 205; markets, 230; museums, 225; nightlife, 225; recreational activities, 226–30; restaurants, 218–19; safety, 203; shopping, 230–31; transportation, 204–7
Rivas Civic Fiestas, 231
Rivas Mercado Municipal, 230
Rivas Museum of Anthropology and History, 222–23, 225
Road House Drinks & Food (Granada), 152
Roca Inculta, 263
Romero, María, 150–51
Rostí Pizza La Frigata (San Juan del Sur), 189
Royal Tepanyaki (Managua), 66
Ruta de las Fincas Verdes, 264
Ruta Maya (Managua), 72

S
safety, 31–32; Carazo, 81; Granada, 119, 121; Isla Ometepe, 233–34; Managua, 53; Masaya, 81; Pueblos Blancos, 81; Rivas, 203; San Juan del Sur, 166–67; Tola beaches, 203
Sailboat Shuttle (San Juan del Sur), 170
Sala Arqueológica Ometepe (Moyogalpa), 266
Salinas Hot Springs, 228
Salomon Tattoo (San Juan del Sur), 200
San Jorge, 226, 232, 236–37; events, 267; lodging, 236; restaurants, 236–37; transportation, 234–36
San Jorge Civic Fiestas, 267
San José del Sur, 260–61; boat travel, 239–40; buses, 235, 239; lodging, 242–43, 250
San Juan de Dios Hospital (Granada), 147
San Juan de Oriente: buses, 85–86; ceramics, 102, 114, 116; events, 116; information, 84; restaurants, 96, 97
San Juan del Sur, 11, 28, 164–201; banks, 199; culture, 189–91; events, 200–201; food purveyors, 189; information, 164, 167; lodging, 170–84; map, 166; nightlife, 191; recreational activities, 193–99; restaurants, 185–89; safety, 166–67; shopping, 199–200;

Spanish schools, 192; spas, 199; surfing, 164, 196–97, 200; transportation, 167–70
San Juan del Sur Beach Camp, 198
San Juan del Sur Guide, 164, 191
San Juan del Sur Horses, 198
San Juan del Sur Mercado Municipal, 185, 199, 200
San Juan del Sur Spanish School, 192
San Juan del Sur Surf and Sport, 195, 197
San Juan del Sur Surf Sand Culture, 164
San Marcos, 100, 104; buses, 86–87; lodging, 91–92, 94; nightlife, 106; restaurants, 97–99
San Ramón Fishing Tournament, 267
San Ramón Waterfall, 248, 264
San Silvestre de Papa (Catarina), 116
San Simian (Laguna de Apoyo), 109
Sancho Sport Fishing (San Juan del Sur), 195
Sandinista Revolution. See Revolution
Sandino, Augusto C., 17, 68, 74, 84, 102, 271
Sandino Airport (Managua), 38, 53; car rentals, 54
Santa Cruz, 235; buses, 238; lodging, 245–46, 251; nightlife, 259
Santa Cruz Hostel and Restaurant, 251
Santa Fe (Managua), 66–67
Santiago Crater, 110
scuba diving, 198–99
sea turtles, 13, 193–94, 216, 226, 228
Seaside Mariana (Montecristo), 229
seasons, 32
Seeing Hands Blind Massage (Granada), 159
Semana Santa, 48–49; Granada, 163; Masaya, 116; Ometepe, 267; Rivas, 231; San Jorge, 267; San Juan del Sur, 201
Sendero del Cráter, 155
Sendero La Puma, 155
Servitour Monimbó (Masaya), 87, 113
shopping, 36–37; Granada, 159–62; Isla Ometepe, 265–67; Managua, 77–79; Masaya, 113–15; Pueblos Blancos, 113, 114–15; Rivas, 230–31; San Juan del Sur, 199–200; Tola beaches, 230–31
showers, 43
snorkeling, 198–99, 229
soccer, 27, 69
social history, 13–20; books, 270–71
Soda Sinai (San José del Sur), 250
Solentiname Tours, 31
Soma (Moyogalpa), 250
Somoza Debayle, Anastasio, 17–18, 50–51, 74
Somoza García, Anastasio, 17, 100
Sonzapote, 131, 156
South Seas Hostal (San Juan del Sur), 183
Spanish Conquest, 15, 143–45, 222
Spanish School House Rosa Silva (San Juan

del Sur), 192
Spanish School Xpress (Granada), 153
Spanish schools: Granada, 152–53; Isla
Ometepe, 259; Managua, 72–73; Masaya,
107; San Juan del Sur, 192; Tola beaches, 225
Spanish Ya (San Juan del Sur), 192
spas: Granada, 159; Isla Ometepe, 265; Playa
Gigante, 230; Playa Guasacate, 230; San Juan
del Sur, 199
special events. *See* events; *and specific events*
special needs travelers, 45
Spices and Sugar (Granada), 160; (Managua),
79
Sport Bar M'Che (San Juan del Sur), 191
Sport Fishing Nicaragua (San Juan del Sur),
195
Sportfishing Charters (Tola), 229
Statue of the Unknown Guerrilla (Managua),
69
Stones and Waves Veterinary Clinic (San Juan
del Sur), 175
strikes, 34
Super Pollo (Rivas), 219
Surf Casino (San Juan del Sur), 191
Surf Sanctuary (Playa Santana), 213
Surf Santana (Playa Santana), 212–13
Surf Zone (Playa Marsella), 181
Surfari Nicaragua Tours (San Juan del Sur),
197
surfing: books, 272; Huehuete, 112; La
Boquita, 112; Managua, 77; Playa Popoyo,
202, 230, 231; San Juan del Sur, 164,
196–97, 200; Tola beaches, 229–31
Swell Beach Hostel (Playa Gigante), 218

T
Tabú (Managua), 44
Tagüizapa Civic Fiestas, 267
Taquería La Jarochita (Granada), 142;
(Masaya), 96
taxis, 42; to/from the airport, 38–39;
Granada, 124; Isla Ometepe, 238–39;
Managua, 53, 55; Rivas, 207; safety, 31–32;
San Juan del Sur, 169
Taxis Oficial Aeropuerto, 38
Teatro Justo Rufino Garay (Managua), 73
Teatro Rubén Darío (Managua), 73
Tele Pizza (Granada), 143; (Masaya), 99
telephone numbers, useful, 34
telephones, 44
Tequila Vallarta (Granada), 142
Tercer Ojo (Granada), 140, 141
Terminal UCA (Managua), 55
Tesoro del Pirata (San José), 243
theater: Granada, 153; Managua, 73; Masaya,
107

Theater Victor Romeo (Managua),
73
Tica Bus, 39; Granada, 122; Jinotepe, 83;
Liberia, 204; Managua lodging, 61; Masaya,
83; San Juan del Sur, 168
Tienda de Artesanías Luna (Moyogalpa),
267
Tienda Olé (Granada), 160
Tierra Tour (Granada), 37, 124, 157
tipping, 47–48
Tiscapa National Historical Park, 73–76
Tisma, 110–11; events, 116
Tisma Lagoon Ramsar Wetlands Preserve,
110–11
toilets, 43
Tola (Tola beaches), 11, 28, 202–31; culture,
222, 224–25; events, 231; food purveyors,
221–22; information, 202, 204; lodging,
207, 208–18; map, 205; nightlife, 225;
recreational activities, 226–30; restaurants,
218–21; safety, 203; shopping, 230–31;
Spanish schools, 225; surfing, 229–31;
transportation, 204–7
Tonalli (Managua), 66
Toro Mixcal Private Wildlife Preserve, 194
Torre Reloj (Diriamba), 104
Totoco (Santa Cruz), 246, 252
tour operators, 31
tourist offices, 28–29. *See also specific destina-
tions*
Toyota Rent a Car (Managua), 54
Transnica, 39; Granada, 122; Liberia, 204–5;
Masaya, 84
transportation, 38–40, 42–43; Carazo, 81–87;
Granada, 121–25; Isla Ometepe, 234–40;
Managua, 53–55; Masaya, 81–87; Pueblos
Blancos, 81–87; Rivas, 204–7; San Juan del
Sur, 167–70; Tola beaches, 204–7. *See also*
boat travel; buses; car travel
Transporte Isla Ometepe, 239
Trip Advisor, 29, 181
turtles. *See* sea turtles
Twain, Mark, 164, 190
Two Brothers Surf (Playa Popoyo), 214–15

U
UCA Tierra y Agua (Granada), 157, 159
Uca Tierra y Agua (Granada), 131
Un Buen Viaje, 31
Unión Guías de Ometepe, 260
Urbaite, 256; events, 267
Urbaite Civic Fiestas, 267
U-Save Auto Rental (Managua), 54

V
Va Pues Tours (Granada), 157

vacation rentals: Granada, 132–33; San Juan del Sur, 181–82; Tola beaches, 217
vaccinations, 46
Valenti's Pizza (Managua), 67
Vanderbilt, Cornelius, 16–17, 189, 270
Velago Nicaragua (Granada), 158
Vía Crucis Acuatico de las Isletas, 163
Viajero Clandestino (Granada), 135
ViaNica, 31, 71
Victoriano Hotel (San Juan del Sur), 176–77
vigarón, 24, 135–36
Villa Aller (Playa Santo Domingo), 250–51
Villa Angelo (Managua), 61
Villa Mar Marsella Beach (Playa Marsella), 181
Villas at Norome Resort (Laguna de Apoyo), 109
Villas de Palermo (San Juan del Sur), 182
Villas del Mar (La Boquita), 95
Villas Mombacho (Granada), 141, 158
Villa's Restaurant (Diriamba), 99
Villa's Rosti Pizza (Rivas), 222
Virgen de la Candelaria (Diriomo), 102, 116
visas, 48
visitor offices, 28–29. *See also specific destinations*
Viva Spanish Schools (Managua), 44, 72–73
Volcán Concepción Natural Reserve, 254, 259–61
Volcán Maderas Natural Reserve, 254, 261; lodging, 245
Volcán Masaya, 80, 110
Volcán Mombacho, 154, 155
Volcano Ranch (Laguna de Apoyo), 112, 159
V!va Travel Guides, 29

W
Walker, William, 16, 68, 133, 146–47, 150, 223, 225, 270
Walker (movie), 144, 271–72
water parks, 112
water taxis. *See* boat travel
weather, 32
websites, 29–31; Costa Rica, 40; Granada, 118; Isla Ometepe, 232; Managua, 51, 71; Masaya, 84; Rivas, 202; San Juan del Sur, 164; Tola beaches, 202, 217
Whiskey Bar (Rivas), 225
wildlife guidebooks, 272

X
Xalteva, 15, 144
Xalteva Condominiums (Granada), 133
Xiloá (Jiloa) Lagoon, 75
Xterra Off-Road Triathlon (San Juan del Sur), 201

Y
Yogi's Café (Moyogalpa), 254

Z
Zagúan (Granada), 141
Zapatera Archipielago, 155–56
Zapatera Tours, 156
Zepeda Guitars (Masaya), 115
Zompopo Dance, 257, 258, 267
Zona Hippos (Managua), 72
Zona ViVa (Managua), 78; nightlife, 72
Zoológico Nacional Nicaragüense (Managua), 75
Zoom Bar (Granada), 152